Y'ALL VS. US

THRILLING TALES OF MISSISSIPPI'S HOTTEST HIGH SCHOOL FOOTBALL RIVALRIES

X.M. FRASCOGNA, JR.
X.M. FRASCOGNA, III
MARTIN FRANK FRASCOGNA

In Memory of

Brigadier General Norman J. Bittner

1922 - 2007

Table of Contents

ACKNOWLEDGEMENTS

We are grateful to many people for their invaluable efforts on this project. Numerous people contributed to the successful completion of *Y'all vs. Us*, from traveling to do interviews with over 500 people, to the tedious job of transcribing 7500 pages of those interviews, to the photo shoots with over 400 football players, cheerleaders and mascots, to proofreading and editing. Our team included: Brenda Marsalis, Betty Orr, Janice Carden, Judy Frascogna, Shawnassey Britt, Freddie Ahrend, Kamel King and Tim Little.

A special thanks to Dr. Ennis Proctor and Dr. Phyfa Eiland of the Mississippi High School Activities Association for their valuable insight into the high schools of our state. Their support and knowledge have been priceless.

Also, our thanks to Buz Phillips (Olive Branch), Walter Thornton (Pascagoula and Moss Point) and Danny Davis (Clinton) for providing important historical data, and to Kay Smythe (South Panola), Kyle Brigance (Olive Branch), Will Crosby (Jackson Prep) and Peter Jernberg (Jackson Academy) for giving valuable feedback as readers of portions of the final manuscript.

Finally, we offer our thanks to the hundreds of interviewees at the rival schools in our book – coaches, players, students, administrators, booster club presidents, broadcasters, sports writers and mayors – who provided important background information, color and facts, without which there would be no book.

X.M. Frascogna, Jr.
X.M. Frascogna, III
Martin Frank Frascogna

CHAPTER
01
THE PERFECT STORM

Arguably, the greatest high school football rivalries in America are played every autumn in the Magnolia State. One reason Mississippi has so many rivalry games can be traced back to the efforts of one man – C.B. "Buck" Cameron.

Considered by many to be the "father of coaching" in Mississippi, Coach Cameron was born in 1902 in Quitman, Mississippi. The longtime coach and educator at Laurel High School was responsible for organizing the Big Three Conference. Originally, the Big Three consisted of the high schools at Laurel, Meridian and Hattiesburg. Later, the conference was expanded and renamed the Big Six. Because of continued growth in its membership, the conference was eventually split into divisions and the name changed for the final time to the Big Eight Conference. Coach Cameron served as the first president of the new super-sized conference. Sporting a membership of the largest high schools in Mississippi, the Big Eight remained the most prestigious conference in the state until its dissolution in the late '70s.

Shortly after organizing the original Big Three, Coach Cameron remarked that the reason he started the conference was "to have something the teams could play for," namely, a championship. For over half a century, the holy grail of high school football in Mississippi was the Big Eight Conference Championship. The schools that were not members of the Big Eight formed their own conferences, thereby establishing a network of conference affiliations across the state. Emerging from the conference schedules each season were critical games that determined conference championships. Consequently, the competitive environment in all the conferences throughout the state quickly led to the development of rivalries between many of the schools. Often, once conference championships were determined, the winners were invited to play in a number of post-season bowl games that were popular between the '30s and '70s.

Coach Cameron is well known for his athletic accomplishments while attending Mississippi A&M (now Mississippi State University), and for his success as a coach and educator; however, his influence goes even deeper into the football subculture of Mississippi. Because of Cameron's efforts in establishing the old Big Three Conference "to give the players something to play for," he helped create an environment that has encouraged football rivalries to flourish throughout Mississippi. From the '20s through the twenty-first century, Mississippi has always been a hotbed for high school football – especially its rivalry games. In many ways, C.B. "Buck" Cameron got it all going way back in the '20s with the old Big Three Conference.

****

After 40 years of coaching high school football, a retired veteran coach compared a good rivalry to a severe storm. In order to have a storm, all the right elements have to come together at the right time. The old coach would say, "It takes a strong cold front colliding with a strong warm front to create the turbulence needed to spawn a storm. Then, if everything comes together the right way, a storm might erupt."

According to the old coach, just like a storm, a good football rivalry needs the same delicate mix of elements. Some of the ingredients needed for a strong rivalry include:

Proximity – The closer the schools are to each other, the higher the volatility index. Three of the rivalries in this book, namely, Brandon-Pearl, Oxford-Lafayette and Vicksburg-Warren Central, rank extremely high when proximity is considered, while one rivalry, Jackson Academy-Jackson Prep, is off the charts.

Longevity – The longer the series history, the more intense the rivalry tends to become due to increased opportunities for controversy, high stakes games, the arrival of big name players and circumstance. Four rivalries in the book started in the 1920's. However, the granddaddy of all rivalries is Biloxi-Gulfport, which began in 1908.

Record – All-time rivalry records are an unusual element. The rivalry can be made more intense by close series records, but also by lopsided ones. After 48 meetings, the Biloxi-Gulfport series was knotted at a perfectly balanced 22-22-4. However, Vicksburg posted only a single win against Warren Central in their first 21 games. Despite the vastly different records, both rivalries burn as two of the hottest in the state.

Controversy – Every rivalry explored in this book has been blessed, or cursed, with some controversy. Elements of controversy help rivalries linger throughout the year as the controversial occurrence is debated over and over by town members. One of the more colorful incidents took place in 1970 in the annual game between Booneville and Baldwyn when the famous, or infamous, Garrett Tackle occurred. The tackle is still regularly discussed 38 years after it happened.

High Stakes – Often, the rivalry game on the schedule has high stakes attached to it in the form of a district, regional or sometimes even a state championship. Such is the case with a number of the rivalries covered in the book, but especially in the case of South Panola-Olive Branch, West Jones-Wayne County, Meridian-Oak Grove and Jackson Prep-Jackson Academy.

Coaches – Colorful coaches can do more than anyone to stimulate the passion surrounding a rivalry. Many an astute coach has used the media to "get in the heads" of their opponents or to motivate his own team. The undisputed king of using the media as a motivational tool and for literally creating a rivalry to energize his program is Coach Mike Justice. Along with Coach David Bradberry, these two men nearly singlehandedly created the Clinton-Madison Central rivalry.

Players – The more big-name, high-profile players coming out of a rival game over time, the better. This helps keep the folklore about the school's football greatness alive. The continued exploits of hometown heroes in college and the pros fan the flames of competition with a school's rival. For example, the Brookhaven teams of the late '50s featured a future Pro Football Hall of Famer and several college All-Americans and is still a topic of conversation more than half a century later.

Pride – The big rivalry games are driven more than anything else by community pride. For example, just ask anyone in Batesville about the Tigers, or over in Greene County, ask anyone if Wildcat football is important. As a matter of fact, ask anybody at any of the schools discussed in this book. You'll get the message. Pride is the primary motivator.

Circumstance – The outcome of many rival games can turn on a circumstance of the moment. Sometimes, a circumstance may appear in the form of an injury; at other times, it may be an accident; sadly, the circumstance may present itself as a death. The weather is a good example of how fickle circumstance can be and how it can influence the outcome of a game. The night the lights went out at Lafayette during the Oxford game, creating a 30-minute delay and allowing the Commodores to regroup and defeat the Chargers, is an example of this. However, Oxford fans saw this not as circumstance, but as a major controversy.

X-Factor – While circumstance cannot be controlled, it can be explained, at least to some degree. However, the X-Factor is unexplainable. Why did the momentum shift? Why did our running back play with a passion never seen before? Was it the ghosts of tradition that pulled the team to victory? Many of the rivalries in this book have had unexplained events occur during their games. Ironically, rivalry games seem to be fertile ground for quirky and bizarre events – the X-Factor at work.

Rivalries, like storms, may not come about even though all the right elements are in place. It takes the proper mix of all the required elements at the exact time to activate the event. Even though there are thousands of teams playing high school football every week during the fall all over America, only a few of those games fall into the special category of a rivalry game.

Y'all vs. Us explores some of the history, traditions, players and coaches surrounding 15 of the most popular high school football rivalries in Mississippi. Each school and each rivalry is unique and special to the players, students and fans of those communities that are fortunate enough to have one of these special games on their schedule every year. Enjoy!

★★ OFFICIAL GAME DAY PROGRAM $5.00 ★★

BRANDON
VERSUS
PEARL

BRANDON

NATIONAL AWARDS

The Recognition Specialists

PROUD SPONSOR OF MISSISSIPPI HIGH SCHOOL FOOTBALL

FRIDAY, AUGUST 29, 2008 ★ 7:00 PM KICKOFF

PIRATE STADIUM ★ PEARL, MISSISSIPPI

EAT DIRT!

"Good evening, football fans, and welcome to Pirate Country."

For 44 years, those familiar words spoken at the start of every game by the public address announcer at Pirate Stadium, Ray Rogers, have greeted Pearl fans and visitors. Since 1964, Ray has entertained generations of Pearl fans with his colorful announcements and play-by-play descriptions of games played on the Pirates' turf. Ray Rogers, or as he is affectionately known, "Mr. Pirate," has become an icon in the Pearl community. However, his notoriety extends well beyond his oratory skills as the voice of the Pirates. Ray Rogers is the personification of Pearl Pirate football.

Ray started school at Pearl in 1938. At the time, Pearl's school consisted of Grades 1 through 6. Before Ray completed the sixth grade, the school added a junior high, allowing him to continue through the ninth grade. Fortunately for Ray, a high school was added right at the time he graduated from junior high school. Prior to the establishment of Pearl High School, all of the high school age students in the Pearl community were bused to Central High School in downtown Jackson. At the start of the 1948-49 school year, Pearl High School officially opened its doors to fewer than 100 students. Ray Rogers was one of 17 students in Pearl High School's first sophomore class. In the spring of 1949, Pearl High School graduated its first senior class – all eight of them.

While Pearl did not field a football team in the fall of 1948, they did start preparing for the 1949 season. Consequently, about midyear, school administrators hired Pearl's first football coach, James Frances Cooper, a graduate of Murray State University in Kentucky. Coach Cooper conducted spring football drills in 1949, which consisted primarily of teaching his players how to put on their equipment, along with basic blocking and tackling techniques.

In the fall of 1949, Pearl High School fielded its first football team. The Pirate squad won the school's very first game, defeating Bentonia 20-0, and went on to post a respectable record of 3-6-1. The lone tie in its inaugural season came on Thanksgiving Day to a school just to the east of Pearl – the Brandon Bulldogs. The Pearl team and fans were pleased with the season-ending tie, since Brandon had been playing football for several years prior to the Pirates' arrival on the gridiron. Little did anyone know what was to come out of that first meeting between the two neighboring schools.

Leading the Pirate team in its first game against Bentonia was its co-captain and Pearl's first quarterback, a junior by the name of – Ray Rogers. In the inaugural game against Bentonia, Rogers was the first Pirate to score a touchdown for Pearl as he led his team to a decisive 20-0 win.

During Ray Rogers' senior season, he co-captained and quarterbacked the Pirates to a 6-5 finish, recording Pearl's first winning season. Rogers was selected to play in the Third Annual Mississippi High School North-South All-Star Game, becoming Pearl's first all-star player. Since Ray Rogers' graduation from Pearl High School in 1951, he has served his community as a representative in the Mississippi Legislature for 25 years and as the voice of the Pirates for the last 44 years.

Ray Rogers – one of the co-captains of Pearl's first football team, Pearl's first quarterback, the first Pirate to ever score a touchdown, Pearl's first quarterback to play in the Brandon rivalry, Pearl's first all-star player, representative to the Mississippi Legislature for 25 years and the voice of the Pirates for the last 44. There is little wonder why Ray Rogers is known throughout the City of Pearl and Rankin County as "Mr. Pirate."

A government teacher at Pearl always tests her students on their knowledge of state government by asking questions about current public officials. When she poses the question "Who is Ray Rogers?" to her class, most of her students answer, "Voice of the Pirates," rather than "Representative to the State Legislature." Comments Rogers, "I've been in the State Legislature for 25 years and the kids here don't know it, because to them I'm the 'Voice of the Pirates.' That's what's most important to them."

Pam Sutton, former Pearl High School student, says, "Ray Rogers has been the Voice of the Pearl Pirates for over 40 years. The minute he gets behind that mic in the press box and says, 'Welcome to Pirate Country,' it's just the most awesome feeling in the world. It's just one of those things that you have to be there to understand. When we honored the first Pearl football team at halftime of a recent game, everybody in the stands went wild when Mr. Ray's name was announced."

Prior to the first game of the season, which is typically the Pearl-Brandon game, all incoming freshmen students and the football team congregate in the school's gym for a special assembly program. Standing in the middle of the gym floor with a mic in his hand, Mr. Pirate greets the students. For the next 30 minutes, Ray mesmerizes his audience with Pirate stories that go all the way back to the beginning of the school's history. He relates how Pearl got the name "Pirates" and why its colors are blue and gold. From the very first game against Brandon in 1949 to the game played last year, Ray creates a timeline for his young audience to help them understand the history of their school. He tells story after story about Pearl High School – the school that has been and will always be the centerpiece of this community. The audience cheers time and again during Mr. Pirate's presentation. Comments Ray, "The kids eat it up. They get up and start clapping and cheering. Gosh, they fire me up."

One of the most interesting stories Ray Rogers tells his young audience is how Pearl ended up with the Pirate mascot. According to the story, there was a young man, Floyd Shearer, who left school at the age of 16 and joined the Merchant Marines right after World War II. For over a year, he toured the world, collecting several tattoos during his travels. On Floyd's left leg, from his knee down to his ankle, was a tattoo of a standing pirate in blue and gold. Well, according to the story told by Ray Rogers, Floyd returned to Pearl after his tour in the Merchant Marines and became a student – age unknown – in the junior class the year the high school opened. While Pearl had no football team that year, it did have a basketball team, and Floyd was on it. Standing 5'11" with long legs and curly hair, and armed with a great personality, Floyd was very popular. Everybody liked Floyd Shearer.

Pearl High School's first principal, L.W. Bright, summoned all the high school students to a meeting in the cafeteria early in the school year to choose the colors and the mascot for the new school. Some of the seniors had already gotten together and drawn up some proposals for the group. After a meeting that lasted over an hour, one of the seniors said, "I think we ought to call ourselves the 'Pirates' and we ought to get a mascot just like the one painted on Floyd Shearer's leg." Everybody went crazy over the name and the pirate on Floyd's leg. Debate continued on the colors until the choices of blue and gold or purple and gold remained. Someone mentioned that Bentonia's colors at the time were purple and gold. Once that information was presented to the group, Pearl immediately and unanimously adopted blue and gold as its colors and the Pirate as its mascot. According to Ray Rogers, "Floyd Shearer was so popular and influential he could have had a damn Tiger on his leg and we would have become the Pearl Tigers."

Floyd never left Rankin County after his return from the Merchant Marines, and he and Ray Rogers remained friends until Floyd's death. Ray comments, "I used to kid old Floyd and tell him all the time, 'Floyd, if anything happens to you, can we have that leg so we can embalm it and put it in the trophy case?' He would say, 'Hell no, you can't have my leg.'"

At a halftime reunion of the first Pirate team several years ago, the public address announcer recognized the old players individually. When he introduced Floyd, he asked, "Mr. Shearer, would you raise your britches on your left leg and show everybody that Pirate?" Floyd pulled up his left pants leg and held up the Pirate for everyone to see. The stadium went wild and 5,000 Pirate fans gave Floyd a standing ovation.

The Pearl football team has enjoyed an advantage over its opponents for quite some time. The Pirates play with 12 players – a twelfth man! The 170-piece Pearl Pirate Band has influenced the outcome of many games over the decades. Jeff Cannon, Pearl's Band Director and former drum major for the Pirate Band back in the '70s, comments, "We like to think we're the twelfth player. On many occasions, the band is the reason for the opposing teams jumping off sides. Our kids are pretty savvy and they know when it's time to crank it up and when it's time to be quiet. We like to feel that we help our guys when they're on the field."

The Pearl Band is a formidable teammate to have as that twelfth man. Over 19 percent of the school's student body is in the band; and over the last 20 years, all but two of the school's valedictorians and salutatorians have been members of the band.

Band Director Cannon gives a good historical perspective of the Pearl Band: "From the very beginning, even as far back as the early

'50s, the Pearl Band has been very active, participating in festivals and traveling to perform. There has always been great support for the band by the Pearl community and the school administration." The Pearl Band has performed in the Macy's Thanksgiving Day Parade, on the Today Show, in the Presidential Inaugural Parade in 2001, in various Mississippi Governors' Inaugural Parades and at several NFL games. The band recently won the MHSAA Class 4A Marching Band Championship.

Band Director Cannon gives insight into the Pearl Pirate Band's attitude as they approach each football game: "A football game is not the time to make an artistic impression. It is the time to entertain the crowd, do something exciting and get the crowd on their feet to keep the energy going. We try to do that at football games, because the band is part of the Pirate team – it's the twelfth man."

A good example of the historical connections between that first Pirate football team of 1949 and all the succeeding teams to take the field for Pearl vividly appears on page 78 of the 2007 Pearl football program. The caption at the top of the page reads, "It's a Pirate's Life for Me." Pictured there, ensconced between a Pearl football helmet and a Wilson football and resting atop a Pearl jersey, is Jack Frazier Durr, age 14 days. Comments Jack's mom, Tiffany Blair Durr, "Pearl is the only place where people have their babies' pictures taken in a football helmet. Our son Jack had his picture taken in his Pearl helmet and jersey when he was two weeks old. We have every intention of him being a Pearl Pirate." Jack Frazier Durr – Class of 2025.

Fifty-nine years after Pearl High School fielded its first team in the fall of 1949, the tradition of Pirate football continues through its players, its band, its fans, the community and, most of all, through the Voice of the Pirates, Ray Rogers.

Welcome to Pirate Country!

****

Louis Gene Strickland Field is located in the middle of the city of Brandon. To many of Brandon's residents, Strickland Field is the hub, the very center of the community. Visitors to Strickland Field at Bulldog Stadium can immediately sense the vintage of the structure by the closeness of the stands to the playing field. Literally, spectators are on top of the action. In today's liability-conscious society, the down side is that maybe fans are too close to the field. Because of liability concerns and the lack of modern conveniences, there is some speculation that Bulldog Stadium might eventually move to the campus of the new Brandon High School several miles away. Even though the high school relocated to Highway 18 over three years ago, the community was not ready to move Bulldog Stadium. There are just too many memories of the numerous games played in the old stadium. For now at least, Strickland Field at Bulldog Stadium awaits the arrival of the next season of Brandon Bulldog football.

Buddy Bailey, Principal of Brandon High School, provides interesting insight into the importance of the old stadium. Bailey says, "Every community is built on a foundation. The people who have come before us have laid the history of this community – its foundation. We continue to build on it." Louis Gene Strickland Field has deep meaning for many people in Brandon. In many ways, the old stadium is a monument to the history created by the people of Brandon, both past and present. It is the foundation upon which the future will be built. According to the wise words of Principal Bailey, "Moving that foundation does affect people. It's sometimes much bigger than we realize."

Legendary Brandon football coach Wally Bumpas describes what it's like to play on Strickland Field: "The stands are right on top of the field and there is very little out of bounds space. There is a chain link fence around the field. That chain link fence has come down a time or two because of so many people pressing against it."

During the 1983 Brandon-Pearl game at Strickland Field, a photograph was taken that appeared in an article about high school football in America for *U.S. News and World Report*. The photographer snapped the picture from the home side, shooting across to the visitor's side. All around the field, especially the end zones, were people eight to ten deep. The photo showed an over-the-top shot of the home crowd, the visitor's side completely full and all those people standing around the fence. The attendance that night was between nine and ten thousand people in a stadium built to hold five thousand. The caption under the photo read, "Brandon versus Pearl. December 1983. Attendance 9500." According to Coach Bumpas, "By the third quarter, the people were up and down the sidelines and mingled in with our players."

Former Brandon student and current Bulldog radio announcer, Jason Scarborough, describes the view of the old stadium from the press box:

I love the stadium because it is so unique. It's kind of down in a hole. When the crowds begin to make noise, the sounds stay within that little hole and it resonates and creates a unique feeling during the game. From the press box, I can see the elementary school I attended. Behind the visitor's bleachers sits the baseball field. The whole school has a campus-like feel to it. The old Brandon High School is now the middle school. The stadium is big; however, there have been many games when there was standing room only. Many times, there are three, four or five people deep around the fence. Every bit of the stadium is slam full for the Brandon-Pearl game.

Only two head football coaches have guided the Bulldog program from 1980 to 2008 – Wally Bumpas and Dan Davis. Both men understand the pride of the Brandon community for the Bulldog football program and the significance of Strickland Field. Coach Bumpas says, "There is a lot of support here. There are many successful people in the Brandon community and they expect their kids to be successful. They expect them to be achievers. It feeds on itself." Coach Davis adds, "Louis Gene Strickland coached at Brandon in the late '50s on through the mid-'60s. He won the overall Little Dixie Conference Championship in 1966. That was a pretty big deal. Most of the 'old time' traditional Brandon area people played for Coach Strickland – Sonny Shamburger, David Tigrett, Robbie McLeod and Watson Purvis. They say he was a great guy to play for. Coach Strickland made a lasting impact on the Brandon community."

Bulldog radio announcer, Jason Scarborough, says, "Brandon has a long history of great football teams. Coach Bumpas had quite a few great teams, and since Coach Davis has been here, there have been even more. Those Jerious Norwood-led teams put up some incredible offensive numbers. Brandon has a long lineage of great football players, and Brandon has always been known as a football town."

Brandon Principal, Buddy Bailey, remarks,

When your students are on the field, you say, "Those are our kids." There is an ownership of those kids by the Brandon community. Those kids on the field are a representation of the community and what it stands for. The community wants them to represent us well and we want them to win because we are winners. They reflect our community values. Their performance relates back to the community. Every Saturday morning when I go downtown, no matter where I go, someone asks about our kids' performance on Friday night. I think that is vital. That is one thing Brandon has always been able to do – keep the consistency of a hometown atmosphere. Everyone in our community invests in our students. I believe the teams on the field today continue to be a reflection of our community. We want them to represent us well, to fight to the end and to win. If we can't win, we want them to display the concepts we stand for, which are never quit, team unity, sticking together no matter what and representing yourself the way the community would want to be represented.

The entire Brandon community expresses the sentiments of Principal Bailey in different ways; however, no other event binds the community in a common cause the way the annual football game with archrival Pearl does. Players, students, fans, administrators, alumni and even retired folks living in the two cities who never attended school at either high school get in the act. The Brandon-Pearl football game is not just a rivalry between two schools. It is a contest between two communities.

Current head football coach, Dan Davis, comments, "Before there was the rivalry in football, there was the rivalry between these two communities. I think the rivalry is so intense because of its longevity. It has even outlived the fact that the two schools are no longer in the same classification. It's still serious business."

Joseph Barnes, current Bulldog football player, says, "The rivalry has been going on for such a long time. My dad played here and it was a big game for him. Dad always used to tell me, 'When you graduate, everybody is going to ask you about your team, but the one question they really want answered is: Did you beat Pearl?'"

Joseph Barnes describes the big game against Pearl from a player's perspective: "It's the first game of the season. All summer you have been hitting the weights, running and putting everything you have into those workouts. There are more people in the stands for that first game against Pearl than for any other game all year. The bands are playing and people are hollering and yelling from both sides. The hair on your head, arms and legs is standing up and you can feel the chill bumps. It makes you just want to go out and play."

Former Bulldog players Ti Garner and Jerious Norwood comment on the involvement of the Brandon community in the Pearl rivalry. Ti Garner says, "I remember how involved the community is during the week of the Pearl game. When you are around town with people who know you, everybody wants to talk to you about the game. During the other weeks of the season it's business as usual, but the week of the Pearl game, the whole community is involved. Everybody is getting ready to play the game. It is huge for the community."

Jerious Norwood, one of Brandon's all-time greats and now a veteran NFL player, sums up his feelings about the rivalry: "Of all the football games I've played in, the most fun I've ever had was being a part of the Brandon-Pearl rivalry."

Brandon's mayor, Carlo Martella, offers his view of the rivalry: "I think it's a big part of the social life of Brandon. You go to the barbershop before the season starts and they are already talking about the game. It always comes down to who wins the Brandon-Pearl game."

Brandon coach Dan Davis says, "It's hard to describe to someone unless they have been involved in the rivalry. Words don't do it justice. It brings out the emotion and pride of our community. It is an exciting, electrifying, extremely competitive series. You just have to be in it to appreciate the experience."

From the school administrator's point of view, the week of the annual clash between the Bulldogs and Pirates is always interesting. Says Brandon Principal Buddy Bailey, "Some of the most memorable moments are the Friday pep rallies and the events leading up to the big game. Like it or not, the Friday of the Pearl game is all about the pep rally. The entire week leads up to the pep rally, which lasts at least two hours. It is not only a school function, but a community function as well. All of the activities leading up to the Pearl game unite the community in a way that very few things can."

One highlight during the week of festivities occurs at the pep rally before the big game. That is when the Brandon Bulldog clashes with, defeats and kills the Pearl Pirate. Enter June Hollis, Brandon teacher and resident Pearl Pirate impersonator. For the last 27 years, June Hollis, like a cat with nine lives, has tripled her feline life expectancy and returned from the dead to taunt Brandon students, only to be sent to her death yet again. Ironically, Mrs. Hollis grew up in Pearl, graduated from Pearl High School and taught in the Pirate Den for two years before coming to Brandon.

June Hollis recalls her early days at Brandon: "When the students found out I had been teaching at Pearl and graduated from Pearl, it was like, 'Okay, what can we do to this lady?' The first year I was here, the cheerleaders asked me if I would play the Pearl Pirate in a skit at the pep rally before the Pearl game, so I did. From that first year and ever since, they have asked me if I would play the Pirate. I've been doing it for 27 years now."

June Hollis a/k/a The Pearl Pirate has suffered all sorts of humiliation at the hands of the Brandon students, and especially the Brandon Bulldog, during the pep rally the week of the Pearl game. No matter the story line of the skit, the Bulldog wins, the Pirate loses and the terrible event ends in the Pirate's demise. June Hollis describes the horror of her last moments: "I made up my own little tacky Pirate suit. Every year the Bulldog beats me up and kills me, and then they drag me off. One year the students put me in a coffin and some football players carried me off."

June Hollis recalls a funny story involving Mississippi Governor Ronnie Musgrove:

> When Governor Musgrove was in office, his children were in school here. Like many parents, he attended the pep rally before the Pearl game. I was in my Pirate outfit with my little plastic sword and I started walking toward a group of fans during the skit, not knowing the Governor was among them. Suddenly, the Governor's two bodyguards jumped in front of him to protect him from the Pirate with the sword. I guess they thought I was going to stab Governor Musgrove with my little plastic sword.

After 27 years of teaching world history and geography at Brandon, June Hollis retired at the end of the 2007-08 school year. As far as her continued theatrics at the annual Pearl pep rally are concerned, she says, "I'm a glutton for punishment. Even though I'm old and have gained too much weight, I would do it for the next 50 years if I'm still around. I think it would be fun."

June Hollis and her husband have attended Brandon home football games for the past 27 years and have sat in the same reserved seats the entire time. At a retirement party honoring June's service as a teacher and Pirate impersonator at Brandon High School, her only wish was that she and her husband be allowed to continue to sit in their reserved seats after her retirement. Coach Dan Davis granted her wish – seats for life! Such an ironic twist for this graduate and former teacher from Pearl to be bestowed seats for life in Bulldog Stadium.

****

Eat dirt, Pearl. Eat dirt!
Eat dirt, Brandon. Eat dirt!
No one knows exactly when it started, but everyone takes credit for starting it – the famous "Eat Dirt" cheer. Today, both the Brandon and Pearl fans scream the chant frequently and loudly. According to former Brandon head football coach Wally Bumpas, "It was here when I came to Brandon in 1980. Both sides would holler that 'Eat Dirt' cheer at each other starting at 6:00 for a 7:30 game. I don't have the foggiest idea where it came from or who started it." Mr. Pirate, Ray Rogers, weighs in on the mystery: "Well, I've been doing it ever since I can remember. It's the most famous cheer at Pearl-Brandon football games. They holler 'Eat dirt' at each other during the whole game. I can't say exactly when it started, but I can't remember a time when it wasn't part of the Pearl-Brandon game." Pearl Principal Raymond Morgigno confirms, "I recall the 'Eat Dirt' cheer being used when my family moved to Pearl when I was 5 years old." Collette Usry, a 2008 graduate and former Brandon cheerleader, adds, "I've been at Brandon from kindergarten through twelfth grade, and 'Eat Dirt, Pearl' has always been drilled into our heads. That's the famous chant. We try to chant it loud enough so they can hear us all the way to Pearl." Tiffany Blair Durr, a 1996 graduate and former Pearl cheerleader, says, "The first cheer you learn at Pearl is 'Eat Dirt, Brandon. Eat Dirt.'"

While the origin of the famous "Eat Dirt" cheer has become obscure over time, urban myths handed down through generations of Brandon and Pearl graduates have kept each school's claim of authorship alive. Even with the conflicting evidence of ownership, the most detailed account regarding the origin of the cheer comes from Tommie Hill, a graduate of Pearl High School and a 31-year veteran teacher at her alma mater:

I'm going to give you the correct answer to

where the "Eat Dirt" cheer started and who started it. I was a junior at Pearl High School in 1970. On Fridays during football season, we were given a 15-minute break from classes and marched around the parking lot and had a little pep rally. The drummers played their drums and we led cheers. One Friday, Signa Chestnut, who had moved to Pearl from Morton, asked us if we had ever done the cheer "Eat Dirt?" I said, "What?" She said, "That's the cheer we've used against some of our rival schools." I said, "How does it go?" She said, "Eat dirt, Brandon. Eat dirt." We started chanting that around the parking lot. Some of the teachers and administrators thought that cheer was rude and told us not to use it, so it kind of started out as taboo. It was as if it was profanity. That's what we chanted at the beginning of our games. Then the other side started to do it. I will never forget it. Pearl started the "Eat Dirt" cheer in 1970.

Regardless of which school receives credit for starting the famous "Eat Dirt" cheer, one fact is certain: both Brandon and Pearl use the chant to harass the other to the fullest extent. Hollering "Eat Dirt, Pearl" and yelling "Eat Dirt, Brandon" at each other has helped keep the rivalry heated and competitive from 1970 to today – or maybe before 1970, depending on whether or not you believe Tommie Hill's version of the story. Did Signa Chestnut really exist?

The Bulldogs and Pirates first collided on the football field on Thanksgiving Day in 1949. The historic first meeting between the schools resulted in a 0-0 tie – the only tie in the 59-year history of the series. According to Ray Rogers, the quarterback of Pearl's 1949 team, "The game was so competitive that afterwards, a lot of fans got into tussles and spats. It grew from there to become one of the greatest football rivalries in the state."

In the 1950 game, the second of the series, Brandon defeated Pearl 27-20 to claim a one-game lead in the series. However, Brandon's lead was temporary. In 1951, Pearl defeated Brandon 21-13 to even the series. The next year, 1952, Brandon won 25-7 to go ahead in the series two to one. However, there were problems on the horizon. According to Ray Rogers, "After every one of those four games there were scuffles and fights – mostly by the fans. Sometimes the players got into it, too. Both teams had players who got kicked out of the game for fighting, but most of all it was the fans."

According to an eyewitness account during the first game in 1949, the Brandon center was Bennie Hill and the center for Pearl was Willie Paul Beason. Throughout the game, both players were all over each other because each played defense against the other. Hill was on top of Beason when Pearl had the ball, and Beason was on top of Hill when Brandon was on offense. By the third quarter, it got so heated both players started fighting in the middle of the field and both were ejected from the game. It was the first game of the series and both starting centers were thrown out for fighting. The tone was set for the rivalry in game one of the series.

The competition got so hostile after only four ball games that the Mississippi High School Activities Association had to step in and stop the football series between the two schools. Consequently, they suspended play between Brandon and Pearl in 1953 and 1954. However, it had become such a big game for both schools that administrators and fans lobbied to get the Brandon-Pearl game back on the schedule. The MHSAA allowed the schools to resume play in 1955 after the two-year suspension. According to Ray Rogers, "Since 1955, it's been dog eat dog."

While the cooling-off period in 1953 and 1954 did create a somewhat calmer atmosphere for the next three decades, there were indications all hell could break loose at any time. In 1988, it happened – all hell did break loose. "The brawl" occurred at Pearl on a wet, muddy field with the Pirates enjoying a comfortable lead with time running down to the final buzzer. Pearl's tailback took a handoff from the quarterback on a straight-ahead dive play in an attempt to kill the clock. After driving a few yards, he was stopped in a pile of Bulldog and Pirate players. The entangled players started pushing, then kicking and then punching one another as the pile started to grow larger. Quickly, players from both teams who were on the field became involved in fisticuffs. Like an amoeba, the pile kept growing. Then both benches cleared as players from both sides rushed toward each other like armies engaged in ancient combat. The next wave of combatants came from the stands as fans jumped fences and rushed to the aid of their teams. The brawl was on. Players, fans and anyone who had a remote affiliation with either school became involved in the incident on the field. It took coaches, administrators and a large contingent of local and state police over 15 minutes to regain order.

A cameraman from a local television station caught all the action.

When the news aired that night, it showed people across the entire field fighting. It was a classic bench-clearing brawl with fans from both sides jumping over the fence and running onto the field to fight.

Pearl's current head football coach, John Perry, was on the team the night of the brawl. He recalls, "I can't remember the score, but I think we were ahead by 14 points with the game almost over. On the last play of the game, a Brandon player hit our tailback late and knocked him out. Then out of nowhere, a melee started. There were people everywhere fighting. I was playing on the offensive line. When the play was over, I was on the bottom of the pile looking up. I couldn't move. The next thing I knew, the pile was getting bigger and people were running around shouting and yelling. I knew we were in a fight."

Coach Perry continues,

> I had a little brother who was on the team as a tenth grader. I was a senior. When the game was over, he was covered in mud. When we got home that night, we started talking about the fight. He told me he was coming on the field to help me, but he got knocked down by a Brandon guy who hit him with his helmet. My little brother didn't know my dad had filmed the entire fight. Well, we rolled the tape. My brother was running around outside the pile and was so scared he kept slipping down in the mud. Then he would get up and run some more. He never touched anybody.

Also on the field as a player the night of the brawl was current Pearl Principal, Raymond Morgigno, who expresses mixed emotions regarding the incident. He remarks, "I remember I felt like this was the way to go out as a senior. This had to be the greatest moment of my life. It's a memory I'll never forget. But now as a principal, I would have a heart attack."

There was an ironic ending to the brawl incident. Two weeks later, Pearl received an invitation to play Southaven in a postseason bowl. The name of the bowl? The Sportsmanship Bowl!

During the period of 1991 to 1993, the Pearl-Brandon series moved to Mississippi Veterans Memorial Stadium as part of the "Super Saturday" high school doubleheader weekend. The first year the Bulldogs and Pirates met at Memorial Stadium, they shared the card with another big Magnolia State rivalry – Mendenhall and Magee. Brandon's head football coach at the time, Wally Bumpas, recalls, "The first year we played at Memorial Stadium we had 17,000 people. Stadium officials told me that was the biggest crowd for a high school game in Mississippi at the time." Over the next two years the Bulldogs and Pirates battled at Memorial Stadium, their games drew record-breaking crowds and expanded the fan base for both schools' football programs.

One of the more humorous stories resulting from a Brandon and Pearl game involved an injured Brandon player or, according to Coach Wally Bumpas, "a not so injured" Brandon player. Coach Bumpas tells the story:

> We played at Brandon in 1987 and got behind 21-0 early in the second quarter. Long story short, we had caught up enough where one score would win the game for us. We were trying to drive for the winning touchdown with a little over a minute to play in the game. We had a receiver who had caught several passes and really hurt them. The ball was somewhere around Pearl's 30-yard line. Our quarterback hit our receiver, Michael Elliott, on an out pattern. As he caught the ball, he was knocked out of bounds on the Pearl sideline. Well, the next thing I knew, our receiver was surrounded by dozens of people, many of whom were paramedics and medical staff for Pearl's team. It took several minutes to clear everybody out and get our medical staff to our player to check him out. When our staff finally got to him over on the Pearl sideline, the paramedics had already put his entire right arm in an air splint. Our team doctor said, "Wait a minute. This is my player. Y'all don't have anything to do with him." When our team doctor got our player to our sideline and examined him, he determined there was nothing wrong with his arm and removed the air splint. During this time, the clock was running down. The game was almost over when we sent Elliott back into the game. On maybe the last play of the game, he caught the winning touchdown pass in the corner of the end zone. I know what they were trying to do, because I've done it before. It wasn't any secret.

Ray Durr, former Pearl football player and current assistant football coach, remembers the Brandon game his senior season in 1993:

We had only won three ballgames leading into the Brandon game. They were already going to the playoffs. If we beat them, they had to go to South Panola to play; however, if Brandon beat us, they would get to play at home against some other team. All we wanted to do was beat Brandon, because we had not had a good year. Brandon was winning 17-0 before we scored a point. Then we came out in the second half and ran the ball right at them and just dominated. We ended up beating Brandon 26-24. I get chill bumps just talking about it.

****

Mr. Pirate, Ray Rogers, offers a startling thought to people who don't really understand the emotional dynamics of a good ole down home rivalry: "Pearl and Brandon folks are not enemies; we're rivals. There is a difference, a big difference. In a good rivalry, longtime friendships are established."

There is no better example of the wisdom of Ray Rogers' statement than the Pearl-Brandon game played on September 14, 2001, at Louis Gene Strickland Field. Many fans simply refer to it as "the 9-11 game."

Following the horrific events at the World Trade Center in New York City; Shanksville, Pennsylvania; and the Pentagon in Washington, D.C. on September 11, 2001, most schools in Mississippi temporarily suspended their Friday night football games. However, school administrators at Brandon and Pearl received numerous telephone calls from people urging them to play the game as scheduled. These folks were not motivated by a zealous competitive spirit for football, but rather by a yearning for a return to some normalcy. Playing the game would be a symbol for everyone in the community, but most of all to those terrorists abroad, that America could take the terrorists' best shot and it still wasn't enough to deter our way of life. Dr. Ennis Proctor, Executive Director of the Mississippi High School Activities Association, was one of the people in support of playing the game as scheduled. According to Dr. Proctor, "The decision to support the schools in playing this game was an easy one. Both schools felt this game could unify and comfort their communities. They were right. It did heal the communities."

Adding to the national drama of the terrible events of the week was the local drama of the annual Brandon-Pearl football game, and the interest in Brandon's superstar running back, Jerious Norwood. Once the MHSAA made the decision to go forward with the game, Mississippians from all over the state converged on Louis Gene Strickland Field to see Norwood play, witness a great rivalry, attempt a return to some normalcy and, most of all, to send a message to terrorists around the world – "You don't scare us!"

Bo Hynes, a Brandon teacher, recalls the evening of the 9-11 game:

> I was working the game as one of the administrators with the school. It became apparent two hours before the game that we were fixing to have problems with the crowd. Shortly before game time, the fire marshal told us, "Don't let another person in the stadium." One of our problems was we had presold a lot of tickets, and many of the folks who had purchased tickets were still outside the gate. We had people screaming mad. It was the largest crowd I have ever seen at a high school football game.

Most of the people attending the game that evening were not from Brandon or Pearl. The crowd that gathered at Louis Gene Strickland Field was from all over the Magnolia State. They came to watch a high school football game in an attempt to get their lives back to normal. There were busloads of kids and fans from around the state that had come to watch the game and to find some peace from the events of the week.

The pre-game ceremonies were chilling. Starting with a moment of silence in memory of the Americans who had lost their lives earlier in the week in New York, Pennsylvania and Washington, D.C., and followed by a prayer, the ceremonies served to punctuate an already somber moment. Then, for the first time in the history of the 50-year rivalry, the Pearl Pirate Band and the Brandon Bulldog Band, together with their respective R.O.T.C. color guards, marched onto the field together, took their formation and played "God Bless America" and the "National Anthem." Red, white and blue balloons were released during the playing of the "National Anthem" by both bands. With an overflow crowd of 12,000 people, everyone in the stadium joined in the singing of the "National Anthem" and "God Bless America." When it was over, there wasn't a dry eye in the stadium. The moment was riveting.

Jeff Cannon, Pearl High School's band director, describes the incredible moment: "You could tell we were all dealing with something a lot more important than a football game. Even though we were on opposing sides, we were teammates that night. It went from 'y'all versus us' to 'us versus the terrorists.' All of a sudden, we weren't rivals anymore. It was amazing."

Bo Hynes says, "It was one of those high school games that you never, ever forget." Pam Sutton, a Pearl graduate, says, "We came together as a community and as a nation and it was really an awesome night."

Raymond Morgigno, current principal at Pearl High School, recalls, "It was a special night. It's the only time I can remember turning people away at the gate because the stadium was stuffed to capacity. The people who could not get in were standing in the streets trying to watch the game. There was such togetherness that night." Another Pearl graduate, Tiffany Blair Durr, says, "It was an extremely patriotic and moving event."

As Ray Rogers said, "Pearl and Brandon folks aren't enemies; we're rivals." There is a big difference. In case you don't understand, ask anybody who was at Louis Gene Strickland Field the night of September 14 and they will explain what Ray was talking about.

God Bless America!

WHAT THE PIRATES SAY ABOUT BRANDON

Eat dirt, Brandon. Eat dirt.

Everybody at Pearl

I did not fully appreciate the Brandon-Pearl rivalry when I was playing because I thought everybody had a rival game like that. You really appreciate it and begin to understand how unique it is once you go to other places.

John Perry
Former Pearl Football Player and
Current Head Football Coach

The chant "Eat dirt, Brandon" really starts the week of the Pearl-Brandon game, but it stays around all year.

Michael Parker
Pearl Football Player

Both the Brandon and the Pearl communities take great pride in their schools. That's what both communities have in common. That's one reason the rivalry is so good.

Jeff Cannon
Pearl Band Director

The Brandon-Pearl rivalry is not only our school versus their school. It's also our community versus their community.

Hannah DeSalvo
Former Pearl Student

I think there is competition between Pearl and Brandon at every level.

Ray Durr
Former Pearl Football Player and
Current Assistant Football Coach

Brandon has a lot of pride and tradition, just as Pearl has a lot of pride and tradition. It's a healthy rivalry. It really is. It's a good thing for both communities and it's a lot of fun.

Raymond Morgigno
Former Pearl Football Player
and Current Pearl Principal

If you have a 1 and 9 season, but you beat Brandon, you might get a raise.

John Perry
Former Pearl Football Player and
Current Head Football Coach

My fondest memory of the Pearl-Brandon game is the fact that even if our football team came out on the short end of the score, our band was undefeated at halftime.

Jeff Cannon
Pearl Band Director

When I was growing up, you really didn't talk to people from Brandon. It was that serious. You didn't even buy gas in Brandon. If you ran out of gas, you pushed your car to Pearl.

Tommie Hill
Former Pearl Student and
Current Cheerleader Sponsor

Brandon and Pearl are two different places. When you ride through the parking lot at Brandon, you see BMWs and other fine cars. When you ride through the parking lot at Pearl, you see trucks that you need a ladder to get into. Our kids are going to be tougher, blue-collar type folks.

John Perry
Former Pearl Football Player and
Current Head Football Coach

I hate the Wing T to this day because Brandon used to run it.

Ray Durr

Former Pearl Football Player and

Current Assistant Football Coach

During the week of the Pearl-Brandon game, even the principals of each school are trash talking back and forth with each other – all in good fun.

Raymond Morgigno

Former Pearl Football Player

and Current Pearl Principal

I attended one Pearl-Brandon game when I was young, and I remember the two mascots got into a fight and the police had to pull them apart. It's an intense game.

Michael Parker

Pearl Football Player

Because of all the trailer sales in Pearl they call us 'trailer trash.'

Ray Durr

Former Pearl Football Player and

Current Assistant Football Coach

Jerious Norwood was one of the best – if not the best – high school running backs I have ever seen.

Ray Rogers

Former Pearl Football Player

and Public Address Announcer

You don't plan your wedding or the birth of your babies for the date of the annual Pearl-Brandon game.

Pam Sutton

Former Pearl Student

WHAT THE BULLDOGS SAY ABOUT PEARL

Eat dirt, Pearl. Eat dirt.

Everybody at Brandon

I think the atmosphere of the Pearl-Brandon game is like the Super Bowl of high school football.

Jerious Norwood
Former Brandon Football Player

The records do go out the window when Brandon and Pearl play football.

Jason Scarborough
Brandon Radio Announcer

It all starts out with friendship between the communities and each one wanting to beat the other one so they can have bragging rights.

Buddy Bailey
Brandon Principal

For years, it has been kind of a tradition that we wear white trash bags on the day of the Pearl game.

Collette Usry
Former Brandon Cheerleader

You have to experience a Brandon-Pearl pep rally, because there really isn't anything quite like it. The game is big, but at the pep rally all the students are so excited. It's a culmination of all the preparations during the week. It puts you on a high for the entire day.

Lane Davis
Wife of Head Football Coach Dan Davis

Pearl is stereotyped as the redneck, white trash school. We are stereotyped as the conceited, preppie school.

Maci Palasini
Former Brandon Student Body President

I know the Pearl folks call Brandon people snooty and preppie and the sweater vest clan. We consider Pearl the country, backwoods folks.

Jason Scarborough
Brandon Radio Announcer

When the two bands go at each other, you have to show out until the end.

Steven Baptiste
Former Brandon Football
Player and Band Member

The first time I met Dan's parents was when I came to a Pearl-Brandon game. When we went into the stadium, I was stunned. It was ten deep in both end zones, and we were there two hours before the game started.

Lane Davis
Wife of Head Football Coach Dan Davis

The football rivalry is big, but the rivalry carried over to other sports, too. Of course, the intensity of football is the biggest.

Buddy Bailey
Brandon Principal

I had a lot of friends who played for Pearl. We were always talking noise back and forth about who was gonna do what. My brother played for Pearl and we bumped heads during the game and almost got to fighting on the field.

Jerious Norwood
Former Brandon Football Player

There was a little joke whenever Pearl beat us. We would say, "Those pink flamingos are flying high over in the trailer parks." All in good fun. Just picking at them.

Steve McCann
Former Brandon Football Player
and Assistant Football Coach

One year there was a toilet placed in front of the school with a sign that said, "Brandon Stinks." We beat them that Friday night, and by the next week we had t-shirts with the score on them that read, "Pearl, flush this."

Lane Davis
Wife of Head Football Coach Dan Davis

It would be easier on the administrators at both schools if we just declared the Pearl-Brandon game day a holiday.

Buddy Bailey
Brandon Principal

There is nothing better than a Brandon-Pearl game on a Friday night.

Jason Scarborough
Brandon Radio Announcer

BRANDON-PEARL
SERIES HISTORY

Year	Brandon	Score	Pearl
1949	Collier Jordon	0-0	J.F. Cooper
1950	Jack Pop Warner	27-20	J.F. Cooper
1951	Jack Pop Warner	13-21	George Dearing
1952	Jack Pop Warner	25-7	George Dearing
1953		*Did not play*	
1954		*Did not play*	
1955	Louis Strickland	31-7	Arthur Baugh
1956	Louis Strickland	19-14	Arthur Baugh
1957	Wade Bass	32-14	Arthur Baugh
1958	Wade Bass	27-19	C.G. Muse
1959	Wade Bass	27-0	Fred Foster
1960	Burnett Blackmon	7-0	Fred Foster
1961	Burnett Blackmon	0-19	Bob Parker
1962	Louis Strickland	6-38	Bob Parker
1963	Louis Strickland	20-7	Bob Parker
1964	Louis Strickland	7-0	Bob Parker
1965	Louis Strickland	9-0	Bob Neblett
1966	Louis Strickland	26-12	Bob Neblett
1967	Troy Greer	21-13	Bob Neblett
1968	Phil Flynn	6-38	Joel Hudson
1969	Danny Neely	7-31	Joel Hudson
1970	Jack McAlpan	13-0	Cotton Robertson
1971	Jack McAlpan	27-7	Cotton Robertson
1972	Jack McAlpan	7-37	John Blaylock
1973	Jack McAlpan	3-26	John Blaylock
1974	Jack McAlpan	21-26	John Blaylock
1975	Henry Rath	14-13	John Blaylock
1976	Henry Rath	14-6	Joe Edwards
1977	Danny Gregory	20-19	Joe Edwards
1978	Danny Gregory	12-10	Doug Merchant
1979	Larry Hancock	0-31	Doug Merchant
1980	Wally Bumpas	20-13	Doug Merchant
1981	Wally Bumpas	17-7	Doug Merchant
1982	Wally Bumpas	13-3	Doug Merchant

Year	Brandon	Score	Pearl
1983	Wally Bumpas	12-21	Doug Merchant
1984	Wally Bumpas	7-3	Bruce Merchant
1985	Wally Bumpas	7-41	Bruce Merchant
1986	Wally Bumpas	6-7	Bruce Merchant
1987	Wally Bumpas	33-29	Bruce Merchant
1988	Wally Bumpas	13-20	Bruce Merchant
1989	Wally Bumpas	7-38	Bruce Merchant
1990	Wally Bumpas	24-10	Bruce Merchant
1991	Wally Bumpas	27-23	Bruce Merchant
1992	Wally Bumpas	13-42	Bruce Merchant
1993	Wally Bumpas	24-26	Bruce Merchant
1994	Wally Bumpas	14-17	Bruce Merchant
1995	Dan Davis	31-20	Bruce Merchant
1996	Dan Davis	27-20	Bruce Merchant
1997	Dan Davis	21-14	Bruce Merchant
1998	Dan Davis	22-31	Marcus Boyles
1999	Dan Davis	10-7	Marcus Boyles
2000	Dan Davis	38-7	Larry Weems
2001	Dan Davis	42-13	Larry Weems
2002	Dan Davis	49-15	Larry Weems
2003	Dan Davis	7-12	Larry Weems
2004	Dan Davis	14-18	Larry Weems
2005	Dan Davis	20-21	Larry Weems
2006	Dan Davis	35-16	Jack French
2007	Dan Davis	35-20	Jack French

★★ OFFICIAL GAME DAY PROGRAM $5.00 ★★

WEST JONES
VERSUS
WAYNE COUNTY

MUSTANGS

42

5

STADIUM WRAP

PROUD SPONSOR OF MISSISSIPPI HIGH SCHOOL FOOTBALL

FRIDAY, OCTOBER 31, 2008 ★ 7:00 PM KICKOFF
WAR EAGLE STADIUM ★ WAYNESBORO, MISSISSIPPI

CHAPTER

03

TWO BULLS, ONE PASTURE

Anyone who is even remotely familiar with the landscape of high school football in Mississippi understands the intensity, importance and excellence of football in Wayne County. The War Eagles of Wayne County High School in Waynesboro, Mississippi, have produced some of the most dominant teams of the past decade. The proud citizens of Wayne County support their teams like nothing else in the community. However, there was a time in the not so distant past when War Eagle football was not only less than dominant on the gridiron, but was also a source of discontent and division off the field.

Like many other areas of Mississippi, Wayne County can be described as a "tough man's" part of the state. It is largely rural and sparsely populated. The entire county boasts a population of a little over 21,000, with the county seat of Waynesboro holding approximately 5,000 of those residents. The primary industries in Wayne County are timber and oil, but the most important natural resource, both past and present, is high school football.

For many years, the citizens of Wayne County drew their identity from their four high schools. Individuals were either a black and gold Tiger from Beat Four, a royal blue and gold Buccaneer from Buckatunna, a maroon and gold Whippet from Clara or a green and white Panther from Waynesboro Central. Coach Tim Blackwell, a 1981 graduate of Clara High School, describes Wayne County as a "clannish" county, especially when it comes to sports. "Everyone wanted to beat the other so badly. Whoever the dominant team in the county was the previous year was who everyone hated the next year. We all wanted to capture county bragging rights for our school and community," says Blackwell.

The three smaller schools (Beat Four, Buckatunna and Clara) competed in the old Sam Dale Conference, while Waynesboro Central resided in the Singing River Conference in the days before district play. Waynesboro Central was the largest of the schools in Wayne County and was viewed as the "city school" by the other three. Despite the difference in size, all the schools in the county competed with Waynesboro Central. Kenny Odom, current radio broadcaster for War Eagle football and longtime resident of Wayne County, recalls an especially heated contest between Clara and Waynesboro Central. "The match-up between Clara and Waynesboro Central was the closest thing to a reenactment of the Civil War. It was nothing more than a controlled fistfight," said Odom.

Odom, whose mother grew up just south of Clara, remembers Clara being a particularly tight-knit and isolated community. Clara's school was built in the early 1900s as an agricultural boarding school, and many of the houses and apartments that were used to house teachers and staff members still stand today. The main part of the old school is presently used as a county junior high. Many of the people in the Clara community worked in Waynesboro during the day and crossed the Chickasawhay River on their way home in the evenings. According to Odom, "It was almost like you needed a passport to go down to Waynesboro if you were from Clara."

Former Waynesboro mayor, Marshall Wood, recalls that students of the four high schools remained separate even in social settings. "I remember being in junior high school at Waynesboro Central and seeing the high school kids from the different schools hang out in self-designated spots. The Waynesboro Central crowd would hang out at the Triple Treat, and the kids from Beat Four, Buckatunna and Clara would hang out at the Humdinger. When they built the Piggly Wiggly, everyone started hanging out in that parking lot, but each school still maintained its own corner of the lot."

Even though a large part of the northern third of Wayne County attended Waynesboro Central, it was still viewed as the "city school" by the other schools in the county. In fact, except for its own students, Waynesboro Central was simply referred to as "Waynesboro" by everyone in the county. It may have been centrally located, but Waynesboro Central certainly did not represent the identities or psyche of the people outside its district lines.

In 1989, the balance of power and equilibrium of the four Wayne County schools was shaken up like a snow globe when consolidation arrived. Although many of the surrounding counties had already gone through consolidation, the strong individual identities and support for the individual Wayne County schools had held it off until a relatively late date. Although consolidation was widely considered inevitable by the populous, it was met with resistance when it arrived. The small high schools, which were the pride of the smaller communities, faced extinction. Some loyalists even discussed creation of separate school districts.

As if the loss of their local high schools was not a painful enough blow, the way in which Wayne County schools were consolidated added insult to injury. The common practice when a county consolidated was to build a brand new school somewhere in the county and to adopt new school colors and a new mascot. However, the consolidation of Wayne County happened quickly, and no new school was built. Rather, all students were sent to the old Waynesboro Central location, which was renamed Wayne County High School. The fact that the old Waynesboro Central Panther mascot and school colors of green and white were replaced by blue and orange and the War Eagle was of little consolation to the former students of Beat Four, Buckatunna and Clara. In their minds, they were still being shipped off to Waynesboro Central, the "city school."

To exacerbate problems, the Wayne County High School cafeteria could accommodate fewer than 200 students per hour. As a result, some students were forced to eat lunch at 10:00 a.m. while others had to wait until 2:00 p.m. to be served. Some parents began opting for private schools as a mechanism to avoid the "new" high school.

Other than the fact that no new school was built, the item that caused the most resentment among the former students and parents of the now defunct small high schools was the fact that Jim McCain, the former head coach of the Waynesboro Central football team, was kept on board to lead the newly formed Wayne County. Although by all accounts Coach McCain was a good man and a good coach, the former players and parents of Beat Four, Buckatunna and Clara saw him as an insider. Still feeling the sting of the loss of their schools, many of these individuals felt they could not get a fair shake from the city school's old football coach and opted not to participate in sports. Thus, Coach McCain was charged with playing a 5A football schedule against the likes of Hattiesburg, Pascagoula and Gulfport, but with a less-than-5A-size squad. As one might expect, War Eagle football enjoyed little success in the years following consolidation.

After struggling for its first four years of existence, Wayne

County made a move that many people consider to be the turning point of War Eagle football. In 1993, Bubba Davis was hired as the new head coach. Coach Davis had fully entrenched himself at perennial power West Point, serving as head coach for the previous ten seasons. During this time, Coach Davis solidified his place among Mississippi's elite high school coaches by winning three straight state championships. Fortunately for Wayne County, Davis was ready for a change and looking for a new challenge.

When Coach Davis arrived in Wayne County, there were several factors in play that set the stage for progress. First, the students who were caught in the crossfire of consolidation and thus harbored the most resentment had been eliminated from the equation through graduation. Second, Davis was an outsider with no Waynesboro Central, Beat Four, Buckatunna or Clara affiliation. Davis's perceived lack of bias, coupled with his championship past, convinced many athletes to continue playing football once they reached the high school level. Third, and possibly most important, Davis recognized the need to unite the splintered communities that lost their high schools only four years earlier. Davis immediately began a dialog with individuals in these communities and began selling the vision of an athletically united Wayne County. The fact that the county's junior highs remained unconsolidated was sold as an advantage, since it allowed for greater athlete participation and development prior to high school.

In his first season, Davis compiled a 5-6 record. However, in his second season, Davis's War Eagles went 10 and 3 and earned the school's first trip to the playoffs. During this season, the team played a pivotal game at home against Pascagoula. Kenny Odom recalls the powerful Pascagoula team making fun of Wayne County's football field before the game and asking, "What happened to all the cows?" Wayne County players overheard the remarks, quickly nicknamed their football field "the pasture", and then promptly dispatched Pascagoula's team on the field of play. Odom recalls this game as the first big win that got the attention of the people of Wayne County. War Eagle fans got a glimpse of the football power they could become if they banded together. Success was just over the horizon and ready to break like the new dawn after a long night.

Unfortunately, before the new momentum reached a point of critical mass, Coach Davis opted for a job in Alabama after his second season at Wayne County. The school took great efforts in hiring its new football coach, but the next two hires were never able to match Davis's success. During those seasons, the program began to slide back into its old ways. Wins decreased, people grumbled, players got discouraged, support splintered and the downward spiral gained speed. Then, at the beginning of 2000, Wayne County was able to land another one of Mississippi's coaching titans – Bobby Hall.

Similar to Davis, Hall arrived in Wayne County with a stellar résumé including multiple championships at Amory and Louisville. More importantly, Hall understood the importance of uniting the small communities and junior highs. He immediately resumed the task of selling the vision of a united Wayne County. Unlike Davis, who exuded more of a quiet confidence, Hall was far more intense and animated. Kenny Odom compares Hall's demeanor to an F-14 pilot who just shot down a dozen Iraqi airplanes. "He came in and basically said, 'You can do anything. I can do anything. And if you follow me, we're going to win the Alamo and turn the Mexicans back.' Coach Hall had a confidence and arrogance to him that you see in folks that are really good at what they do," says Odom.

Traveling from town to town like a snake oil salesman pushing War Eagle football paid quick dividends. By the end of the 2000 season, participation had once again increased, people had stopped referring to the school as "Waynesboro" and the proud people from the community of Clara now formed the backbone of the War Eagle booster club. In a nine-month period, the program was ready to explode and become a dominant force in Mississippi high school football. Then, as quickly as he arrived, Bobby Hall left for the head coaching job at Northeast Mississippi Community College.

Coach Hall's departure had all the makings of a repeat of Coach Davis's departure six years earlier. However, Hall was able to make one crucial move during his tenure that would have significant and lasting effects. Shortly after he was hired at Wayne County, Hall was able to lure Marcus Boyles from his head coaching post at Pearl High School to serve as an assistant on the War Eagle staff. When Hall left for Northeast Mississippi Community College, Wayne County hired from within and Coach Boyles took over the head coaching position. This move would ultimately lead to the completion of Wayne County's football masterpiece.

Coach Boyles served as head coach at Pearl from 1998 to 1999, but most people knew him for his success at Taylorsville. From 1993 to 1997, Coach Boyles was the architect of two state championships at the 2A school. Ultimately, it was the similarities to Taylorsville that convinced Boyles to uproot his family from Pearl and move to Wayne County. "I often compare Wayne County to Taylorsville. In Taylorsville, the kids grow up tough working in the watermelon fields. In Wayne County, they're cutting pulp wood and hauling timber. The kids in both places are just tough. They are mentally and physically tough because of the work they do themselves and because they observe the work habits of their parents," says Boyles.

Because of the relatively isolated location of Wayne County, there are not many distractions, which helps create more of an interest in football and school activities in general. Coach Boyles describes Wayne County as follows:

> Our community is very athletic-minded. They love sports, not just football. When it's basketball season they support it. When it's baseball season they support it. They love sports. We are a large school, but we still have a community feel, which I think is extremely important. I'm not knocking the big cities by any means, but when you have that sense of community, it means a lot. That feeling pulls the community into school events like football games. We have 700 reserved seats in our stadium and we have people on a waiting list to buy them. We even sell reserved tailgating spots in our end zone, and there is a waiting list for those as well. We had a longtime supporter who held four reserved tickets. When he retired and made it known he was going to be moving to Georgia, everyone started jockeying for position to get his seats. But he told me that he wanted to keep paying for them so he could come back for a couple of games a year. The stadium is slam-packed every Friday night. It just means so much to the people here. This place will really spoil you as a coach.

If Wayne County spoiled Boyles as a coach, he certainly returned the favor in his second season. In 2002, the team began its assault on a brutal 5A football schedule. This was to be the season all the hard work of Bubba Davis, Bobby Hall and now Boyles himself would pay dividends on the field, as the War Eagles were able to go 10-1 in the regular season. Once the playoffs arrived, Boyles' team ripped through the preliminary rounds, setting up a final collision with South Panola. In a colossal showdown in Veterans Memorial Stadium in Jackson, the War Eagles handed South Panola its first loss of the season and took the biggest prize in Mississippi high school football home to the people of Wayne County.

Elected in 1999 as mayor of Waynesboro, longtime Wayne County resident Marshall Wood describes the importance of Wayne County football:

> Nothing has galvanized this community like Wayne County football. It has been the flash point for this county. We don't find our identity in the University of Mississippi, Mississippi State, Jones Junior College, Masonite or any industry. Wayne County's identity is formulated from and founded on Wayne County football. I recognized this when I became mayor, and that's why I made the decision to start buying police cars that were painted orange and blue in honor of the War Eagles. I wanted the new fire trucks to be the same orange and blue as well, but I couldn't get it passed before I left office. When I was mayor and we were winning football games, there were fewer complaints in the community. People weren't as worried about the mosquito problem, garbage pick-up or if the water wasn't smelling quite right. All that mattered was that we had a football game on Friday night and that we were chasing a state championship. That feeling and excitement is real and it matters. It sends chills over me just thinking about it.

The game against South Panola and the 5A championship crown had a deep impact on the Wayne County community. After over a decade of struggling to unite the old supporters of Beat Four, Buckatunna, Clara and Waynesboro Central, the championship was the equivalent of removing the last splints and bandages from a patient who had been in a traumatic accident. Says Kenny Odom, "The championship undid all those bad feelings from the previous ten years." After the 2002 season, Wayne County football was permanently on the map and currently on top of the mountain.

****

Jones County, Mississippi, is a special place for high school football. The county contains approximately 65,000 people and has an impressive four high schools in the 4A classification. The high schools include Laurel, which is its own school district, South Jones, Northeast Jones and West Jones. Of the four schools, Laurel has the deepest tradition, with its football roots firmly planted in the old Big Eight Conference. South Jones experienced football success in the late '80s, playing for a state championship. Northeast Jones enjoyed a golden age in the '90s, playing for two state championships and winning one.

West Jones was created in the 1960s when Soso, Calhoun and Shady Grove high schools consolidated. West Jones, like Northeast Jones and South Jones, began as a small county school whose football teams lived in the shadow of mighty Laurel. However, unlike the other two county schools, West Jones never achieved measurable football success.

In 2002, things began to change at West Jones. First, Mark Herrington, who had been employed for 15 years at West Jones, was assigned to the supervising principal position over the entire school. Herrington, a former kicker at Mendenhall in the 1970s, was an avid supporter of high school football. Second, Scott Pierson was hired to replace the retiring Mike Taylor. Pierson had established himself as a successful coach at 2A Bay Springs High School from 1994 to 2001, leading the Bulldogs to the state championship game in 1999. While at Bay Springs, Pierson regularly did battle with perennial 2A power Taylorsville who, at the time, was led by Coach Marcus Boyles.

The fact that Mike Taylor would no longer prowl the West Jones sidelines was a significant change. After all, Coach Taylor had served as head coach for an amazing 28 years and had been the face of Mustang football for most of its existence. However, the transition between the two coaches was smooth, and Pierson recalls Taylor being an invaluable resource during the change. According to Pierson,

> I would go over to his house and we would sit down and talk. I learned what he did to motivate his players, many of whom were now the fathers of kids currently on the team I would be coaching. He gave me the phone numbers of people I could contact to make my job easier. Coach Taylor truly cared about West Jones football and wanted to make sure it prospered in the future.

Like many coaches when they arrive at a new school, Pierson changed both the Mustang's uniforms and their offensive attack. West Jones had always used Kelly green and old gold as their uniform colors. Partly due to a preference of style, and partly due to the scarcity of Kelly green uniform suppliers, Pierson elected to go with a darker forest green and Vegas gold look. In addition, the old "WJ" was removed from the helmet and replaced with a silhouette of a mustang in full stride.

The offensive change was a bit more complicated. West Jones was traditionally a run-oriented team that lined up in the "I" and pounded the opposing defense for four quarters with athletes like Ronnie Ducksworth. However, Pierson elected to go in the opposite direction and installed the spread attack. Such an offense was more complicated and would take total commitment from the players and coaching staff. To aid in the transition, Pierson assembled a crack staff of assistant coaches, including Bud Blackledge, Bruce Adams and Wayne Graves. Blackledge, a holdover from the previous staff, was utilized as the offensive coordinator; and Adams, former head coach at Stringer, was hired to work with the wide receivers. Graves was brought on board to work with the defense. Not only was Graves a graduate of West Jones, but he also had experience coaching at in-county rivals South Jones and Northeast Jones. He was an excellent guide to the ins and outs of the community.

Just as soon as Pierson had assembled his coaching staff and was preparing to build a new foundation for Mustang football, the West Jones area was rocked by a tornado. Fortunately, the tornado hit during spring break and no students were at the school on that particular day. Unfortunately, school facilities were so badly damaged that classes could not be conducted at that location for the remainder of the school year. While the campus recovered, classrooms were relocated to the local Wal-Mart. The move prompted one of the West Jones teachers to write a song entitled "Wal-Mart High School." Interestingly, local radio stations played the song, and it eventually received enough attention to be played on the Paul Harvey Show.

The turbulence of the spring semester continued into the summer as Coach Pierson and his staff attempted to train their players under less-than-ideal conditions and simultaneously install a complicated new offense. The entire process was a race against the clock as the opening game against formidable 2A Taylorsville grew closer with every passing moment.

By the time the season arrived, the school was somewhat settled back on its own campus and the spread offense was installed to the extent time and circumstances would allow. Pierson knew that they were far from perfecting the high-flying offensive attack, but believed two factors would allow his team a chance to get to the .500 mark for the season. First, he enjoyed the service of some talented players such as Brett Hyatt, Britt Barefoot and Archie Sims. Second, besides West Jones, the only other school in the area that was attempting to run the spread was 5A Oak Grove. This meant that opposing defenses would experience at least some amount of difficulty preparing for their games against the West Jones offense.

However, just as Pierson and his staff started believing in their possible advantages, they quickly reminded themselves of a number of disadvantages they faced. Namely, they were going to start three ninth graders and eleven tenth graders for the opening game. If that alone wasn't enough cause for concern, the opening game was against Taylorsville. Although Taylorsville was a 2A team and West Jones was a 4A team, West Jones had not beaten Taylorsville in almost a decade. The Taylorsville game would be a stiff test and an important barometer of how much the West Jones players and coaching staff had achieved in their short time together. As Pierson put it, "The kids and the community as a whole were in a wait-and-see mode. They wanted to see if this coaching staff really knew what it was doing."

The Taylorsville game finally arrived, and by the time it was over, the West Jones family realized it had entered a new era of football. West Jones won the game and the spread offense worked . . . sort of. "It wasn't pretty. We were not a polished team by any means. However, it was enough to beat a team that had beaten us for the past nine or ten years in a row, and it was enough to convince our players and community to buy in to what we were doing," said Pierson.

The upcoming weeks were very similar to the opening game. West Jones wasn't winning any style points; they were, however, winning. Pierson describes his team's play: "We were winning games that we didn't have any business winning. We had athletes that could play, but not to the level our record indicated. But the players didn't know that, and we weren't going to tell them."

The Mustangs of West Jones ultimately finished the 2002 season with an amazing 10-0 record. The patchwork team that included a bunch of underclassmen running a brand new, sophisticated offense installed by new coaches working under the constraints of a devastating tornado, was able to produce one of the most successful seasons in West Jones history. The remarkable run, which ultimately ended in the second round of the playoffs, caused tremendous excitement in the community and caused support for the football program to reach a new high.

In addition to the success on the field, Pierson was simultaneously endearing himself to current and future Mustang fans off the field. Coach Pierson's wife, Angela, a first grade teacher at West Jones Elementary School, explains the importance of West Jones football to her younger students:

> I've had Scott send a few players down to my classroom to read to my students. You would have thought Hollywood had come to town. These young kids go to the games on Friday and they know who the players are. They know number 99 is Ira Lee Keys, and Ray Ray Pickering is so popular with the kids he might as well be President of the United States. Scott gives out special tickets or passes to the kids and tells them, "If you wear a Mustang jersey to the game and use this pass you will get in free." That means a lot, too. You see these little first and second graders in their jerseys walking through the gates and they feel important. At the end of the games, these kids line up along the fence to see the players. I'm so impressed by the players because they take time, win or lose, to come over and shake hands and take pictures with these little kids. It's a great dynamic from top to bottom. There is so much support for Mustang football that by the end of July, you can't buy anything green anywhere in Jones County.

After only one season, Pierson and his staff had successfully injected an unprecedented excitement and optimism into West Jones football. The community was bleeding forest green and Vegas gold in preparation for a stampede of winning seasons.

✶✶✶✶✶✶✶✶✶✶✶✶✶✶

On the heels of an undefeated 2002 regular season, the 2003 football season couldn't arrive fast enough for the West Jones faithful.

Expectations and excitement were through the roof. This was going to be the year the Mustangs would run the table in 4A and produce the first state championship in school history. Then, it happened.

Every two years the Mississippi High School Activities Association (MHSAA) reclassifies schools based on enrollment. They begin with 5A, place the largest 32 schools in this class and then work their way down to the 1A schools. When the schools were ranked in order of enrollment, absent from the top 32 was defending 5A state champion Wayne County. Their enrollment had dipped just enough to drop them out of the 5A classification, thus making them one of the largest 4A schools. This shift immediately changed the landscape of 4A football in Mississippi for the upcoming season. Dealing with mighty Wayne County was a tall order for any team in the state, but even more so for the smaller 4A schools, which were unaccustomed to playing the War Eagles.

For West Jones, the classification shift had a greater impact. Wayne County is directly adjacent to Jones County. Wayne County High School is only 30 miles down Highway 184 from West Jones. Not only was Wayne County now in the same size classification as West Jones, their geographic location placed them right into the same district as the Mustangs. Forget the possibility of the two teams meeting at some point in the playoffs; these two were going to have to get it on in the regular season – October 24, 2003, at Wayne County, to be exact. The date and location were set and the players, coaches and communities circled their collective calendars.

Kenny Odom, radio announcer for Wayne County, asks,

> Have you ever seen it when a farmer puts a new bull in an older bull's pasture? Country folks understand. When you buy a new bull and you roll up to your pasture and drop the tailgate, your old bull doesn't like that one bit. The old bull will ram into the new bull and try to push him out of the pasture. I've seen them run down the side of the road alongside the trailer moving the new bull, bang into the side of the truck and run into the trailer. For someone who has never seen it, it's scary. Well, we got dropped into their pasture. That tailgate dropped down and out we came – an 1800-pound bull just blowing and snorting. They didn't like it, but we really didn't care. We were just looking for someone to play and they were on our list.

The match up fell in week number nine for both schools, a fact that would make the game that much more intense and that much more difficult to deal with throughout the season. The anticipation was so great in both communities that it was the talk of both towns for literally months before the game was played. People began predicting a collision between two undefeated teams late in the season. Both coaching staffs were aware of the danger of looking past earlier games, and they knew failure to reach week nine without a blemish would seriously dampen the explosive excitement that was quickly building. Says Coach Pierson,

> I never really sensed any pressure from the players; it was the community. I knew we couldn't drop the ball before that game. Every week it was a grind on the staff to stay focused. We knew we had to get to week nine without a loss. Otherwise, this was all for naught. The real pressure was just getting to that game. If we both got there undefeated, I knew it would be anyone's game to win. It would also mean that both teams were already qualified for the playoffs. I could reason that in my mind, but with the community, it just didn't matter. The anticipation and intensity was the dangdest thing I've ever seen.

In line with recent tradition, West Jones opened the 2003 season with Taylorsville. While the Mustangs broke their ten-year losing streak to the Tartars in 2002, they did so in a close game highlighted by a couple of critical errors committed late in the game by their opponent. No errors were needed in 2003 as the Mustangs exploded past Taylorsville 31-0 in the opener. The Mustangs continued to put up points and roll past opponents in the weeks leading up to the highly-anticipated week nine contest. While West Jones piled up victories, Wayne County lived up to their No. 1 overall ranking in Mississippi and rolled over teams in the 4A classification. When week nine arrived, both teams entered a perfect 8-0.

Justin Graves, a 2007 graduate of West Jones, remembers the day of the epic 2003 game between the Mustangs and War Eagles:

> Mr. Herrington, the school principal, is a very structured guy and very good at what he does. I remember coming to school that day and he came over the intercom and said, "Today is not a normal day." It

was very unusual for him to do something like that, and it made it clear how important this game was. Right after he made that announcement, the band came marching down the school halls playing the fight song along with the cheerleaders and football players. We didn't even have class that day. It was an all-day pep rally for the game. We had a phenomenal pep rally and a phenomenal day. It started off with him saying, "Today is not a normal day." I will never forget that. It was incredible.

While the West Jones student body was busy working itself into a frenzy on its own campus, the West Jones fans were busy preparing for the game by tailgating on the Wayne County campus at 11:00 in the morning! West Jones booster club president, Dr. Harlon Mathews, Jr., recalls rumors in the community that Wayne County was going to let their students out of school at noon on the day of the game. "West Jones fans travel strong to out of town games, and we were concerned that we would have trouble getting parking spots at their stadium; so a bunch of us went over that morning. The security guard wouldn't let us on their campus and directed us to the Wal-Mart parking lot across the street. The whole parking lot was filled with green and gold. There were RVs and cars everywhere with grills set up." At the same time, the special reserved parking area located next to the stadium for the Wayne County faithful saw its usual influx of tailgaters. Said Coach Marcus Boyles, "It's the same every week. They come in, set up and cook all day. People actually leave work on their lunch breaks and come to our stadium to eat lunch on Fridays."

In the face of all the obvious excitement, the coaches attempted to keep their teams focused on the game. Coach Pierson remembers preaching to his team that this game was just like any other game and should be treated the same as each of the previous 18 consecutive regular season games won by the Mustangs. "I wanted them to treat this like a normal game, but we all knew it wasn't. When our bus pulled up to their stadium, the entire crowd in the stadium and the parking lots stood up and cheered like we had just scored the game-winning touchdown. Just getting on and off the field was an absolute circus."

The excitement was so great and the lines to get into the stadium were so long that both principals felt the need to stand at the gates and monitor the crowd. Wayne County students mocked their

Mustang opponents by riding around on stick horses, while the West Jones students honored the War Eagles by donning Kentucky Fried Chicken buckets on their heads with the words "war chickens" written on the front. Said Dr. Mathews, "People were just so excited about what was fixing to happen. I have been to a lot of high school, college and professional games, but I'm telling you, the atmosphere inside and around that stadium – if you could have bottled it that night, it would have powered the state of Mississippi. It was one of those games where the feeling was Kick the football, quit the warm-ups and get the mascots off the field. Just kick the football!"

All 10,000 tickets to the game were pre-sold well ahead of time, but the actual number of people in the stadium is anyone's guess. The game was so big and so anticipated that Governor Ronnie Musgrove was present for the opening coin toss – an act made more interesting by the fact the Governor was from Tocowa, Mississippi, a place nowhere near Wayne or Jones Counties. By all accounts, this particular crowd remains the largest single gathering of people in the history of all of Wayne County. Says Kenny Odom, "The only thing I can imagine that would attract anywhere close to this number of people would have been a tent revival by Billy Graham during his prime, or a Wal-Mart grand opening that also featured a goat roping."

As hyped as the game was, the play on the field lived up to the anticipation. In a stadium flooded with green and gold and orange and blue, the teams battled nip and tuck for a full four quarters. In the end, maybe Wayne County was a little overconfident. Maybe West Jones felt it had more to prove. Final score: West Jones 23, Wayne County 15.

Coach Pierson says, "Although we had won a bunch of games in the past couple of seasons, we still had not established ourselves as one of the big boys. We still had something to prove. That game was kinda like little brother going up against big brother looking for some respect. We got it that night, but Wayne County certainly made us earn it."

As big as the week nine battle was, it immediately became almost completely irrelevant. Just as Coach Pierson predicted before the season, both teams had already qualified for the playoffs and would likely face one another again. In fact, if they were to meet again, it would be for the south state championship. By a strange twist of fate, the way the playoff brackets were set up, if West Jones and Wayne County did meet in the south state championship game, it would be played the day after

Thanksgiving at . . . Wayne County. Obviously, West Jones was furious that they would somehow fail to earn home field advantage throughout the playoffs and would ultimately lose the advantage to a team they had already beaten in the regular season. Wayne County didn't try to explain their stroke of good luck, but just accepted it and began preparing all over again for the monster event.

Both teams finished the rest of the regular season without losing a game. When it came time to prepare for the playoff games, the Wayne County coaching staff took a slightly different approach. Says Kenny Odom, "That regular season loss just devastated our folks. I'm good friends with Coach Todd Mangum (Wayne County assistant coach) and I thought he was going to go insane. He was watching West Jones film constantly. The coaching staff was preparing for each playoff game, but they were also installing a little bit of the West Jones game plan each week, as well." As Coach Pierson had predicted, the spread offense was difficult to prepare for. The Wayne County coaching staff was making sure they would be better prepared for it the second time around.

Just like the regular season match up in week nine, the south state championship game arrived according to plan. West Jones entered undefeated and Wayne County showed up furious about their one loss. Because school was out the day after Thanksgiving, nothing prevented the fans from coming to campus early to get ready. Dr. Mathews and his traveling band of Mustang faithful arrived at 8:30 in the morning to begin their tailgate preparations. Even though the weather was now bitter cold, the feast was even larger with the abundance of Thanksgiving leftovers.

Unlike the regular season game, the playoff match up was a little more intense between players and fans. After all, there would be no third chance after this game was over. The winner of this game would go on to play for the state championship in Jackson and the loser would go home. In addition, West Jones – particularly their fans – arrived with more of a swagger, having already proven they could dispense with the War Eagles on the gridiron. Wayne County arrived without a shred of overconfidence, a steely-eyed focus and a lingering pain that could only be cured by a victory over the Mustangs. The atmosphere at the stadium was once again electric. Security guards were on site to escort War Eagle players from their cars to the locker room through the hoards of West Jones and Wayne County tailgaters.

The game was another close-fought contest. Final score: Wayne

County 15, West Jones 14. As the final horn sounded, the Wayne County sea of orange erupted in cheers of jubilation released simultaneously for the trip to the state championship game they had just earned and for the demon they had just exorcised. The West Jones fans on the other side did the only thing they could do; they went home.

Dr. Mathews recalls going back to his truck after the game with his five-year-old daughter Alise. "We got back to the car and it was muddy, so Alise had to take off her shoes. When she took off her shoes, she started crying. I asked her what was wrong and she pointed to her socks. She was crying because she realized that she had inadvertently worn a pair of socks with orange and blue on them. She pulled them off, threw them on the ground and cried herself to sleep in the back of the truck. She blamed herself for the loss."

The next week the War Eagles dismantled Oxford in the state championship game and took their second straight title home to the people of Wayne County, thus completing the transfer of their dominance from the 5A to 4A level. West Jones watched the championship game from a distance and was left to wonder, What if? By all accounts, West Jones would have also easily defeated Oxford had they made it to the big game.

The West Jones-Wayne County rivalry blew up overnight and has never let up. Kenny Odom says, "This rivalry is like Tang. You just open up the jar, pour in some water and – Bang, you've got Tang! It's instant. There are some rivalries that take time to build, but everything with this one just fell into place. There was no slow build to it. It was like pouring gasoline over a fire. It was going to happen; and when it did, it just blew hot and ran hot."

In 2004, West Jones decided to move the game to the brand new stadium at Jones County Community College in order to accommodate the huge crowds. Even at the much larger stadium, the game produced a standing room only crowd. The attendance was so great that the visiting fans of Wayne County attempted to go to the home side gate to find seats. However, in an effort to prevent altercations, stadium security turned fans away from their respective gates if they were wearing the wrong colors. Wayne County fans resorted to returning to their vehicles and changing into non-blue and orange apparel in order to get in the stadium. Wayne County won the game, handing West Jones its only loss of the season. Both teams again made the playoffs, but were knocked out in consecutive weeks by a Jimmy Johns-led Brookhaven team before they could meet again.

The 2005 season played out similarly to the 2003 season. The teams squared off in the regular season and then collided again in the playoffs in the south state championship game. Wayne County won both games and prevented West Jones from having another shot at a state championship. In a span of three seasons, the dominant West Jones teams suffered only six losses – four of those were to the War Eagles. After the loss to Wayne County in the 2005 south state championship game, Angela Pierson remembers her husband's unique response: "He took his lucky game pants and shirt and burned them in front of the players. He told the players 'I'm burning the loser off. We are going to get a fresh start. We are going to work even harder this year.'"

Unfortunately for Pierson and the Mustangs, the hard work did not pay off in 2006. Not only did they lose to Wayne County, but the War Eagles went on to win another 4A state championship. However, 2007 favored the Mustangs in another memorable game. Unlike previous years, other schools in the division produced particularly strong teams, and both West Jones and Wayne County were fighting for the final playoff spot in the final contest of the season. The game, played at Mustang Stadium, had been a defensive struggle. The game was knotted at 6-6 late in the fourth quarter when West Jones began their final drive. With 40 seconds left, West Jones faced a 4th and 5 situation on Wayne County's 26-yard line. Coach Pierson elected to send out his field goal team led by kicker Adam Herrington.

West Jones principal, Mark Herrington, enjoys a special bond with his son Adam. On Sunday afternoons, father and son go to the West Jones stadium and kick field goals. For years, they have teed it up and competed against each another. Father visualizes his playing days, kicking for his Mendenhall Tigers in their annual grudge match with Magee, while son Adam practices nailing the winning kick for West Jones over Wayne County. "It's something we have done for years. It's a very special tradition for both of us," says the elder Herrington.

So with the game on the line in 2007, Adam strode onto the field, teed it up and nailed a 42-yard game-winning kick against Wayne County, just like he and his dad had practiced so many times on Sunday afternoons. The result: West Jones advanced to the playoffs and Wayne County went home. Says Principal Herrington, "You can accomplish all kinds of things in life yourself, but to watch your kid do those things is second to nothing."

West Jones' offensive coordinator, Bruce Adams, remembers the moments after the 2007 victory:

> After the clock had ticked off and all the fans were rushing the field, somebody came and grabbed me around my waist. My feet were dangling off the ground as this person was spinning me around. I looked down and saw it was the parent of a kid who graduated a couple of years ago. He didn't even have a dog in the fight anymore, but it was still important. I understood his feelings. During the course of my lifetime, I have been overwhelmed emotionally probably seven or eight times. Four of those would be when my sons were born. Two would be for the wins over Wayne County.

Each match up between the Mustangs and War Eagles is important when it happens, and it remains important for years. Michael Thigpen was a two-way starter for the Mustangs during his high school career and was on the field during the epic battles in 2003. Now a student at Jones County Community College, Thigpen says the match ups with Wayne County are still topics of conversation. Says Thigpen,

> Sid Jones and a couple other players from Wayne County ended up here at Jones CC with me. I rag them about the regular season game in 2003 when we beat them. I'll put the game film on before they come in my room. One day Sid came in and asked, "Is this the game we beat y'all?" I said, "No. This is the one where we beat y'all." The next thing I knew, everybody from Wayne County was sitting in my room watching the game and flashing their championship rings at me. At that point, I had to tell them to get out. I have to admit I would rather have lost the regular season game and beaten them in the playoffs so we could have played for a ring. That regular season game was a life changing experience. I will never forget it.

Wayne County is still one of the largest 4A schools in Mississippi, and reclassification is quickly approaching once again. With a shift in population here and a drop in population there, Wayne County could find itself back in 5A. What would happen to this instant rivalry then? Well, the farmer would pull the trailer back up to the field, drop the tailgate, shove the 1800-pound snorting bull back in and drive off to another pasture.

WHAT THE WAR EAGLES SAY ABOUT WEST JONES

I've never coached anywhere that always had so much on the line every time you were playing a particular team. Our kids love to compete against West Jones in any sport, and they respect the athletes at West Jones. My staff and I have a great deal of respect for Scott and his staff. But we want to beat them.

Marcus Boyles
Wayne County Head Football Coach

After we beat West Jones in the playoffs in 2003, we went on to beat Oxford 30-7 for the state. There is no doubt in my mind West Jones would have beaten Oxford by two touchdowns easy. We have kept them from winning at least one state championship.

Kenny Odom
Wayne County Football Radio Announcer

You can look at a map of Mississippi and see where the champions come from. This is a very good region for high school football.

Marshall Wood
Former Mayor of Waynesboro

We're hungry for more championships. We want to be able to have ten fingers full and maybe even be able to put them on our toes. That's how many more championships we want. West Jones will never be our stopping point again. They are just like a stumbling block that you can easily overcome.

Katerra Stephenson
Wayne County Cheerleader

West Jones sees us as the country bumpkins.

Myra Boyles
Wife of Head Football Coach Marcus Boyles

When West Jones and Wayne County play, you can expect a big crowd.

Donta Chambers
Former Wayne County Football Player

There are actually fans from the other county schools in Jones County that will come and watch this game.

B.R. Jones
Wayne County Principal

During the Wayne County-West Jones game, the noise is so loud you can't hear yourself when you take the field. Everything about Wayne County and West Jones playing is just indescribable.

Brandon Jordan
Former Wayne County Football Player

With my occupation, I am on the phone with clients across the state that come to Ellisville just to see this game. There are literally people traveling from north Mississippi just to watch this football game.

Marshall Wood
Former Mayor of Waynesboro

There are people who get into the game more than they have ever gotten into a game in their lives when it comes to the West Jones-Wayne County game.

Katerra Stephenson
Wayne County Cheerleader

When I graduated and went on to college with the same guys I played against from West Jones, I realized they were much like us – just good ole boys that loved to play football.

Brandon Jordan
Former Wayne County Football Player

West Jones are the rich boys and we're the country hicks.

Keith Smith

Wayne County Football and Baseball Player

The rivalry between West Jones and Wayne County goes on all year long in all sports. We just want the bragging rights.

Tracy Lampley

Wayne County Football Player

It never gets old beating West Jones.

Keith Smith

Wayne County Football and Baseball Player

Sometimes at the movies I'll have a Wayne County jacket on and I'll see a person from West Jones with their jacket on. We both cut our eyes at each other. People you don't even know from there, you dislike.

Katerra Stephenson

Wayne County Cheerleader

Wayne County's football program is better than West Jones's because we have the best coaching staff and they know what it takes to win games. They know how to get us ready.

Tracy Lampley

Wayne County Football Player

WHAT THE MUSTANGS SAY ABOUT WAYNE COUNTY

When they dropped down to 4A, it put a new spin on our district. Obviously, they were such a power. We would prefer that they stay in 5A.

Bruce Adams
West Jones Offensive Coordinator

I know they are dirty when they play football. They play rough. They are just not nice. They are seen as the bullies on the block.

Kaleigh Byrd
West Jones Cheerleader

The crowds are just amazing. If you are in the south part of the state during week 10 of the football season, you need to visit Mustang Stadium or War Eagle Stadium for some good football.

Nicholas Carr
West Jones Student

Instead of War Eagles, we like to call them "War Chickens." We wear KFC buckets on our heads.

Chase Headrick
West Jones Football Player

We like to think that Wayne County got in our way of winning one – maybe two – state championships.

Mark Herrington
West Jones Principal

When they fell to 4A and got put in our district, they felt like they were the only big dog in the hunt.

Dr. G. Harlon Mathews
West Jones Booster Club President

When they moved down to 4A after winning the 5A state championship, they weren't expecting anybody to beat them. Then we came in and beat them the first time we played. I think that really sparked the rivalry.

Adam Herrington
West Jones Football Player

They have big trucks and coon dogs.

Kirby Mauldin
Community Leader

They are arrogant and real cocky. They have shirts that say, "It's like taking candy from a baby." Their cheerleaders made a sign that said, "Do we have to keep embarrassing you year after year?"

Maylen Musgrove
West Jones Cheerleader

Scott and Marcus respect each other enough to know, "I'm going to play you just as hard as I can, because I know that's how you are going to play me."

Angela Pierson
Wife of Head Football Coach Scott Pierson

The first game was a game of wills. I think we just wanted to prove that we belonged, so we played a little bit harder. We were fortunate to win. To be honest with you, they were every bit as good in 2003 as they were in 2002.

Scott Pierson
West Jones Head Football Coach

There is no love lost between the two schools. You either eat crow for 364 days or you get to brag.

Bruce Adams
West Jones Offensive Coordinator

Wayne County is always big and fast. Most of the time, they think they have more talent than we do. They think we are small and overrated.

Chase Headrick

West Jones Football Player

It's more than just football; it's a school rivalry. Football led the way, but they don't like us in nothin'.

Michael Thigpen

Former West Jones Football Player

They had t-shirts that said, "We don't rebuild. We reload." That's really evident in their program. Every year they just reach down and pull up another group of athletes.

Mark Herrington

West Jones Principal

I have two sons and they love Auburn, but they won't wear anything from Auburn because it looks too much like Wayne County.

Bruce Adams

West Jones Offensive Coordinator

One of the best t-shirts we ever had said, "The reason football was invented – West Jones vs. Wayne County." Even their fans wanted to buy that shirt.

Dr. G. Harlon Mathews

West Jones Booster Club President

WEST JONES-WAYNE COUNTY
SERIES HISTORY

Year	West Jones	Score	Wayne Co.
2003	Scott Pierson	23-15	Marcus Boyles
2003*	Scott Pierson	14-15	Marcus Boyles
2004	Scott Pierson	14-23	Marcus Boyles
2005	Scott Pierson	16-24	Marcus Boyles
2005*	Scott Pierson	6-34	Marcus Boyles
2006	Scott Pierson	14-34	Marcus Boyles
2007	Scott Pierson	9-6	Marcus Boyles

* *Playoff Game*

BROOKHAVEN
VERSUS
McCOMB

ESTABLISHED 1933

MOAK-MASSENGILL CLINIC
INTERNAL MEDICINE

PROUD SPONSOR OF MISSISSIPPI HIGH SCHOOL FOOTBALL

FRIDAY, SEPTEMBER 19, 2008 ★ 7:00 PM KICKOFF
C.C. MOORE STADIUM ★ McCOMB, MISSISSIPPI

CHAPTER
04
LEGENDS OF HIGHWAY 51

Ole Brook fans refer to it as "The Golden Era." The names of so many great players come to mind when stories are told about the Panther teams of the '40s and '50s. Remarkably, over five decades later, residents of this southwest Mississippi town just off Interstate 55 remember the heroes of that distant era.

Starting in the late '40s, the gridiron feats of Joe Tuminello amazed thousands of Panther fans gathered at King Field. Then, in the early '50s, Harol Lofton, to the delight of hometown fans, raced up and down King Field on his way to becoming Brookhaven's first High School All-American. Immediately following Tuminello and Lofton came more Panther legends in '56, '57 and '58. Beginning their careers as mere high school players, Lance Alworth, Ralph "Catfish" Smith, Don "Red" Estes and Norman Minton would exit three years later as hometown heroes. These star players and many of their teammates continued their careers at the college level. Stated in simple football terms, the '56, '57 and '58 Brookhaven High School football teams were "loaded."

One of Ole Brook's players, Lance Alworth, nicknamed "Bambi," became a three-time Southwest All-Conference and All-American player for the University of Arkansas and runner up for the Heisman Trophy. Following his stellar career as an Arkansas Razorback, Alworth played for the San Diego Chargers, earned All-Pro honors nine times and was inducted into the Pro Football Hall of Fame in Canton, Ohio. The records set by Lance Alworth stood for decades until another Mississippian, Jerry Rice, finally broke them. Amazingly, several of Alworth's teammates from Ole Brook also had pro football careers.

Everything and everybody in Mississippi is connected in some way, no matter how slight that connection may be. Lance Alworth's hero as a kid was Harol Lofton. Lofton wore No. 19 and Alworth wanted to wear the same number when he got to high school. No luck – Ole Brook had retired No. 19 by the time Alworth played for the Panthers. Consequently, Alworth wore jersey No. 30 while playing at Brookhaven. Many years later, the school board in Brookhaven decided to retire Alworth's No. 30 during a halftime ceremony at the annual homecoming game. According to Bob Massengill, Brookhaven's mayor, "I was president of the school board at the time the decision was made to retire Lance's jersey. I got a call the afternoon of the homecoming game. The caller reminded me that Joe Tuminello had worn No. 30 and his number had been retired 20 years before. So, No. 30 has been retired twice – once for Tuminello and once for Alworth."

Interestingly, the manager of the '56, '57 and '58 teams was a fellow named Billy Peavey, father of current Brookhaven head football coach, Tucker Peavey. Panther great Ralph "Catfish" Smith recalls an incident involving Peavey and some of his teammates:

> On Tuesday before our Thanksgiving game against McComb, seven or eight of us loaded up in two cars and drove down to McComb. During those days, the equipment managers for the teams washed the uniforms and hung them on a clothesline to dry. Well, we found the jerseys and stole all of them. We were stupid enough to drive by McComb High School and wave the jerseys at everybody. The police caught us before we got out of Pike County. Of course, Billy Peavey was trying to talk us out of doing it the whole way down there.

The Golden Era made an impact on Panther head football coach, Tucker Peavey. The football players and the fans at Ole Brook still feel that impact today. Coach Peavey recalls,

> I grew up seeing photos and hearing about Lance Alworth, Ralph Smith, Don Estes and all that crew because my dad was in high school here during those glory years. I also remember seeing old photos of when Brookhaven played McComb on Thanksgiving Day with people just as far as you could see standing around the field. So for me, the importance of that game was instilled at a very young age. Back in those days, you knew a lot of the kids playing against you, so that made it personal. You knew the history. It was important to come out on top. It meant a whole lot to me and it's

something I've never forgotten.

The connection of today's team to the Panther teams of the Golden Era is vital to Coach Peavey. "The Ole Brook legacy is important. We are representing our town, our school and all the people who have been here before us," says Coach Peavey. In 2003, new goalposts were installed at King Field. The old goalposts, which had been installed in the '30s, were taken down but not discarded. A portion of the historic posts hangs today over the door of the Panthers' locker room. When a player exits the locker room and heads for the field, he touches that old piece of metal to honor the past players and coaches of Ole Brook; because to Coach Peavey and the folks of Brookhaven, the past is important – it's "golden."

There are so many links in the Ole Brook legacy chain that connect today's players, students and fans to their counterparts of the past. Take for example the architecture of the building where Brookhaven High School is located or the stadium where the Panthers play their home football games. The connections are everywhere.

King Field was named after John M. King, who came to Brookhaven as a coach in 1930 and was one of the founders of the Big Eight Conference, of which Brookhaven was a charter member. In 1938, King began building one of the finest football stadiums in the state. The stadium was a byproduct of President Roosevelt's Works Progress Administration, aimed at providing jobs and income to the unemployed during the Great Depression. When construction of the stadium was complete in 1939, the field was named "King Field" in John King's honor. King died in 1984 as a result of a stroke. However, his legacy lives on as thousands of Ole Brook fans gather each autumn at one of the most historic gridiron shrines in the country.

Visitors to King Field today will immediately appreciate the perfect blend of storied tradition and modern embellishments. Take, for example, the "Monster Board." Panther PA announcer Stan Patrick says, "It's one of the largest high school football scoreboards you will find anywhere. It has a message panel across the top that I affectionately refer to as our 'Jumbotron.' We have pre-game music and all kinds of events on game day. It is a very festive environment. We have a blast on Friday nights here at Brookhaven."

For an extra dash of excitement, the Monster Board growls every time the Panthers score. Tethered to the Monster Board is Prowler, the huge blow-up panther complete with snarling puffs of smoke, through which the team runs onto the field.

Another architectural link to the past is the building in which the high school is located. Originally constructed in 1927, the school was rebuilt on the same site after a fire in 1937. The bricks used in the construction of the school after the fire were fired in Brookhaven and the color referred to as "Brookhaven Brick." In the late '90s, a school bond issue was defeated, mainly because it called for the location of the school to be moved from its historic site. However, in 2000 an $11 million bond issue passed. Instead of requiring that the high school relocate, it called for renovation of the existing structure and additions to the building on the same site. According to long-time Brookhaven resident and current high school principal, Susan Chapman, "The people in Brookhaven did not want the school to be anywhere other than right here. They identify with this structure and the position it holds in the downtown community."

In addition to the interior renovation in 2000, two new wings were added to the building. Even though the brickyard where the original brick had been made had closed, great pains were taken to match the color of the Brookhaven Brick on the wings to the original structure. The look of the Brookhaven High School building is right out of the movie *Grease* – a classic Riddell High structure. Says Chapman, "There is a lot of history sitting on this piece of property."

Just to the southwest of King Field is Panther Park, which accommodates hundreds of tailgaters and festivities for fans prior to home games. Panther fan Stan Patrick comments, "The tailgating starts about 3:30 the afternoon of the games and goes on until the game is over. It's a big deal. The band comes to perform. It's just a lot of fun." Lee Ann Peavey sums it up: "Brookhaven is the most fun place in the state to be on a Friday night."

Across High School Street on the east side of the campus lies Rose Hill Cemetery, circa early 1800s. The mere location of the cemetery in proximity to King Field and the classic building housing the high school seems to punctuate the historical link the community has to its high school's football tradition. Longtime fan Tom Moak, age 84, has not missed a game in over 40 years. He sits in the same seat every football season. Principal Chapman reflects, "This community loves its football. While there are a lot of people who like baseball or basketball or track – everybody loves football." It seems fitting that the

Panther fans of today are linked to the traditions handed down to them by their hometown heroes and Ole Brook fans of the past, and that the residents of Rose Hill cemetery have a great view of all the Friday night action at King Field.

****

"Pride Runs Deep Here, Sir" is the motto of the students of McComb High School. Evidence of Tiger pride seems to be everywhere on the McComb campus located on tree-lined Seventh Street in downtown McComb. Starting in the principal's office, Tigers are everywhere – peering down from the top of bookcases, hiding in the bookshelves, staring from table tops, sizing you up directly from Dr. Sharon Slater-Smith's desk, making sure you are one of them. Comments Principal Slater-Smith, "If you notice the main office, it has a beautiful Tiger on the wall. My office has Tigers – lots of them. Everyone here has Tiger pride in his or her heart. We want to exemplify that pride so that visitors to our school see and feel the pride we have for our school. Everybody in this town believes in McComb High School."

To appreciate fully the depth of the Tigers' motto, one has to understand the history of not only McComb High School, but another school as well – Burglund. During the pre-integration era in Mississippi, all the white students of McComb attended McComb High, while the black students attended Burglund. Interestingly, even though the black and white students of McComb remained segregated during this era, both schools proceeded down parallel tracks toward the same objectives – football championships.

It appears that McComb High School started playing organized football around 1920. Beginning in the late '30s, the Tiger football program started picking up momentum under head coach C.C. "Hot" Moore. Over a ten-year period, Coach Moore posted an impressive record of 87 wins and 12 losses while winning several Big Eight Conference titles. During Coach Moore's highly successful career, McComb played St. Stanislaus (Bay St. Louis) in 1941 in the Toy Bowl in New Orleans. Doc Blanchard, who later became an All-American halfback at Army, led St. Stanislaus. Former McComb player Bobby Maddox recalls the event: "We stopped Doc Blanchard and won the game. Folks from McComb rode the train down to New Orleans and rode it back after the game. The ladies got on that Illinois Central train looking like six million dollars with their dresses and corsages just ready to see McComb win the Toy Bowl." In 1968, the stadium at McComb High School was named in honor of Coach C.C. Moore for his outstanding service on behalf of the Tigers.

During the 1946 regular season under the direction of Coach Dutch Binion, McComb fielded a team that went undefeated, untied and unscored upon while trouncing archrival Brookhaven on Thanksgiving Day. McComb was invited to play Clarksville (Tennessee) in the Memorial Bowl in Jackson (Mississippi). McComb dominated the game and held a decisive 33-0 lead late in the game when Coach Binion started clearing the bench with Tiger subs. Right at the end of the game with McComb deep into its roster of substitute players, Clarksville scored. That lone touchdown in post-season play resulted in the only points scored on McComb's 1946 team.

Numerous Tiger players have dazzled the hometown fans over the many years of McComb's storied football program. Many of these star players went on to play collegiate and professional football. Some of the names of former Tiger greats that regularly pop up in conversations regarding McComb football include Louis Guy, John Lowery, Tommy Parker, Harry Case, Douglas Spence, Bobby Rhedd, Warner Alford, Jerry Stone, Bobby Robinson, Pete Young, Bucky Moore, Jerry Butler, Cooper Carlisle, Hawkeye Webb and David McIntosh. Tommy Parker, one of McComb's all-time great players, remarks, "David McIntosh may be the best all-round athlete to ever come out of McComb. He played football, basketball and ran track. David was a Little All-American football player at Millsaps College. He was drafted by the Los Angeles Rams, but declined because he was going into the ministry."

"It's really amazing how close I came to never playing football at all and never going to college," says David McIntosh. Until the spring of his junior year, McIntosh attended a small county school outside of McComb. When his family suddenly moved to McComb after Christmas in 1943, McIntosh found himself at a new school in the city. While he played basketball and ran track for the Tigers, he had no desire to play football. However, a friend of McIntosh's, Albert Lancing, convinced him to work out with him during the summer, just in case McIntosh changed his mind about playing football in the fall. By the time the '44 season rolled around, McIntosh wore a blue and gold Tiger jersey and was the star of the team. His outstanding senior season earned him scholarship offers to play football at Ole Miss, Mississippi

State, Alabama, Auburn, LSU, Vanderbilt and Tulane. "It was just unbelievable, because my family didn't have any money to send me to college," recalls McIntosh. Subsequently, he turned down the offers to play big-time college football and, instead, attended Millsaps College to prepare himself for the ministry. McIntosh played three years for the Majors, earning Little American honors his junior and senior years, and received an offer to play professional football with the Rams. Instead, true to his original plan, he opted not to play professional ball and entered the ministry. Comments McIntosh, "The years playing football at Millsaps were three of the happiest years I have ever spent."

While the great players at McComb High School were entertaining the hometown fans, that was only half the story. Just a short distance from McComb High School was Burglund High School, located on Elmwood Street. Burglund was the high school for the black children in McComb. During the pre-integration era, Burglund was a member of the Negro Big Eight Conference and competed against other black schools, many of which were in the same towns where McComb found its competition. The big rival of the Burglund Lions was a school just up the road in Brookhaven, the Alexander Golden Panthers. McComb's mayor, Zach Patterson, recalls, "At some point Burglund was renamed 'Higgins' in honor of its principal, C.D. Higgins, but that didn't occur until much later in the school's history. When you hear 'Burglund,' it's the same as 'Higgins.' My class of 1970 was the last class of Higgins (Burglund) High School. The rivalry with Alexander in Brookhaven dates back as far as I can remember."

Throughout their existence, the Burglund Lions were writing their own entries in the football history books of Pike County. Star players, exciting rivalries, colorful mascots, thrilling bands, big games and events were all a part of the football tradition being created by the Burglund Lions. Former Burglund player and coach, James Brooks, relives some of those special moments. The Lions' legendary Brooks recalls, "There were a number of great players coming out of Burglund before I got there in '51, and they were still turning them out after I graduated. I remember Theodore Bullock, Arthur Jobie Anderson, A.C. Washington, Julius Nobles, Clarence Steen, Robert Jones and Thurston McLeod, just to name a few."

James Brooks, whose nickname was "Dick" while at Burglund, says, "We won the Negro Big Eight Conference my sophomore year by defeating Oak Park of Laurel in 1952. I played quarterback for the

Lions. Of course, our big rival was the Alexander Golden Panthers in Brookhaven." Later, Brooks learned that the two schools' principals, C.D. Higgins and A.A. Alexander, were college roommates back in the '20s. The two roommates and teammates at Jackson College had their own personal rivalry going between their respective schools – Higgins at McComb Burglund and Alexander at Brookhaven Alexander. The already intense rivalry between the two black schools, fueled by their proximity, was supercharged by their respective principals.

Brooks recalls, "There was only one stadium in McComb, and both Burglund and McComb used it. We went to their games and they came to ours. We used to practice on their track because there was no track at Burglund."

Louis Guy, former McComb football great, recalls, "I remember going out and watching some of their games. Sometimes they would come over and play at McComb's field. The Burglund team played a different style of football from ours, but the skill level was definitely there. They had some good teams."

Beginning in 1967, the schools in McComb started the integration process. As events unfolded, school administrators felt the classroom transition for the students was proceeding very well. Their main concerns were with activities like sports and band, mainly because these were social events. According to Robert Vick, Jr., Burglund's band director, "Sometimes people get highly upset when you destroy the social aspect of the school. The school superintendent told us to 'work it out.' So instead of having a head band director, Joe Daniel from McComb and I were co-directors."

In order to "work it out," a number of issues – some extremely sensitive – had to be resolved without alienating the folks from either Burglund or McComb. Mr. Vick explains,

> The Burglund and McComb bands marched to different styles. Burglund performed commercial, hot music from the radio charts and marched to a fast cadence. To make matters worse, we had just purchased brand new green and gold uniforms. To complicate matters further, McComb High had just purchased a new Tiger mascot suit. School colors, mascots and band marching and music styles were just some of the things we had to resolve as we sat around the table during an endless number of meetings.

After numerous discussions, the transition team of coaches, teachers, band directors and administrators from McComb and Burglund high schools finally made some recommendations. After consolidation, the new school would stay at the site of the old McComb High. The Tiger would survive as the mascot of the new school; however, to achieve some balance, they would abandon the blue and gold of McComb High and replace it with the green and gold of Burglund. As for the band uniforms, a decision was made to discard the Burglund design and adopt a new uniform that was black with green and gold overlay. When Mr. Vick carried the proposals back to the black community, many people were not pleased. As Mr. Vick recalls, "We were not dying to integrate. We enjoyed our way of doing things." Fortunately, the transition team worked through all the issues and the consolidation of McComb High and Burglund moved along with minimal difficulty.

Mr. Vick recalls the tension surrounding the band's first performance at the opening home football game:

> Both bands had their own style. At McComb High, they marched a 6 to 5 step – 6 steps every 5 yards. Burglund marched an upbeat 8 to 5 step. We had a high-stepping march with knees up. Theirs was a stride step like the military. We did something peculiar at the first game. The co-band directors decided to have one band under one goal post in their old uniforms and the other band at the opposite end in their old uniforms. Each band would march its style coming onto the field and meet at the 50-yard line where they would merge for the first time and play "Tiger Rag."
> The stadium was packed; both sides were full. Basically, all the blacks were together and all the whites were together. Everybody was wondering just how we were going to work things out. Both bands came on doing their own things. McComb High came onto the field playing "Raindrops Keep Falling on my Head" and marching 6 to 5 military style. Burglund took the field to "Fever," marching at the faster 8 to 5 pace. Both bands came to midfield, merged and struck up "Tiger Rag." When we hit that tune together, you just felt a great sigh of relief across the entire audience. The band marched off the field to a standing ovation. As the band was getting set up back in the bleachers, everybody – both black and white – wanted us to play "Fever" again.

From that game on, every time our defensive unit took the field, we played "Fever." It became our trademark.

Several years after the band's first command performance, Mr. Vick retired as band director at McComb High School. He now pastors a church in Summit, Mississippi. He says, "When your community can make things work, God has a way of helping out. You always want to be sincere about what you are doing. There are always going to be differences, but we prayed about our performances and things really worked out for our band."

During the state band competition the first year McComb and Burglund consolidated, the band received all superior ratings for its performance. In 1976, the McComb High School Band was invited to Washington, D.C. to represent the State of Mississippi in the bicentennial celebration. The Tiger Band also received an invitation to perform at the opening of Disney World and was one of the first high school bands to play in the Louisiana Superdome.

Through all the turmoil of the consolidation of McComb High and Burglund, "Our band program held together; and the night we marched off the field to a standing ovation, we brought the community together," says Mr. Vick.

Principal Slater-Smith sums it up this way:

I would love to say that our school community stands as one all the time, but we don't. No school does. There are times when parents are angry with teachers and times when the teachers get angry with parents. However, when our boys are on the football field, everybody throws away their differences and becomes one family because every one of those boys is ours. It's the one thing that pulls us all together. It makes us forget our differences and brings out the best in all of us. Parents and teachers are sitting in the stands side-by-side, cheering together. When one of our boys scores a touchdown or makes a big play, it doesn't matter who it is because it's McComb's child who did it. He belongs to all of us. It's the one factor that promotes unity and togetherness. The only thing that matters is beating the opponent.

The words of Principal Slater-Smith bear repeating – ". . . it doesn't matter who it is, because it's McComb's child. He belongs to all of us . . . every one of those boys is ours."

Yes, pride does run deep in McComb, sir!

****

The gridiron rivalry between Brookhaven and McComb began in 1920 with the teams playing each other twice that year. McComb won both games by the same score – 6-0. In 1921, Brookhaven returned the favor by beating the Tigers 12-6. By 1927 when the teams started to play the annual game on Thanksgiving Day, the series was tied with each school having claimed four victories. The first Thanksgiving Day game in 1927 created a backdrop for one of Mississippi's most colorful football rivalries. The annual Brookhaven and McComb Turkey Day battle quickly became one of the biggest sporting events in the Magnolia State. While the first Thanksgiving Day game between the Tigers and Panthers ended in a 14-14 tie, the following 35 games proved to be full of excitement, thrills and intensely-waged gridiron wars. Not until 1963 was the game moved to a Friday night in lieu of the Thanksgiving Day date on the schedule.

In an article written by Carroll Case for the *Enterprise-Journal* in 1985, he described in vivid detail the atmosphere surrounding the big game:

> For 36 years on Thanksgiving Day, the McComb Tigers and the Brookhaven Panthers met either in McComb or Brookhaven to play football. It was a rivalry that has never been surpassed. It was billed as, and was, the greatest sporting event of the year.
>
> On Turkey Day nearly one-half of each city's population came down or either went up Highway 51 to support their teams. Bumper to bumper in caravans, cars were decorated with colorful crepe paper streamers.
>
> The event had all the spectacle of a King Arthur legend, the color, the pomp, the splendor. Ladies wore mums and men wore school colors. The spectators came dressed in their Sunday best to watch young Lancelots from each team do battle in the arena for southwest Mississippi's greatest event.
>
> Even in the war years there was standing room only and in McComb, if you were not fortunate enough to find standing room, you could go to Kramertown and

listen to the game over loudspeakers at Pete's Place.

Fans would hurriedly eat their turkey and dressing, leaving dirty dishes for later, and head for the stadium. For months prior to the event, Tiger fans had been worked into a white heat by the columns of Charlie Gordon. In Brookhaven, the Panthers were honed to a fine edge by the writings of Jimmy McDowell.

Football was at its best. Both teams were always strong Big Eight contenders. Over the 36 years that the two teams met on Thanksgiving Day the Tigers would end the tradition by winning the most games. When Brookhaven did win, the victory was even sweeter and the supporters from Brookhaven never seemed to be disappointed.

The series was hard hitting and tough. Friendships were made among players that would last a lifetime.

Former Brookhaven football player Bob Allen recalls the Thanksgiving Day ritual: "There were two things I always remember. You had to get back and eat Thanksgiving lunch because Mama never wanted to serve it before the game, which started at 1:00. Then we had a dance that night, and afterwards we left for deer camp about 2:00 in the morning. We didn't hunt with those SOBs from McComb either."

Miriam Moyer, a teacher at Brookhaven for 42 years and wife of legendary Brookhaven football coach Paul Moyer, reminisces about the big holiday event:

As a child, our entire Thanksgiving revolved around the big game. My mother was from McComb and had family still living there. When the game was played in McComb, we ate lunch at my aunt's house and then we rushed to get a seat for the game. When the game was played in Brookhaven, we ate lunch at my house in Wesson and came to the game in Brookhaven. These were exciting times and we prepared ourselves by wearing our very special new outfits for the big event. Of course, my perspective on all this took on a new and more significant meaning when I became a coach's wife and cheerleader sponsor – such great times and fond memories.

Bobby Maddox, former McComb football player, remembers

the Thanksgiving Day festivities: "When the fans came to that football game, the women wore their Sunday best with a corsage. It was really a very special occasion, not only to play football, but for the ladies to dress up. That was a special time and a special part of the history of football in McComb and Brookhaven."

Former McComb football player Tommy Parker recalls, "The ladies from McComb wore gold corsages with a blue 'M'. Brookhaven had white corsages with a red 'B'. The dress was real important back then. Our band marched through downtown McComb with some of our players."

Parker continues, "Try to envision Highway 51 so crowded with cars – 3500 people trying to get up there on Thanksgiving Day. The highway was just jammed. A highway patrol trooper got in front of the line of cars starting at 12:00, and we followed him to Brookhaven doing about 45 miles per hour. That's the way it was coming back, too."

Louis Guy, one of McComb's great players in the '50s, recalls the excitement in the community surrounding the Tigers' football games, especially the game against Brookhaven. Guy says, "If you couldn't pick up the game on the radio when McComb played out of town, somebody would always figure a way to get the information back to McComb. The storeowners in downtown McComb put the scores in their windows as information was received. Fans went downtown to find out the score."

Anyone who ever witnessed these Thanksgiving Day extravaganzas has a favorite game. Perhaps it was in 1947 when, only two days before the big game, McComb's football uniforms caught fire and burned up. That year the Tigers played in uniforms borrowed from their cousins down the road, the LSU Tigers, and scored one of their greatest upset victories over Brookhaven. Maybe it was one of the games of the '50s when Brookhaven fielded powerhouse teams resembling thundering herds that trampled the Tigers on several occasions. Conversations among fans and football aficionados invariably lead to the 1949 game played before an estimated crowd of 6,500, when underdog McComb defeated Brookhaven 33 to 27 at C.C. Moore Field. In the words of Carroll Case writing for the *Enterprise-Journal*, "Remembering and looking back makes memories of this game even more special. It seems like the crowd was bigger, the game was better and smiles of victories brighter, but if you talk to anyone who either played or watched the game, you, too, would be convinced that this surely was football at its best."

Sadly, the Thanksgiving Day event ended in 1963. However, the rivalry kept right on going when the game was moved to Friday night. While old timers still reminisce about the well-dressed, standing room only crowds gathered at King Field or C.C. Moore Stadium on Thanksgiving Day for the big game, the players today wearing the colors of Ole Brook and the Tiger green and gold play just as passionately as their predecessors did decades earlier.

Stan Patrick, former Brookhaven player in the '70s, recalls his first time to play in a Brookhaven and McComb game his sophomore year: "The game was well in hand, so Coach put me in at middle linebacker toward the end of the game. The McComb quarterback dropped back and hit me right in the chest with the ball, so I took off running and got knocked out of bounds on the McComb sidelines. Well, I thought I was going to die; there was kicking and stomping and all sorts of problems before I got out of there."

Former Brookhaven football player Roderick Henderson, who graduated in 1990 and is now an assistant coach for the Panthers, says, "The week of the Brookhaven-McComb game was a rallying time for the whole town. We always had people come by and give motivational speeches. People came up to you on the street and said, 'You've got to win this one.' After you hear that over and over from people, the pressure builds up and you know it's a big-time rivalry."

Karen Sullivan, wife of legendary Brookhaven head football coach Doug Sullivan, and Miriam Moyer both describe how important winning the McComb game is to the Brookhaven community. Karen Sullivan recalls, "At a booster club meeting during our first year at Brookhaven, a member got up and said, 'You know, Doug, we folks here at Brookhaven have a tendency to have a bad memory and wipe out all the losses . . . if you beat McComb.'" Miriam Moyer and her husband, Paul, had a similar experience their first year when a group of neighbors told them, "If you beat McComb you can hang the curtains; if not, don't bother. Just pack 'em along with everything else." Ms. Moyer says, "I just laughed, but they told me it really wasn't funny."

During the 88-year history of the Brookhaven and McComb rivalry, there have been two Monday night games – 1963 and 2005. In 1963, officials cancelled the regularly scheduled game due to the assassination of President John F. Kennedy. Hurricane Katrina disrupted the game in 2005, causing officials to reschedule it to a Monday night two weeks later.

Another piece of Tiger and Panther trivia involves the 1957 game between the two schools. In the '57 game, four future college All-Americans played for Brookhaven and McComb. Lance Alworth (Arkansas), Ralph Smith (Ole Miss) and Red Estes (LSU) played for the Panthers, while Louis Guy (Ole Miss) played for the Tigers. Alworth, Smith and Guy all went on to play professional football.

Since the creation of the state championship format in 1981, McComb has captured two state championships – 1984 and 2000 – while Brookhaven has one gold ball in its trophy case for their title in 2004.

The Brookhaven Panthers and the Tigers of McComb have been engaged in gridiron battle for 88 years. During that long period, each team has won its share of games. Stories created from those exciting events are still told to this day, but perhaps the greatest legacy of this classic high school rivalry are the players who have proudly worn, and who will wear, the colors of two proud towns in southwest Mississippi – Tuminello, Guy, Lofton, Parker, Brooks, Alworth, Spence, Estes, Rhedd, Minton, Young, Smith, Alford, Stockfisch, Robinson, Greenlee, Brister, Butler, Jones, Brueck, Carlisle, McKissack, White, McGill, Case, McIntosh, Sutton, Shaw, Bullock, Carr, Catlin, Pope, Cain, Clark, Case, Strothers, Ramsay, Stewart, James, Crawford, Johns, Brice, Bowman, Robinson, Wilson . . . and many more yet to come.

WHAT THE PANTHERS SAY ABOUT McCOMB

The ritual was we would go down and date their girls; they would come up here and date our girls and then we would meet at Dixie Springs and fight about it.

Bob Allen
Former Brookhaven Football Player

I would rather beat McComb than eat a good meal.

Susan Chapman
Brookhaven Principal

At C.C. Moore Stadium, the McComb band sits in the south end zone and they are real close to the field. Of course, when you are driving toward them, the band cranks it up to raise the noise level.

Don Coleman
Former Brookhaven Head Football Coach

There are a few schools we play that create a great atmosphere. McComb is one of those schools. When you go to McComb you can feel a football atmosphere. They bring that same atmosphere when they come to Brookhaven.

James Dennis
Former Brookhaven Student Body President

McComb-Brookhaven is still the biggest rivalry.

Charles Rancifer
Former Brookhaven Football Player

I hate playing at McComb because they have those obnoxious cannons. Every time they score, they shoot them off and they are really loud.

Abby Fisher
Former Brookhaven Cheerleader

Brookhaven and McComb is a war.

Roderick Henderson
Former Brookhaven Player and
Current Assistant Football Coach

We want to beat McComb in everything – football, basketball, baseball, tax revenue, church attendance – everything.

Rob Fisher
Brookhaven Radio Crew

The hospitals, banks, doctors and just about everyone in Brookhaven and McComb has some kind of rivalry going on. I believe it stems from the football rivalry.

Mark Lewis
Brookhaven Radio Crew

A couple of years ago when McComb beat us, you would have thought they won the Super Bowl. It was a huge, huge deal to them.

Shannon Aker
Brookhaven Radio Crew

McComb has always had those lean, long, tall athletes who can run. When you see McComb on film, the first thing you say is, "They can run."

Roderick Henderson
Former Brookhaven Player and
Current Assistant Football Coach

The Brookhaven and McComb football game is as aggressive as it can be without someone going to prison.

Rob Fisher
Brookhaven Radio Crew

WHAT THE TIGERS SAY ABOUT BROOKHAVEN

We want to welcome our friends from Ole Brook – Home Seekers' Paradise.

Bobby Maddox

McComb P.A. Announcer

We love playing Brookhaven, but better than anything, we love whooping Brookhaven. If we don't beat anybody else on our schedule, we have to beat Brookhaven.

Dr. Sharon Slater-Smith

McComb Principal

When I talk to some of those older former players, they tell me how much better McComb is than Brookhaven. Of course, when I go to Brookhaven, they tell me the opposite. The intensity is still there because everyone knows each other.

Randy Martin

McComb Head Football Coach

I'm sure we're gonna win this year.

Zach Patterson

Mayor of McComb

When you are getting dressed to go to the Brookhaven game it's just a different feeling. I can't describe it.

Dr. Sharon Slater-Smith

McComb Principal

Brookhaven always has huge linemen.

David Varnell

McComb Athletic Director

Back in the early days, McComb was beating the tar out of Brookhaven.

Tommy Parker

Former McComb Football Player

We've got to beat Brookhaven every time. I heard one of our players say, "We want to win every game, but Brookhaven is the one game we will not lose." We just don't want to lose against Brookhaven.

Dr. Sharon Slater-Smith

McComb Principal

I think the rivalry is going to heat up more and more. No doubt about it.

Zach Patterson

Mayor of McComb

Brookhaven High School is wide open. That panther is right there in front of the school. It's an easy target. I think it looks better pink.

Anonymous

BROOKHAVEN-McCOMB
SERIES HISTORY

Year	Brookhaven	Score	McComb
1920	*NA*	0-6	Frank Lee
1920	*NA*	0-6	Frank Lee
1921	*NA*	12-6	Frank Lee
1922	*NA*	0-20	Frank Lee
1923	*NA*	0-31	*NA*
1924	Coach Nevins	6-0	*NA*
1925	*NA*	9-7	*NA*
1926	*NA*	6-0	*NA*
1927	*NA*	14-14	Coach McGowan
1928	*NA*	0-9	Coach McGowan
1929	*NA*	0-0	Coach McGowan
1930	*NA*	6-7	Coach McGowan
1931	*NA*	14-26	Coach McGowan
1932	*NA*	12-7	Coach McGowan
1933	*NA*	2-19	Coach McGowan
1934	*NA*	12-6	Coach McGowan
1935	*NA*	12-7	C.C. Moore
1936	Coach King	0-48	C.C. Moore
1937	Coach King	13-19	C.C. Moore
1938	Coach King	0-25	C.C. Moore
1939	Coach King	0-20	C.C. Moore
1940	Coach King	0-27	C.C. Moore
1941	*NA*	0-61	C.C. Moore
1942	*NA*	0-39	C.C. Moore
1943	*NA*	6-7	C.C. Moore
1943	*NA*	7-7	C.C. Moore
1944	*NA*	0-21	C.C. Moore
1944	*NA*	0-33	C.C. Moore
1945	*NA*	0-26	Dutch Binion
1946	*NA*	0-29	Dutch Binion
1947	Hartince McPhail	0-33	Sammy Bartling
1948	Hartince McPhail	0-13	Sammy Bartling
1949	Hartince McPhail	27-33	Sammy Bartling
1950	Hartince McPhail	14-19	Sammy Bartling

Year	Brookhaven	Score	McComb
1951	Charles Armstrong	34-6	Melvin Hemphill
1952	Charles Armstrong	0-25	Melvin Hemphill
1953	Jim Sinclair	20-6	Melvin Hemphill
1954	Paul Moyer	0-6	Melvin Hemphill
1955	Paul Moyer	34-21	Melvin Hemphill
1956	Paul Moyer	25-7	Melvin Hemphill
1957	Paul Moyer	37-13	Calvin Triplett
1958	Paul Moyer	12-34	Calvin Triplett
1959	Paul Moyer	13-33	Calvin Triplett
1960	Leonard McCullough	13-14	Calvin Triplett
1961	Leonard McCullough	19-7	Calvin Triplett
1962	Leonard McCullough	6-46	Calvin Triplett
1963	Leonard McCullough	6-13	Claude Harrison
1964	Charles McArthur	6-0	Claude Harrison
1965	Charles McArthur	6-28	Frank Halbert
1966	Charles McArthur	14-14	Frank Halbert
1967	Charles McArthur	0-14	Frank Halbert
1968	Charles McArthur	13-13	Frank Halbert
1969	Charles McArthur	0-48	Frank Halbert
1970	Doug Sullivan	2-23	Jimmy Robertson
1971	Doug Sullivan	8-36	J.W. Beck
1972	Doug Sullivan	26-0	J.W. Beck
1973	Doug Sullivan	38-0	J.W. Beck
1974	Larry Thomas	14-7	Wally Bumpas
1975	Larry Thomas	0-14	Wally Bumpas
1976	Larry Thomas	7-18	Wally Bumpas
1977	Larry Thomas	7-22	Wally Bumpas
1978	Les Bumgarner	20-29	Wally Bumpas
1979	Les Bumgarner	21-0	George Blair
1980	Les Bumgarner	12-28	Chet Bergalonski
1981	Bud O'Hara	0-18	Chet Bergalonski
1982	Bud O'Hara	7-10	Chet Bergalonski
1983	Bud O'Hara	41-6	Chet Bergalonski
1984	Bud O'Hara	7-31	Chet Bergalonski
1985	Charles McCollum	14-24	Chet Bergalonski
1986	Charles McCollum	3-6	Chet Bergalonski
1987	Charles McCollum	13-17	Chet Bergalonski
1988	Don Coleman	9-21	Chet Bergalonski

Year	Brookhaven	Score	McComb
1989	Don Coleman	27-19	Chet Bergalonski
1990	Don Coleman	21-42	Chet Bergalonski
1991	Don Coleman	27-29	Lee Bramlett
1992	Don Coleman	7-10	Lee Bramlett
1993	Russell Funk	22-53	Lee Bramlett
1994	Russell Funk	0-24	Lee Bramlett
1995	Russell Funk	12-6	Lee Bramlett
1996	Russell Funk	0-34	Lee Bramlett
1997	Greg Wall	21-14	Lee Bramlett
1998	Greg Wall	20-14	Lee Bramlett
1999	Greg Wall	6-28	Lee Bramlett
2000	Greg Wall	8-40	Lee Bramlett
2001	Andrew Hickman	21-28	Ted Milton
2002	Tucker Peavey	12-14	Ted Milton
2003	Tucker Peavey	41-7	Ted Milton
2004	Tucker Peavey	52-13	Ted Milton
2005	Tucker Peavey	21-14	Randy Martin
2006	Tucker Peavey	28-31	Randy Martin
2007	Tucker Peavey	35-21	Randy Martin

NA - Information Not Available

★★ OFFICIAL GAME DAY PROGRAM $5.00 ★★

LAFAYETTE
VERSUS
OXFORD

Trustmark
Banking and Financial Solutions

PROUD SPONSOR OF MISSISSIPPI HIGH SCHOOL FOOTBALL

FRIDAY, SEPTEMBER 19, 2008 ★ 7:00 PM KICKOFF
BOBBY HOLCOMB FIELD ★ OXFORD, MISSISSIPPI

CHAPTER

05

SLUGFEST ON THE SQUARE

Perry Arrington, the oldest son of Coach Jimmy and Gale Arrington, was born on May 17, 1967. Two years later, Perry's younger brother, Alan, joined the Arrington team. During Perry's entire childhood, he and his family lived in a mobile home on the campus of Lafayette High School. It wasn't until midway through Perry's senior year that his family moved away from the Lafayette location. Luckily, Perry enjoyed 18 years of "pure childhood paradise." The entire athletic complex of Lafayette High School was Perry and Alan's personal playground. The Commodores' football stadium accommodated the boys during the fall for games of roughhouse. When winter arrived, Perry and Alan had the keys to unlock the gym to shoot hoops and play games of one on one. In the spring, the Commodores' baseball diamond was manicured and ready whenever the boys had the urge to play ball with their buddies. Perry and Alan's entire world revolved around Commodore athletics.

As elementary kids, Perry and Alan stood down by the fence to watch football practice almost every day. As the ritual continued throughout their childhood years, certain things made impressions – deep impressions – on the Arrington boys. These were impressions that would not, nor could not, be erased from their young minds. As the boys approached their high school years, many of those youthful impressions were reduced to simple rules – rules to live by and to follow as young men. It became clear that the first rule was the most important. It became known in the Arrington household simply as Rule No. 1.

Beginning in the seventh grade at Lafayette, football players begin preparing for the Oxford game. Since there are no junior high games between Oxford and Lafayette, the first game doesn't occur until three years later during a player's sophomore year of high school. Nonetheless, preparation for a Lafayette football player begins in seventh grade. Each player understands that he and his class of teammates will get three shots at Oxford. To ensure that they make the most of those shots in the tenth, eleventh and twelfth grades, preparations start well in advance. Losing to Oxford is not an option for any Lafayette football player, and especially for Coach Arrington's boys. The thought of a loss to the Chargers is simply unthinkable. Perry and Alan had been taught well. Don't violate Rule No. 1.

Finally, after years of playing imaginary games against the Oxford Chargers, Perry's turn arrived for real in 1983 and Alan's turn came two years later. As many times as they had experienced the excitement surrounding the annual Oxford and Lafayette game, they were overwhelmed with the school spirit and the excitement of the rivalry as high school players. The pep rallies, the parades on the square and the incredible heart-pounding rush of adrenaline on game days were the best times of a young man's life. The pressure came with the thrilling anticipation of each Oxford game – the pressure to win for the community, the school, the team, the family and themselves. Pressure on Perry and Alan started with the impressions made on them while watching football practice for so many years as their dad coached his players. Now they were more than Coach Arrington's boys. Perry and Alan were two of their dad's Commodore players ready to follow Rule No. 1 – Beat Oxford!

At Meet the Commodores Night prior to Perry's senior season, when he stood up to introduce himself he said, "My name is Perry Arrington and I play center. I'm a senior and I've never been beaten by Oxford." Following Perry's proclamation came 60 of Perry's teammates with the same statement accompanying their introduction, ". . . and I've never been beaten by Oxford." The stadium just exploded with cheers and applause each time a Commodore player made his proclamation. When it was Alan's turn his senior year, he started Meet the Commodore Night with the same introduction, followed by ". . . and I've never been beaten by Oxford," just as his brother Perry had done. The reaction in the stadium was the same as before – pure jubilation.

After Perry and Alan completed their playing days as Commodores, they departed Lafayette High School having never lost to Oxford. Coach Arrington's boys had learned well during their childhood days growing up on the Lafayette campus to always follow Rule No. 1. Perry and Alan did just that . . . by beating Oxford!

Perry would go on to play for Northwest Community College and win a state juco championship in 1987. Following his juco career,

Perry played for Ole Miss and ended his football playing days with the Rebels in the 1989 Liberty Bowl. From his childhood days standing by the fence at Lafayette watching football practice to his final college game in the Liberty Bowl, Perry reflects on his football career: "Even after playing major college football, I still show up at the Oxford and Lafayette games and get chill bumps. At age 40, I still want to put on that red and gold No. 55 jersey. There's nothing better than an Oxford and Lafayette game on a Friday night."

Almost 20 years after Perry and Alan played in their final games for the Commodores, current head football coach Anthony Hart arrived on the Lafayette High School campus. After three years at the helm of the Commodore football program, Coach Hart reflects on his early days: "One of the funny things I remember was during the entire interview process nothing was ever mentioned about the Oxford rivalry. So when I accepted the job I told everybody that each of our games was important and that we would prepare the same way for every opponent." However, after talking to several Commodore fans and supporters, the reality of the situation became apparent. Kent Littlejohn, a longtime Commodore fan, told Coach Hart, "That's fine to prepare the same way for the other nine games, but for this one game, it's not." Coach Hart's wife, Traci, recalls someone telling her, "Lafayette is the only place where you can go 9-1 and lose your job or go 1-9 and keep your job." During Coach Hart's first year at Lafayette, his Commodore team lost a very close, hard-fought game to Oxford. Coach Hart remembers a comment made by a fan at a meeting several weeks later about Lafayette being the easiest place in Mississippi to coach, because all you had to do was win one game a year – Oxford. It didn't take Coach Hart long to figure it out. He says, "If it's important to the community, then it's important to me. We're going to do the very best we can every year to win the Oxford game. I didn't really realize how big the rivalry was at first. I do now. Bottom line – if you lose enough times in a row, people probably are not gonna want you around here anymore." Following Coach Hart's first-year, heartbreaking loss in 2005 to Oxford, the Lafayette Commodores won the next two games against the Chargers in thrilling overtime nail biters.

Coach Hart and wife Traci try to keep it all in perspective. Traci says, "We always kind of joke and say, 'We are here for another year because we beat Oxford this season.'" According to Coach Hart, "There is no rivalry in Mississippi bigger than Oxford and Lafayette." Coach

Hart and Traci have both learned the importance of following Rule No. 1 – Beat Oxford!

****

Brad Freeman was in the eighth grade at Oxford when the Hill boys came to town. Walt, Chad, Jake and Stan were Johnny and Linda Hill's sons. Johnny Hill just happened to be Oxford's new head football coach. Brad and the Hill boys virtually grew up together, especially Walt, who was the oldest of the Hill boys and only one grade behind Brad in school. During Brad's eighth-grade year, all of them were sitting in the stands on the top row watching an Oxford and Lafayette football game when they were startled by a ruckus below the bleachers. There, in full view of all the boys, was a sure enough old-fashioned fistfight between boys from Oxford and Lafayette. It was at that point in Brad's life that he realized there was bad blood between Oxford and Lafayette folks, especially when it came to football.

Since that shocking event beneath the bleachers during Brad's eighth-grade year, it seemed like he and the Hill boys stayed in the center of the Commodore and Charger feud. Brad recalls opening his locker during his junior season the week of the Lafayette game to find notes purportedly written by Lafayette fans that said insulting things to him and his teammates. Messages from the hated Lafayette opponents saying such things as, "Freeman Sucks," "Lafayette Rules" and "We're Gonna Kill Freeman" were some of the more complimentary phrases. To make matters worse, his best friends, the Hill boys, received the same disrespectful treatment. Of course it never crossed Brad's 17-year-old mind that maybe someone other than Lafayette fans might have placed those insulting and inflammatory postings in his locker and the lockers of his friends. Instead, it was just another rallying cry to avenge the many disrespectful acts dumped upon Oxford by those lowlifes over at Lafayette.

During Brad's senior year, Walt Hill had torn his ACL and was unable to play in the Lafayette game. Instead, Walt was on the sidelines standing on crutches. Early in the second quarter of the game, Brad was run out of bounds. At the end of the play, a Commodore player put a late hit on him that sent him rolling to the fence. The next thing Brad remembered was a commotion directly over him involving several Lafayette players and some man who appeared to be swinging two giant sticks. It was Walt beating the Commodore player with his crutches as he hopped on his one good leg. Brad recalls, "I just sat there and thought, Only in the Oxford and Lafayette game would a crippled man get into a fight and try to hit someone with his crutches."

After his high school days at Oxford, Brad Freeman went on to play football and baseball at Mississippi State University. During his baseball career at State he played in the 1997 and 1998 College World Series. As a collegiate athlete, Brad was fortunate to play in front of tens of thousands of fans at Dudy Noble Field in Starkville and Rosenblatt Stadium in Omaha, Nebraska. However, according to Brad Freeman, the sporting event that he would most want to relive is "to get back out there for an Oxford-Lafayette game."

Jake Hill, the Hills' third son, was a sophomore when his brother Chad was a junior and older brother, Walt, was a senior. Jake recalls, "It didn't matter what we were doing, it was always competitive. Even if we were taking a leak, we were gonna see who could pee the longest. Being competitive really helped us when it came to athletics."

Jake describes the intensity of the Lafayette game: "As a player you put so much into that game. When the time comes, you don't stand around at all. You better have your head on a swivel or else you're gonna get flattened. My junior year the word was out that Lafayette was out to get Chad and me. I remember several times when Chad went down and some player for Lafayette would come in to get a cheap shot. I got some good licks on several Commodores that night just trying to protect my brother. It was fun."

Coach Johnny Hill describes the feeling the week of the big game: "It's one of those games where you don't have to motivate the players because they are already motivated. They are motivated at home, in their neighborhoods and at church. The night of the game you can cut the tension with a knife. I mean you can feel it in the air. There is so much tension between fans, players and coaches. It is a very unique feeling."

Coach Johnny Hill recalls a funny incident involving a Lafayette fan one season:

> I went over to Lafayette on a Saturday to trade out film. On the way I noticed I was about to run out of gas, so I pulled over at a convenience store out on Highway 334 to fuel up. I went inside the store to pay

for my gas wearing an Oxford jacket since it was chilly outside. Some big guy wearing overalls and a t-shirt with the sleeves rolled up came over to me, grinned, stuck his finger in my chest and said, "We're gonna whoop y'all's ass Friday night." I wasn't worried about Friday night; I was more worried that I was about to have my ass whooped right at that moment. I stood there a second and then put my finger in his chest and said, "Just remember one thing. You've got to bring some ass to get some ass." This big guy just died out laughing. I knew it was all right, but before that moment, I didn't know if we were gonna get to swinging at each other in the convenience store or not. I didn't know that guy from anybody.

The Hill boys never lost to Lafayette in football. "The year I was a sophomore and Walt and Chad were upperclassmen, Lafayette had a sign on their school that said, 'We are going to top the Hills!' I loved it because we just put it in their face and beat them," recalls Jake.

Coach Steve Herring has coached on both sides of the Oxford and Lafayette rivalry. He recalls one ballgame in particular when Oxford was playing at Lafayette during a first-round playoff game:

Right before halftime in what was an extremely tight game, I noticed my wife coming toward me with tears in her eyes. When she reached me she said, "You've got to go. Your sister just called, and your mom may not make it. Go now." My mother lived in Sardis and was battling cancer. I immediately went to Coach Hill and told him the situation. He told me to go, so I took off for Sardis. When I arrived at my mom's house, I went straight to her bedroom. When I got to her room, there she was, sitting up in bed, drinking iced tea and listening to the game on the radio. Her exact words to me were, "What the hell are you doing here?" I said, "Mom, Denise called and said you may not make it and that I needed to get over here now." Mom said, "Oh, she must have heard me moaning and groaning when Lafayette had the ball inside the five and your defense wasn't holding them. I already told you I'm not gonna die on a Friday night." We listened to the rest of the game together. It was real exciting, because the game went into overtime. Unfortunately, Oxford lost.

I'll never forget that Oxford-Lafayette game. It was a special night for me and my mom. She died two days later.

****

The Oxford and Lafayette rivalry did not begin until 1972, even though Oxford High School had been playing football since 1929. Lafayette did not come into existence until 1965 when a number of small county schools were consolidated into one high school. From 1965 until the date of the first gridiron clash between the Commodores and Chargers, the two schools played football in different conferences. Oxford competed in the well-established Little Ten with schools such as West Point and Amory. For several years during the beginning of Lafayette's football program, it played a five-game season, taking on whatever opponents it could find with open dates. Eventually, Lafayette became a member of the Tri-Lakes Conference and competed against neighboring schools such as Bruce, Calhoun City, Independence, Coldwater, Coffeeville and several others.

The first meeting between Lafayette and Oxford's football teams occurred on November 18, 1972, in the Civitan Bowl played in Oxford, Mississippi. Omar Craig, an Oxford lawyer and a big Lafayette supporter, convinced his local Civitan Club to sponsor a post-season bowl game to help raise money for medical equipment needed in the emergency room at the local hospital. Both the Commodores and the Chargers were coming off good seasons, so Craig's idea was generally well received. Once the Civitan club decided to go forward with sponsoring the bowl game, concerns started to surface in the community. Some people believed the Lafayette team could not stay on the field with the more established Charger football program. There were also serious concerns that the game might get out of control. Due to the proximity of the schools and the fact that this would be the first time the teams would compete, many thought the game could get out of hand, both on and off the field. However, all the naysayers were proven wrong. The Commodores and Chargers treated the huge crowd to a spectacular defensive struggle. The game was a big success and established Oxford and Lafayette as a "must play" rivalry game every year. The first contest between the football teams from Oxford and Lafayette literally set the tone for the next three and a half decades to follow. According to sports writer Harvey Faust, "The Oxford Chargers rode the toe of Ray Poole to a 3-0 victory over the Lafayette Commodores Monday night in the first annual Civitan Bowl as a crowd estimated at 4,000 watched two of the finest teams in north Mississippi battle for top honors."

The *Oxford Eagle* newspaper's account of the game described it as a defensive struggle with neither team able to generate much offense. Many of the fumbles during the game came as a result of the intense contact on the field. The Most Valuable Player of the game, Charger guard Bill Lawhorn, received such a blow late in the game that he was still groggy in the locker room an hour after the game ended. Lawhorn said, "I don't remember too much about the game . . . somebody really put a lick on me." The first Civitan Bowl in 1972 set the stage for Oxford and Lafayette to continue their rivalry, which is acknowledged as one of the classic high school football games in Mississippi each year.

Oxford defeated Lafayette again in 1973 to go ahead 2-0 in the series; however, in 1974 Lafayette beat the Chargers 16-0 to notch its first victory against its cross-town rival. Except for a seven-game winning streak by Lafayette between 1983 and 1989, the winner of the annual game has bounced back and forth between the two sides. Originally, the game was scheduled as the last game of the season; however, since Mississippi high schools moved away from conference schedules into district and size classifications in 1981, the Oxford and Lafayette game has moved around on the teams' schedules. Of course the date of the game is of no concern for the fans or the players of either team. Once the schedules for the Commodores and Chargers are published each year, the game between the two teams is circled and the anticipation starts to build, no matter when it's played.

From the moment the announcement was made that Oxford and Lafayette would play each other in the Civitan Bowl, the fun began. Even though the two schools are less than two miles apart and have the same zip code, some type of continental divide seems to exist between them. As in most rival games, whether at the high school or college level, out come the stereotypes to help fuel the fires of competition – superficial labels attached to each side in the "y'all against us" contest. In the Oxford and Lafayette game the labels were established quickly – "rednecks" versus "city slickers." According to Timmy Pruitt, a former Commodore player in the early '80s,

When I was a player, all the Oxford people were

the preppies and wore Izod shirts and penny loafers. Mostly lawyers' and doctors' kids attended Oxford. The country folks went to Lafayette. Of course we were the hicks and they were the little preppies. For the most part, we were all pretty good friends, but during the week of the game, all that ended and we didn't talk to them. Every once in a while a few fights resulted. You might have a big brawl up at the Square. As soon as it was over, we were back out there sitting on the Square talking about who hit who in the game.

Former Lafayette coach Doug Vanlandingham offers his perspective: "I think the proximity of the schools has a lot to do with it. The rivalry was portrayed as rich kids versus poor kids. A lot of the parents of the Lafayette students worked for the parents of the kids at Oxford. At the time I coached at Lafayette, the difference in the household income of both schools would have favored the Oxford folks. Defeating the Oxford kids in athletic competition was one way Lafayette kids could have something to be proud of."

Lessie Belk, former Oxford Booster Club president, describes the perception by Lafayette fans of the Oxford folks this way, "They probably view us as maybe snobby and preppie." According to Don Brooks, television broadcaster, "Oxford people see Lafayette people as the 'rednecks.' Lafayette people see Oxford people as the 'preppie city guys – got plenty of money types.' They are good friends off the field, but when it's game time, a whole year's worth of bragging rights are on the line."

Former Oxford head football coach, Tim Carter, describes the situation this way, "You've got families moving into town and they're trying to decide where to buy a house. One of the unique aspects of this rivalry is that both schools are academically and athletically excellent. Both schools are highly desirable. A lot of times one school will be way ahead of another; but these two are on equal footing."

Rivalry games have certain characteristics that set them apart from regular games. Big rivalry games such as Oxford and Lafayette are always hard-fought contests to the end – the bitter end. Consequently, it is common to see more overtime games when two rival teams are matched up. Regardless of which team is favored in a rival game, toss out the won-lost records coming into the game. It doesn't matter. Along with the record and ranking, throw away the home field advantage. It doesn't matter. Rivalry games are always toss-ups, and therein lies much of the appeal for the fans. A true rivalry game is never a gimme game for either team, especially the favored team. It seems that weird things occur more frequently in a rivalry game. For coaches, these games are nightmares because, more often than not, the unexpected will occur. Uncertainty is at its highest in the classic rivalry games.

Over the years, certain games in the Oxford and Lafayette series stick out as "unique" or maybe "bizarre," depending on what side of the score a fan finds his team. One such game occurred in 1989 while Jimmy Arrington was coaching at Lafayette and Dennis Dupree was coaching at Oxford. The game was the first one of the season at Oxford. It was hot – extremely hot. The Chargers jumped out to an early 10-0 lead and then it started to rain, then it poured and then it began to flood. The deluge continued all the way to halftime. The teams retired to their respective locker rooms soaking wet. Not only did the downpour continue during halftime, but the temperature turned bone-chilling cold. The officials delayed the start of the second half for 45 minutes. After the delay, the officials called a conference with both head coaches and announced that they needed to end the game. Coach Arrington said, "What do you want to do? Come back tomorrow morning and finish it?" Coach Dupree said, "No, Coach, that's not what they're talking about. Let's just end it right now. You know we can't go back out there in this kind of weather." Coach Arrington responded, "Then you're asking me to forfeit? No, we will play it Saturday, Sunday, Monday or tonight." It wasn't 15 minutes later that the rain stopped. While it was still cold, wet and muddy, the rain and lightning had stopped. When the teams came back on the field, no one was left in the stands. Everybody had gone home thinking the game was called due to the weather. Lafayette immediately shifted to an unbalanced line and ran inside dive plays all the way down to the Oxford 1-yard line. However, they fumbled the ball and Oxford recovered. The playing conditions were just horrible. On the very next play the Oxford ball carrier fumbled and Lafayette recovered in the end zone and scored. The Commodores kicked the extra point and, all of a sudden, the score was Oxford 10 and Lafayette 7. After Oxford received the kickoff and brought the ball out to its 14-yard line on the first play from scrimmage, the Chargers fumbled at the 6-yard line. When the Lafayette defense fell on the ball, it squirted out and went into the end zone where the Commodores fell on it and scored again. After Lafayette kicked the extra point, the Commodores had somehow managed to score 14 points without running an offensive play and were now ahead 14-10. The teams slopped around for the rest of the game without either Oxford or Lafayette scoring again. Final score: Lafayette 14, Oxford 10.

The next day, most of the folks in town thought Oxford had won the game 10-0. Folks all over the county assumed the 14-10 score reported in the paper was simply a misprint. It took several days for word to get around that Lafayette had really come back to win the game. Coach Arrington recalls the scene at *The Beacon* on Saturday morning. "All the coffee drinkers were there and they said, 'Tough one to lose.' I said, 'You're another one who wasn't there.'" To this day there are still some Oxford fans who do not believe Lafayette really won the 1989 game. It was simply a misprint!

During the 2004 playoff game at Lafayette, a bizarre event occurred involving the lights. Oxford had defeated the Commodores during the regular season 28-14. Oxford took the lead 6-0 early in the game, but, more importantly, controlled the momentum. Suddenly, the lights went out. The stadium was pitch black. Lafayette principal Adam Pugh recalls the event: "It was a nightmare. You never expect something like that to happen. It was probably 20 to 40 minutes before we got the lights back on, but it seemed like six or seven hours. People actually turned on their car lights so we could see."

After the long delay, the lights were restored and the game resumed. When the teams returned to the field, Oxford had lost all of its momentum and had gone flat. On the other hand, Lafayette had found its momentum and was on fire. The Commodores went on to defeat Oxford 22-6. Charger fan Lessie Belk was at the game. She comments, "The momentum of the game shut down and we had to wait about 30 minutes before the lights came back on. We ended up losing the game. We always thought that it was intentional, because we were beating them at the time the lights went off." Of course, Lafayette fans view the loss of power as divine intervention to help the Commodores overcome the cross-town rival Chargers. Oxford fans view the event quite differently. Lessie Belk says, "I don't think God would have done that to us."

The two most recent Oxford and Lafayette games – 2006 and 2007 – have both been overtime thrillers. In 2006, Lafayette edged out the Chargers 29-28 when the Commodores went for a two-point conversion to win the game. The 2006 game will go down as one of the classics in the series. Then again in 2007, the teams treated the fans to another nail-biter overtime game when, on Lafayette's first possession, the Commodores were able to score a touchdown and extra point to go up by 7. In a monumental defensive stand, the Commodores kept the Chargers out of the end zone to win the game 21-14.

Pat Patterson and Jeff Busby, the owners of University Sporting Goods located on The Square in Oxford, have been helping keep the Commodore and Charger rivalry alive for almost four decades. Just outside their store is a post holding up the New Orleans style balcony located over the front door to the store. On that post are painted all the scores of the Oxford and Lafayette football series, dating back to 1972. It's a vivid reminder of the colorful history surrounding one of Mississippi's classic high school football rivalries.

WHAT THE COMMODORES SAY ABOUT OXFORD

Oxford is always gonna be good and we're always gonna be good – just a healthy competitive spirit for the community.

Anthony Hart
Lafayette Head Football Coach

Oxford is the city school while Lafayette is considered the farm school – Lafayette, the hicks; and Oxford, the city slickers.

Jim Smith
Former Lafayette Football Player

Any time a team from Oxford steps on the field, they are gonna be good.

Kent Littlejohn
Former Lafayette Football Player

When we rode up in our bus, the Oxford fans started hollering, "Hicksville, hicks, country hicks."

Jimmy Arrington
Former Lafayette Head Football Coach

Oxford High School has the impression that we are just a bunch of rednecks that wear overalls and straw hats and have hay sticking out of our mouths.

Vincent Anderson
Lafayette Student

It's kind of ironic. In the last three to four years, Oxford has adopted the cowbell as a way of making noise at their games.

David Kellum
Former Lafayette Football Player

They are both good schools with good athletic programs. There isn't any need to crow too loudly unless you are willing to eat it the next year.

Jimmy Mills
Former Lafayette Football Player

All of them seem to think they are better than us. They really wish they were at Lafayette.

Blair Hunt
Lafayette Student

It is the biggest rivalry that I have been involved in during my 18 years of school administration.

Adam Pugh
Lafayette Principal

In the early years, Oxford viewed Lafayette as their stepchild – just a bunch of country bumpkins that didn't know how to play football.

Jimmy Murphy
Former Lafayette Football Coach

Both Oxford and Lafayette are strong in their divisions. This rivalry is just gonna get better and better and bigger and bigger.

Doug Vanlandingham
Former Lafayette Head Football Coach

We respect them, but on Friday nights we want to kill them and they want to kill us. On Sunday morning we shake hands at church and get along fine . . . but we are gonna both pray for each other's downfall.

Jimmy Mills
Keith Littlejohn
Former Lafayette Football Players

WHAT THE CHARGERS SAY ABOUT LAFAYETTE

Even if you don't make the playoffs, if you beat Lafayette it's a good year. You can go 1 and 10 and beat Lafayette and it's still a good season.

Taylor McGraw
Former Oxford Football Player

They're talking real big. We want to stick it to them.

Adrian Agnew
Oxford Football Player

Oxford people see Lafayette as the country school – the rednecks. Lafayette people see Oxford as the preppie city guys with plenty of money. They are good friends off the field, but when it's game time a whole year's worth of bragging rights are on the line.

Don Brooks
Oxford TV Broadcaster

The excitement of this rivalry matches any that I've been around in high school. There is nothing like Lafayette versus Oxford.

Tim Carter
Former Oxford Head Football Coach

You can throw the records out the window when it comes to Oxford and Lafayette. The records do not seem to matter.

Johnny Hill
Oxford Head Football Coach

It's kind of like a feud way back in the hillbilly days. You just know you're supposed to hate Lafayette. When somebody asks you why, well, you don't know – it's just because they're Lafayette.

Ulysses Howell
Former Oxford Football Coach

When Oxford and Lafayette are playing each other, you see the best of both teams. They are great games.

Linda Hill
Wife of Oxford Head Football Coach

We don't necessarily feel like they have a lot of respect for us.

Taylor McGraw
Former Oxford Football Player

They are serious about lifting weights.

Adrian Agnew
Oxford Football Player

The Lafayette-Oxford rivalry resembles the State-Ole Miss rivalry.

Bill Hovious
Oxford Principal

I spent a large part of my career in Georgia and witnessed a lot of intense rivalries, but I don't think any of them compare to the Oxford and Lafayette rivalry.

Bill Hovious
Oxford Principal

The intensity of the rivalry has grown because both sides have had good football programs and the winner of the Oxford and Lafayette game has played a big part in who's gonna be the district champion.

Robert Youngblood
Former Oxford Football Coach

They're country and we're preppie.

Poinesha Barnes
Former Oxford Student

LAFAYETTE · OXFORD
SERIES HISTORY

Year	Lafayette	Score	Oxford
1972	Jim Buck Aven	0-3	Bobby Sanders
1973	Jim Buck Aven	12-28	Bobby Sanders
1974	Jim Buck Aven	16-0	Bobby Sanders
1975	Jim Buck Aven	27-28	Bobby Sanders
1976	Bill Scott	35-35	Bobby Sanders
1977	Bill Scott	12-6	Bobby Sanders
1978	Bill Scott	26-7	George Blair
1979	Bill Scott	23-28	Buz Morrow
1980	Danny Patterson	18-3	Buz Morrow
1981	Doug Vanlandingham	0-0	Walter Denton
1982	Doug Vanlandingham	0-13	Walter Denton
1983	Doug Vanlandingham	21-0	Walter Denton
1984	Doug Vanlandingham	26-13	Walter Denton
1985	Doug Vanlandingham	13-0	Walter Denton
1986	Doug Vanlandingham	14-0	Bob Tyler
1987	Jimmy Arrington	33-8	Dennis Dupree
1988	Jimmy Arrington	19-7	Dennis Dupree
1989	Jimmy Arrington	14-10	Dennis Dupree
1990	Mike Moore	0-21	Dennis Dupree
1991	Mike Moore	18-7	Dennis Dupree
1992	Mike Moore	0-28	Johnny Hill
1993	Mike Moore	6-35	Johnny Hill
1994	Mike Moore	10-13	Johnny Hill
1995	Mike Moore	13-19	Johnny Hill
1996	Mike Moore	0-7	Robert Youngblood
1997	Boyd Bayles	22-6	Robert Youngblood
1998	Boyd Bayles	41-35	Tim Carter
1999	Scott Samsel	29-21	Tim Carter
2000	Scott Samsel	14-12	Johnny Hill
2001	Scott Samsel	13-27	Johnny Hill
2002	Scott Samsel	20-21	Johnny Hill
2003	Scott Samsel	12-7	Johnny Hill
2004	Scott Samsel	14-28	Johnny Hill

Year	Lafayette	Score	Oxford
2004*	Scott Samsel	22-6	Johnny Hill
2005	Anthony Hart	25-28	Johnny Hill
2006	Anthony Hart	29-28	Johnny Hill
2007	Anthony Hart	21-14	Johnny Hill

* *North Mississippi Class 4A Championship Game*

★★ OFFICIAL GAME DAY PROGRAM $5.00 ★★

WARREN CENTRAL
VERSUS
VICKSBURG

mississippi
web
radio
www.VisitMississippi.org

PROUD SPONSOR OF MISSISSIPPI HIGH SCHOOL FOOTBALL

FRIDAY, SEPTEMBER 5, 2008 ★ 7:00 PM KICKOFF
VICKSBURG MEMORIAL STADIUM ★ VICKSBURG, MISSISSIPPI

CHAPTER

06

RIVER RATS AND REDNECKS

Vicksburg, Mississippi, is a city where the voices of history whisper to you around every bend, over each hill and beneath each tree. Located in Warren County, Vicksburg sits on bluffs 250 feet above the Mississippi River. The city is in a perfect defensive position by military standards, and the Confederate Army used this advantage to control the flow of supplies down the river during the Civil War. President Abraham Lincoln understood the importance of the city's location and commented, "Vicksburg is the key. The war can never be brought to a close until that key is in our pocket." After many failed attempts to take the city directly, the Union forces of Ulysses S. Grant elected to trap the Confederate forces of John C. Pemberton in the confines of the city. Grant then laid one of the most famous sieges in military history. The Confederate forces dug in and hung on for over six weeks before succumbing to disease and starvation on July 4, 1863. The Union victory effectively cut the Confederacy in half, opened supply lines all the way to the Gulf Coast and accelerated the end of the war.

Signs of the famous battle can still be seen all over the city of Vicksburg today. Many businesses have battle-themed names, and a stroll through the woods can still net you an authentic Civil War bullet if you have a sharp eye. Vicksburg's National Military Park and the riverboat casinos remain the top tourist attractions to the city. Although tourism dollars lured by the military monuments and roulette tables may be the economic lifelines of the city, they are not the city's passion. The nation will forever see Vicksburg as a "Civil War town," but the people of Vicksburg will quickly tell you they are a "football town."

With around 26,000 people in the city and about that many more located out in the county, Vicksburg boasts an impressive four high schools. Porter's Chapel is a private school, St. Aloysius is a parochial school and Warren Central and Vicksburg High School are the two large public schools. Each school has its own rich heritage and tradition of winning on the gridiron. In fact, so much athletic ability exists in the Vicksburg area that it prompted legendary Jackson State University head coach W.C. Gorden to say, "I could go downtown to the corner grocery and gather up 11 boys and win a state championship."

Of all the schools in Vicksburg, Vicksburg High School is the oldest. You don't have to look too far before you find people, both young and old, who bleed green and white. However, not all green and white is the same in Vicksburg. A little more investigation is necessary before one can truly understand the origins of the individuals' allegiances.

In the days prior to integration, the two primary high schools in Vicksburg were H.V. Cooper High School and Rosa A. Temple High School. Cooper was the white school and Temple was the black school; however, both schools wore green and white as their colors. The Cooper Greenies competed in the powerful Big Eight Conference and played against other conference teams such as Jackson Central, Murrah, Provine, Natchez, Hattiesburg, Greenwood and Greenville. Similarly, the Temple Buccaneers competed in the equally stout Negro Big Eight Conference. Both schools enjoyed success in their respective conferences, but they never played each another. Alonzo Stevens, current head football coach at Vicksburg High School and a 1970 graduate of Temple High School, remembers the two teams: "Both schools had excellent football teams. Temple had some amazing football success, especially in the mid to late '60s. From 1964 to 1970, Temple only lost four games, and in 1966, W.C. Gorden was the head coach before Jackson State offered him a position. Even though we didn't get to play Cooper on the field, their players and our players would get together on Sundays and play pick-up football. We all got along great. There was never an issue between the kids."

Although Cooper had plenty of great opponents within the Big Eight, their attention was somewhat diverted in 1965 when a new school named Warren Central was formed out in the county. When Warren Central began to have some football success in the Little Dixie Conference, debate began over how the team would fare against mighty Cooper. John Newton, a 1969 graduate of Cooper High School, recalls the attitude of the Cooper players towards Warren Central:

There was an attitude that they were in the Little Dixie Conference and that they were playing lesser competition. Everyone in the Big Eight just felt like a Big Eight team would roll over any team from any other conference. We were probably more interested in just having a good in-town rivalry than anything. We thought that would have been great. Everyone in the city referred to the Warren Central people as rednecks, and they referred to us as river rats. We wanted a piece of Warren Central so bad, but for whatever reason, they just couldn't arrange it where we could play one another. After I graduated, the schools did play each other in some sports, but that football game never happened. It would have really been something.

In 1971, integration hit the state and students from Cooper and Temple were mixed together. In an effort to give the schools new identities, Cooper was renamed South Vicksburg High School and Temple was renamed North Vicksburg High School. However, both schools kept green and white as their colors and Greenies and Buccaneers as their respective nicknames. As part of the transition, some of the students from Temple ended up at Warren Central. Many residents credit the addition of these players to the rise of Warren Central's football program.

Within a couple of years, everyone realized that running North and South Vicksburg High Schools was not the most efficient path, so they consolidated the two schools to form Vicksburg High School in 1973. Maintaining tradition, green and white remained the school colors, but the Greenie and Buccaneer mascots were retired in favor of the newly selected Gator. The 1973 season marked the first time all the black and white players from the city of Vicksburg were on the same team. After years of these guys playing together on Sunday afternoons in unofficial pick-up games, their gridiron forces were now unified. It did not take long for the new teammates to gel. In their first campaign, the newly formed Gator army went undefeated and won the Big Eight Conference.

Vicksburg's success continued in upcoming years as talented athletes poured from the banks of the Mississippi. Future NFL players such as Sylvester Stamps (Atlanta Falcons), Mark Smith (Arizona Cardinals), James Jones (Dallas Cowboys), Richard Blackmore (Philadelphia Eagles) and Michael Myers (Dallas Cowboys) were all groomed for greatness at Vicksburg High School. Countless other Gator athletes were sent to the college ranks as well. In fact, the University of Alabama regularly invites so many Gators to visit that Nick Saban's secretary was prompted to ask Vicksburg's Alonzo Stevens, "Coach, what exactly are y'all doing over in Vicksburg? Nobody else has this many players come through here."

Coach Stevens is quick to point out that attention to detail is what sets his players apart. "When we travel to away games, we look sharp and we act right. It's all about the details. When we go out in public, we are representing our community, Vicksburg High School and all the people who came before us that love the green and white," says Stevens.

Coach's wife, Linda Stevens, who is also a Vicksburg alum, describes the total family effort put towards running the Gator program:

> When we first applied for the head coaching position, our daughter Jasmine was six. All three of us had a role with the program that we were responsible for. Alonzo was to coach and run the team. I was to work with the booster club, help with decorations and help the guys with their homework. Since we were spending a lot of time at the field house, Jasmine's job was to be quiet, sit down, do her homework and make her grades. It was a partnership among the three of us and it has worked out. The players have been successful both on and off the field. I remember one summer one of the principals was talking to one of our coaches and he said, "Why doesn't Coach Stevens come over and check on his players in summer school the way some of the other schools' coaches do?" Our coach responded, "He doesn't come over because we don't have any in summer school. All our kids are eligible, so we didn't have to send them." Things like that make me feel good and let me know we are doing our job. We are all committed to the Gators.

****

For many years, Vicksburg High School and its predecessor schools, Cooper and Temple, dominated the football landscape in Warren County, Mississippi. The mighty green and white, with its membership in the elite Big Eight Conference, cast a long shadow across the county from the high bluffs on which the city of Vicksburg sits. Living in the coldness of that shadow were the county schools, namely, Culkin, Redwood and Jett. Although each of these small schools had its own proud heritage, none would ever grow to a size large enough to challenge formidable Vicksburg. In the eyes of the Vicksburg students, Culkin, Redwood and Jett would always just be county redneck schools. Not surprisingly, many of the county students developed a strong distaste for the city school, its athletic teams and everything else the school represented.

Like many other counties in the state, officials soon determined that running three schools in Warren County made little sense and that eliminating duplicative services through consolidation would better serve the populous. In 1965, Culkin, Redwood and Jett each sacrificed their own individual school pride and came together to form Warren Central High School.

Sidney Beauman, a member of Warren Central's first graduating class, remembers his initial impression of the new school:

> There was really a tradition of excellence at Warren Central from day one because it took the best of Culkin, Redwood and Jett and combined them. The staff at Warren Central was made up of the best of the best from the three smaller schools. When we walked through the doors of Warren Central for the first time, we didn't know what to think. Keep in mind the schools we had just come from were each probably around 100 years old. We walked into Warren Central and we thought we were in California or somewhere. We didn't know how to act. The facilities were extremely nice. It was pounded into you from day one that you didn't throw paper on the floor, you didn't write on the walls and you didn't mess up the toilets. I don't think we would have anyway, because we were all so proud of the school.

Culkin's Ernie Albritton was retained as the first head football coach for Warren Central's Viking team before he turned the position over to Dewey Partridge the following season. Although the academic facilities were brand new, the same could not be said for the athletic facilities. Coach Albritton faced the daunting task of building them from scratch before the 1965 football season.

Having attended Jett High School prior to his senior year, Sidney Beauman was at the center of the effort to help Warren Central establish an athletic toehold. Beauman says,

> I never got to play a game on the Warren Central football field because it was not finished the first year the schools combined. We played at Vicksburg or at St. Aloysius. We didn't even have a practice field. Someone owned some land just across the highway and they gave us permission to practice on it. It was a big hollow and we went out there and cut it with a bush hog to get it ready. The whole thing slanted down toward a creek. Our warm-up for practice each day was to jog the quarter mile or so from the locker room to the practice field. We'd run down the hill and jump the creek, and then we'd practice. Guys suffered more injuries from falling and tripping over little sapling stumps than they did from the hitting that was going on. Since our nickname was the Vikings, and since that practice field was anything but heaven, the guys jokingly nicknamed the practice field Valhalla (a mythical place for the souls of slain Vikings).

The Viking football team became a member of the Little Dixie Conference and competed against foes such as Clinton, Brandon, Pearl, Magee and Mendenhall. Warren Central also had regular contests against St. Aloysius High School, located right in its own backyard. Because St. Aloysius was an older school with a more established football program, it dominated Warren Central in the early years. At the same time, the Vikings also struggled with their peers in the Little Dixie, managed to win only a handful of games in the first several years of its existence and produced no winning seasons. However, in 1971 all losing officially came to an abrupt halt.

A veteran of nearly two decades of high school coaching in the state of Texas, Coach Lum Wright was hired to lead the Viking forces in 1971. In Wright, Warren Central found one of the best football coaches in the country, as he was ultimately inducted into the National High School Sports Hall of Fame in 2004. Coach Wright's arrival on the Warren Central campus had an immediate and lasting effect on the school and its young football program.

Wright recalls the attitude that permeated the Warren Central community when he accepted the coaching position:

> The school had a losing attitude when I arrived. Part of that was due to the strength of Cooper and Temple, and part of that was due to the division of support from the Culkin, Redwood and Jett people. I remember the first day I got to the school I was confronted by an old lady in the parking lot. She was known as Granny Wells and she was a serious football fan and a Redwood loyalist. She shook her finger at me and said, "I'm watching you. I'll find out whether you can coach real quick." There were plenty of people here who wanted to win. They just hadn't figured out how to do it yet.

Granny Wells may have been the first fan to challenge Wright, but she would not be the last. In need of some wood for his home stands, Wright visited the local lumber yard before the start of his first season. The owner of the yard approached Wright and said, "So, you are the new football coach. I tell you what; I'm going to let you have the lumber, but the first game you lose I am going to come and get it." Wright accepted the deal and took the lumber back to the school. Wright didn't see the owner again until a PTA meeting a couple of months later after the Vikings had opened the season a perfect 8-0. The owner again approached Wright and said, "I don't guess you are ever going to give me a chance to come back and get that lumber, are you?" Wright smiled and simply responded, "Nope."

Warren Central ultimately finished the 1971 regular season 8-1, with their sole loss coming to a tough Mendenhall team. When the team was invited to play in the prestigious post-season Red Carpet Bowl, the school principal commented to Wright, "Well, you have gone and ruined a great regular season, because now we have to play St. Aloysius. We've never beaten them." Not knowing or caring who St. Aloysius was, Coach Wright responded, "I don't know anything about St Aloysius. All I know is that we are going to play them, and we are probably going to kick their tails." Coach Wright's confidence in his own team was accurate. The Vikings held a 38-0 lead at halftime. According to Wright, that particular victory was the final piece of evidence needed to convince the Warren Central faithful of his coaching ability and the bright future their program had if they all fully committed themselves to the new school.

Coach Wright ultimately spent 14 seasons at Warren Central, during which time the Vikings piled up victories at a breakneck pace. The team was performing so well that the students even started to embrace the derogatory term "rednecks" that had been bestowed upon them by students at the city schools. Bursting with newfound confidence, Warren Central's students began a tradition of mocking this nickname by wearing red overalls to pep rallies on Fridays. In addition, as the team got progressively stronger, members of the Little Dixie Conference began to complain that Warren Central was too big and too strong to continue being a member school. However, the other members of the Little Dixie never voted the Vikings out of the conference. As the Vikings were becoming more powerful on the field of play, their fan base was also growing and clogging up opponent's ticket gates. The Little Dixie schools may have grumbled about Warren Central's football prowess, but no one dared cut the cord and lose the valuable dollars spent by the traveling hoard of Viking fans.

While Wright was the spark that ignited the Viking fire, the bedrock on which the future of the program was built came in the form of two of his assistant coaches. In 1968 (three years before Coach Wright), Robert Morgan accepted a job as an assistant football coach at Warren Central under Dewey Partridge. In 1970, Curtis Brewer, a graduate of Culkin High School, came to Warren Central as a junior high coach. Both men served the Viking football program faithfully for an astonishing four decades and created what would become a true family atmosphere.

During the early years while Morgan and Brewer were busy helping build the Warren Central program, several sets of important eyes were carefully watching them. Morgan's three sons – Rob, Josh and Brett – literally grew up in the field house and learned firsthand what it meant to be a Viking. Says Josh Morgan,

> My brothers and I lived on the Warren Central campus. As far back as I can remember, we were out at the field house holding up dummies and playing football. If they had a meeting, we would be in the middle of it, kind of watching things from under my dad's legs. When we were little, the players were our biggest role models besides our parents. They were everything to us. They were like NFL players. I can remember all the

players in 1985 and 1986, and I was only six years old. Those memories stick with you. That's how much they meant to us. In addition to the players, we were really close to the assistant coaches. We called Coach Brewer "Uncle Curtis" and his wife "Aunt Janice." We still call them that even today. That closeness really helped build a trust and chemistry within the program. It makes a difference when you are coaching with, or playing for, someone you love and respect.

To add to the family feeling, Robert Morgan's brother-in-law, Johnny Hill, was also part of the coaching staff. Hill had four boys about the same age as the three Morgans. The boys were natural born athletes and competed incessantly against one another in pick-up football games right there on the sidelines of the Warren Central practice fields. These family games on the sidelines may have rivaled the quality of play of the Vikings themselves. Remarkably, all seven of the Morgans and Hills developed into SEC football and baseball players. Uncle Johnny later went on to his own coaching success at Tupelo and Oxford High Schools.

Robert Morgan took over the head coaching duties from Coach Lum Wright in 1985, and he utilized the athletic ability of his three sons as his signal callers. In fact, for almost a decade there was a Morgan under center for the Vikings. During those years, Warren Central produced some of its most talented and formidable teams. Coach Morgan was able to capture Warren Central's first state championship in 1988, and then chased down a second in 1994. The Vikings also played in the championship game in 1993 against South Panola in what many people believe was the greatest high school football game ever played in the state of Mississippi.

Like its coaches, Warren Central's style of play has remained consistent and straightforward over the years. The Vikings traditionally line it up in the Power I and challenge their opponents to go toe-to-toe with them in an effort to see who has the better conditioning, the most guts and the most courage. The approach has served them well as numerous opponents have ventured into imposing Viking Stadium on Highway 27 to face the team in red, only to leave battered, bruised and one loss heavier. One of the favorite post-home-game traditions of former Warren Central football players is the memory of Coach Morgan entering the locker room and telling the team that Coach Brewer was about to speak. At that point, Coach Brewer climbed on top of the lockers and yelled at the top of his lungs, "Another one has crashed and burned on Highway 27 South!"

A far more cerebral coach than his old post-game celebrations may indicate, Curtis Brewer assumed the position of head coach in 2005 after 35 years as an assistant. Although Brewer is now the head coach, his staff still includes his good friend Robert Morgan, as well as Coach Morgan's middle son, Josh. The family continuity in the Warren Central program remains intact, and the path of the Viking ship under Brewer is still clear and well defined. Says Brewer, "Some very tight-knit coaches have come through Warren Central and have given a real family feel to this program. I believe that is why we have been successful. I am a firm believer that athletics is extra. The kids are not here to play football, and my job is not to produce players for State, Ole Miss or Southern. My job is to make sure these kids work hard, take responsibility for their actions and are able to look over their shoulders and say, 'I have a responsibility to that guy because he's on my team.'"

****

In 1981, the Mississippi High School Activities Association overhauled the structure of high school sports in the state. For years, schools competed in self-formed conferences like the Big Eight and the Little Dixie. Each team's goal was to win their conference and then to be invited to one of the many post-season bowl games throughout the state. There were no divisions and there were no true state champions. But in 1981, the conferences were abandoned in favor of "division play." Similar to the systems many other states used, the MHSAA placed Mississippi high schools into divisions based on size. Teams of similar size played one another in the regular season to qualify for the statewide playoffs that ultimately produced the state champions. When the MHSAA eliminated conferences and divided the schools, Vicksburg and Warren Central found themselves in the same size classification. For the first time in the history of the two schools, their collision on the gridiron was now unavoidable. The people of the city of Vicksburg and all of Warren County braced themselves for the football game they had wanted to see for so many years.

The 1981 Vicksburg team was led by junior running back/ receiver Robert Green, who was widely considered to be the fastest player in the state at the time. Green remembers the events leading up to the kick-off of the first game:

> ·I will never forget leaving the field house and getting on the green and white bus escorted by the Vicksburg police. The county sheriff picked us up on Highway 27. I have never seen that many cars from 27 all the way to the school. Cars were lined up way back as far as you could see. I was sitting next to my cousin on the bus and I looked at him and I felt a calm come over me. At that moment I really felt like I would play well that night. During pre-game there were people all around the field. A bunch of them were yelling at me and telling me that they were going to keep me out of the end zone the entire game. We had played in front of big crowds, but that was astonishing.

Jim Sizemore had come to Warren Central with Lum Wright in 1971 and served as an assistant coach while the Vikings were building their program. Prior to the 1981 season, Sizemore accepted the invitation of Vicksburg head coach Rush McKay to become part of the Gators' coaching staff. Being intimately familiar with the Warren Central offensive attack, McKay and Sizemore determined that Vicksburg's best strategy for this particular game was to change their own offensive attack to match that of the Vikings. They shuffled players around and implemented the new offense for the highly anticipated contest.

Robert Green vividly recalls the Gators' first offensive play.

> When the coaches installed the new offense, they moved me from receiver to tailback. On the first play, I got into my stance at tailback and looked over at Warren Central's linebackers. They were so used to seeing this offense during their own practices, and I guess they were so familiar with Coach Sizemore's tendencies, that they knew what play we were about to run. Joe Nathan Shelly yelled out, "They're running 38 Power!" Shelly and their other linebacker, Jim Warren, shifted down to their right. I thought to myself, Lord, they know exactly where I'm going. You have to understand; these were two very good linebackers and I didn't want them to have any idea where I was going. Fortunately, I had Eddie McGowan and Malcolm Harris in front of me. They both got shoulders on the Warren

Central linebackers and opened a hole. I went 70 yards for a touchdown on the first play. Nobody touched me. That quieted the whole stadium to the point you could have heard a pin drop.

After that first play from scrimmage, the power of the former Big Eight Conference team was affirmed in the minds of the Vicksburg fans, and the Warren Central faithful momentarily wondered if they had ever really evolved from their days as a "little redneck county school." Then the confidence of the Gators was blown to pieces as if General Grant's entire battery of artillery had just opened fire at point blank range.

A penalty marker lay innocently on the field, well behind the action of the play. The call negated Green's touchdown sprint and changed the mood of this rivalry for the next nine years. "That penalty killed the spirit of our fans and our players. It really affected us mentally and we could never get back on track after that. I hate to admit it, but I had another touchdown pass that went right through my hands later in the game," says Green.

Alonzo Stevens echoes the sentiments of Green: "It's amazing what that call did to the minds of Vicksburg fans. In their minds they felt like it was a bad call and that Warren Central had stolen the game from them. From that point forward, it's like the fans were just waiting for something to go wrong when we played Warren Central."

The final score of the first contest between the Vikings and Gators was 17-0. Robert Morgan recalls the headline of the Vicksburg Post the following morning. "It simply read 'Poof!' referring to the myth that the former Big Eight Conference teams were too dominant for anyone to stay on the field with them."

The following season, Warren Central traveled to Vicksburg's stadium for the first time. With the Gators still in knots mentally over the penalty and the loss the previous season, the Vikings dealt Vicksburg a crushing 55-15 defeat – a score that still stands as the most lopsided in the history of the series.

Robert Green was an injured senior in 1982 and stood helplessly on the sideline as his teammates suffered at the hands of the Vikings. Green remembers,

At the end of the game they were down deep in

our territory when Coach Lum Wright called a timeout. All of their fans were yelling, "Score, score, score!" The chant kept getting louder. We were all on the sideline thinking they would surely take a knee since the game was already in hand, but they ran another play and they put it in the end zone. I wish I would have had one more year to play and I would have beaten them myself. This is a great rivalry and I'm glad I have been a part of it, but I still hurt from those two games.

Warren Central's winning streak over Vicksburg ballooned to nine over the upcoming seasons as the psychological anguish of the Gators continued. Lum Wright was responsible for the first four wins in the series before he turned control over to Robert Morgan in 1985. Morgan continued the streak as his teams posted shutout victories in each of his first three seasons. However, in 1988 the structure of the high school system in the Vicksburg area shifted once again and had a significant and lasting affect on the rivalry.

Similar to the reasoning that consolidated Culkin, Redwood and Jett into Warren Central, officials decided running two school districts in Warren County was an inefficient strategy. Therefore, the Warren County and Vicksburg school districts were consolidated into the Vicksburg-Warren School District. As a result, Vicksburg was no longer a city school that drew its students exclusively from inside the city limits, and Warren Central was no longer a county school that drew its students exclusively from outside the city limits. New district lines were drawn so that the county was divided equally between the two schools based on both population and race. The change caused instant turmoil.

The redistricting of the county required many students to switch schools. Kids who had grown up wearing Viking red were now forced to attend Vicksburg and wear Gator green. Similarly, many longtime Vicksburg High School families found themselves squarely in the middle of Warren Central's district and were forced to switch schools and allegiances. Students were not required to make the switch if they were entering their senior years, but juniors and younger were fair game.

On the football field, players now stared down their former teammates as many on each team suffered an identity crisis. Robert Morgan recalls that many of his best 9th-grade players were turned against him as the change ripped them out of his system and sent them to Vicksburg. Many people at Warren Central felt the Vikings were on the verge of fielding teams that would be unstoppable by anyone in the state when consolidation occurred, and that the shift not only watered down their talent, but also sent much of it to their biggest rival. Interestingly, this was the same sentiment expressed by the people who attended Cooper and Temple almost two decades earlier when their consolidation sent key players out to Warren Central.

In 1989, James Knox, Jr. assumed the role of head coach at Vicksburg High School and changed the Gators' approach to the Warren Central game. Said Knox,

> In the early part of the rivalry, I think we were over-preparing. We didn't treat it like a regular game, and I really think we tried to do too much. They had some good athletes and we had some good athletes. But I think mental preparation was the biggest reason for them winning the first nine games. We were just trying too hard and got out of our rhythm. Finally, we told the kids to just go out there and treat it like a normal game. We just needed to play the way we were playing against everyone else.

In 1990 in a game played in Vicksburg's stadium, the Gators' Mr. Everything, Ronnie Taylor, ripped off a 40-yard run on the first play from scrimmage. This time there was no penalty to call the early offensive strike back, and the Gator players and fans were once again energized and optimistic. After hanging on for dear life with a tough defensive effort, Vicksburg was finally able to capture their first win against Warren Central. Final score: Vicksburg 10, Warren Central 9.

Regarding the importance of the historic win, Coach Knox comments, "I never had another victory in my coaching career that was as important to me as that one. I just feel fortunate to have been part of this rivalry. It was special to me because I grew up in Warren County during segregation. I ended up being the head coach of a high school where I never thought I would have a chance to be a head coach. This was a special win for me and the entire Vicksburg community."

Prior to the game, a Warren Central player had commented to the media, "Vicksburg can talk the talk, but they can't walk the walk." The comment was well circulated in the media and provided additional motivation to the Vicksburg team. At the end of the game, many Vicksburg fans carried signs that read, "We can talk the talk AND walk the walk!" To add additional insult to injury, Warren Central fans were forced to eat t-shirts prepared in advance that read "A Decade of Dominance."

The euphoria of the Vicksburg players and fans did not go unnoticed by key members of the Warren Central football program. Coach Robert Morgan's wife, Cathy, describes the events she witnessed after the Vicksburg victory:

> Even before the final clock went off, the Vicksburg players and fans rushed the field. They had really sold too many tickets because there were people already in the field area standing around the sidelines. Security couldn't control them. Before our players could get off the field, all these Vicksburg players and fans rushed our sideline and taunted our players and cussed Robert. My three boys, who were small at the time, were standing next to their father when this happened. It all happened so suddenly that they couldn't get away. They saw the whole thing up close and saw those Vicksburg players taunting their daddy. That lit a fire under them to kick that butt when they were old enough to play.

The following season the grudge match returned to Viking Stadium on the Warren Central campus, and the Viking coaching staff kicked the team's mental preparation into overdrive. Joel Neely, a sophomore defensive end in 1991, remembers an unusual announcement that came over the school intercom the day of the game. Says Neely,

> The principal got on the intercom and said, "All football players need to report to the football stadium." When we got to the stadium, there were two sheriff's cars parked on the track and they had their lights on. Coach Morgan and some of the school administrators were out there and there was a large brown box sitting on the track. Coach Morgan said the package was addressed to the Viking football team and they had originally thought it might be a bomb. When they opened the box, it was full of huge pairs of pink panties

individually labeled with the Warren Central players'
jersey numbers on them. There was also a long poem
included in the package that read:

To Coach Morgan and All the Vikings
(Personal)

Hey Vikings. It's time.
You can run but you can not hide
You are going to see a real team
You are going to wish you had died.

Load up your wagons
And try to find your way to town
Come on out of those hills
Because you are going down.

Just follow the signs
If you know how to read
Get ready to hurt
Get ready to bleed.

Put on that red
That matches your neck
And after the game
Pick yourself off the deck.

Come on down to the swamp
And find that real men wear green
Friday night you'll see
A real football machine.

The Gators are strong
Just look at the polls
We'll run it down your throat
We'll open up some holes.

We'll pass short and long
You had better try to get hurt
Because if you stay in the game
You are going to eat some swamp dirt.

You had better practice going backwards
The Gators are bad to the bone
The whole game will be played

In your end zone.
And if you ever get the ball
Hold on for dear life
Because when the Gators hit you
They stick like a knife.

Put your linemen in the backfield
Let them block or run
Try anything you like
It won't help you none.

Play all of your quarterbacks
They can run it or pass
You'll find that little red machine
Just ran out of gas.

And when the game is over
And you go back to the sticks
The news will tell you how the Gators
Crushed some country hicks.

Rest your mules and fix your wagons
So you can carry a load
Because when the playoffs begin
We're home while you hit the road.

So when you lay down tonight
And your mama hears you scream
Just tell her you had a nightmare
All you could see was GREEN!

We know you are scared
But try to give us some competition
We could use a little practice
As we move up our poll position.

But as we come out Friday night
Just keep your eyes peeled
We'll show you how a fired up team
Takes to the field.

Try not to run or hide
Stick around for two hours
But there's one thing you better understand
YOUR BUTT IS OURS!

Vicksburg entered the contest highly ranked in the state polls and with one of their best teams in school history. The team was receiving a great deal of attention throughout the state due to talented senior running back Ronnie Taylor and because of a particular photo that was taken at the beginning of the season. At some point during summer practice, several of the star Gator players were prompted to wade out in some swamp water near their practice field while wearing their full uniforms. The photo was widely circulated, and the 1991 Vicksburg team was dubbed the "Swamp Thing."

Warren Central was dressed in their customary head-to-toe red uniforms for the game and even took the field that night through a thick cloud of red smoke produced by a military-grade smoke canister secured from Camp Shelby by a Viking fan. As the Warren Central players took out a year's worth of frustration on the Vicksburg players, they delivered a special gift with each big lick. Remembers Neely,

> The players had kept those pink panties with their numbers on them from earlier in the day. The guys had jammed them up under their shoulder pads before the game. When they would knock a Vicksburg player to the ground, they would pull the panties out and throw them at him. The memory I have is just the total shock on the faces of the Vicksburg players. One of my good friends played wide receiver for Vicksburg. To hear him tell his side of the story is just hilarious. He had no idea what was going on and was just freaked out by the whole thing. That may have actually helped us win the game.

It was later revealed that the individual responsible for the package on the track, and all of its contents, was in fact Joel Neely's father.

Warren Central ultimately won the 1991 contest 21-14. Towards the end of the game, a special announcement was made over the Warren Central public address system in response to the Gators' declaration the previous year that they "talked the talk AND walked the walk". Says Neely, "When the game was in hand, the announcer got on the mic and said, 'Ladies and gentlemen, please turn your attention to the press box.' When everyone turned around, a big sign unfurled that read,

'Short walk, wasn't it?'"

The walk taken by Vicksburg was a short one indeed, as Warren Central responded to the ending of their nine-year winning streak over the Gators by starting a new streak that would last 11 years. During much of that time, the Vikings were led by a trio of Morgans – the same three boys who stood on the sidelines and watched Gator players and fans taunt their father after the 1990 game. Says middle son Josh, "I never lost to Vicksburg as a player. From seventh grade up, I never lost. Neither of my brothers ever lost to them either. There was a lot of pressure within our house. I definitely didn't want to be the brother to lose to them. If one of us had lost and we were sitting at the dinner table right now, that loss would get brought up."

Sean Murphy, sports editor of *The Vicksburg Post*, has a unique perspective on the rivalry and on Mississippi high school football in general. Originally from Peekskill, New York, Murphy decided to attend the University of Southern Mississippi after watching Brett Favre lead the Golden Eagles to a win over Auburn. Says Murphy, "Football in New York was nowhere near what it is in Mississippi. Games were played on Saturday afternoon, and football was always second fiddle to basketball. I had never been to a Friday night football game until I got to Mississippi. The games in Mississippi are amazing. You pull up to a game here and the cops are out and the traffic is backed up. It's an adrenaline rush. It's much more important to the people in Mississippi than it was in New York."

Murphy witnessed one of the more memorable Warren Central and Vicksburg games in 1996. During that game, Vicksburg jumped out to a lightning quick 23-0 lead. Everything went right for Vicksburg as the bottom just fell out for Warren Central. Murphy remembers going to the Vicksburg locker room at halftime to avoid the cold and to organize his stats. "The Vicksburg players were really fired up over the way they had performed during the first half. They had never jumped on Warren Central like that before and they definitely smelled blood in the water," says Murphy.

The Warren Central locker room was an entirely different scene. By the time Coach Morgan and the rest of the staff could get in the locker room to sink their teeth into their players, there was nothing left. Immediately upon entering the locker room from the field, the Viking players were confronted by past Viking players wearing their old letter jackets. The football alums took turns passionately communicating the importance of beating Vicksburg. Many of the speakers moved themselves to tears by their own words. Warren Central responded by playing an inspired second half, as several key players fought through serious injuries to stay on the field. Final score: Warren Central 35, Vicksburg 23.

By 2001, the series history stood at an imbalanced mark of 19-1 in favor of the Vikings. However, that same year marked a new beginning for Vicksburg High School, as the highly successful James Knox, Jr. elected to retire and assistant coach Alonzo Stevens was promoted to the head-coaching slot. Coach Stevens brought a new enthusiasm to the program and an open-minded approach. In 2002, Coach Stevens recruited an All-American from the school's soccer team to kick field goals for his gridiron forces. There is certainly nothing unique about football coaches finding kickers on the soccer field, but in this case the player, Brandi Head, was a girl. In that season's contest with Warren Central, Head converted numerous extra points as the Gators downed the Vikings 27-12 to notch their second victory in the history of the rivalry. The points by Head were the first ever scored by a girl in Mississippi 5A high school football.

With a rare win over the Vikings already in his hip pocket, Stevens now focused on getting Vicksburg over its next hurdle: beating Warren Central in Viking Stadium. Says Stevens,

> Warren Central is an intimidating place to play. They pack their fans into that stadium and they have great tradition. They put on those red helmets, jerseys, and pants when they're at home and they come out with a swagger. We may have beaten them a couple of times, but we had never beaten them in their own place. They used that to their advantage in motivating their players. It was important that our players and school got over that mental obstacle.

It took Stevens a couple of tries, but in 2005, the Gators finally went into Viking Stadium and came out with a win. Just to prove it wasn't a fluke, Stevens repeated the feat two years later in 2007, although the second win required a bit of mind games on the part of the Gators. Prior to the 2007 season, Stevens had purchased some new black pants as part of his team's uniforms. Gators defensive coordinator Stacy Sizemore (son of former Gator head coach Jim Sizemore), suggested to

Stevens that the team warm up in their traditional white pants during pre-game, and then change into the new black pants in the locker room just prior to retaking the field for the opening kickoff. Stevens agreed to the tactic, and the pants were laid out in the lockers and waiting for the Gators when they returned from pre-game. Surprised and charged by the new threads, the Gators gutted out a 7-0 victory in Viking Stadium, highlighted by a 75-yard interception return for a touchdown by Les Lemons. Some Viking fans grumbled after the game that the Gators had violated an obscure rule, and that since black was not an official school color for Vicksburg, the Gators should forfeit the game. As of the printing of this book, the Gator victory still stands. It marks the first time in the history of the series that a graduating class from Vicksburg can say they beat Warren Central twice in their tenure.

As if Warren Central and Vicksburg High Schools are not intermingled enough, they are brought even closer together by the unique existence of the Red Carpet Bowl. One of the few, if not the only, remaining high school bowl games in the state, the Red Carpet Bowl was started in 1962. It began as a post-season bowl formed to raise money to help pay the medical expenses of a local high school player named Leo Puckett who broke his neck during a game. After Puckett's death, and after the post season bowls were eliminated in favor of a playoff system, the Red Carpet Bowl moved to the beginning of the season as a kickoff classic game. The bowl is now a doubleheader that rotates between the Warren Central and Vicksburg stadiums. The first game is played at 6:00 and the second is played at 8:30. One game features the Vikings, and the other features the Gators against out-of-district opponents. The bowl creates interesting match-ups and a unique situation where Vicksburg may open its season in Warren Central's stadium against a team other than Warren Central. The following year, the game rotates and the Vikings will open their season in Vicksburg's stadium.

Because the Red Carpet Bowl takes place the first game of the season before district play begins, the local schools are typically pitted against high-profile teams from some of the more distant areas of the state. In 2007, Vicksburg took on the always-powerful Clarksdale Wildcats, while Warren Central went head-to-head with South Panola, winner of the last four 5A state championships. The existence of the Red Carpet Bowl ensures that both Warren Central and Vicksburg will open their seasons with hard-fought, emotional games. This fact is made even more important since Vicksburg dropped down to the 4A size classification.

When the MHSAA last ranked the high schools based on student enrollment, Vicksburg was a few students shy of being in its familiar 5A classification. Because it was no longer in 5A, it meant it would have to play Warren Central as one of its early non-district games. With the Red Carpet Bowl being the first game of the season, the Vikings and Gators were forced to move their annual grudge match from the final game of the season to the second game of the season. Although Vicksburg's drop to 4A means the outcome of the Warren Central game has no bearing on either team's qualification for the playoffs, it has not affected the emotion of the players or the attendance of the fans. Says Vicksburg history teacher and stadium public address announcer, Ed Wong, "Some people say this game is less intense when it is played at any time other than the final game of the season. I say it doesn't matter. You could play it in the middle of July and it would still be packed. You could play it on Christmas Eve and the stadium would be full."

As interesting as the past and present of the rivalry between the Gators and Vikings is, it is the possible future of this rivalry that may be the most interesting. Coach Alonzo Stevens describes the current trends:

> All the growth in the area is going towards Warren Central. Rivers surround Vicksburg in three directions – Mississippi River to the West and Big Black River to the South and East. It can't grow anywhere but north, which is towards Warren Central. It's only going to be a matter of time until the two schools combine and there is only one school. Because of the direction of growth, Warren Central is in the better geographic location to be the surviving school. People are going to be split right down the middle as to whether or not this is a good thing. If it weren't for football, the combination of the two would be a no-brainer. But it's a tough issue. It is something that will end some politician's career.

Ricky Mitchell, radio announcer for Warren Central, offers his opinion on the situation:

> This rivalry has a wonderful history, but I don't think it has a long-term future. I think one day they are

going to merge these two high schools and have one big school. When that happens, it will be a sad day for a lot of fans in Vicksburg and Warren County when there is no more Vicksburg High School and there is no more Warren Central High School. That will be a sad day for many people, but that, too, will pass quickly, because Vicksburg is a town that supports its athletic teams in whatever event they are playing. It may take a few more years for people to warm up to the notion, but I think that somewhere down the line, these schools are going to merge. It is inevitable. It's like Redwood, Culkin and Jett coming together to form Warren Central many years ago. History will repeat itself.

WHAT THE GATORS SAY ABOUT WARREN CENTRAL

The game with Warren Central is an absolute war, both physically and emotionally. It takes until Wednesday of the following week to either get our players to come down off the high of a victory, or to pull them up out of the dumps after a loss.

Alonzo Stevens
Vicksburg Head Football Coach

We've had some really, really good teams come through Vicksburg High School in the past. For some reason, it took us a while before our kids realized that Warren Central puts their pants on one leg at a time just like we do.

Stacy Sizemore
Vicksburg Defensive Coordinator

I graduated from Warren Central in 1989, and now I'm the principal at Vicksburg. I have friends from high school that rag me about being a Gator now. I correct them and say, "I am not a Gator, I am THE Gator."

Derrick Reed
Vicksburg Principal

Eventually they will combine these two schools. When they do, it will be like trying to combine good and evil.

Sammie Rainey
Vicksburg Booster Club President

I love beating Warren Central. I could be playing ping pong and I would want to beat them. I created Warren Central and Vicksburg on "NCAA Madden" so I could whip the pants off them every day.

Delmon Robinson
Vicksburg Football Player

My grandchildren are in elementary school in the Warren Central school district, but they still have a Gator mindset in enemy territory. During football season, they wear green and white shirts under their school uniforms that say, "My Granddaddy is the head football coach."

Linda Stevens

Wife of Vicksburg Head Football Coach

They've dominated the series. I can't take anything away from them. There have been years where we knew we had the better team and they found a way to win. Some people say we have had a monkey on our back, but I say it's more like a dragon. Some teams have your number; Warren Central had our whole phone book.

Sammie Rainey

Vicksburg Booster Club President

When we play Warren Central, I tell our players that we know exactly what to expect out of them. Warren Central is not going to do anything to surprise you. They are going to play with intensity and hustle, and they aren't going to make many mistakes.

Alonzo Stevens

Vicksburg Head Football Coach

My sophomore year was the first time we ever won in Viking Stadium. After the game, I saw a Vicksburg man that was so happy he was throwing money in the air.

Christian Price

Vicksburg Cheerleader

The players at Warren Central are cocky. They act like they know they are going to win. I guess that's because they have won so many times in the past. But I bet they are second guessing themselves a little bit and not feeling so cocky since we have won the past two out of three. The tide is turning.

Adam Farrish

Vicksburg Senior Class President

WHAT THE VIKINGS SAY ABOUT VICKSBURG

People can try to sugarcoat it as a friendly rivalry. It's not a friendly rivalry. You do not want to lose that game. That's what makes rivalries.

Josh Morgan

Former Warren Central Football Player

and Current Assistant Football Coach

There were a lot of hard feelings between the people who came to Warren Central and the Big Eight Conference, who looked down on everyone. Those first six or seven years it wasn't a rivalry; it was a war.

Curtis Brewer

Warren Central Head Football Coach

We certainly try to be cordial with this rivalry, but there is an urgency to beat them. We have to beat them in everything. It's not just football.

Pam Wilbanks

Warren Central Principal

I had butterflies two weeks before this game. You never knew how things were going to go, and this was a game we simply could not lose. I stayed focused and didn't talk to anyone during the week of the game. I told my girlfriend we had to get a divorce for that week.

Corey Wilson

Former Warren Central Football Player

and Current Junior High Football Coach

For the players at Warren Central, the winning streak against Vicksburg and the one-sided series history got to be somewhat of a burden. Instead of being excited about the game and the atmosphere surrounding it, you were so worried that you were going to lose and be remembered as "the team that lost to Vicksburg."

Joel Neely

Former Warren Central Football Player

The joy of beating Vicksburg is nowhere near the pain of losing to them.

Josh Morgan
Former Warren Central Football Player
and Current Assistant Football Coach

For Vicksburg to even the series history with Warren Central, they would have to win every year until I'm 85 years old. By then somebody will probably be feeding me and I won't even know about the rivalry.

Curtis Brewer
Warren Central Head Football Coach

The only thing that could stop this rivalry is consolidation of the two schools; but there are a lot of people in this area that would have to die before that would ever be allowed to happen.

Sidney Beauman
Former Warren Central Football Player

We have to beat Vicksburg. It's just not right when we lose to them. We have been winning every year up until the last few years, and Vicksburg has beaten us two out of three. It can't happen again. It won't happen again. It just can't.

Amanda Suell
Warren Central Cheerleader

We lost 7-0 to Vicksburg last year and our senior class had a really hard time dealing with that. No one wants to be remembered as a class that lost to Vicksburg. The underclassmen work extra hard to send the seniors out the right way, but we just couldn't get it done last year.

Clay Koestler
Warren Central Football Player

WARREN CENTRAL-VICKSBURG
SERIES HISTORY

Year	Warren Central	Score	Vicksburg
1981	Lum Wright	17-0	Rush McKay
1982	Lum Wright	55-15	Rush McKay
1983	Lum Wright	17-0	Jim Sizemore
1984	Lum Wright	15-2	Jim Sizemore
1985	Robert Morgan	24-0	Jim Sizemore
1986	Robert Morgan	3-0	Jim Sizemore
1987	Robert Morgan	13-0	Jim Sizemore
1988	Robert Morgan	10-6	Jim Sizemore
1989	Robert Morgan	6-0	James Knox, Jr.
1990	Robert Morgan	9-10	James Knox, Jr.
1991	Robert Morgan	21-14	James Knox, Jr.
1992	Robert Morgan	27-21	James Knox, Jr.
1993	Robert Morgan	35-13	James Knox, Jr.
1994	Robert Morgan	24-0	James Knox, Jr.
1995	Robert Morgan	20-12	James Knox, Jr.
1996	Robert Morgan	35-23	James Knox, Jr.
1997	Robert Morgan	9-0	James Knox, Jr.
1998	Robert Morgan	27-7	James Knox, Jr.
1999	Robert Morgan	10-0	James Knox, Jr.
2000	Robert Morgan	30-7	James Knox, Jr.
2001	Robert Morgan	27-14	James Knox, Jr.
2002	Robert Morgan	12-27	Alonzo Stevens
2003	Robert Morgan	35-6	Alonzo Stevens
2004	Robert Morgan	37-0	Alonzo Stevens
2005	Curtis Brewer	0-10	Alonzo Stevens
2006	Curtis Brewer	29-9	Alonzo Stevens
2007	Curtis Brewer	0-7	Alonzo Stevens

★★OFFICIAL GAME DAY PROGRAM $5.00★★

BOONEVILLE
VERSUS
BALDWYN

Trustmark
Banking and Financial Solutions

PROUD SPONSOR OF MISSISSIPPI HIGH SCHOOL FOOTBALL

THURSDAY, AUGUST 28, 2008 ★ 7:00 PM KICKOFF
LATIMER PARK ★ BALDWYN, MISSISSIPPI

CHAPTER

07

HATE FOR NO GOOD REASON

48 Sweep – That's the first play taught to every kid who has ever played football at Booneville High School under "The Legend." 48 Sweep is so engrained in the fabric of the Booneville community that almost every man, woman and child can diagram the play against any basic defense. "When a male child is born in Booneville, he learns 48 Sweep coming down the birth canal," says longtime Booneville assistant football coach Riley Presley. The importance of executing 48 Sweep to perfection is readily accepted by the folks in Booneville, because they have been well coached by "The Legend." Not only is "The Legend" a highly successful football coach, he is also considered the most influential man in the community. On July 7, 2008, the town of Booneville will share their local treasure with the entire nation. "The Legend," Blue Devil head football coach Jim Drewry, will be inducted into the National High School Sports Hall of Fame in Washington, D.C. Coach Drewry has won more than 300 games, along with three state championships, over his 43-year career. "Coach Drewry's career record of 327-151-5 makes him the most successful coach in the history of the Mississippi High School Activities Association," says its Executive Director, Ennis Proctor. At age 77, Coach Drewry is the oldest active head coach in Mississippi.

While the many accolades bestowed on Coach Drewry for his professional accomplishments are quite impressive, the most meaningful praise comes from the people who know him best. Steve Beavers, Sports Editor of the *Daily Corinthian*, says, "Coach Drewry not only personifies the Booneville football program, he personifies the whole community as well. The town has named a street after him. He is so humble you would never know he has won more games than anyone else."

All three of Coach Drewry's assistant football coaches – Rick

Coggin, Riley Presley and Mike Mattox – played for him in high school. Edna Drewry comments, "They are just like our children. We are the godparents of Coach Coggin's son. It is because of those three coaches that he has been able to continue coaching for so long. They have each had opportunities to move into head coaching positions, but they won't leave him. We love them just like they are family." Assistant football coach Mike Mattox says, "Coach Drewry's youngest son and I were best friends in high school; so not only did I play football for him, I was over at his house all the time. I consider him my second father. He reinforced so many of the things my dad taught. I have so much respect for him and don't want to disappoint him." Mattox continues, "He has always done it right. I want to pattern myself after him. I will stay with him until he retires." Coach Mattox is the rookie on Coach Drewry's staff of loyal assistant coaches. He's only been aboard for 16 years. Coach Coggin has coached with Drewry for 21 years, along with Coach Presley, who has been on Drewry's staff for 19.

Coach Mattox offers these words to describe his mentor: "Coach Drewry is a man of integrity and character. He is fair-minded, demanding, professional and loyal. Yes, sir, we're loyal to him just like he's loyal to us."

According to Rickey Neaves, Booneville High School Principal, "Jim Drewry is a great man. The kids love him and the entire community respects him. We've won a lot of football games because he is still coaching here. Coach Drewry supports what goes on in the classroom. His players know if they get in trouble at school they are in trouble with him. He is a disciplinarian. Our graduation rate is the highest in the state."

Principal Neaves comments about the loyalty of Coach Drewry's assistant coaches, "All of his assistants played for him and have come back to coach with him. Every one of them could have been a great head coach, but they love him and are loyal to him."

Longtime assistant football coach Riley Presley reveals the secret to Coach Drewry's success, "He lives and breathes football. He makes a kid believe that he can do things that he should not be able do." Former Booneville football player, Don Williams, explains, "Football is Coach Drewry's life. He loves to coach kids. He knows how to motivate the kids and how to make great players out of average players. The kids don't realize at the time what he is doing for them, but years later they get it. My son thinks the world of Coach Drewry; of course my son is

47 years old now.

Mike Mattox says, "He always taught me when you do the little things right, the big things will take care of themselves. That advice has always stuck with me. I know all his assistants now on staff have had chances to go other places, but they prefer to stay and continue learning from the coach who has done it longer than anyone else. It's not just the Xs and Os, but how to deal with kids and how to deal with people. It has been a great experience for me."

Former Blue Devil player Dwight Hastings, who played for Coach Drewry in the early '70s, says, "He expected you to know your role and to carry out your responsibilities. In a team environment, each person depends on the next person to do his job. He taught us the meaning of teamwork and commitment. I still carry these concepts with me today. When I deal with my children I use the same philosophy."

Jim Drewry has only missed one football game in 47 years of coaching. On that particular night he was in the hospital under lock and key, so to speak; otherwise, he would have been with his Blue Devil players and coaches. Jim Drewry, "The Legend," winner of over 300 games, three state championships, numerous conference and district titles and the latest inductee from Mississippi into the National High School Sports Hall of Fame, credits all of his success to his former players and assistant coaches. However, Coach and Edna Drewry do admit they have a special place in their hearts for Mike Mattox, Rick Coggin and Riley Presley, all long-time loyal assistants and friends who have stood shoulder to shoulder with Coach during the twilight of his highly successful career. Loyalty is important to Jim Drewry – a trait he highly respects in others. Jim Drewry may think his successful career is due to his loyal assistants, as well as the hundreds of loyal players who have worn a Blue Devil jersey. However, the truth is, Jim Drewry must credit every school administrator, every parent and every fan who recognized the character of Jim Drewry and believed he was the man capable of making a difference in the lives of their young men. They were right. He has paid them back with something he values greatly – loyalty.

****

Coach Jimmy Dillinger is a quiet, mild-mannered man. Coach D and his wife, LaRane, moved to Baldwyn in 1972. It was Coach D's first coaching job. After the Dillinger's fourth child was born in 1984, he and LaRane made the difficult decision that Jimmy would leave coaching for a more lucrative career in business. So after 12 years as a Baldwyn assistant football coach, Jimmy Dillinger left his coaching career behind and entered the business world. However, it was just a matter of time – a very short time – before Coach D realized where his passion in life was, and it wasn't in money and business. Instead, his brief detour from coaching only clarified what Coach D cared about most in his professional endeavors – coaching and mentoring kids. In 1986, Coach D returned to Baldwyn and resumed the same duties he had performed two years previously as an assistant football coach. Here he would stay – a football coach for the Baldwyn Bearcats – influencing hundreds of kids over the next two decades.

During the first 25 years of his coaching career at Baldwyn, Coach D served as an assistant to some of the great coaches who led the Bearcat football program. With each coaching change, Coach D was always supportive and eager to soak in all the knowledge and wisdom brought to the program by a new coach. During the 13 years following his return to coaching in 1986, Coach D was privileged to assist Coach Hubert Tucker, who was tragically killed in an automobile accident in 1994, and his successor, Coach Larry Cain. Both of these men helped shape Coach D's coaching style and philosophy. All the while, he waited patiently for his chance to lead the Bearcats. Upon the retirement of Coach Cain in 1999, Coach Jimmy Dillinger became the head football coach of the Baldwyn Bearcats. In just nine quick years, Coach D has become the second most successful coach in Baldwyn's storied history and is well on his way to breaking the record of the beloved Hubert Tucker. However, in the world of Coach Jimmy Dillinger, personal records and honors are just secondary, if even that. To truly understand the man they lovingly call Coach D, you have to know the definition of the word "class." Coach D, through his quiet, mild-mannered, patient approach to life and coaching, has set a world-class standard for his staff, players and fans.

Edna Drewry, wife of Booneville head football coach Jim Drewry, says, "We love Coach Dillinger. He was one of the first ones to the hospital when Jim had problems. Coach Dillinger is such a nice person and has really been a good friend over the years."

Praise for Coach D throughout the Baldwyn community and the Mississippi coaching profession is not uncommon. According to former Baldwyn player and assistant coach, Carl Reynolds, "Coach Dillinger is the finest person in coaching. If someone came to Baldwyn and said, 'Pick out the finest individual you know in Baldwyn,' I would not hesitate. That person is Jimmy Dillinger."

Baldwyn Mayor Danny Horton comments, "Jimmy Dillinger is an outstanding citizen of our community. As a coach he has the uncanny ability to take a team of small, mediocre players and get the best out of them. He has surrounded himself with a great coaching staff. Mike Gray, Jeff Palmer, Greg Tucker and Neal Allen all grew up in Baldwyn. They are well known in the community and very involved in it. Baldwyn is their home. They know the tradition and want to keep it going. Coach Dillinger is responsible for attracting these quality men."

Baldwyn High School principal, Ronnie Hill, offers his thoughts regarding the character of Coach Dillinger, "He's such a mild-mannered person that he leads the kids and they don't even realize it. He just blends in and takes care of everything. Things run smoothly. Whether it's a good day or a bad day, Coach D is always the same. He is one of those rare people who can teach and get his point across without ever raising his voice. Coach D is the type person kids don't want to disappoint."

Principal Hill continues, "I don't think you could find anybody anywhere who would say a bad word about Coach D. I've never heard anybody complain about him. He is just a quality person – a class act." Principal Hill offers the ultimate compliment for any coach when he says, "I would want my son to play for Coach Dillinger. He loves the kids and treats all of them fairly."

Graduating senior football players Dominique Davenport and Jarvey Grice comment about their experience playing for Coach Dillinger. Dominique says, "It's great playing for Coach D. He is not the type coach to yell; he is a quiet leader. Coach D is a great coach." Dominique's teammate, Jarvey Grice, says "Coach takes the situation and then puts himself in your shoes. He understands everybody. It has been a good experience playing for him."

One of Coach Dillinger's favorite quotes is from legendary Dallas Cowboys coach, Tom Landry. Coach Landry was asked in an interview one day, "What did football teach you?" He said, "Well, it taught me to learn how to lose without losing the will to win." Coach D teaches his kids that you are not going to win every football game – no one does. However, you can always maintain the desire to win. Coach

D believes competition makes a person successful even though he might be on the losing side. Once you give your best, you are a success regardless of the outcome. Spectators attending a Baldwyn game can see Coach D's quiet, well-mannered leadership style at work following the game. His Bearcats meet their opponents at midfield for the customary shaking of hands. Then everyone takes a knee, joins hands and prays. The lessons of competition are kept in perspective after a rough, tough, hardnosed game of football through Coach D's quiet, well-mannered style.

Coach D and his wife, LaRane, have four children. Not surprisingly, all four are teachers or coaches. Their daughter, Whitney, is a teacher and cheerleader sponsor at New Site just east of Baldwyn and still works with the Baldwyn Band. Ricky is the new head football coach at Wheeler. Adam is the head football coach and athletic director at Ackerman. Their youngest son, Patrick, is an assistant football coach at Ethel. Ironically, all of Jimmy and LaRane's children are doing what he has done – coaching and teaching children the Coach D way – with class.

****

It appears from old records, along with the fading memories of some of Baldwyn and Booneville's most senior citizens, that the first football game between the two schools took place in 1928. In the first clash between these two neighboring towns, Baldwyn defeated Booneville 7 to 6. The victorious Bearcats were led by their team captain, fullback Bradford White, and head coach Melvin Shirley. At the time, no one could possibly imagine the gridiron storms that would be spawned from this first football game that would last for the next 80 years. The gridiron clash between Baldwyn and Booneville in 1928 would set in motion a fierce athletic rivalry between these neighboring schools in northeast Mississippi that quickly spread from the football field to every type of competition imaginable. Eighty years later, there is no indication that the Baldwyn and Booneville rivalry is slowing down. While the intensity of the game has ebbed and flowed throughout the years, there is evidence that the rivalry is starting to pick up momentum again as it approaches its 100-year anniversary.

There are similarities between the Baldwyn and Booneville communities that help explain, at least to some degree, why these two towns are such fierce competitors. First and foremost is their proximity to each another. A mere ten miles separates the two incorporated entities. Consequently, there is frequent interaction among the residents of both towns at restaurants, convenience stores, the Wal-Mart and churches. The subject of their conversations remains consistent – the results of the last Baldwyn and Booneville football, basketball, baseball, soccer and any other competitions that have occurred between the two schools. While both schools are located in the same county, the city of Baldwyn literally straddles the line dividing Prentiss and Lee Counties. Booneville is entirely in Prentiss County, while Baldwyn is located half in Prentiss County and half in Lee County. At this point the similarities end.

The differences between the two towns seem to be the engine driving the rivalry. There are economic differences. At least there is a perception of economic differences – blue collar versus white collar – that tends to be used as a rallying point to fan the flames. According to Michael Gray, former Baldwyn player and current assistant football coach, "Baldwyn is the 'Used Car Capital of the World.' We've got used car businesses all over town. My dad's a car dealer. Then we have all those automotive support businesses such as mechanics and auto detailers."

"Several businesses in Baldwyn buy used cars by the truckload from up North, clean them up and ship them out. It's big business in Baldwyn and has gone on here for generations," says Ronnie Hill, Baldwyn High School Principal.

In contrast, Booneville is the home of Northeast Community College, which attracts thousands of students and teaching faculty to the area. Booneville has attracted an unusually large number of attorneys for a town its size. Consequently, the overall population of Booneville is greater then Baldwyn's. Edna Drewry comments, "We always laugh about how many beauty shops, florists and attorneys are located in Booneville." Of the two towns, Booneville is considered the more cosmopolitan because it offers a greater variety of specialty stores, restaurants and professional services. To further contrast the two schools, Baldwyn plays its home football games at Latimer Stadium, a stadium constructed in the '50s, while Booneville utilizes the modern stadium of Northeast Mississippi Community College. In addition, Booneville sports it owns basketball arena, which is second to none in the nation for a school its size.

Given the fact that Booneville is larger than Baldwyn and offers more economic opportunities due to a greater number of retail stores and professional offices, together with the community college, it is easy to make the transition to the convenient stereotypes of the Booneville folks as "full of themselves" and "the preppies," and the Baldwyn folks as "from the country." It's an easy leap to the Hatfields and the McCoys where neither of them like the other, but don't know why. All anyone can remember is that their parents, their grandparents and their neighbors just don't like 'em and that's enough to start, and keep, a good rivalry going. In the case of the Baldwyn and Booneville rivalry, it's been strong for 80 years.

Legendary Booneville head football coach, Bill Ward, offers an account of the rivalry:

> I attended Booneville from 1944 through 1948. For as long as I can remember, the two teams have been bitter rivals. Deep-running emotions and attitudes surface in the competition between the Booneville Blue Devils and the Baldwyn Bearcats. This is evidenced by the intense competitive spirit of not only the players, but the fans as well. Many times, fistfights have broken out among the fans. When I played at Booneville High School, our last game of the season was always against Baldwyn. Whichever team won that game, their season was considered successful. The same was true when I coached at Booneville from 1954 to 1960. Even our pee wee teams and junior high teams knew the importance of beating Baldwyn; and the tradition of winning was learned at an early age. The fact that these schools are in close proximity to each other and are both in Prentiss County only enhances the rivalry as a must-win competition for both schools for bragging rights. As a coach, I knew to be on guard at the school the night before the game, because our school was often the target of vandalism with spray-painted messages on the sidewalk or building. Also, I had to be on alert to my own team's pranks on Baldwyn. Up until the classification systems started, which created different divisions, the competition stayed heated. Even today when these two teams meet for any competition, the flame of the rivalry is still there. Actually, many friendships were created by the participants of these two schools, and good sportsmanship was shown on both sides.

Baldwyn principal Ronnie Hill says, "I have been in school administration for over 30 years, and even if you put together all the rivalries I've ever seen, it still would not compare to the intensity of the Booneville and Baldwyn rivalry."

The long history of the Blue Devil and Bearcat rivalry has produced numerous tales that have helped enhance the folklore surrounding these games. At times, the rivalry has gotten out of control, taking on the characteristics of a hostile, even nasty event. Stories about fans getting into fistfights are colorful and, in most instances, probably exaggerated; but such incidents have occurred. However, more often than not, the Baldwyn and Booneville games are friendly contests between two well-prepared football teams. During the 48 minutes of on-the-field competition, the intensity is at a fever pitch, but when it's over, it's over. The recent games between these two teams have been extremely hard-fought contests with both squads exhibiting good sportsmanship. The coaching staffs of Jim Drewry and Jimmy Dillinger have done an outstanding job of managing the conduct of their players on and off the field. Because of the high standards of sportsmanship set by these two veteran coaches, most, but not all, of the fans follow their example. Nonetheless, the lid has blown off enough times to keep the stories of the rowdy events of the past alive and well in the minds of today's players and fans.

Booneville assistant coach Mike Mattox recalls an incident early in his career:

> I was driving the bus home from a game down at Baldwyn when I came to a railroad crossing. As required by law, I stopped the bus, opened the door and listened for the train. I happened to notice seven or eight kids standing there on the side of the road. Just as I closed the door, I heard something go, "bang, bang, bang." Immediately, one of our players came up to me holding his hand over his nose and said, "Coach, they threw rocks through the window and one hit me!" It broke his nose and it was really bleeding. When I stopped the bus and got out to confront those kids, they just scattered. The bad thing was the Booneville police were right behind us in a squad car escorting us out and they didn't see it happen. Two years later, it happened again; but, fortunately, none of my players were hurt.

The intensity of the rivalry is not confined to the players on the field. It can spread like wildfire to the fans seated in the stands and standing along the fence. Mike Mattox explains, "Yes, it's an intense rivalry that can turn hostile, which is why we don't hesitate to jerk a kid off the field if we catch him jawing."

In order to help prevent any incidents between the fans after the big game, the restaurants in Booneville close except for their drive-through lanes. However, extraordinary precautions such as these don't always prevent confrontations. Mike Mattox recalls one such event:

> After the Baldwyn game one year in Booneville, we received a report from a police officer that there had been a fight at the McDonald's. All the coaches immediately assumed some of our football players were involved. So off to McDonald's we went to check it out. To our surprise, it wasn't any of our football players; instead, it was one of our cheerleaders. Some girl from Baldwyn who was behind her in the drive-though lane blew her horn and yelled at her. Our cheerleader parked her car, drug the Baldwyn girl out of her car and whipped her right there in the McDonald's parking lot. I guess you might consider that hostile.

Over the years there have been some unusual, if not bizarre, events associated with the Baldwyn and Booneville games. The 1957 game was canceled due to an influenza epidemic that sent the majority of the players on both teams home or to the hospital. During a two-year period from 2001 to 2002, the big game was not scheduled. Depending on which side you ask, there are conflicting reasons why the two teams did not play. The Booneville version for the hiatus stems from the fact that Booneville moved up to the 3A division, leaving Baldwyn in a 2A division. Because of the shift in size classification, something Booneville had no control over, it disrupted the scheduling of many of its previous non-division games. Baldwyn, on the other hand, has a different explanation. According to sources at Baldwyn, the Bearcats were loaded and Booneville wanted no part of them during those two years. Either way, Baldwyn and Booneville did not play in '01 and '02.

Current Booneville assistant football coach, Rick Coggin, tells about a motivational stunt he was involved in his junior year as a Blue Devil player:

A friend of mine, Brad White, came up with an idea of writing a letter downgrading the Booneville coaching staff, its players and basically the entire community. I typed the letter and Brad was the author. We gave it to our teammate, Sid Stevens, who taped it to our locker room door on Wednesday night before the Baldwyn game that Friday. The letter questioned our players' manhood – and everything else. It was just a motivational ploy.

It just so happened that one of our players who lived close to the school spotted the Baldwyn quarterback in Booneville on the Wednesday night the letter was left on the locker room door. When I got to school on Thursday morning, the letter had been found and read. Rumors were flying about the Baldwyn quarterback being in town. By the time classes started, the Baldwyn superintendent was in the office of Booneville's principal, trying to convince him that no one in Baldwyn had anything to do with the inflammatory letter. Of course no one in Booneville believed him, so Baldwyn took all the blame. That Thursday afternoon we had a great practice! On Friday we went on to beat Baldwyn 24-8 on a rain-soaked, muddy field. It was just one of those nights when everything went our way and nothing but bad happened to Baldwyn. We played as well as we could have played on that Friday night. After the game, Baldwyn's head coach, Hubert Tucker, came over and assured us no one from Baldwyn had written that letter. Brad, Steve and I never told anybody about the letter until after we graduated a year and a half later. We have our 30-year reunion coming up soon, and the "letter" incident will be one of the things that will be discussed and laughed about time and time again.

One of the most bizarre and controversial plays to unfold in the Baldwyn and Booneville football series happened at Tiger Stadium on September 11, 1970. Depending on one's affiliation, the strange event is referred to as the famous, or infamous, "Garrett Tackle." Butch Caldwell, Sports Editor of the *Banner-Independent*, recalled the event in his 1995 article marking the 25th anniversary of the event. He wrote, "Baldwyn took an early 12-0 lead. Midway through the second quarter, IT happened. Halfback Robert Momert fielded a Baldwyn punt at the

Booneville 25-yard line and raced around left end down the Baldwyn sidelines behind a wall of blockers. Suddenly, Jerry Garrett – watching the play – pulled down his facemask and came off the sideline from the Bearcat's bench to tackle Momert. Bearcat teammate David Bradley, seeing Garrett come off the bench, ran off the field."

According to spectators at the game, the officials took a player count following the play and determined there were 11 Baldwyn players on the field – which there were – Garrett, minus Bradley. Momert never saw the tackler. He just came out of nowhere – nowhere being the Baldwyn sideline. Booneville Coach Jim Drewry couldn't figure out what had happened from field level either, but when he saw the game film on Monday, it was apparent where the phantom tackler came from. Caldwell wrote, "When asked why he did it, Garrett explained, 'I was dating a Booneville girl named Judy Barnes and I wasn't about to let Booneville beat us that night.'" In the second half Booneville made a run at the Bearcats, scoring two touchdowns, but missing both extra point attempts. Late in the game with the score tied 12-12, the Blue Devils tried a field goal, which was wide. In the end, the Blue Devils and Bearcats left the field with a sister-kisser 12-12 tie. To this day the Garrett Tackle is still remembered by both Baldwyn and Booneville fans; however, whether it's a good memory or a nightmare depends on which side of the field you were on at Tiger Stadium back in 1970.

Another colorful event in the Blue Devil and Bearcat gridiron series took place in 1986 when the game was moved, in anticipation of bad weather, from Friday to Saturday night. Surprisingly, the weather turned out to be fair and clear on Friday night, the originally scheduled game time. But 24 hours later on Saturday night of the game, the worst happened – tornadoes. Coach Dillinger recalls that evening:

Bad weather was predicted, so we brought all our rain gear and wore it during pre-game. However, after pre-game the sky was so clear we took everything off and left it in the locker room. By the end of the first quarter you could not see the midfield it was raining so hard. Our defensive coordinator, Coach Reynolds, had to wait for our middle linebacker to come to the hash mark on our sideline to see the signals. During the game, a tornado came through town.

Other observers described the officials having to hold the ball down to keep it from floating away until the center could get to it. The game didn't stop; both teams played to the end. Baldwyn won 23-0 in the "Flood Game," or as some call it, the "Tornado Bowl."

Dwight Hastings, a Booneville football player in the early '70s, recalls his very first play in the big game:

> It was intense. I was on the kickoff team at the end on the right side. I was hyped up and keyed up to the max. I kept telling myself, "First game. Just run down the sideline and if the ball comes my way, get the tackle." Well, I ran down the field on the kickoff and the ball carrier started in my direction. Somebody from Baldwyn just bumped me and I fell on the ground and passed out. That's the last thing I remember. I was so hyped up that little bump just knocked me out. I had to get smelling salts to bring me back before I could get back in the game.

It takes a lot of history to keep a good rivalry going; and the Baldwyn and Booneville series certainly has a long history of many colorful, bizarre and exciting events. From one extreme to the other, the rivalry between these two schools has provided fans with much excitement and many thrills. However, one thing is certain; anybody who played in this special game as a Blue Devil or a Bearcat – whether he played in the '40s, '70s, '90s or today – will always have exciting memories. Former player Dwight Hastings reminisces, "It was so good for the community. It was just great to see everybody rally around their team and pull in one direction. It is a special memory."

WHAT THE BLUE DEVILS SAY ABOUT BALDWYN

I think it means more to the people in Baldwyn if they beat Booneville. They seem to get a little bit more enjoyment out of it.

Steve Beavers

Sports Editor, Daily Corinthian

We always thought those guys in Baldwyn ran their mouths a lot.

Lee Bethay

Former Booneville Football Player

I remember my junior year when we played at Baldwyn. We were on the bus going through a subdivision to get to the school. There were two little kids, maybe third graders, walking down the street. When they recognized it was the Booneville team, they started throwing stuff at our bus.

Bill Hawkins

Former Booneville Football Player

I don't have a better friend in the coaching profession than Jimmy Dillinger.

Jim Drewry

Booneville Head Football Coach

We don't wish them any harm. We just want them to win every game except when they play us.

Rickey Neaves

Booneville Principal

We get tagged as the preppy school.

Kyle Robbins

Former Booneville Football Player

You can't find better men than Coach Drewry and Coach Dillinger.

Steve Beavers

Sports Editor, Daily Corinthian

Man for man, Baldwyn has Booneville beat speed-wise every year. But remember; you might be the fastest horse on the track, but that doesn't mean you are going to cross the finish line first.

Jacques Calamese

Former Booneville Football Player

Hubert Tucker was one of my best friends. I would go to his home on Sunday during the season and he would help me get ready for the teams that he had played that were still ahead of us.

Jim Drewry

Booneville Head Football Coach

If Baldwyn beats Booneville, they are going down to our restaurant – Mitoro – and hang out in their letterman jackets. Of course if we beat them, we are going to the Pizza Factory in Baldwyn and do the same thing.

Kyle Robbins

Former Booneville Football Player

The Pizza Factory has pretty good pizza.

Bill Hawkins

Former Booneville Football Player

Baldwyn – Home of white socks, rednecks and Blue Ribbon beer.

Banner Placed on the Baldwyn Sideline

by Unknown Booneville Operatives

WHAT THE BEARCATS SAY ABOUT BOONEVILLE

When we are playing them, the rivalry is nasty. But when we are just hanging out, it's okay.

Becky Bishop
Former Baldwyn Cheerleader

It's a unique rivalry due to the closeness of the two communities. Our kids know each other; so do entire families. The rivalry has been there for years and years and it has built and built. Regardless of the size of the respective schools, we still have to play this game.

Jimmy Dillinger
Baldwyn Head Football Coach

It doesn't matter if it's jacks, hopscotch, Tiddlywinks, football, baseball, basketball or whatever; if it's Baldwyn and Booneville, it's going to be a clash.

Danny Horton
Mayor of Baldwyn

When I was in high school at Baldwyn in the early '70s, there was a Baldwyn boy dating a girl from Booneville. If she came to Baldwyn, that girl got her tail whipped by a bunch of girls. You didn't date anybody from up there and they didn't come down here. You just didn't do that.

Melanie Long
Former Baldwyn Student

The adults don't have any animosity toward Booneville folks. However, to beat Booneville is really something that makes you feel good. After we win, it's more enjoyable going to Booneville to shop or eat out and wear your Baldwyn shirt.

LaRane Dillinger
Baldwyn Head Football Coach's Wife

Booneville thinks they are better than us. They are kind of snobbish.

Clay Gholston
Former Baldwyn Football Player

This rivalry is unique because you know you are fixing to get 48 minutes of hard-fought football. We've been on the end of getting kicked for 48 minutes and we've been on the other end of kicking back.

Michael Gray
Baldwyn Assistant Football Coach

You have two coaching staffs that really prepare their kids, not only for the Booneville-Baldwyn game, but for all their games. Once the game is over, many of the coaches play golf together and are close friends.

Ronnie Hill
Baldwyn Principal

The Booneville cheerleaders act like they are trying to compete against us, even though they are not in our division. They act like, "We are better than y'all." We say, "Not really, but whatever you want to think!"

Becky Bishop
Former Baldwyn Cheerleader

They look at us like we are a small little town and we can't do anything. They view themselves as a big town that has everything. We don't see it that way.

Jarvey Grice
Former Baldwyn Football Player

Coach Drewry has done a great job year after year. He is one of the best coaches in Mississippi.

Jimmy Dillinger
Baldwyn Head Football Coach

There is something about the way they act. It seems like they are arrogant.

Dominique Davenport
Former Baldwyn Football Player

Everybody in Baldwyn thinks Booneville is preppy. I think we get stereotyped as just the opposite.

Brody McCreary
Former Baldwyn Football Player

Over time growing up, you know each other because the towns are only 10 miles apart. You play Little League baseball against each other. You develop a love-hate relationship. You love to beat them and you hate to lose to them.

Gregg Tucker
Baldwyn Assistant Football Coach

BOONEVILLE-BALDWYN SERIES HISTORY

Year	Booneville	Score	Baldwyn
1928	*NA*	6-7	*NA*
1929	*NA*	*NA*	*NA*
1930	*NA*	*NA*	*NA*
1931	*NA*	*NA*	*NA*
1932	*NA*	*NA*	*NA*
1933	*NA*	*NA*	*NA*
1934	*NA*	*NA*	*NA*
1935	*NA*	*NA*	*NA*
1936	*NA*	*NA*	*NA*
1937	Carson Pyle	0-28	*NA*
1938	Carson Pyle	6-0	*NA*
1939	Carson Pyle	2-13	*NA*
1940	Carson Pyle	0-7	*NA*
1941	Carson Pyle	0-34	*NA*
1942	Paschal Box	0-7	*NA*
1943	Paschal Box	0-34	*NA*
1944	Paschal Box	21-18	*NA*
1945	Paschal Box	6-13	*NA*
1946	Paschal Box	19-0	*NA*
1947	Paschal Box	19-7	*NA*
1948	Paschal Box	19-0	*NA*
1949	Paschal Box	32-12	*NA*
1950	Paschal Box	6-36	*NA*
1951	Paschal Box	6-27	*NA*
1952	John Mac Curlee	14-14	*NA*
1953	John Mac Curlee	0-48	*NA*
1954	Bill Ward	0-21	Jimmy Jobe
1955	Bill Ward	6-37	Jimmy Jobe
1956	Bill Ward	14-12	Jimmy Jobe
1957	Bill Ward	*NA*	Jimmy Jobe
1958	Bill Ward	59-6	Jimmy R. Harris
1959	Bill Ward	28-0	Jimmy R. Harris
1960	Bill Ward	13-21	Jimmy R. Harris
1961	Doug Herbert	0-26	Jimmy Deakle

Year	Booneville	Score	Baldwyn
1962	Doug Herbert	0-21	Ned Holder
1963	Doug Herbert	14-28	Ned Holder
1964	Doug Herbert	0-19	Ralph Mitchell
1965	Jim Drewry	0-12	Ralph Mitchell
1966	Jim Drewry	0-13	Ralph Mitchell
1967	Jim Drewry	0-6	C.L. "Red" Shelton
1968	Jim Drewry	13-0	C.L. "Red" Shelton
1969	Jim Drewry	6-20	C.L. "Red" Shelton
1970	Jim Drewry	12-12	Jackie Spradling
1971	Jim Drewry	20-0	Jackie Spradling
1972	Jim Drewry	12-20	Jackie Spradling
1973	Jim Drewry	35-6	Hubert Tucker
1974	Jim Drewry	21-7	Hubert Tucker
1975	Jim Drewry	9-32	Hubert Tucker
1976	Jim Drewry	29-8	Hubert Tucker
1977	Jim Drewry	17-14	Hubert Tucker
1978	Mac Curlee	6-7	Hubert Tucker
1979	Mac Curlee	0-27	Hubert Tucker
1980	Mac Curlee	3-7	Hubert Tucker
1981	Doc Gullett	16-22	Hubert Tucker
1982	Doc Gullett	21-14	Hubert Tucker
1983	Wayne Jones	0-46	Hubert Tucker
1984	Wayne Jones	3-28	Hubert Tucker
1985	Wayne Jones	0-28	Hubert Tucker
1986	Wayne Jones	0-23	Hubert Tucker
1987	Andy Greening	10-31	Hubert Tucker
1988	Andy Greening	6-33	Larry Gann
1989	Andy Greening	13-10	Larry Gann
1990	Jim Drewry	33-7	Larry Gann
1991	Jim Drewry	14-28	Larry Gann
1992	Jim Drewry	19-12	Larry Gann
1993	Jim Drewry	35-20	Larry Gann
1994	Jim Drewry	41-7	Larry Gann
1995	Jim Drewry	42-6	Larry Gann
1996	Jim Drewry	26-12	Larry Gann
1997	Jim Drewry	3-21	Larry Gann
1998	Jim Drewry	29-18	Larry Gann
1999	Jim Drewry	35-13	Jimmy Dillinger

Year	Booneville	Score	Baldwyn
2000	Jim Drewry	44-7	Jimmy Dillinger
2001	Jim Drewry	*Did Not Play*	Jimmy Dillinger
2002	Jim Drewry	*Did Not Play*	Jimmy Dillinger
2003	Jim Drewry	20-27	Jimmy Dillinger
2004	Jim Drewry	32-7	Jimmy Dillinger
2005	Jim Drewry	42-7	Jimmy Dillinger
2006	Jim Drewry	28-43	Jimmy Dillinger
2007	Jim Drewry	7-21	Jimmy Dillinger

NA - Information Not Available

★★OFFICIAL GAME DAY PROGRAM $5.00★★

GREENE COUNTY
VERSUS
GEORGE COUNTY

PROUD SPONSOR OF MISSISSIPPI HIGH SCHOOL FOOTBALL

FRIDAY, SEPTEMBER 5, 2008 ★ 7:00 PM KICKOFF
GILL-MARTIN STADIUM ★ LUCEDALE, MISSISSIPPI

CHAPTER

08

THE REAL GC

A close look at the helmets worn by Coach Johnny Ainsworth's Greene County Wildcats tells you a lot about his team – and him. From a fashion standpoint, the design of the helmet is plain. However, from a purely football perspective, the helmet is stunning. Though it may be spartan in appearance, the solid navy blue headgear without the clutter of any decals, stripes or numbers efficiently records and displays each player's "battle scars." Whether it's a defensive player sticking an opposing running back or an offensive lineman pancaking an enemy linebacker, the navy blue helmet records it all. It is the ultimate performance scorecard. The scuffmarks of the opposing teams' colors on the surface of the navy blue helmets quickly tell the story about the Wildcat players' efforts.

Upon a deeper inspection of the plain navy blue helmet, one begins to understand the philosophy of Coach Ainsworth when it comes to building championship teams and transforming boys to men. Greene County football is not about which team has the best-looking uniforms or padding the schedule with patsy teams to boost the players' egos, but quite the contrary. Wildcat football under Johnny Ainsworth is all about knocking heads with the biggest and best teams in America and letting the chips fall where they may. At Greene County, it's about winning football games the old-fashioned way – scrappin', clawin' and fightin' to the end – or, simply put, just gettin' after it. As one Wildcat player expressed, "We ain't afraid of nobody."

One has to have a grasp of the geography of the county and a little slice of its history before totally understanding the value of Wildcat football to the folks of Greene County. From a historical perspective, the relevant periods pertaining to football in the county are divisible into three periods – pre-consolidation, post-consolidation and the Ainsworth era. First, a short geography lesson is necessary.

Greene County is one of the largest counties based on land mass in Mississippi. The county covers 719 square miles and encompasses 460,160 acres. It is a very sparsely populated county with only about 13,000 people. Greene County is very rural with a number of border communities. For instance, Sand Hill is a community located close to the Perry County line. Wayne and Greene Counties split the little community of State Line down the middle. McCain sits right on the Perry County line. The Windburn Chapel community in the south end straddles the George County line. The largest town in Greene County is Leakesville, which is located in the center of the county. In essence, Greene County is large in land mass and sparsely populated with many of its communities dispersed to its borders and its largest town located in the middle.

From a historical perspective regarding a study of Greene County football, the first relevant time period is the pre-consolidation phase. Prior to the formation of Greene County High School, there were four high schools in the county. The largest was Leakesville High School located in the big city of Leakesville. The students who attended Leakesville proudly sported the school's colors of navy blue, white and gold. Their mascot was the Bears. Twenty miles up the road on Highway 63 was Sand Hill High School. The Bucks wore uniforms of royal blue and gold. Then over off Highway 98 was McLain High School, whose students were proud to be the Rams and display their school's maroon and white colors. To the north of the county was State Line High School, home of the proud Warriors.

Under the old high school athletic classification system, Leakesville was a BB school, while McLain, State Line and Sand Hill were included in the smaller B class. Because all four of the schools were in the same county, rivalries quickly developed. For example, State Line and Sand Hill were only 18 miles apart. They developed a heated rivalry in no time. The smaller schools played and developed a rivalry with the big city school, Leakesville High. During the pre-consolidation period, the big game for Leakesville was not with one of its neighboring schools in the county, but a team farther south in George County, the Lucedale Panthers. The annual football game between Leakesville and Lucedale was the most anticipated event of the year for the people of both counties. The rivalry probably started in the early '30s.

The post-consolidation phase began in 1987 when Greene County High School came into existence. The opening of the new

Greene County High School meant the closing of the schools at Sand Hill, McLain and Leakesville, while the school at State Line had already closed prior to consolidation. There was a great deal of opposition to consolidation by the smaller schools in the county. Even though the new school would be located in a new modern facility, the consolidation plans bogged down in debate over its location and, more importantly, whether to consolidate at all. The consolidation didn't gain the necessary approval until the third time it was addressed at the polls.

Because of the geography of the county with the smaller schools located a considerable distance from the site of the new school in Leakesville, the consolidation measure was a subject of hot debate. Unfortunately, there were still many people with hurt feelings over the consolidation process when Greene County High School opened its doors. Many students arrived at school harboring resentment for having to abandon their community schools for the new mega school. Abandoning their loyalties to their old schools was bad enough, but they also had to give up the rivalries created over the years among all the county schools. They couldn't swap their allegiance to the Bears, Bucks, Rams or Warriors overnight for the Wildcats. The result was a general reluctance of the students to get involved in extracurricular activities, namely, football. While there was a general attitude of indifference about football on the part of the students, there was a concurrent epidemic of coaching changes at the head football coaching position for several years. The unfortunate result of all these factors was that Greene County football did not perform well on the field during the post-consolidation period. In short, the Wildcat football program was in the tank.

The Ainsworth era began at Greene County High School in 1997. Johnny Ainsworth overhauled the Wildcat football program overnight, bringing a completely new mindset and approach to the players. He came with a plan – the Ainsworth plan. Under the plan, the Wildcats' football season would be divided into three mini seasons. During the non-district part of the schedule, Coach Ainsworth informed the team that the Wildcats would "play up", regardless of the consequences. Ainsworth told his players he was going to schedule the biggest and best teams he could find. According to the plan, the second part of the schedule featured district games. Shockingly, Ainsworth told the team he fully expected that they would win every game against district opponents. The third mini season would be the playoffs. To everyone's surprise,

Ainsworth announced that the Wildcats would be in the playoffs every year from that point forward. David Chatham, a sophomore player at the time Ainsworth arrived, recalls his reaction: "I thought this guy was an idiot."

True to the plan, Coach Ainsworth began scheduling bigger teams for the Wildcats to play. David Chatham continues, "The first season Coach Ainsworth was here we played St. Martin, East Central, George County and one more school much larger than we were. We ended up winning two of those games."

One of the most memorable games for Coach Ainsworth's Wildcats during his first year was a victory over archrival George County. The Rebels were riding a ten-year winning streak against Greene County when they arrived in Leakesville in 1997. David Chatham recalls the night of the game: "George County ran out on the field with 60 or 70 players in their flashy uniforms. There we were – all 35 of us – just wondering how in the world we were going to beat these guys. Coach Ainsworth stayed confident the whole time and told us, 'You can beat them.' We drummed them that night. It was the first time in ten years Greene County had beaten George County."

Coach Ainsworth had administered shock therapy to the Wildcat football program. Everyone was now on board, including the players, fans, administrators and even the apathetic people in the county who were bitter over consolidation. All of a sudden, the Wildcats were out of the tank and stalking 5A school prey. The people of Greene County were proud to be part of Greene County High School. The navy blue and silver colors of the Wildcats even started to look pretty good to the old McLain, State Line and Sand Hill diehards.

Russell Turner, sports writer for the *Greene County Herald*, whose family has owned the newspaper since the '20s, offers his perspective on the impact of Coach Ainsworth on the community:

> People from Sand Hill, McLain and State Line came to the same spot on Friday nights, wore the same colors and cheered for the same team. They truly bonded. You can see it today, because when we travel to away games, Greene County oftentimes outnumbers the home team's crowd. Our people embrace this school. It has just been centralizing; it's the glue for the community. Having that "us versus them" mentality is very good for building camaraderie and trust, which had

not previously developed in Greene County. I think that, because of the geography of the county, our people did not bind together after consolidation until this school started having a successful football program. I give Johnny Ainsworth credit for it.

G.L. Dearman, longtime supporter of the Wildcats and former Leakesville High School football player, says,

> When Coach Ainsworth came here, we maybe won one or two ballgames a year. The program was in desperate shape with only 15 to 20 boys playing football. He got the program organized and got the kids' confidence up, and they started coming out to play. Most importantly, he got the parents involved. He built this program from scratch. Coach Ainsworth has instilled a will and a want in these kids to play football. He did it by working closely with the parents, faculty and local people. The fact that we have 75 boys on the roster has a tremendous amount to do with Johnny Ainsworth.

The voice of the Greene County Wildcats, Brent Walley, offers his explanation regarding the success of Coach Ainsworth: "Somehow he convinced the boys, the school and the community that we could win. I'm not sure how he did it. All I know is that when our boys put on that blue helmet and come on the field, they are ready to play with anybody."

After the amazing turnaround of the Wildcats' football program during Ainsworth's first year as head coach, he directed the team's attention back to his plan. Consequently, he continued to load the non-district portion of the schedule with even bigger and better football schools like Wayne County, Biloxi, D'Iberville, Petal and Moss Point. Ainsworth didn't stop with the big schools in Mississippi. He went looking for national competition, too. The folks in Greene County learned quickly that their coach was serious about playing the biggest and the best when national power Niceville (Florida) High School appeared on the Wildcats' schedule for a two-year run in 2002 and 2003. According to Coach Ainsworth, "We will play anybody. It doesn't matter if they are ranked nationally every year." To drive the point home, they played both games against Niceville in their stadium in Florida, all according to the plan.

As Greene County matched up with the big boys locally and nationally, they beat George County four straight years and became a perennial playoff contender. Wildcat football exploded with confidence and pride. Then Greene County was reclassified during this period from a 4A school to a smaller 3A classification, while George County moved up to 5A from 4A. Nothing could have suited Ainsworth better. He ignored the classifications and proceeded with the plan of scheduling up whenever the opportunity presented itself. It was as if the smaller 3A Wildcats were stalking the larger 4A and 5A schools. Many of the larger schools that had fallen into the trap and scheduled Greene County in the past refused to reschedule them after falling prey to Ainsworth's Wildcats. The hunted had now become the hunter. David Chatham, former Wildcat player, says, "Yeah, we've beaten some bigger schools and we have lost some games, too, but we always leave the field feeling those big schools know they were in a fight for their lives."

Assistant Greene County football coach Michael King sums up Ainsworth's philosophy: "We don't care who the team is; we'll go play anybody." King continues, "I don't know any other place that would ask their starting quarterback to play defense; but our guys just say, 'Yeah.' It's hard to get any of them off the field."

Colby O'Neal, senior offensive lineman for the Wildcats, says, "The way we look at it, if we play bigger schools, we are going to get better. That's the reason we do so well when we get to district."

Bill Ricks, Greene County High School Athletic Director, states, "Johnny brought a sense of winning to our football program. In doing so, he built a tradition. As the tradition became bigger and bigger, it reached the point where the kids said, 'We can beat anybody.'"

John Turner, III, former Wildcat player, echoes the Ainsworth philosophy: "We don't play down. We always play bigger schools in the non-district part of our schedule to make us better. Most of the time we win those games, too."

The plan paid big dividends for the Wildcats in 2003. On a cold December morning at 11 a.m. at Mississippi Veterans Memorial Stadium, Greene County collided with superpower Cleveland High School. The north Mississippi champion was loaded with talented players at every position and was the favorite to win the 3A state championship. The Wildcats trailed Cleveland 7-6 late in the game. Coach Ainsworth describes the action:

Cleveland was ahead 7-6 all the way through the game. We were an option football team, but we used a set with trips to one side. The player who carried the play in called it to go away from the trips – the exact opposite of what I had called. Cleveland seemed confused by the formation and sort of shifted to the trips side of the formation. Our quarterback, Tommy Lott, took the ball around the end away from the trip set and ran 75 yards down to the 3-yard line. On the next play, Travis Hicks scored. We made the extra point and led 13-7 at that point. On the next series, Lance Moore picked off a Cleveland pass and returned it for a score. That was a big moment for Greene County Wildcat football.

Greene County finished the 2003 season 11 and 4 and captured the school's first 3A state championship – all according to the plan. The Wildcat tradition established by Coach Ainsworth of playing up against the bigger schools and scrappin', clawin' and fightin' 'til the end to get the win paid off. In ten years at Greene County, Johnny Ainsworth has almost 100 wins to his credit – proof that his plan works. However, Coach Ainsworth's most important accomplishment is not in the staggering number of victories, but the fact that Wildcat football is the pride of Greene County – all of it. From State Line to Sand Hill to McLain and to Leakesville, they love their navy blue and silver Wildcats.

There was another tradition started that Saturday morning in Jackson when the Wildcats stormed onto Butch Lambert Field at Mississippi Veterans Memorial Stadium. To most observers other than the Greene County fans, the moment probably went unnoticed. As Greene County took the field, they were led by a senior player, Josh Jordan, who was carrying a large cross on his back. The cross was a symbol that Jesus Christ had changed Jordan's life when he became a Christian. To this day, the Greene County Wildcats continue that tradition by carrying that same old beat up cross – now held together by athletic tape – when they take the field before every game.

The plain blue helmet, the plan and the cross have all become the foundation of Greene County Wildcat football under Coach Johnny Ainsworth.

****

Al Jones is a patient man.

In 1960, the Lucedale Panthers defeated the Leakesville Bears 7 to 0 to win the big rival game between the two neighboring high schools. The annual cross-county grudge match was played in front of a standing room only crowd at Josey Ratliff Field in Lucedale. Up in Wayne County that same year on May 12, Al Jones was born to Albert Ray and Helen Jones at Wayne General Hospital in Waynesboro, Mississippi.

The high schools in George County were consolidated and integrated in 1964 when the largest high school in the county, Lucedale Central, was rolled up with a number of smaller county schools. Eight miles northeast of Lucedale, the high school at Rocky Creek was pulled into the consolidation process. Agricola High School, ten miles south of Lucedale, along with the schools at Basin and Broome, were all pulled into the vortex of consolidation. Oak Grove, the black high school located in Lucedale, also became part of the giant mass of school consolidation. Together, all of these schools made up the new George County High School, which sported a new nickname – the Rebels. About the time George County High School was being forged into existence, Al Jones was only four years old.

In the mid-'70s, while the Rebels and Bears were duking it out on the gridiron, Al Jones was engaged in his own football warfare. As an offensive lineman for the Clara Whippets, his entire focus was on defeating their inner-county rivals at Waynesboro, Beat Four and Buckatunna. Al's coach was a young fellow named Johnny Ainsworth, himself a graduate of Clara High School, who was just starting his coaching career.

Then, in 1988, the annual George County and Leakesville game ended and was replaced with a newer, bigger match up with Greene County. Just as George County had done 24 years earlier, Greene County followed suit with consolidation of its schools, thereby ending the colorful history of the Leakesville Bears and the other small high schools in the county.

Beginning in 1988, the George County Rebels and the Greene County Wildcats clashed for the very first time. The Wildcats defeated the Rebels 20 to 18 in the first football game between the two schools. During this time, Al Jones was on the staff of Hal Holmes as an assistant football coach at Vancleave High School. Ironically, the same year George County and Greene County started their new rivalry, Vancleave defeated George County in what many considered a shocking upset.

Before the season was over, the George County Rebels had their sights set on bringing Hal Holmes and his staff to Lucedale to build their football program. If the Rebels were successful in luring Holmes away from Vancleave, in all likelihood, Al Jones would move to Lucedale with him. As fate would have it, Holmes accepted the George County offer, and he and his staff were eager to start the building process with the Rebel football program.

Al Jones arrived at George County High School in 1989 as an assistant football coach on the staff of Hal Holmes, the Rebels' new head coach. During the next 12 years, Al Jones would serve as an assistant to six head coaches at George County, beginning with Coach Holmes and followed by John Watkins, Fred Gill, Steve Buckley, Greg Freeman and Andrew Hickman. During the entire succession of coaches, Al Jones remained confident that the football program at George County could be a perennial playoff contender. While the rapid succession of turnovers at the head coaching position was disruptive to the Rebel football program, it was positive for Jones. As the head coaches came and went, Al learned another philosophy of coaching, new offensive formations, different defensive schemes and organizational methods from each of them. All the while, he was listening, learning and waiting patiently for his opportunity.

As Al gained more experience and observed the head coaches passing through the Rebel program, he became confident that he could make a difference in bringing success to George County on the gridiron. Upon the resignation of Coach Hal Holmes in 1991, Al applied for the head coaching position. However, his application was declined and the Rebels hired John Watkins as the new head coach. Two years later when the head coach position became available again, Al applied a second time; and for a second time, school officials rejected his application. Although disappointed, Al was not discouraged. He diligently and patiently went about his job as an assistant football coach. The head position came available again 1995. Again, Al applied; and again, the Rebels hired someone else – Steve Buckley. Al didn't miss a beat, always remaining confident that his time would come. Then, in 2000, Coach Hickman decided to retire. Al applied for the head coaching position a fourth time. During the entire time in the past when he had applied and been rejected, one overriding thought kept him on track – his players. Because of the confidence they had always shown in him and his relationship with them, Al remained calm and patient with the process.

To Al Jones, his relationship with his players was, and will always be, the most important element of coaching. That's really all Al Jones cared about. In the spring of 2001, Al Jones became the head football coach of the George County Rebels. His patience and confidence finally paid off – and, oh, boy, did it pay off for the Rebels.

George County football immediately entered a new era – a big time winning era. From Jones's first season in 2001 through the 2007 season, the Rebels turned in double-digit wins. To put Coach Jones's accomplishment in perspective, in the 15 seasons preceding Jones, the program had only recorded one double-digit-win season. To put an exclamation mark on a stunning record, Coach Jones led the Rebels to the south Mississippi 5A championship and a shot at the state championship against national superpower South Panola. Prior to the December showdown in Jackson to cap off the 2007 season, prognosticators didn't give the Rebels a chance of defeating the Tigers. South Panola sported a 74-game winning streak and four consecutive state championships and was loaded with several Division I college prospects. The hope of the Rebels staying on the field with the Tigers was doubtful.

At the start of the game, South Panola came out blazing. It looked as if the Tigers had the Rebels outmatched in size, speed and championship experience and had just too much firepower for George County. However, the Rebels had developed a trait – something they picked up from their head coach – patience. No matter how great South Panola played or how far ahead the Tigers got, George County stayed calm and played in a patient, methodical manner. With about a minute left in the game and the score at 28 to 21, the Rebels had the ball and were driving. They had a chance to win the game, beat nationally-ranked South Panola, snap the Tigers' 74-game winning streak and win George County's first state championship. As time was running down on the clock, the Rebel quarterback called an audible and lofted a pass to Alonzo Lawrence, who was running a sideline route. As the nose of the ball started its downward trajectory, the Tiger defensive back nudged, pushed and mugged the Rebel receiver, but there was no flag – no call – pass incomplete – game over – South Panola won! It was a heartbreaking loss for the Rebels, but the Rebel team never buckled. They didn't fold. They were like their coach – patient and calm under pressure – a trait of a team destined for championships.

According to Coach Jones, the fast turnaround was primarily attributable to finally having some stability on the staff from top to bottom. For instance, one of Jones's assistants, Darwin Nelson, has been coaching with Jones for 17 years. Another assistant, Chris West, has been on staff for 12. Once Jones became the head coach, the communication already in place among these three men flowed freely and efficiently without any need of translation or decoding. In short, they were all already on the same page.

The population growth in George County has provided a larger pool of athletes for the Rebel program to select from and to expand the size of the squad. However, one of the most important factors fueling the success of the program is the support in the community. Jones explains, "George County folks love football and they are going to support the team. This is just a football-loving county and they are hungry for victory." From a player's perspective, community support validates the importance of his sacrifices to work for the success of the team. Ethan Eubanks, a George County football player, comments on the day the Rebels traveled to Jackson for the state championship showdown with South Panola: "The day we left, everybody was standing on the street corners and you just knew the town was behind you. Leaving to go to Jackson, we knew the community was behind us 100 percent – win or lose. We were gonna play our hearts out for those folks, no matter what – and we did." Former George County football player in the '70s, Derrick Scott, recalls, "Walking into the stadium in Jackson to play South Panola was the crowning moment of my memories as a George County Rebel. I was just so proud of the team, coaches and our community." Scott offers his comments about Coach Jones, the man who gives credit to everyone other than himself:

> He brings emotional stability to the boys. He is not distant from them. Coach Jones is so patient and grounded. After we beat Meridian to go on to play South Panola, I watched Al come back across the field and go over to where the cheerleaders had left a spirit sign on the fence. As everybody was up on the hill talking and celebrating, he rolled up the sign, put it on his shoulder and carried it up the hill. He didn't send somebody back down the hill to get it, nor did he just walk off and leave it. That's the kind of guy Al Jones is.

Yes, Al Jones is a patient man – and a damn good football coach!

****

George "Little Buck" Green, a 1943 graduate of Lucedale High School, remembers going to see his older brother, "Big Buck," play football against the Leakesville Bears in the mid '30s. According to Little Buck, who attended school at Lucedale from first grade through high school, "Those two teams were playing as far back as I can remember, but I can't tell you exactly when they started playing."

Little Buck played halfback and wingback in the single wing formation run by the Panthers at the time he was attending Lucedale High. Of course, on a 15-man squad, everyone played both ways. He proudly wore his red and white No. 31 Panther jersey.

During the four years Little Buck played in the Lucedale-Leakesville series, both communities turned out in mass for the games. He recalls, "Oh, yeah, it was always a big game when we played. Hundreds of folks would attend those games. I don't remember exactly, but we kind of split. We didn't win them all and they didn't either. It was a friendly rivalry." However, how can it be a friendly rivalry when current George County assistant coach Darwin Nelson says, "We want to beat their brains out and they want to beat our brains out"? As strange as it sounds, the rivalry between Greene County and George County is as intense and competitive as you will find anywhere, yet friendly. To understand this phenomenon in the highly competitive world of sports, it is necessary to study a little history again. While Little Buck Green is certainly a credible witness to the atmosphere surrounding the rivalry in the late '30s and early '40s, the genesis of this friendship between the folks in Greene and George Counties predates Little Buck. Actually, it goes back to 1910. At the time, there was no George County. George County was later carved out of the existing counties of Jackson and Greene. So from its very inception, George County has been grateful to the people in Greene County, because without the generosity of its neighbors to the north, George County wouldn't exist. Essentially, it is difficult to hate yourself. George County is Greene County, and Greene County is George County. It is confusing, paradoxical and odd, but how can the unique love-hate relationship otherwise be explained?

Fast forward from 1910 to 2001 – 91 years later – and consider the experience of Paul Wallace during his first year as principal of George County High School. Wallace says,

I was very nervous before the first ballgame, because the Greene County game was our first ballgame my first year as principal. I remember talking to the principal at Greene County at the time, David Dearman, who has since passed away. He told me, "Paul, it's going to be a packed house, but I promise you will not have a single problem. We are going to have to find a place to put all these people, because you don't have enough bleachers to seat them. Knowing where you are coming from, you are going to be uncomfortable letting people inside the fenced area, but we are going to have to come up with something." David and I determined that we would allow Greene County people to come on the track area outside the field. I would leave him in charge of his people. Basically, we had enough seating and standing room for our crowd. Our concern was for the visiting crowd. We had absolutely no problems that night. In the six years I've been involved as principal we have not had any problems. It's probably one of the friendliest rivalries around. It's because a lot of the people are kin to each other. They work together. These kids hunt and fish together. That first game, there were over 8,000 people in attendance. As Mr. Dearman predicted, there were no problems. When the game was over, the kids shook hands and the adults shook hands. Everyone walked through the parking lot together, talking and joking. We just don't have problems.

Another recent example of the friendship and cooperativeness of these two schools and communities occurred in 2005. Due to Hurricane Katrina, the game between the Wildcats and the Rebels was cancelled. Both sides attempted to reschedule the game later in the season, but they couldn't find a mutually-acceptable makeup date. Consequently, the game, which was scheduled to be played at Greene County, was lost. Since the Greene-George game is by far the biggest game for both schools, the loss of the revenue to Greene County had a devastating financial effect, because the home team gets 100 percent of the gate. To make matters worse, under the rules governing the schools' scheduling, a lost game had no effect on the schedule for the next year. Based on the home and home schedule, George County would get the game and the gate in 2006. Under the rules, Greene County was just out of luck. In a fiercely competitive dog-eat-dog rivalry, such a situation would be too bad for the team suffering the loss. However, while competitive on the field, the Greene-George rivalry ends on the field and a more humane attitude takes over. According to Al Jones, "We technically didn't have to do it, but we split the gate with them in 2006. That was just the right thing to do. Again, this is a friendly rivalry."

Larry Shirley, owner of WRBE radio station in Lucedale, offers his observations about the Greene County-George County football rivalry and both schools' head coaches. Shirley says,

> Johnny Ainsworth and Al Jones are both men of solid character. They are both grounded. They know how to handle kids. Some need to be handled with some gentle care, while others need more discipline. They teach the kids the sport of football and the lessons about life that can be learned from the game. These two coaches have a lot to do with this being a friendly rivalry. Both have taught their kids to do their best to win, but in the same vein, they have also taught respect and they expect their kids to give it to the other team. The fans follow the lead of the players and coaches.

Throughout the series of the Greene County and George County rivalry there have been a number of exciting games, controversial games and disappointing games for both Wildcat and Rebel fans. Regardless of the era, whether it was the Lucedale Panthers playing the Leakesville Bears, or the George County Rebels fighting the Leakesville Bears, or the games today between the Rebels and the Greene County Wildcats, this exciting rivalry continues. It's a rivalry covering three eras, but it still lives on today in the same thrilling way it did for Little Buck Green in 1943. Each player and fan has a special memory. Maybe it was the excitement of the first Greene County victory over George County in 1988, or the four straight Wildcat victories under Coach Ainsworth in 1997, 1998, 1999 and 2000. Perhaps it was the rain game won by Lucedale 12-7 over Leakesville, or maybe the spectacular performance of Greg Wash in 1999 at Leakesville. There are just so many memories and so many special moments for the fans in Greene and George Counties.

At the outset of the Greene-George rivalry, someone suggested that the schools establish a trophy to exchange each year. The idea was to have the scores engraved on the trophy to keep track of the series record. One suggestion for the trophy design was a spittoon. However, school officials rejected that one. The next suggestion, a bell, received a more positive response. Consequently, they decided that the sides would exchange a bell as a trophy each year, with the winning team taking possession of the trophy until the next annual game. The plan also called for the loser of the first game in 1988 to purchase the bell. Greene County won the first Rebel-Wildcat match-up. However, to this day, the bell trophy has not materialized.

The cheerleaders for both the Rebels and Wildcats taunt one another every year with the cheer "GC what?" which begs the question: Who is the real GC? The answer is: They both are. The George County Rebels and the Greene County Wildcats are both "for real."

WHAT THE WILDCATS SAY ABOUT GEORGE COUNTY

I've been involved in a lot of rivalries, but this has to be the friendliest.

Johnny Ainsworth

Greene County Head Football Coach

It's just a good rivalry. We don't like those guys down the road and they don't like us.

David Chatham

Greene County Assistant Football Coach

I'd rather beat George County than win our homecoming game.

Colby O'Neal

Greene County Football Player

Lucedale is rural like we are, but then it has a city atmosphere that we don't have in Greene County.

Mike Chatham

Greene County Principal

The only thing more important than beating George County is the state championship.

Alex Cooper

Greene County Football Player

It's fun to have an enemy.

Timothy Cooper

Greene County Band Member

They are more of a prank school.

Lee Hill

Former Greene County Football Player

The Leakesville-Lucedale rivalry is the underpinning of today's rivalry between Greene County and George County.

G.L. Dearman
Former Leakesville High School Football Player

The administrators of both schools sit together in the end zone.

Richard Fleming
Superintendent of Greene County Schools

Their pep rallies are like two hours long.

Charly Rogers
Greene County Cheerleader

They stick their noses up and walk around like they are better than us. We look at them as snobs.

Alex Cooper
Greene County Football Player

I think their stereotype of us is "inbred rednecks."

David Chatham
Greene County Assistant Football Coach

You have families that usually don't get along during that week; and, depending on how the game goes, may be on the outs the rest of the year until the game rolls around next year.

Frederick McCann
Greene County Assistant Football Coach

Even though it's a heated rivalry, our fans get along really well. We are friends all the time except for one night out of the year.

Richard Fleming
Superintendent of Greene County Schools

They do a lot of trash talking.

Alex Cooper
Greene County Football Player

They think they are "GC what" and we think we are.

Ashley Smith
Greene County Cheerleader

The football game between George County and Greene County is the biggest event in Greene County.

Kevin Richie
Greene County Football Player

George County thinks we are a bunch of inbreds.

Jill Vest
Greene County Cheerleader

They call us white trash.

Alex Cooper
Greene County Football Player

It's a friendly rivalry.

G.L. Dearman
Former Leakesville High School Football Player

I don't like George County.

Colby O'Neal
Greene County Football Player

WHAT THE REBELS SAY ABOUT GREENE COUNTY

They are like the country hicks. At our pep rallies, people dress up in overalls and have signs that say, 'I date my sister!'

Lainey Leggett

Former George County Cheerleader

They think we are like preps and, supposedly, they dress up like preppie people or snobs on their pep rally day.

Alicia Byrd

Former George County Student Body President

The Leakesville-Lucedale game was always a packed house. People would have to stand. It wasn't nasty, but it was highly competitive. I don't remember an actual fight ever breaking out.

Tony Caldwell

Former George County Football Player

We think of them as a bunch of dumb rednecks. They probably think of us as a bunch of thugs and troublemakers. We give them a hard time about being in the sticks.

Ethan Eubanks

George County Football Player

Coach Ainsworth is always calling our home. He and my dad are friends.

Rae Ann Jones

Daughter of George County Head Football Coach

After every game we meet each other at midfield and shake hands, joke about the game and laugh about different plays.

Chris West

George County Assistant Football Coach

Even in two of our double-digit winning seasons, we still got beat by them. That takes some of the shine off the season, even when you go 11-3 or 10-3 and make a run through the playoffs.

Darwin Nelson
George County Assistant Football Coach

A team might not be very good, but you can throw the records out. The closeness of the communities and the fact that a lot of the people are kin in George and Greene Counties make it the rivalry it is.

Poochie Stringfellow
Former George County Head Football Coach

It has never gotten out of hand. It's just a good contest and an enjoyable week. When it's over, everybody shakes hands and we start getting ready for next year. We don't rub it in if we win, because we know next year it could turn around.

Donnie Howell
Former George County Football Player
and Superintendent of George County School District

Everybody thinks people from Greene County are just redneck and backwoods. I'm sure they say stuff about us. We all know that's just part of a good rivalry.

Chris West
George County Assistant Football Coach

I don't think these two teams ever hated each other. It's been a good rivalry from the standpoint of pure sports emotion.

Derrick Scott
Former George County Football Player

Coach Ainsworth is the king of poor mouthing.

Chris West
George County Assistant Football Coach

They just don't quit. We were up by several touchdowns in the fourth quarter and they just kept coming. They don't quit.

Ethan Eubanks
George County Football Player

Let me just say Greene County is country.

Poochie Stringfellow
Former George County Head Football Coach

My wife told me way back when we came to Lucedale in the '60s, "I will go anywhere that you go to work except Leakesville. I won't go to Leakesville."

Fred Gill
Former George County Head Football Coach

We are both country folks. We like to say they are more country than we are, but both of us are country.

Al Jones
George County Head Football Coach

People say, "If you don't win another game, you better beat Greene County."

Melody Jones
Wife of George County Head Football Coach

Rivalries don't start with the kids; they start with the parents.

Fred Gill
Former George County Head Football Coach

Never in my recollection has anything really gotten out of hand. There has never been a fight.

Derrick Scott
Former George County Football Player

When Coach Ainsworth came, they got to be good and got good in a hurry. All of a sudden, they started beating us and beat us four times straight.

Al Jones
George County Head Football Coach

They are hillbillies.

Ryan Scott
Former George County Football Player

It's probably one of the friendliest rivalries going.

Paul Wallace
George County Principal

It's a friendly rivalry where the winner wins with pride and the loser loses with pride.

Fred Gill
Former George County Head Football Coach

If there is one game we don't want to lose, it's to Greene County.

Donnie Howell
Former George County Football Player
and Superintendent of George County School District

Greene County is the enemy you don't really hate.

Derrick Scott
Former George County Football Player

We would dress out 70. They would dress out 20. All of them would go both ways. It was embarrassing that they would hang with us and always make the games interesting.

Derrick Scott
Former George County Football Player

Year	Greene County	Score	George County
1927	*NA*	0-7	Coach Lumpkin
1927	*NA*	6-13	Coach Lumpkin
1928	*NA*	0-7	Coach Bailey
1928	*NA*	14-0	Coach Bailey
1929	Coach McDaniel	25-0	*NA*
1930	*NA*	*NA*	R.J. Hinson
1931	*NA*	0-6	R.J. Hinson
1932	*NA*	*NA*	*NA*
1933	*NA*	*Did Not Play*	*NA*
1934	*NA*	*NA*	*NA*
1935	*NA*	*NA*	*NA*
1936	*NA*	*NA*	Jakie Miller
1937	*NA*	18-0	Jakie Miller
1938	*NA*	27-13	W.C. Griffith
1939	*NA*	7-0	W.C. Griffith
1940	*NA*	26-6	W.C. Griffith
1941	*NA*	20-0	Coach Dennis
1942	*NA*	*Did Not Play*	*NA*
1943	*NA*	*NA*	*NA*
1944	*NA*	*NA*	*NA*
1945	*NA*	*NA*	*NA*
1946	*NA*	14-7	*NA*
1947	*NA*	*Did Not Play*	Bracy Smith
1948	*NA*	*NA*	Rice/Stevenson
1949	*NA*	0-14	Coach Roberts
1950	*NA*	*NA*	Coach Roberts
1951	*NA*	38-0	Coach Roberts
1952	*NA*	13-0	M.T. "Tick" Tatum
1953	*NA*	0-21	M.T. "Tick" Tatum
1954	*NA*	0-39	M.T. "Tick" Tatum
1955	*NA*	14-6	John King
1956	*NA*	6-12	Ray Nobles
1957	*NA*	0-41	Ray Nobles
1958	*NA*	*NA*	Ray Nobles

Year	Greene County	Score	George County
1959	*NA*	14-7	Ray Nobles
1960	*NA*	0-7	Jimmy Taylor
1961	*NA*	0-20	Jimmy Taylor
1962	*NA*	0-45	Fred Gill
1963	*NA*	*NA*	Fred Gill
1964	*NA*	0-40	Fred Gill
1965	*NA*	7-27	Fred Gill
1966	*NA*	0-28	Fred Gill
1967	*NA*	0-25	Fred Gill
1968	*NA*	*Did Not Play*	Bill Martin
1969	*NA*	*NA*	Bill Martin
1970	*NA*	*NA*	Bill Martin
1971	*NA*	*NA*	Bill Martin
1972	*NA*	17-30	Bill Martin
1973	*NA*	15-14	Bill Martin
1974	*NA*	14-27	Bill Martin
1975	*NA*	0-20	Bill Martin
1976	*NA*	6-28	Bill Martin
1977	*NA*	3-14	Bill Martin
1978	*NA*	14-13	Bill Martin
1979	*NA*	20-42	Bill Martin
1980	*NA*	6-33	Bill Martin
1981	*NA*	6-39	Bill Martin
1982	*NA*	0-42	Bill Martin
1983	*NA*	0-48	Bill Martin
1984	*NA*	*Did Not Play*	Bill Martin
1985	*NA*	*NA*	Poochie Stringfellow
1986	*NA*	*NA*	Poochie Stringfellow
1987	Hilton Baucum	15-26	Poochie Stringfellow
1988	Barry Sharpe	20-18	Poochie Stringfellow
1989	Roy Gene Hicks	0-28	Hal Holmes
1990	Steven Stringfellow	8-49	Hal Holmes
1991	Hilton Balcum	8-34	Hal Holmes
1992	Hilton Balcum	6-14	John Watkins
1993	Hilton Balcum	6-13	John Watkins
1994	Danny Adams	7-21	Fred Gill
1995	Mike Chatham	14-20	Steve Buckley
1996	Mike Chatham	14-24	Steve Buckley

Year	Greene County	Score	George County
1997	Johnny Ainsworth	12-0	Greg Freeman
1998	Johnny Ainsworth	27-18	Andrew Hickman
1999	Johnny Ainsworth	42-22	Andrew Hickman
2000	Johnny Ainsworth	22-20	Andrew Hickman
2001	Johnny Ainsworth	7-17	Al Jones
2002	Johnny Ainsworth	28-21	Al Jones
2003	Johnny Ainsworth	14-7	Al Jones
2004	Johnny Ainsworth	6-35	Al Jones
2005	Johnny Ainsworth	*Did not play – Hurricane Katrina*	Al Jones
2006	Johnny Ainsworth	17-49	Al Jones
2007	Johnny Ainsworth	21-42	Al Jones

NA - Information Not Available

Leakesville consolidated into Greene County in 1987.

Lucedale consolidated into George County in 1964.

★★ OFFICIAL GAME DAY PROGRAM $5.00 ★★

JACKSON PREP
VERSUS
JACKSON ACADEMY

Mississippi Vein Institute

PROUD SPONSOR OF MISSISSIPPI HIGH SCHOOL FOOTBALL

FRIDAY, AUGUST 29, 2008 ★ 7:00 PM KICKOFF
PATRIOT FIELD ★ FLOWOOD, MISSISSIPPI

CHAPTER

A House Divided

In 1970, Jackson Prep opened its new school on Lakeland Drive in Rankin County. Its mission was to establish one of the finest academic high schools in the state of Mississippi. History confirms the school has achieved its mission. Over its 38-year existence, Jackson Prep has produced 461 National Merit Semifinalists, more than any other school in the state.

Prep's goal was not only to be a great academic school, but also to be a great school overall. From its inception, Prep made extracurricular activities a priority and invested resources in a number of athletic, artistic and performance-based activities. Prep's desire to excel in athletics was made particularly evident when they hired their first football coach, Jack Carlisle.

During the 1960s, Coach Carlisle led the gridiron forces of the Murrah High Mustangs in Jackson. Murrah was a statewide power and was regularly vying for, and winning, championships in the powerful Big Eight Conference. The idea of even approaching such a well-known, well-established and successful coach would be considered brazen by any school's standards. However, considering that Jackson Prep was a brand new private school that had yet to play a single down of football, the notion was darn near preposterous. However, Prep had an ace up its sleeve. Not only would Carlisle receive a $3,000 raise, he would also be given the position of athletic director and, more importantly, full control over the layout and design of all the new athletic facilities. The lure of designing practice fields, locker rooms and, of course, the football stadium, was too much to resist for Carlisle and he accepted Prep's offer, sort of.

Carlisle had a special group of football players at Murrah that would be playing their senior year in 1970 – the same year Prep wanted him to start coaching their football team. Carlisle told Prep he would accept their offer to become their first athletic director and head football coach, but that he could not assume the position until after the 1970 football season. Prep agreed to Carlisle's terms and Jerry Richardson was put in place as a one-year interim coach. Carlisle went on to coach a loaded Murrah team to a Big Eight Conference championship in 1970 before leaving mid-semester for Prep in January of 1971. With Carlisle came nine of his best players from Murrah.

Upon arriving at Prep, Carlisle immediately went to work designing the athletic facilities. In fact, the home stands at Jackson Prep today are the same ones that Carlisle designed and built in 1971. In addition to taking on the challenge of creating athletic facilities out of thin air on Lakeland Drive, Carlisle also struggled to find opponents for the upcoming season. Many of Prep's opponents from the inaugural 1970 season began canceling their scheduled contests with Prep for 1971. Carlisle's success at Murrah and the caliber of the Murrah athletes was well known throughout the state, and schools in the young Mississippi Private School Association were apprehensive about going head-to-head with what amounted to remnants of the reigning Big Eight Conference champions. Carlisle was forced to employ drastic measures to find games.

Armed with a high school directory and pen and paper, Carlisle began writing to every school in Mississippi and surrounding states that wasn't currently on Prep's schedule. Finally, Carlisle received a response, hand-written in pencil, from a school in England, Arkansas. The letter accepted Prep's offer to pay the school $1,000 cash; pay for their travel to Jackson, Mississippi, via bus; and put them up overnight in a motel on Highway 80 in Pearl (a motel that has since been converted to a women's prison). Including the food that would be provided to the team, the entire package was worth a whopping $2,500.

The team from England, Arkansas, arrived at their motel on Thursday night before the game and then came out to Prep to walk the field on Friday morning. Carlisle remembers his first impression of the visitors: "They showed up in a bobtail school bus. I counted all 16 of them as they got off the bus. I know the biggest one did not weigh 175 pounds. I wouldn't let my team come out there. I didn't want their team to see our players and get back on the bus and go home."

Carlisle's assessment of the mismatch proved to be accurate, as the score was 40-0 at halftime. Prep's first string had hardly played the first half, and Carlisle didn't plan to use them in the second half in an attempt to make the game more competitive. However, at the start of the second half, Prep was the only team that came out of the locker room and back to the game field. One of the officials approached Carlisle and explained that the other team had just informed him, "They're not coming out." Knowing that the large home crowd would be highly disappointed if they were cheated out of a second half of entertainment, Carlisle decided to pay a visit to the opponent's locker room.

According to Carlisle, "I opened the door to their locker room and asked their head coach what the trouble was. He told me his players refused to come back out. I said, 'They can't do that. The stands are full of people. The guarantee doesn't hold up unless you finish the game. Do you mind if I talk to them?'" At that point Jack Carlisle gave a pep talk to the players of the opposing team in an attempt to motivate them to retake the field for the second half against his Jackson Prep Patriots. "I told them I was only going to play my third team during the second half and I was certain they were better than my third teamers. I told them they didn't want to go back to Arkansas and tell everyone they quit because they were scared of a bunch of boys from Mississippi," said Carlisle. Finally the biggest player on the team stood up and said, "I ain't scared of them" and led his team back on the field.

Prep's third team promptly hung another 26 points on the boys from Arkansas, gave them their contracted post-game meal and sent them back home on their bus with a 66-0 defeat in tow.

Carlisle's first Prep team ultimately had ten athletes sign college scholarships. Six of those players signed with Ole Miss, including Ricky Kimbrough, Dan Murff and George Stewart. Carlisle started the trend of great athletes coming out of Prep, but it did not stop there. Upcoming Patriot seasons produced NFL players like Ken Toler, Paul Lacoste, Todd Wade and Will Overstreet. The athletic program designed by Carlisle has ultimately become the most successful in the Mississippi Private School Association and has produced more overall state championships than any other member school.

Jackson Prep's coaching excellence continued after Carlisle under the subsequent guidance of head coaches Buddy Crosby, Randy Rucker and John McInnis. In 1997, Prep pulled another legendary coach from the public school ranks and began what would become a decade of unprecedented excellence. Coach Ricky Black enjoyed coaching success at Kosciusko from 1975-1979 and at Tupelo from 1980-1990. When Jackson Prep came calling, Coach Black was part of Jackie

Sherrill's staff at Mississippi State University. Says Black,

> I never really thought about coming to a private school or being involved with a private school. I was in public school when most of the private schools started up. I saw the development, but never really paid that much attention to the private schools at all. I played at Ackerman and coached at Kosciusko and Tupelo. I didn't have to deal with many private schools in those areas. Then, when I was coaching at Mississippi State, a couple of people I really respected asked me to interview at Prep. When I took the job, I thought I would stay for a couple of years. I've been here 11. It's a very good institution. I've learned a lot about independent schools and private school education. I am very impressed with Prep.

Coach Black describes the unique qualities of Jackson Prep:

> There are several unique factors about coaching at Prep as compared to the other places I have been. First, top to bottom, this is the hardest-working group of players I have been around. Eighty-five to ninety percent of the team is involved in the off-season training and doesn't miss workouts. That's unusual for any program, but even more so when you consider all the other distractions and opportunities the kids at Prep have available to them. Second, the family involvement here is tremendous. It's a given that the parents are going to be involved; and many of the grandparents are, too. So a "broken home" here is when you don't have grandparent participation. Because of the parents' desire to participate, we have a film session on Monday nights for them. We have anywhere from 20 to 60 parents show up. We show them the tape of the previous week's game and we talk about what we tried to do, why we were successful and who played well. We don't get into personnel issues and decisions. We also talk about the upcoming game and any conflicts that may occur during the week.

Since Prep's formation in 1970 and the subsequent expansion of the Mississippi Private School Association, there has been a great debate regarding whether or not public and private schools in Mississippi should compete against one another and, if they did, whether or not private schools could stay on the field with public schools. True to its progressive nature and history, Jackson Prep was the first of the private schools to attempt to answer that question. In 1997 during Coach Black's first season, Prep scheduled and played George County, a 4A public school. For perspective, Prep would be classified as a 3A school under the MHSAA system of classification. George County won the game 27-14 and went on to make a run deep into the playoffs at the end of the season. Although Prep lost, the game was a significant event in the history of Mississippi high school football and helped crack the door for additional match-ups between public and private schools in other sports. However, football games between public and private schools did not occur again until 2007 when Prep crossed association lines and scheduled both Newton County and Pearl High School.

The game with Pearl was especially significant because both Prep and Pearl are located in Rankin County. In addition, Pearl has its own decorated football history and possesses a very strong fan base. While teams like George County and Newton County certainly wanted to beat Prep, due to proximity, they didn't possess the same level of desire or need to beat Prep as did Pearl. For all the public schools in the central Mississippi area, the game between Prep and Pearl was to finally be the game where public school dominance over private schools was firmly established.

Jackson Prep senior player Scott McVey remembers the back-to-back games with Newton County and Pearl:

> The week before the Newton County game we were getting a lot of press about the game. A lot of people doubted us and said we couldn't compete with public schools. However, we went into that game with a positive attitude, came out strong and shut them out. Once we had beaten them, we realized that maybe we could beat Pearl, too. Everyone in the media and around town was saying that Pearl was going to kill us. Their students showed up at the game wearing ties with no shirts. They were standing at the fence and yelling at us and calling us preppies. It made us mad and made us want to win the game even more. When Bryant Salmon took the opening kickoff back 97 yards for a touchdown, you could see the air come out of their whole team and

I knew we had them. By halftime it was 43-0 and their fans and players weren't yelling at us anymore; they were too busy yelling at each other. That game proved to everyone, without a doubt, that we could play.

With his coaching background in public and private high schools (as well as experience at the major college level), Prep's Ricky Black is uniquely qualified to compare public and private high school football in Mississippi. Black says,

> When I talk about the great work ethic of the players at Prep, that's not to suggest that they aren't also great athletes. I think speed is the biggest factor year in and year out in determining the success of your team. Public schools probably have more speed overall year after year than the private schools, but my 2006 and 2007 Prep teams have been the fastest overall teams that I have ever coached anywhere. That tells you everything you need to know about the athletic ability of these kids.

During Coach Black's 11 seasons at Jackson Prep, the football program has experienced excellence at a level never seen before in school history. Coach Black's first team went undefeated and then lost in the first round of the playoffs. In each of the next ten seasons, his teams have played for the state championship, winning the championship in five of those seasons. Prep is currently riding a 25-game winning streak that resulted in back-to-back championships in 2006 and 2007. Black has won more games and more championships than any other coach in Prep's history.

The original mission of Jackson Prep was to create a school that was excellent from top to bottom in every facet of the high school experience. With 100 percent of its graduating students going on to college, a record number of National Merit Semifinalists, athletic teams that dominate the private schools and successfully compete with the public schools, the early founders of Jackson Prep can confidently say, "Mission accomplished."

****

Nestled comfortably on the corner of Ridgewood Road and Sheffield Drive in the middle of an affluent northeast Jackson neighborhood, Jackson Academy currently boasts the largest student body of any private school in Mississippi. With 1,450 students in kindergarten through twelfth grade, JA's campus has slowly transformed into what looks like a small college. However, this is a far cry from the school's humble beginnings in 1959 when it occupied a small house and taught phonetic reading to ten first graders.

Through the years, Jackson Academy grew its kindergarten and elementary school to one of the finest in the state and served as the primary feeder school to the junior high and high schools at Jackson Prep. The two schools enjoyed a symbiotic relationship through much of the 1970s until a letter allegedly sent from a Prep administrator changed the dynamic forever. The letter was sent to parents of elementary school students at Jackson Academy and informed them that if they failed to register their children early for seventh grade at Prep, a spot would not be saved for them. Although the exact timing, reasoning and author of the letter are unclear, the effect of the letter is not. In the late 1970s, key parents in the JA community came together and decided JA would form its own high school.

In true Deep South style, a football program was immediately put in place for the new high school and Ron Jurney was hired to lead the first Raider team in 1980. During this first season, Jurney had a 21-man team comprised of 12 sophomores, 9 juniors, and 0 seniors (since the new high school had not yet formed a twelfth grade). Jurney's team competed in the smallest division of the private school ranks and finished the season with an unimpressive 4-5 record. In 1981, Jurney took a team with a mere 18 battle-hardened players and produced JA's first undefeated season, going 10-0 and earning a playoff birth in only their second season of play. However, the event that sparked the transformation of Jackson Academy football was not the undefeated season in 1981. In fact, this spark didn't take place on the JA campus, nor did it involve coaches, players or administrators from the school.

In 1981, Brian Baker remembers his father informing him and a group of his friends that their junior high and high school coaches had a disagreement with the administration of their school and were thinking about leaving. Baker and his friends immediately said they would leave, too, and go wherever the coaches were going. The school where this event transpired was the now defunct Brandon Academy, a private school that was located off Highway 80 in Brandon, Mississippi. The head high school football coach involved in the disagreement was Sammy Dantone. More importantly, the head junior high coach who would be leaving with Dantone was Sherard Shaw.

Both Brandon Academy and its collection of coaches are interesting. The small private school was an athletic powerhouse and enjoyed phenomenal success in the mid- to late '70s. They regularly played against, and beat, larger private schools, including Jackson Prep. Brandon Academy won a state title in 1979 under the guidance of Sammy Dantone. They were also producing their own impressive roster of college and professional athletes.

Coach Dantone enjoyed success at Pillow Academy from the '71 to '78 football seasons. During his tenures at Pillow and Brandon Academy, Dantone was joined at the hip with his good friend and assistant coach, John McInnis. Dantone and McInnis regularly traveled the country in search of good coaching clinics and were regulars at Bear Bryant's clinic in Tuscaloosa. The two men were certifiable football junkies. In addition, McInnis was a genius track coach.

Dantone and McInnis were on a constant quest to rub elbows with the famous college coaches that attended the clinics as guest speakers. Both men, but Dantone in particular, were masters at finding their way behind the scenes at these events. Each trip produced quick two-on-one Q&A sessions with the Bear in his office or chalk talk with Joe Paterno over coffee. Some of the encounters resulted in lasting friendships. After meeting Notre Dame's Ara Parseghian at one particular clinic, Dantone actually maintained a phone relationship with him and consulted with the great coach on game plans prior to some of his high school contests.

In 1982, newly formed Jackson Academy called on Dantone. As luck would have it, Dantone was interested in leaving Brandon Academy and Ron Jurney was interested in leaving JA. Jurney's focus at the time was to become a college coach as quickly as possible, and the place where he could best take his next step toward this goal was Brandon Academy. So, in 1982, Dantone and Jurney switched jobs.

When Dantone left Brandon Academy, he asked several of his coaches to come with him, including Sherard Shaw, Phil Sheppard and John McInnis. Both Shaw and Sheppard accepted Dantone's offer and followed him to Jackson Academy. McInnis declined and instead took a job as junior high football coach and head high school track coach at

Jackson Prep.

Just as important as the Brandon Academy coaches who came to JA were the families from Brandon Academy that followed the coaches. Although JA had just completed an undefeated season under Coach Jurney, the team was still small and lacked a sufficient number of talented players. In addition, the school had grown so quickly that it was going to jump from A to AAA in one season – a feat never seen before or since in the private school association. Gone from the schedule were Heidelberg, East Holmes and Woodland Hills. In their place were larger schools, including MRA, Pillow, Washington, Indianola and, possibly, Jackson Prep. An injection of talent from Brandon Academy would certainly help JA immediately field a more competitive team. Some of the key players that transferred to JA included Chris Lawrence, David Dantone, Stennis Wells, Mike Shirley, Scott Coker, Stacy Phillips and Brian Baker. These individuals would ultimately form the backbone of some of Dantone's best Raider football teams.

Brian Baker, who came to JA as an eighth grader in 1982, remembers the transition from Brandon Academy and some of the early days at Jackson Academy:

> We all lived in Brandon and drove past Prep each morning to get to JA. I rode to school with Coach Dantone and his son, David. The reception was phenomenal. It was the best move I ever made in my life school-wise. We developed some fantastic friends. It was kind of like when all those coaches got here, everybody just wanted to work hard for them. We met up here at 5:30 in the morning and lifted weights with Coach Shaw. It's pretty cool when your coaches are as committed as you are and they are coming up here before school and working out with you and meeting you for breakfast.

Dantone, Shaw and Sheppard were the perfect coaching staff for the growing school. The hardworking trio was a stickler for details. Dantone cut and watered the football field constantly and produced what many believe was the prettiest grass in the entire state. Shaw also coached baseball and literally built the baseball field and stadium with his bare hands. In addition, the group was creative. They began a tradition of loading up the team and traveling to Holmes County State

Park for two-a-days. The week-long getaway was one big male bonding trip punctuated by grueling practices during the day and motivational war movies at night. Recalls Dantone, "We started with movies about General Patton and then moved on to the ones featuring Clint Eastwood and Charles Bronson. Coach Shaw could imitate Patton and he wore a little army suit with a steel-potted helmet and a cigar and made speeches to get the guys fired up. It was a really great time and those are great memories."

Dantone and Shaw's creativity spilled over into the pep rallies as well. Dantone remembers a few of their techniques: "I always liked to have very spirited pep rallies when I was at Pillow and at Brandon Academy. When I got to JA, the headmaster, Glenn Cain, was worried that we would go overboard. We had a pep rally where Coach Shaw did his Patton imitation and the students went wild. We had another one where we turned off all the lights in the gym and had a fake funeral procession for the Raider football player. Then the player came to life, jumped out of the coffin in his jersey and fired a shotgun filled with blanks. You couldn't get away with that now, but it sure was great then."

While Dantone was molding the high school team, Shaw was leading the junior high squad, which featured a number of the transfers from Brandon Academy. In 1982, JA's eighth and ninth-grade team went undefeated and un-scored upon. The following year the team maintained the streak. Brian Baker remembers the final game of the season his ninth-grade year:

> We were absolutely blowing people out every game. Whenever an opponent crossed the 50, Coach Shaw called the whole team over and told us, "It's time to buckle up and get at it." He challenged us and we responded. Coach Shaw had us all 100 percent convinced that we were unbeatable and that no one was ever going to score on us. In the last game of the season, we put our second string defense in toward the end of the game, and their running back broke a long touchdown run with only minutes remaining. We won the game, but everyone was crying in the locker room after the game. Coach Shaw was upset, crying and hugging everyone. We just had a great relationship and great time with Coach Shaw. He was meant to be a coach.

The following season in 1984, Coach Shaw's juggernaut junior high team would move up to the high school and it would mark the first year that the entire group of Brandon Academy transfers was on the same team. Dantone felt good about his team, but there were two components he needed to address: uniforms and a punter. Dantone is a well-known uniform connoisseur and had made great looking uniforms a priority at all his previous coaching stops. At Pillow Academy, Dantone relentlessly tracked down the secret formula and ingredients used to paint the gold helmets at the University of Notre Dame. Once he secured both items, he turned his garage into a paint shop and individually painted every Pillow helmet until it was a perfect match with the Fighting Irish. Since Brandon Academy was also green and gold, Dantone used the same technique there as well. He even went so far as to match Notre Dame's 1970's high-rise hip pads and belts. In fact, Dantone got to know the equipment manager at Notre Dame so well that he placed some of his orders along with the Irish. According to Dantone, one of his orders was even mistakenly paid for by Notre Dame.

Dantone recalls that upon arriving at JA, his tendency toward uniforms was so well established that JA's headmaster, Glenn Cain, made a point to tell him that JA was blue and silver and Dantone wasn't allowed to spray any of the helmets Notre Dame gold. Dantone complied and instead sprayed them silver, using the same secret process. Before the 1984 season, he perfectly matched the Dallas Cowboys uniforms and substituted Dallas's famous star on the helmet with the now familiar JA logo.

With sharp new uniforms neatly stored in the Raider equipment room, Dantone now only needed to find a punter before the start of the 1984 season. During spring training, a junior-to-be named Tony Shell caught Dantone's eye. Dantone begged Shell to come out and punt, but Shell was reluctant because he didn't want to get hurt and miss baseball season. Always persistent, Dantone finally convinced Shell to come out only to punt, which he did for the first two games in 1984. However, after a couple of weeks, Dantone caught a glimpse of Shell's arm and his God-given talent for throwing the ball. "I immediately put Tony at quarterback and moved the current quarterback to tailback," said Dantone.

Little did Dantone realize what he had found in Shell. After graduating from JA, Shell earned a football scholarship to Mississippi State, where he directed the Bulldog's offense. But that would come later. In 1984, Dantone, Shell, Shaw, the Brandon Academy transfers and the rest of the Dallas Cowboy-looking Raiders posted a 9-1 regular season record in the competitive AAA division. After avenging their only regular season loss with a come-from-behind win over MRA in the playoffs, Jackson Academy catapulted itself into its first state championship game.

The game would be played at JA against a nearby school the Raiders had yet to face at any level in football.

****

When Jackson Academy started playing football in 1980, it didn't play Jackson Prep, because the schools were of vastly different size and, thus, in different divisions. In 1982, Jackson Academy had grown significantly and moved to the AAA size classification – the same as Prep. However, the two schools still did not play. The reason why varies depending on whom you ask.

Says Jackson Prep's second head football coach and athletic director, Buddy Crosby, "JA had the numbers to move up to AAA a year earlier, but they lobbied to stay A. When they did finally move up to AAA, they lobbied to be in the north since Prep was in the south. They didn't want to play us."

JA's Sammy Dantone remembers the situation differently. "The MPSA put us in the north because they wanted to prevent us from playing Prep in the regular season. The thought was that there were too many families that had high school kids at Prep and elementary kids at JA, and making the two schools play each other in football would just be too tough on the families. The only way we were going to meet on the football field was in the championship game."

Regardless of why JA and Prep did not play in the regular season, it didn't take long for the two schools to find each other in the playoffs. In 1984, both teams made it to the AAA championship game and set up the first contest of what would quickly become one of the state's best high school football rivalries.

No individual has been as closely involved with every JA-Prep football game as Will Crosby, son of former Prep head coach Buddy Crosby. Will now serves as an assistant football coach and athletic director for the Patriots and was in junior high the night JA and Prep played for the first time. "I remember that first game at JA in 1984 for the championship. It was really cold and the stadium was packed. I was just a naïve junior high kid going to the game and I remember thinking, We are about to kill them. We kill everybody. We're Prep."

So both teams entered the stadium – Prep, confident in its already rich tradition and athletic success laid by the legendary Jack Carlisle, and JA, an upstart bursting with adrenalin resulting from the motivational techniques of Dantone and Shaw. Families were tightly packed in JA's small stands and crowded deep around the fence line. The stadium was a powder keg of anticipation, everyone knowing that this inevitable train wreck would certainly change allegiances and friendships through northeast Jackson communities forever.

JA received the opening kick-off. Keith Parker, JA's resident tough guy, carried out the instructions given to him by Coach Dantone, "Take out the first Prep player you see coming down the field." Parker annihilated Prep's kicker and opened up a gaping hole in the middle of Prep's kickoff coverage. JA's Stacy Phillips fielded the kick, found the hole created by Parker's vicious lick and raced all the way to the end zone. The JA-Prep football rivalry had barely been alive 10 seconds and JA had already snagged a surprising 6-0 lead. Then the play was brought back. It seems that the introduction of Keith Parker's shoulder to the Prep kicker's face was a bit less cordial than the referee preferred. The somewhat controversial penalty was actually an appropriate way for the rivalry to begin, as future contests between the two teams produced plenty of debatable calls and questionable strategies.

As the game settled into a rhythm, Coach Buddy Crosby employed his usual multiple-front defensive strategy and Dantone countered with four wide receivers and the arm of Tony Shell. The game was a tightly contested match until Prep put up a late touchdown and put the game out of reach. Final score: Prep 21, JA 6.

After the game, Will Crosby remembers finding his father on the field:

> I remember two things pretty vividly. First, I remember thinking the game was far closer than I anticipated, and JA was really pretty good. Second, I remember seeing my dad. He's not a very emotional guy. He does not wear his emotions on his sleeve, but I will never forget the smile on his face after the game. He came up and gave me the biggest hug. I thought, I've never seen him this happy. I think he understood

the significance of the game. I think he probably knew where this rivalry was headed. He knew that one day JA and Prep were going to play in every sport every year. He understood and felt the significance of that first win.

The following season JA and Prep did not play because neither team made it out of the playoffs into the championship game. In 1986, the MPSA shuffled teams around and JA was moved to the south division with Prep. This move guaranteed that the teams would meet in the regular season from here on. The first regular season game was also played at JA and featured a defensive struggle in the mud. Prep led the game late 3-0 when JA's stud place-kicker, Sean Tracy, missed a difficult field goal that would have tied the game. Prep escaped Raider stadium with its second victory in the rivalry.

Prep's Buddy Crosby understood the importance of this blossoming rivalry and the urgency of Prep gaining quick control over all aspects of it. According to the elder Crosby, "The more success JA had, the more confidence they gained. All of a sudden, they thought they could beat us. Like I used to tell my guys, 'Let's just beat the hell out of them early and get it over, because if you let them stay in there and start thinking they're pretty dad gum good, then towards the end they are fighting for their lives and you are, too.'" Crosby continues his reflection on the rivalry:

> As athletic director, I just hoped something didn't explode at one of those games. It was just so intense, especially with the parents. I used to say, "I wish this son of a gun would hurry up and get over with so that everyone would get home safely." It got to the point that it wasn't fun at all. I think back to my high school days when Laurel and Hattiesburg played for the Little Brown Jug the day after Thanksgiving. You looked forward to 2:00 on that afternoon when the two towns came together. When the game was over, the two towns parted and went back to their respective homes 30 miles apart. But with JA and Prep, everyone lived and worked right on top of each another. There was no separation and you could never get away from the rivalry. It made it that much more intense. I never really looked forward to the JA game. I didn't feel like we had anything to gain. We were supposed to win, and if we

didn't, we were considered a total loser and they were king of the hill. All they had to do was play well against us, and it was considered a victory for them and a loss for us.

Randy Rucker succeeded Crosby in 1987. Rucker's teams racked up a couple more wins over Dantone's Raiders. In 1989, Kim Alsop became head coach at Jackson Academy. The same year, Prep promoted their junior high football coach to the head coaching position. That junior high coach was Dantone's old buddy from Pillow and Brandon Academy, Coach John McInnis. More than any other coach on either side of this rivalry, McInnis' teams absolutely laid the wood to JA. During his eight years as Prep's head coach, McInnis' Patriots outscored JA 265-93 and produced the series' most lopsided victory in 1991 when Prep beat JA 54-0. At the time of this shellacking, Prep's win streak over JA had grown to seven, and JA had still yet to notch a victory in the series.

McInnis' success can be explained from a couple of different perspectives. Jackson Academy athletic director Bobby West recalls the coaching style of JA's new head coach, Kim Alsop:

> Coach Alsop was strictly professional; there was no rah-rah to him. He tried to make the game with Prep just another game. He wanted everyone to keep a very even keel from week to week and never get overly excited about any one particular game. After Coach Alsop left, it was almost comical to think about his efforts in trying to make the kids believe this was just another game; because it wasn't just another game; it's never been just another game and it never will be.

Prep's athletic director, Will Crosby, believes JA's desire to beat Prep began working against them. He says,

> It was clear they wanted to beat us so bad, and every time they lost, it just made the following year's game that much more critical. The pressure really started mounting and the monkey on their back just kept getting bigger and bigger. Any little mistake injected doubt into their minds. What people don't realize is that the monkey on our back was getting bigger, too.

Players and coaches at Prep began to feel the pressure
of keeping the streak alive. People tightened up a little
bit and started thinking, At some point they are going to
win. My God, I can't let it happen while I'm playing.

In 1994, Jackson Academy replaced Kim Alsop as head football
coach and found in his successor a familiar face – Sherard Shaw. Only
three years earlier, Shaw had been out of coaching, selling insurance.
However, Shaw's competitive spirit and desire to coach, coupled with
JA's need for a junior high coach, led Shaw to return to his old post with
the Raider's junior high squad. After coaching the junior high team for
two seasons, Shaw was then promoted to the head high school position.
Shaw was born to be a coach, and this particular job was meant to be
his.

When Shaw took over as head coach, there was really little
doubt what his mission was: beat Jackson Prep. Assistant coach David
Blount reflects on Shaw's approach to coaching the Raiders: "First of all,
I've never seen a coach more loved by his players than Sherard Shaw.
Second, I've never been around someone so passionate about beating
Jackson Prep." Unlike Alsop before him, Shaw knew the game with
Prep was not just another game and he didn't pretend to treat it like one.
After all, Shaw was a product of the Sammy Dantone coaching tree, and
motivational ploys were a coaching tool with which he had extensive
experience. Before one particular game, Coach Shaw loaded up the
entire team and took them to a field out in Byram for practice. There he
installed a brand new offense for the game. Relocating the practice was
partly to keep the new offense secret, but mostly to get in the players'
heads. Shaw was a master motivator, and under his direction, the future
of JA football was extremely bright and promising.

In late 1994, JA President, Peter Jernberg, was in San Antonio
when he received a phone call from a close friend. The caller told Jernberg,
"Peter, this is not good news. Sherard Shaw has been diagnosed with
cancer of the esophagus. It's aggressive. Very few people survive this."
Jernberg remembers getting off the phone and immediately breaking
down.

Unfortunately, the caller's assessment of the situation was
accurate and Coach Shaw began treatment for the cancer. The treatment
and the wicked disease itself took their toll on the ultimate players'
coach, but the ever-committed Shaw still made it to practice during

the 1995 season. When Shaw was not present, assistant coach David Blount led the team. When Shaw returned to practice weakened by his treatments, he sat on the field in a lawn chair and the team gathered around him for instructions. The instructions were clearly good ones, as Shaw's 1995 Raiders were unbeaten and unscored upon when they entered the regular season match-up with Prep. Before the game, Shaw entered the locker room, clearly in the latter stages of his fight with cancer, and mustered the strength to give a pep talk to the team. This was many of the young players' first time to compete against Prep. Sadly, it would be Shaw's last.

In an emotional battle played on their home field, Jackson Academy lost for an eleventh straight time to their cross-town rivals. The consensus among those who watched the game is that JA had the better team, but the heavy hearts carried onto the field that night by the Raider players were just enough to prevent them from securing the victory. Final score: Prep 10, JA 7.

JA was able to regroup after the loss to Prep and win the remainder of its games, but in the final game of the regular season, Jackson Academy played at home against two-time defending state champion Parklane Academy. The Pioneers entered the contest with a 25-game winning streak, and after a tough defensive struggle against the Raiders, left with a 26-game winning streak. Four days after JA's regular season ended in defeat, Sherard Shaw died.

Despite their loss to Parklane, Jackson Academy still earned a spot in the postseason. In a twist of high school football playoff fate, JA's first round opponent was Parklane, but this time the game would be played in McComb, and it would be played only three days after Shaw's death. Similar to the game played seven days before, this was a closely contested game that carried a 0-0 score late into the fourth quarter. Parklane had been shutting down JA's bread-and-butter toss sweep all night, but Coach Blount stuck with the play and kept feeding running back Jeffery Lohmeier the ball. On a carry late in the fourth quarter, Lohmeier once again carried the ball around the left end and was immediately dropped by Parklane defenders. However, on his way to the ground, Lohmeier landed on a Parklane defender, spun back to his feet and raced down the sideline and into the end zone. Final score: JA 7, Parklane 0. The miraculous run set up a semifinal game with Jackson Prep.

Unlike the regular season game, the playoff game with Prep

would be played at the Patriots' stadium. Unlike the regular season game, Coach Shaw was not with his Raider team. Unlike the previous 11 games between the two teams, JA would refuse to allow Prep's winning streak to reach 12 games. On a memorable night in November of 1995, JA made the series with Prep a true rivalry, honored its heroic fallen coach and captured a 21-7 victory over Jackson Prep. The following week, the Raider team completed the story by beating Carroll Academy 14-7 to earn JA its first state championship.

Brian Eubanks, current radio broadcaster for Raider athletics and 1993 graduate of Jackson Prep, remembers his reaction to JA's first victory: "It was heartbreaking when Coach Shaw passed away. I actually cheered hard for JA to win that game against Prep. I cheered even though I was a Prep graduate. You couldn't help but want those kids to win."

The win was a watershed moment in Jackson Academy's history. It finally eliminated the gigantic monkey that had been clinging to JA's back since the first meeting between the two in 1984. The JA victory also took pressure off the students and coaches at Prep who had been feeling the pressure of maintaining the streak each year. Of course no one at Prep wanted to lose, but the great admiration that everyone felt for Coach Shaw made the loss palatable. In addition, Prep was returning what many considered to be the most talented team in school history for the 1996 season, and focus was already being shifted forward.

The 1996 season saw Jackson Prep get right back on track as it rolled over teams in the regular season. The Patriots put up points at an unprecedented pace and smoked through the season undefeated, highlighted by double-digit blowout victories over Jackson Academy and Trinity High School in Dallas, Texas. Constantly in the shadow of the talented Prep team, JA flew under the radar all season and clawed its way back to the championship game played at Prep. Those who attended the game fully expected JA's performance against Prep to be the equivalent of a feather pillow being tossed into a wood chipper. But JA coach David Blount developed an outstanding game plan, and the remnants of Shaw's 1995 championship team executed it flawlessly. Final score: JA 14, Prep 7.

JA's 1996 win over Prep in the championship game is widely considered the biggest football upset in the history of the MPSA. The effect of the game on the JA-Prep rivalry was even greater. Unlike Prep's loss to JA the previous year, this one really hurt. Possibly for the first time in Prep's football history, it began to doubt itself. The following season, Prep hired Ricky Black as its new head coach and the rivalry entered a new era of competitiveness.

A number of interesting trends in the rivalry began in 1995. First, the 1995 season was the first time in series history that JA and Prep played twice in one season (once in the regular season and once in the playoffs). In fact, they played twice a year nine times from 1995-2007. Second, the heightened competitiveness between JA and Prep helped strengthen both programs. The two schools have distanced themselves from every other private school in the state and have dominated the league now for over a decade. From 1995 through 2007, every MPSA football championship game except one has featured either the Patriots or Raiders. Prep has won five championships during that period and JA has won six. They have played each other for the championship seven times during that span. In 2001, JA promoted its junior high coach, Joey Hawkins, to the high school position and promptly won four championships in five years. Similar to Coach Black, his counterpart at Jackson Prep, Hawkins has now coached more years at JA than any other coach and has achieved more wins and championships as well.

The growing intensity of the rivalry has also led to increased student activity and controversy, both on and off the field. As the schools matured, more and more families in northeast Jackson were divided. Just because a student lived next door to one of the high schools didn't necessarily mean he would attend that school. Most of the students have cars because of the relatively high income level of their families and are able to transport themselves to the school of their choosing. The widespread availability of cars also led to the development of what the students dubbed "Fight Night."

While the exact origins of Fight Night are unclear, the protocol is not. On the Thursday night before the JA-Prep football game and after JA's big bonfire, several dozen students (typically seniors) drive to the Eastover neighborhood in northeast Jackson. Dressed in camouflage and armed with paintball guns, shaving cream, water balloons, eggs and toilet paper, participants prowl the neighborhood streets in an effort to hunt each other down. If JA students can identify a car as belonging to a Prep student, then it becomes a victim of semi good-natured vandalism. Predictably, the activities of Fight Night produce some collateral damage. When the yards and property of any of Eastover's million dollar homes begin feeling the fury of Fight Night, an officer of the Jackson Police Department is usually dispatched to break up the activities. The administrations and coaches from both schools frown on the whole concept of Fight Night, but the lure of the tradition seems to entice just enough participants to keep it alive each year.

Prep football player Scott McVey lives in the middle of the Fight Night zone. With four older brothers and sisters who are Prep graduates, Scott and his house have lived through plenty of Fight Nights. Says McVey,

> I know most everyone that is involved in Fight Night. My cousin Scott Gresham is a Raider Rowdy (JA's male cheerleaders) and one of the JA cheerleaders lives a couple houses down from my family. On the night before the JA Prep game, she can basically walk out of her house, come down to my house and vandalize it and it's acceptable. That has to be the only day of the year you could do that and get away with it.

The spirit of Fight Night sometimes spills over to the Friday morning of the game when students from Prep form a large caravan and parade down the neighborhood street that runs right in front of Jackson Academy. However, it only took a year or two of this activity before the JA students began lying in wait for the caravan. Armed with their own water balloons and garden hoses cranked up to full force, JA students quickly put an end to Prep's caravan tradition.

The students from both JA and Prep are smart, tech-savvy and very creative. The pep rallies they produce would impress even Coach Dantone and Shaw. Students gather video footage specifically for their pep rallies for this game. The footage is edited by the students into an adrenaline rush highlight reel set to current music and then shown on two large projectors in the packed gyms at the respective pep rallies. Videos may include highlights from recent games against their rival, scenes from Fight Night or even footage of one of Prep's guy cheerleaders running through one of JA's practices with a Prep flag. Videos are often built around movie themes such as *Braveheart* or *300*, and then coordinated with dances choreographed by the cheerleaders. Some videos, like the one JA produced for its 2007 championship game against Prep, include embedded video messages from celebrities such as Deuce McAllister and sports performance specialist and Prep graduate, Paul Lacoste.

The JA-Prep rivalry could thrive based on physical proximity and championship implications alone, but add the thrill and controversy of on-the-field events as well, and the rivalry explodes in super nova fashion. In just the past five years, the JA-Prep game has produced numerous moments that fall into the all-time-greatest category. In the 2003 championship game, JA came back from a 21-0 deficit at halftime to force the game into overtime and then win the game. In 2007, Prep returned the favor by scoring on a Hail Mary pass on the final play of the game to force overtime and subsequently win the game. JA fans still swear that the muddy field conditions at Prep for the regular season game in 2002 were the result of Prep constantly running fire hoses and a team of Clydesdales over the field all week. Of course, the Prep staff adamantly denies this allegation and reminds the JA folks of the six tons of Diamond Dry that were dumped on the field in an attempt to get it ready for the game.

Says Prep's Ricky Black,

Managing this rivalry is a real challenge. With most other rivalries, there is some distance between the two communities. You live in one town and your rival lives in another. But here, there is no dividing line. Even households have students at both schools. So families sit around the dinner table and talk about those devils at JA, but then they have one sitting right next to them living under the same roof. It's so intermingled that it's a real family feud. If it's not brothers and sisters competing against one another, it's at least cousins and neighbors. Losing this game is devastating because you can't get away from your opponent. You have to live with it every day. You go to a law firm and half the attorneys have kids at JA and the other half have kids at Prep. Heck, the team doctors for JA and Prep are in the same office. You couldn't find a better fan than JA's radio guy, Brian Eubanks. He hates us and he is a Prep graduate! To me, this is the most intense rivalry I have ever been a part of, and because there are no district lines, it is also the most difficult rivalry to manage. There's simply no escaping it.

WHAT THE PATRIOTS SAY ABOUT JACKSON ACADEMY

When it comes to Prep, JA has an inferiority complex.

Coach Buddy Crosby

Former Prep Head Football Coach and Athletic Director

In the early years when I first got here, they called us "Flowood Tech." Of course, Flowood was not nearly the city it is now. They don't do that anymore, since Flowood is one of the richest cities in Mississippi.

Coach Ricky Black

Jackson Prep Head Football Coach

I've noticed a difference in the attitude of the students when we play someone other than JA for the championship. They still play hard and it's important, but you can tell they really want to be playing JA.

Susan Lindsay

Jackson Prep Headmaster

The cheerleaders from both schools get together and have a dinner before the game on Friday. It's kind of fake in a way. Everybody pretends to be friends, and then you get back to being enemies at the game.

Rachael Borne

Jackson Prep Cheerleader

Cheerleaders aren't really allowed to participate in Fight Night. It's not very classy and the police sometimes get involved. It wouldn't look very good for a cheerleader to get arrested.

Alice Blackmon

Jackson Prep Cheerleader

Our team focuses on making plays in the game. JA focuses on making excuses.

Scott McVey

Jackson Prep Football Player

I'll never forget Cory McGee's performance against us in 2003. We were up 21-0 in the second half and then he just took over. That probably has to be one of their greatest victories ever.

Coach Ricky Black

Jackson Prep Head Football Coach

This game is more competitive than others are because it often involves people in the same households. It's one room in the house versus another room down the hall.

Susan Lindsay

Jackson Prep Headmaster

It was mainly the JA students who were rolling people's houses on Fight Night. We have a lot more class. They even rolled Coach Black's house, and that's totally unacceptable.

Alice Blackmon

Jackson Prep Cheerleader

WHAT THE RAIDERS SAY ABOUT JACKSON PREP

I cannot imagine a football season without Jackson Prep on our schedule. I absolutely cannot. There would be a void in life and a void in our school year.

Peter Jernberg

Jackson Academy President

The coaches they've had at Prep are just incredible – starting with Carlisle and then on to McInnis and Black. Buddy Crosby is a distant cousin of mine. I mean, have they ever had a bad year?

David Blount

Former Jackson Academy Head Football Coach

I lived in Rankin County when I first started coaching at JA, so I would drive through the Prep parking lot the week of the game to make sure nothing happened the night before. I was trying to prevent that call from Buddy Crosby that start's off, "Guess what your kids have done?"

Bill Bunch

Former Jackson Academy Assistant Football Coach

This rivalry has grown significantly in the past 10 to 12 years because JA has risen to a level of competitiveness that makes it possible for either team to win almost every time we play.

Bobby West

Jackson Academy Athletic Director

When the rivalry first started, so many families were caught straddling the fence. The whole thing was just so explosive and I don't think anyone really knew how to handle it.

Joey Hawkins

Jackson Academy Head Football Coach

This is the game you look forward to all year. Even during the season when you are supposed to only be thinking about the game that week, you're still thinking about Prep. You can't stop thinking about it.

Bobby Peterson

Jackson Academy Football Player

Our daughter Holly is 11 and is a Raider to the core. We drive down Lakeland and she holds her breath when we pass Prep.

Kim Hawkins

Wife of Jackson Academy Head Football Coach

If Prep wasn't on our schedule, things would be miserable around here. What would we have to look forward to?

Tommy Blair

Jackson Academy Booster Club President

Prep Week is such a big deal. When the football schedule comes out, the first question everyone asks is "When do we play Prep?"

Casey Chinn

Jackson Academy Cheerleader

When I first got to JA, I wrote everything down in a big playbook. I quit doing that because it didn't take long for the Prep kids to get their hands on it. They were always over at the homes of the JA kids.

Joey Hawkins

Jackson Academy Head Football Coach

If Prep didn't exist, JA wouldn't be as good as it is, and vice versa. Both schools make the other better.

Joey Hawkins

Jackson Academy Head Football Coach

Year	Prep	Score	JA
1984*	Buddy Crosby	21-6	Sammy Dantone
1985	Buddy Crosby	*Did Not Play*	Sammy Dantone
1986	Buddy Crosby	3-0	Sammy Dantone
1987	Randy Rucker	20-10	Sammy Dantone
1988	Randy Rucker	21-0	Sammy Dantone
1989	John McInnis	38-9	Kim Alsop
1990	John McInnis	42-7	Kim Alsop
1991	John McInnis	54-0	Kim Alsop
1992	John McInnis	42-7	Kim Alsop
1993	John McInnis	17-7	Kim Alsop
1994	John McInnis	24-14	Sherard Shaw
1995	John McInnis	10-7	Sherard Shaw
1995*	John McInnis	7-21	Sherard Shaw
1996	John McInnis	24-0	David Blount
1996*	John McInnis	7-14	David Blount
1997	Ricky Black	21-0	David Blount
1998	Ricky Black	0-7	David Blount
1998*	Ricky Black	28-12	David Blount
1999	Ricky Black	30-14	David Blount
2000	Ricky Black	14-0	David Blount
2001	Ricky Black	21-20	Joey Hawkins
2001*	Ricky Black	7-12	Joey Hawkins
2002	Ricky Black	14-6	Joey Hawkins
2002*	Ricky Black	21-3	Joey Hawkins
2003	Ricky Black	28-21	Joey Hawkins
2003*	Ricky Black	24-27	Joey Hawkins
2004	Ricky Black	24-34	Joey Hawkins
2004*	Ricky Black	0-21	Joey Hawkins
2005	Ricky Black	23-28	Joey Hawkins
2005*	Ricky Black	8-29	Joey Hawkins
2006	Ricky Black	28-7	Joey Hawkins
2007	Ricky Black	24-6	Joey Hawkins
2007*	Ricky Black	17-10	Joey Hawkins

* *Playoff Game*

★★OFFICIAL GAME DAY PROGRAM $5.00★★

TUPELO
VERSUS
STARKVILLE

BancorpSouth®
Member FDIC

Right Where You Are

PROUD SPONSOR OF MISSISSIPPI HIGH SCHOOL FOOTBALL

FRIDAY, OCTOBER 3, 2008 ★ 7:00 PM KICKOFF

YELLOW JACKET FIELD ★ STARKVILLE, MISSISSIPPI

CHAPTER

10

BULL'S-EYE

The old football stadium used to be located on Church Street in a little neighborhood nestled inside the city limits of Tupelo. Parking for the fans attending games at Robbins Field was very limited; only 160 spaces were available. Most everybody parked on the streets surrounding the stadium and walked to the game. The demand for Golden Wave home football game tickets was overwhelming. Season ticket holders gobbled up the entire home side, along with the seats between the 30-yard lines on the visitor's side. Ricky Black, Tupelo's head football coach from 1980 through 1990, recalls the rush for Golden Wave tickets while he was at Tupelo. Black says, "Every seat on the home side was sold out to season ticket holders and so were over half the seats on the visitor's side. If you came from Starkville to see the Yellow Jackets play Tupelo, you only had seats from the goal line to the 30 on each end of the visitor's side. Tupelo fans divided the visitors' seating down the middle."

Veteran Starkville assistant football coach, Danny Carlisle, recalls taking his Yellow Jacket teams to Robbins Field at Noble Stadium to play Tupelo:

The dressing room was so small we had to dress in shifts. We sent about 20 of our players at a time to get dressed. The rest of the team waited in the parking lot. The field and the stadium were just awful. Tupelo sold reserved seats to the season ticket holders. Not only did those tickets cover the home side, they sold out half the visitor's side, too. One year, a bunch of our fans got to the stadium early so they could get good seats on the 50-yard line. About 15 minutes before kickoff, all those Tupelo people with reserved seats arrived holding their tickets. Our fans were sitting in the seats. I could hear the yelling and shouting down on the field: "I got here first" and "I've got my ticket." Finally, security had to come and break 'em up and move the Starkville fans out of the reserved seats. To make matters worse, when Starkville fans walked up to the stadium, Tupelo people sitting at the top of the bleachers on the visitor's side threw eggs at them. They had to dodge and duck as they approached the stadium. I guess it was kids, but it might have been adults throwing the eggs.

Since the seating at Robbins Field was limited and the crowds that attended the home football games were well beyond the seating capacity, it wasn't unusual for spectators to stand behind the fence around the field. When Tupelo was hosting a big game opponent, or if it was the annual homecoming game, there could be as many as ten deep around the fence. The result was a packed stadium with an exciting football atmosphere.

The atmosphere at Robbins Field on game nights was electric for Tupelo players, the players on the opposing teams and all the fans in the stadium. However, the time eventually came in the early '90s to upgrade or replace Robbins Field to accommodate the growing number of Golden Wave fans. As the Tupelo football program started gaining more and more success on the field, there was increasing momentum to upgrade the facility or possibly build a new stadium.

Ricky Black was leading the Tupelo football program at the time of the rising popularity of the Golden Wave on the gridiron. He constantly pushed for improvements to Robbins Field or the construction of a new stadium. Shortly after Richard Thompson took over as the superintendent for the Tupelo schools, which occurred in the middle of Black's push for stadium improvements or replacement, Thompson voiced his agreement with Black. Consequently, Superintendent Thompson appointed a committee to study the matter and awaited its recommendations. As months passed, the committee presented its findings and recommended the construction of a new stadium. Thompson's reaction shocked Coach Black and the other members of the study committee. Black recalls, "Mr. Thompson not only endorsed the idea to build a new football stadium, but he went a step further and said, 'Man, we've got a lot of support and enthusiasm from the community for the new stadium. Let's just build a new school. We can build both.'" Of course, Coach Black was fine with a new school, just as long as the Golden Wave got its new stadium.

As good fortune would have it, a local businessman and Golden

An official state marker in Yazoo City commemorates the first high school football game played in Mississippi. Yazoo City defeated Winona 5-0 in 1905.

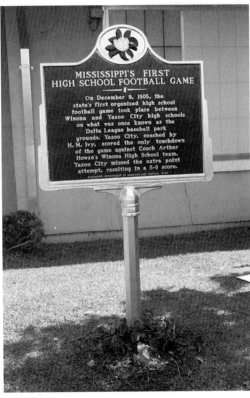

C.B. Cameron, founder of the famous Big Eight Conference - the crucible of many of Mississippi's greatest high school football rivalries.

**BRANDON
BULLDOGS**

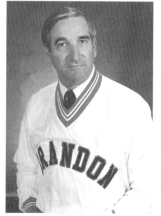

Coach Dan Davis and future NFL running back, Jerious Norwood.

Coach Wally Bumpas.

Louis Gene Strickland Field.

Mr. Pirate, Ray Rogers.

Indoctrination could hardly begin any earlier at Pearl.

Pearl's first captains, Rogers and Dunnam.

Left to Right: Principal Ray Morgigno, Coach Perry Liles, Ray Rogers, Coach Woody Barnett.

The 1949 Pearl Pirates.

WEST JONES
MUSTANGS

Adam Herrington, son of West Jones' principal Mark Herrington, nails the winning field goal for the Mustangs in 2007.

Mustang head coach, Scott Pierson, preparing his troops.

West Jones students honor the Wayne County "War Chickens" by wearing Kentucky Fried Chicken buckets on their heads.

WAYNE COUNTY
WAR EAGLES

Wayne County head coaches: Bubba Davis, Bobby Hall, and Marcus Boyles

The pride of Wayne County:
War Eagle Stadium.

Former mayor of Waynesboro, Marshall
Wood, stands with one of the city's police
cars, painted blue and orange in honor of
the War Eagles.

**BROOKHAVEN
PANTHERS**

Tucker Peavey and his Panther coaching staff.

Coin toss before the Thanksgiving Day classic.

Graveyard next to the Brookhaven campus.

Panthers celebrating a victory over McComb.

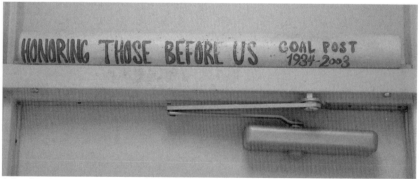

A piece of the old goal post above the locker room door reminds players of their program's history.

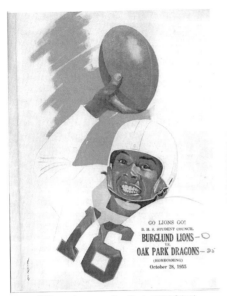

Vintage 1955 game day program from Burglund High School.

McComb's Coach Randy Martin and Principal Dr. Sharon Slater-Smith.

Thanksgiving Day action in McComb.

Former Tiger greats: 1959 graduate Louis Guy and 1945 graduate David McIntosh.

LAFAYETTE
COMMODORES

This post outside University
Sporting Goods in downtown
Oxford keeps track of game scores
between Lafayette and Oxford.

Lafayette vs. Oxford, circa 1970.

Perry, Jimmy, and Alan Arrington.

OXFORD
CHARGERS

Coach Johnny Hill works with his passing attack.

Coach Johnny Hill.

The Charger offense on the move against Lafayette.

WARREN CENTRAL
VIKINGS

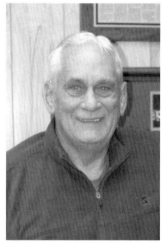

Coach Lum Wright.

The joy of beating Vicksburg.

In the Viking equipment room. Coach Robert Morgan with author Mike Frascogna, Jr. holding old helmets from Culkin and Jett.

Members of the most feared defensive
unit in the state in 1991, Vicksburg's
"Swamp Thing."
Photo Courtesy of the Vicksburg Post.

Bumper stickers display the closeness
of the Gator program.

The Pride of Vicksburg

VHS

We Are Family

Alonzo Stevens is the only Vicksburg coach to taste victory more than once against Warren Central.

**BONNEVILLE
BLUE DEVILS**

Standing beneath the Jim Drewry Drive street sign in Booneville, Mississippi, is the Blue Devil coaching staff. From left to right: Mike Mattox, Jim Drewry, Riley Presley, and Rick Coggin.

48-Sweep has been the bread-and-butter play of the Blue Devils under Jim Drewry for so many years that virtually everyone in Booneville can run it or teach it.

BALDWYN
BEARCATS

Coach Jimmy Dillinger and his Bearcat coaching staff.

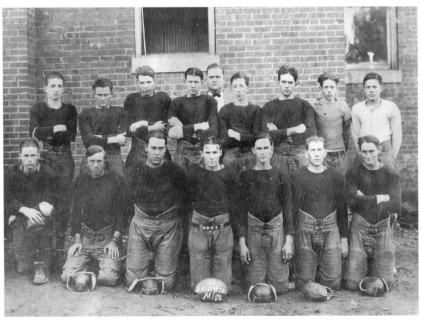

One of the earliest Baldwyn football teams.

GREENE COUNTY
WILDCATS

Off-season workouts in Leakesville, MS.

Coach Johnny Ainsworth leads the Wildcats out for the state championship game in Jackson.

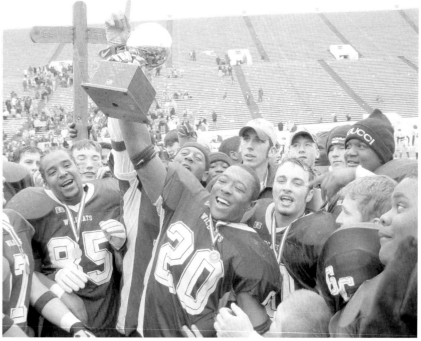

Greene County captured the 3A state title in 2003.

George County's Al Jones and Greene County's Johnny Ainsworth regularly put their rivalry aside for a meal together at Rock Creek Catfish Restaurant.

Virtually the entire city of Lucedale traveled to Jackson to support the Rebels during their run at the 5A championship in 2007.

JACKSON PREP
PATRIOTS

Coach Buddy Crosby led Jackson Prep to victory over JA in the first ever meeting in 1984.

Coach John McInnis, the man
responsible for the most lopsided
wins in the series.

Prep's touchdown catch on the final play of regulation in
the 2007 championship game against JA. The score forced
overtime in a game the Raiders had led the entire way.
Prep ultimately won the game and extended their overall
winning streak to 25 games.

Coach Ricky Black and his truckload of championship trophies.

Dedicated to Coach Shaw, the Raider statue greets visitors at the entrance of the stadium.

Sammy Dantone led the Raiders to their first ever championship game in his third season as the Raider's head coach.

A commemorative plaque immortalizes Coach Sherard Shaw on the Jackson Academy campus.

**TUPELO
GOLDEN WAVE**

Tupelo quarterback, Chris Garrett.

Tupelo students leave no doubt about their feelings.

The most popular t-shirt on campus during Starkville week.

A more sensitive version of the popular t-shirt.

Tupelo's head coach from 1991-1995, James "Booty" Sloan.

Starkville head coach, Bill Lee.

A ball carrier is swarmed under by the Yellow Jacket defense.

Victory celebrations are commonplace in Starkville.

**PASCAGOULA
PANTHERS**

A stiff defensive effort earned Scott Sisson's Panthers a 20-10 victory in 2007.

Coach Bill Matthews' 1987 Panther's set the standard by which all other Pascagoula teams will be measured.

Graduates of Pascagoula and Moss Point combine their efforts to produce warships for the U.S. Navy at the Northrop Grumman shipyard in Pascagoula, Mississippi. The shipyard is a fertile environment for discussions about high school football.

The Moss Point Tigers.

A 1990 graduate of Moss Point, coach Lewis Sims will jump from the role of assistant to head coach of the Tigers in 2008.

Coach Jerry Alexander.

Coach Billy Wayne Miller.

ACKERMAN
INDIANS

A 1978 graduate of Ackerman, Coach Ricky Woods was the head coach at Eupora before returning to his alma mater where he produced multiple championships. Woods later left for South Panola where he began their run of 5 straight state titles.

A school display dedicated to the 1947 team.

An early Indian team in their offensive formation.

E U P O R A
E A G L E S

Silver football commemorating Eupora's landmark victory over Ackerman in 1953.

1956 Choctaw Conference Champion Eupora Eagles.

Metal chair from where William Foots Ford used to enjoy watching his Eupora Eagles.

Mr. William Foots Ford.

Coach Will Roberson and Coach Robert Lightsey oversee junior high off-season training.

Willis Wright: considered by many to be the best high school football coach in Mississippi.

The 2007 team, owners of a 5th straight state championship and a national best 75-game winning streak.

From left to right: Dr. Gearl Loden, Willis Wright, Lance Pogue and Dr. Keith Schaffer.

Students from the "University."

Record-setting Conquistador running back, Sammy Jones.

From left to right: Principal Kyle Brigance, Greg "Buz" Phillips,
Coach Leslie Pool and Coach Scott Samsell.

The state-of-the-art Conquistador weight room.

Olive Branch graduates, Willie Anderson and Dustin Bobbitt,
architects of the Conquistador weight room.

The 1928 Olive Branch team, at the time known as the DeSoto County Agricultural High School "Aggies."

**MERIDIAN
WILDCATS**

Bob Tyler coached the Wildcats during one of their many reigns of terror.

Mac Barnes was a success at Meridian both as a quarterback and as a head coach.

Incomparable Ray Stadium.

Oak Grove still hasn't been around long enough to gain the respect of some Meridian students.

Nevil Barr (top center) and the
Warrior coaching staff.

Oak Grove played their games in the "Dungeon" before their incredible success inspired the community to build palatial Warrior Stadium (below).

CLINTON
ARROWS

ARROWS

JOLT

the

JAGS

Game day ribbon.

Clinton's new football stadium and field. Additional sports facilities can be seen behind the far end zone.

Coach David Bradberry led the Arrows against Mike Justice and the Jaguars in some of the series' most memorable games.

Coach Mike Justice.

MADISON CENTRAL
JAGUARS

Mike Justice's 1999 Jaguar team posted a 15-0 record, won the 5A state champonship, finished 12th in the nation and produced an amazing 5 NFL players.

Madison's Mayor Mary Hawkins-Butler and Coach Bobby Hall at Jaguar Field during installation of artificial turf.

B I L O X I
I N D I A N S

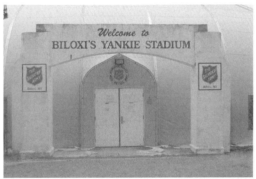

Biloxi quarterback, Sean Murphy, evades a Gulfport defender in the 2007 game.

A.J. Holloway, 1958 Biloxi High School graduate and current mayor of the City of Biloxi.

The friendly gates of Yankie Stadium now funnel visitors into a makeshift building erected by the Salvation Army to assist with relief after Hurricane Katrina.

Vintage 1931 game program.

Once a victim of constant vandalism (allegedly at the hands of Gulfport students), Biloxi's carved Indian head is now housed safely in the foyer of the new high school.

Manager turned kicker, Chad Edwards, stands on the 31 yard line in Milner Stadium. where he launched the last second kick that defeated Biloxi in 1990.

Coach Lindy Callahan.

1964 Gulfport Commodores, 11-0, Big Eight Champions.

Coach Callahan and his 1957 seniors beat Biloxi 19-10. The schools then quit playing each other for a decade.

Pictured in the Frascogna Courtney law firm conference room in Jackson, Mississippi are *Y'all vs. Us* authors Marty Frascogna, Mike Frascogna, Jr., and Mike Frascogna, III.

Wave supporter, L.D. Hancock, donated a tract of land to the school district for the new school and the city of Tupelo floated a bond issue that passed with 92 percent approval of the voters. The result was the Tupelo High School that exists today and, of course, the new football stadium. Ricky Black, looking back at the entire process, observes, "That's the only school I know of that was built because of a football stadium."

It is ironic that the action set in motion by Coach Black to improve Robbins Field would be met by such enthusiastic support of the community that it would ultimately result in the building of the new Tupelo High School. However, to merely describe the school as "new" does not do the community of Tupelo justice. The gift of land by Mr. Hancock, coupled with the passage of the bond issue, resulted in a "super school." Today, Tupelo High School resembles a college campus with its numerous modern buildings and spacious parking facilities all embedded in finely manicured grounds. The school has a reputation as one of the most progressive in the nation. Of course, the community is extremely proud of its 7500-seat football stadium, which can fully accommodate Tupelo fans and the many visiting fans who come to the Golden Wave campus on Friday nights in the fall. All of the facilities on the campus of Tupelo High School are a reflection of the community's priorities. As one looks at the landscape of the campus, it becomes obvious that the people of Tupelo place an extremely high value on education, and part of a well-rounded education are sports programs. Tupelo High School offers 32 men's and women's sports programs ranging from the primary sports of football, basketball, baseball, track and soccer to a number of secondary sports such as golf, bowling, swimming and volleyball. Since 1987, the coveted *Clarion-Ledger* All-Sports Award has recognized Mississippi high schools for their athletic excellence. The *Clarion-Ledger* gives the award each year to the school that accumulates the most points in championship ratings in all sports. Tupelo High School has been the recipient of the All-Sports Award 15 times in the award's 20-year history, making it the most dominant school for all sports in the state. Tupelo's athletic excellence has also been recognized on the national level. A listing of the top ten high school sports programs in the nation in the May 26, 2008, edition of *Sports Illustrated* ranked Tupelo as the third best high school sports program in the country.

Current Superintendent of Tupelo Schools, Randy McCoy,

expresses the educational philosophy of his school district:

> I think over the years there has been a perception that Tupelo has lots of money and we can do anything we want to. I would invite anyone with those thoughts to come up here and help me balance the budget each year. We do believe that if the facilities are nice, the kids are going to start off feeling good about themselves when they come to our campus. It does make a difference to a kid when he or she puts on that nice, shiny uniform or plays in a 7500-seat stadium or performs with the show choir in a 1000-seat performing arts center. It tells our kids that we think everything they do is important. We are not going to spend money just on athletes; we are also going to spend money on singers and dancers. That's why we have a 200-seat drama auditorium on campus. We are going to put you in a nice place to perform and give you the things you need to perform well. Because of our nice facilities, we have a target painted on our backs. I think opposing teams are going to bring their "A" game when they play Tupelo in anything. That's why we tell our kids, "When you go on that field, the other team is going to try to beat you because you are Tupelo." We tell our kids they are something special because they're here and because they are part of the Tupelo tradition.

Will Kollmeyer, former Tupelo TV sportscaster, echoes the sentiment of Superintendent McCoy: "Everyone always compares their school to Tupelo. That's why Tupelo has a big bull's-eye on its back when it comes to Starkville, Columbus or anybody else. They all want to take down the big boy."

"The thing about being a part of Tupelo is its commitment to excellence in everything in which we participate. We want to be good and we want to be very competitive," says Superintendent McCoy.

The commitment to excellence to which Superintendent McCoy refers in his description of Tupelo High School couldn't be more evident than on a Friday night during football season when the Golden Wave takes the field. He comments,

> I touch more people on Friday night at the stadium than I'll speak to individually all year. That

means our uniforms need to look sharp and they need to be clean, the scoreboard needs to work, the PA system should be adjusted so people can hear it, the field should look pretty, the band uniforms should look nice and the flag should go all the way to the top of the flag pole. That's what 7500 people see every Friday night. If all those things aren't right, then those 7500 people ask, "What in the world are these people doing?" They want it done right – excellence.

Another interesting point made by the administrators at Tupelo High School, which is repeated by veteran school personnel, is that depending on how well your football program starts the year dictates to some degree how the school year goes. When a football team wins, especially early in the season, everyone associated with the team enjoys the feeling of success. It starts a chain reaction of positive vibes and attitudes about everything throughout the community. McCoy explains, "You've got something that the whole student body can point to with pride and support. It does have an impact on the overall community. That's why it's so important that we make sure students have a connection to the school, whether they are in the bleachers as fans, in the band or actually performing on the field. They are connected to the success."

The people of Tupelo are proud of their high school and, most importantly, the students are proud to be part of the tradition of excellence created by the community. Nothing symbolizes the loyalty of the Golden Wave faithful more than the ritual at the end of each football game. No matter the outcome of the game, the football team assembles in front of the Golden Wave Band. Together, players, students in the stands and band sing the alma mater. It is a monumental symbol of support for Tupelo High School's "tradition of excellence."

****

"Coming to you live from the campus of Mississippi State University in Starkville, Mississippi . . . "

Several times during every football season, a sports commentator for ESPN, ABC or a host of other television networks introduces a college football game of the week to millions of viewers featuring the Bulldogs of Mississippi State University as they battle an SEC opponent. Whether the Dogs are going against the Alabama Crimson

Tide, the Tigers of LSU or their archrival up the road in Oxford, the Ole Miss Rebels, there is nothing like the pageantry of college football. The excitement of the big crowds, colorful mascots, acrobatic cheerleaders, crisp marching bands and big time players all bundled into one package attracts millions of television viewers every Saturday. Because of such frequent national and regional television exposure, it is understandable why college football fans across America associate Starkville with Mississippi State University. However, in the world of high school football in Mississippi, Starkville is the crossroads for any team trying to advance to a district, regional or state championship. Even back in the '50s, '60s and '70s, the road to the Little Ten Conference championship ran straight through the Starkville city limits. Starkville is, and has always been, the Emerald City of Mississippi high school football championships. But beware; a swarm of angry Yellow Jackets guards the city! To get through the Emerald City to capture a championship, contenders must first endure "Jacket attacks," which can be deadly.

Prior to 1981, Starkville High School competed in the Little Ten Conference along with schools such as West Point, Columbus Caldwell, Corinth, Amory, Aberdeen and Oxford. From the 1950s until 1981 when the current state championship format was established, the Yellow Jackets dominated the Little Ten Conference. Starkville football was a force as far back as the late '50s and early '60s under the direction of Jack Nix. Jim Craig, who followed Nix as head coach, continued to engineer championship-caliber teams. Coach G.T. Thames maintained Starkville's superiority in the Little Ten Conference throughout the '70s. According to Jim Ellis, Starkville High School radio announcer, "Starkville was the football power in this part of the state for a long, long time. They had a brief down period of three years or so, but won the conference championship in 1978. When Willis Wright came aboard, he really got things going."

The arrival of Willis Wright as Starkville's head football coach in 1981 coincided with the new state championship format. Current Starkville assistant football coach, Danny Carlisle, recalls Coach Wright's arrival: "My first impression of him was, where did this guy come from? I had never seen anyone with so much football knowledge. When he talked, football knowledge just flowed out of his mouth. He had a remarkable way of working with the kids." Jim Ellis says, "Willis Wright was the best motivator I've ever seen as a football coach. He could really get a team ready to play, particularly for the big games."

Under the direction of Coach Wright, the Starkville team had numerous opportunities to play in big games. In 1981, Wright's first year as head coach, Starkville won the north state and played South Natchez for the state championship. South Natchez, under legendary coach Ed Reed, defeated the Yellow Jackets in the first 5A state championship game under the new format. Two years later, Starkville again won the north state and earned the right to play Moss Point in the championship game. The Panthers defeated Starkville for the state title in 1983. The following year, Willis Wright had his Yellow Jackets in the state championship game for an unprecedented third time. Starkville defeated Jackson Callaway 26-0 to capture its first state championship. The Yellow Jackets returned in 1985 for a fourth time and played powerhouse Meridian under the direction of another legendary coach, Mac Barnes. The Yellow Jackets fell to the Wildcats in the title game, yielding the state championship to Meridian in 1985.

What is so remarkable about Starkville's championship run is their dominance of the north state in four out of five years. The teams Starkville faced during the 1981, 1983 1984 and 1985 state championship games were all different – South Natchez, Moss Point, Jackson Callaway and Meridian. The only constants were Starkville and Willis Wright. This consistency only highlighted the bull's-eye that was already painted on Starkville's back.

Following Willis Wright, Coach Tommy Lucas guided the Starkville football program for nine years. During Lucas's tenure, he led the Yellow Jackets to eight playoff appearances. Then in 1994 and 1995, double lightning struck when Chuck Friend guided Starkville to back-to-back state championships. Coach Bill Lee's Starkville team captured another state championship in 2001. Coach Lee eventually left Starkville to take a coaching position at Mississippi Gulf Coast Community College. However, he returned to Starkville in 2004, where he remains the Yellow Jackets' head football coach.

Starkville High School football was a consistent contender for the Little Ten Conference championship. Since the inception of the state championship format in 1981, the Yellow Jackets have been a fixture in the state championship picture. Starkville has produced some impressive winning streaks throughout its storied past, one which numbered 57 consecutive wins in the late '50s and early '60s, and multiple state championship appearances, some of which occurred in back-to-back fashion. It is instructive to hear the comments of some of the opponents of the Yellow Jackets to appreciate the impact of Starkville on the gridiron landscape of Mississippi high school football.

Legendary coach Ricky Black offers an interesting perspective, first as a player at Ackerman in 1966, and then later as a coach at Kosciusko and Tupelo. Coach Black says,

> I grew up close to Starkville in Ackerman. When I was in high school, we played Starkville in a bowl game in Columbus in 1966. I threw a touchdown pass with 39 seconds left in the game to the take the lead. Starkville scored on the last play of the game to win. That was the only game we lost when I was a senior in high school. They won on the very last play of the game.

Black continues, "When I started coaching at Kosciusko, we played Starkville the very first game and lost. That was the first loss as a coach that I had when I was at Kosciusko. Of course, when I was at Tupelo we were constantly getting into it with Starkville."

Mac Curlee, Principal of Tupelo High School, tells about his history with Starkville: "I attended high school at Aberdeen. Starkville was one of our big games. When it came down to the Little Ten Championship, it was Starkville and Aberdeen. Just the mention of the name 'Starkville' back when I was in high school would get all the juices flowing."

A long line of quality players has fed the success of the Yellow Jacket football program. Many of the athletes who played for Starkville went on to play college football, and some played professional football – players like Joe Carter, David Fair, Marcus Bush, Freddie Milons, Breck Tyler, Chris Correro, Lance Freeman, Richard Daniel, Jessie Laurie, John Rice, Calvin Young and Tee Milons, just to name a few. Coach Ronnie Cuevas, who coached at Starkville from 2002 to 2003 before returning to coach on the Mississippi Gulf Coast, commented that he only had one player on his Gulf Coast teams that could have played for Starkville. One of the things Coach Cuevas was most impressed with during his time in Starkville was the players' work ethic. He opened the weight room during the summer from 7 a.m. until 7 p.m.; even then, he would have to run the players out and make them go home. The Yellow Jacket players' dedication to the Starkville tradition, coupled with a strong work ethic, continues to make their football program one of the best in the state.

Great football programs always have great fans. Starkville has received high marks for its cheerleaders, marching bands and fan support. Borrowing from their college town tradition, Starkville High School tailgates before games. In fact, it has an official club at the high school – the Global Cookout Consortium – with its own school sponsor and elected officers. The tailgating usually begins around 4 p.m. and lasts until 12:30 or 1:00 the next morning. The GCC members set up their trucks, tents and grills right next to the main parking area. Some GCC members even dress up in costumes to show their school spirit. Since Starkville High School has many Mississippi State fans, most of the GCC members are armed with cowbells. As the Yellow Jacket team arrives, they ring the cowbells and hold up signs of support. Upon the arrival of the opposing teams' buses, according to GCC member Andy Brown, "We pull out all the stops."

****

In an article written in Tupelo's *Daily Journal*, sportswriter Danny McKenzie sets up the first big game between Starkville and Tupelo for his readers the day of the contest. McKenzie writes: "Put the storm windows on your homes, tie down your trailer houses and wrap up all your perishables, 'cause, folks, there's gonna be a collision tonight at Robbins Field – Noble Stadium that's liable to shake the fillings right out of your teeth."

The rivalry between Starkville High School and Tupelo High School is relatively young – only 30 years old. It all started in 1975 in the modern day meeting of the two schools in the Sight Bowl sponsored by the Lions Club of Tupelo. They played at the old Robbins Field in Tupelo on Thursday, November 20, 1975. Although there are references to a game played some 30-plus years before the clash in 1975, circa 1945-ish, no exact score is available. Nonetheless, prior to the historic bowl game between the Golden Wave and the Yellow Jackets, both schools competed in different conferences. Tupelo was a member of the prestigious Big Eight Conference, which included high schools located in the larger cities in the state. Powerhouse programs such as Laurel, Meridian, Hattiesburg, Gulfport, Natchez, Vicksburg and Greenville, along with the Jackson schools of Provine, Murrah and Central, were some of the schools that were members of the elite Big Eight

Conference. Starkville and the schools in its area were members of the Little Ten Conference. All of the member schools were located in cities smaller than the schools in the Big Eight. In most instances, the larger conferences that had member schools beyond one geographic area had a north division and a south division. Typically, the winners of the two divisions would meet in a postseason bowl game to determine the overall conference champion. There were many instances of cross-conference match ups in postseason bowl games, but those usually occurred among teams from the smaller conferences without north-south divisions.

From the time of the creation of the Big Eight Conference until its demise in the late '70s, there was always animosity between Big Eight member schools and the schools in the other conferences in the state. Since the Big Eight members were the largest schools located in the most populated cities, they touted themselves as the best football schools in Mississippi. The winner of the Big Eight usually claimed the title of "mythical state champion." The media, which was primarily located in the same towns as the Big Eight member schools, promoted this attitude of superiority. The non-Big Eight schools, especially schools in the Little Ten Conference and the Little Dixie Conference, took great offense to the self-proclaimed superiority of the Big Eight. To say that schools in the other conferences contested the Big Eight's claim to fame would be an understatement. Whenever a school in one of the many other conferences got an opportunity to play a Big Eight school in football, which was rare, it was a big, big deal. All the past animosity fueled by the declarations of football superiority of Big Eight members made the contest a "holy war."

Toward the mid-'70s, it became obvious that the Mississippi High School Activities Association would eventually adopt a new championship playoff system. Consequently, many of the conferences started to disband in anticipation of a new classification of schools based on size and geographic proximity. Tupelo elected to join the Little Ten Conference in 1976 and was placed in the division opposite Starkville. At the end of the regular season, both schools had won their respective divisions and played each other for the first time in the championship game. However, the Sight Bowl game preceded the Little Ten Conference collision by one year. In short, it was a big deal. Thus, the build up given to the game by sportswriter McKenzie was well deserved.

The Starkville Yellow Jackets overwhelmed the Tupelo Golden Wave 34-7 at Robbins Field to claim victory in the Sight Bowl. The

Jackets were paced by quarterback Keith Bolin and split end Breck Tyler, who was named the most valuable offensive player. "Tyler amassed 140 yards single-handedly by the end of the first half and finished with 172 yards, including six receptions and a touchdown," wrote Clay Harden for the Tupelo *Daily Journal*.

Yellow Jacket great, Breck Tyler, describes the events leading up to the big game with Tupelo:

> The Sight Bowl was my junior year. We had tied West Point in our last game. They were our big rival. We had lost one game that year to Louisville by one point. We voted on whether to go to the Sight Bowl or not. If my memory serves me correctly, it was a very close vote whether to go or not. Even though we had never played Tupelo in football as far as we could remember, for some reason, we were told we didn't like Tupelo. We weren't sure why we didn't like them, but we just didn't. We felt as if we were the underdog and it was our opportunity to end our season on a better note than a tie with West Point.

Tyler continues, "It was a very cold night. I do believe there were snowflakes. The Starkville side was full. I think the game pulled from other cities and towns, since the game was played after the regular season was over. It was a big game from a regional standpoint in Mississippi." Starkville defeated Tupelo in 1975. The next year, after Tupelo joined the Little Ten Conference, the two schools met again at the end of the regular season. Recalls Tyler,

> The game in 1976 was played in Tupelo again. I had to play quarterback. We won the game, but on the last play of the first half I ran the option. Tupelo had a very good linebacker named Felix Rutledge. He hit me before I could pitch it and the hit broke my shoulder. The trainers wrapped my shoulder, but I couldn't lift my left arm, so I was only able to play safety. Fortunately, we were able to win, but I did not enjoy it as much as I did the Sight Bowl the year before.
>
> When you play Tupelo you are going to get hit and you are going to get hit hard. They are going to help you up and then hit you hard again. Tupelo, both years we played them, was a very physical team. They were

well coached. Tupelo was very professional in their demeanor.

In 1980, Tupelo hired Ricky Black to lead the Golden Wave, and Starkville named Willis Wright as its head coach. It was at this point that the Starkville-Tupelo rivalry went into overdrive. Both Tupelo and Starkville were fielding championship-caliber teams during the Black-Wright era, and each time the two teams collided, state championship implications were on the line for both programs. Two of the classic games of the Black-Wright era occurred in 1983 during the regular season and in the playoffs. Many Tupelo and Starkville football aficionados pinpoint the two games in 1983 as the genesis of the rivalry. Both games were thrilling and have left indelible images in the minds of fans on both sides.

Former defensive coordinator for Tupelo, Bob Monroe, was on the Golden Wave sideline for both games in 1983 and gives his account of what unfolded during the regular season game:

> We played the last game of the year down at Starkville. We had a real good football team and were undefeated going into the last game. Fred Hadley caught a 96-yard touchdown pass early in the game. However, late in the game Starkville was ahead of us 24-21 and had the football down on their 20-yard line. It was fourth and one. Coach Wright made the decision they were gonna go for it and try to pick up the first down. If they had made the first down, they would have run the clock out and that would have been the game. As it turned out, on that particular play we got in a goal line defense and pinched everybody inside. Eric Maloney got through before their guard could get his head across and in front of him. He hit the quarterback, Chris Correro, just about the time he took the snap. When they measured, it was about a knuckle short. So we got the football on their 20-yard line with less than two minutes to go in the game. I believe we ran three plays and didn't pick up a first down. We lined up to kick a field goal, which would have tied the game. That very week we had put in a play that you have heard people call the "huddle play" where you line up the team on one side and send out the center to hold for the snapper. We told our guys if they didn't come over and defend against the huddle,

we were going to snap the ball across the field to a guy named Terry Hadley, Fred's brother. We ran the play as instructed and scored. We won the game 28-24. That was the first undefeated football season that Tupelo had had since 1945 when they were playing in the Big Eight Conference.

The Golden Wave victory completed their first undefeated regular season since 1945 and turned Tupelo upside-down. The whole town was excited, and the team was going to the playoffs riding an undefeated record. Prior to the Starkville game, the Tupelo Booster Club had been talking about purchasing a Continental Trailways bus to use for the school's athletic teams. However, over the previous two years the Booster Club had been unable to raise the money necessary to purchase the bus. Two weeks after the Starkville game, the Tupelo football team rode to the playoff game in its new Continental Trailways bus with "Tupelo High School Golden Wave" painted in large blue lettering on each side. The magic of an undefeated season can work wonders in booster club fundraising. Ironically, the bus purchased in 1983 remained in service at Tupelo High School for 25 years until it was retired in 2008. However, as exciting as the regular season was, and as proud as everyone was of posting an undefeated record, not to mention getting a new bus, the euphoria had to be managed, because the first ride on the new bus was to meet up again with . . . Starkville.

Coach Monroe recalls the playoff game against Starkville:

> We played them in the first round of the north half playoff at a neutral site in Aberdeen. I can remember coming out of the dressing room a little after 6 p.m. and both sides of the stands were full – all around the field behind the fence – completely full. Starkville was contending we had received a break on the huddle play in winning the regular season game. The playoff game was a real tough one. It went back and forth and then back and forth again. Starkville scored to tie the game 21-21. When they kicked off to us, it was late in the fourth quarter, as I recall. Our kid caught the kickoff, but when he got hit, he fumbled. They got the ball around our 20-yard line. We held them to third and long. They threw a pass – a post route – and our cornerback had the receiver covered up. Our guy broke in front of the receiver and was in position to intercept the pass, but

the receiver just knocked him forward. The ball hit our guy on the shoulder pads and popped up in the air. The Starkville kid caught it and fell backwards into the end zone. The official on our side of the field reached into his pocket to pull his flag. Then he turned to Coach Black and said, "It's his call" and pointed to the back judge. The official in the end zone didn't call anything. They ended up scoring on that play and kicking an extra point. Then they held us and won the game 28-21. Starkville played Southaven for the north half championship and beat them badly. Then they played Moss Point for the state championship and lost to the Panthers 6-0.

To rub more salt in the wound, after our loss to Starkville and in preparation for that playoff game in Aberdeen, we had installed some new plays. As I look back, the plays were much like the spread offense you see today. When we got down there and jumped into that formation the first time, Starkville didn't hesitate to make their adjustments. That happened throughout the game. It was only after the game was over that we began to hear that Coach Wright's friends from Saltillo, where he had coached previously, had been down during the week when we were practicing over at the old school. Apparently, they had watched practice and reported what they saw to Coach Wright. I know Coach Wright didn't actively ask those guys to come and watch our practice, but when they offered the information he surely didn't turn it down. So when word of that spread around, it made it even worse. When we played them the next year, we were still seething from the previous year.

From 1983 through 1990, Starkville and Tupelo went after each other in the regular season as if it were the Super Bowl. Often, they got to do it again in the playoffs. Both teams were in the state championship hunt almost every year. Coach Monroe states, "The hardest football team for us to beat was wherever Willis Wright was coaching, and during the '80s it was Starkville."

In 1990, the Starkville and Tupelo rivalry was at a boiling point. To make matters worse, Starkville was ranked No. 1 all season until the Yellow Jackets dropped a game late in the year. The Starkville loss catapulted Tupelo into the No. 1 spot. However, the usual hostility that existed between the two schools was multiplied by a disregard for sportsmanship that permeated throughout the high schools in the state during the 1990 season. A number of fights had broken out at games between players and, often, between the fans. There seemed to be trouble erupting at every game during the fall of 1990. Tupelo coach Ricky Black suggested to Starkville coach Tommy Lucas that they try to keep a lid on the upcoming Yellow Jacket and Golden Wave game and send a message about good sportsmanship to schools throughout the state. Black recalls, "I called Tommy Lucas at the beginning of the week and said, 'Tommy, why don't we have a salute to sportsmanship? When the third quarter ends, let's break like boxers coming out and touching gloves at the beginning of the last round. Let's go out and shake hands!'"

So at the beginning of the fourth quarter of the 1990 Starkville-Tupelo game, play was stopped and the players and coaches went to midfield and shook hands. Play resumed with Starkville in the lead, only to have Tupelo tie the game and send it into overtime with the Yellow Jackets eking out a victory.

According to Coach Black, "It was such an intense rivalry. I thought it was a great time to show a tribute to sportsmanship – two teams in a heated rivalry shaking hands at midfield during the game. It was a great way to control the heat of a very intense game."

During the following weeks, newspaper articles appeared throughout the state about the salute to sportsmanship that occurred at the Starkville-Tupelo game. From the very first meeting of the Starkville and Tupelo football teams at the Sight Bowl in 1975, all the way down to the thrilling 2007 game won by Tupelo as time ran out on a Starkville comeback, the games have been hard-fought contests between premier programs. It comes down to two big time high school football programs colliding each year.

Jeremy Weaver, former Starkville football player, sums up the attitude of the two programs: "We feel we are one of the best teams in the state. Tupelo has the same aura about them. Every other team is taking aim at Tupelo and Starkville and has them directly in their crosshairs."

WHAT THE GOLDEN WAVE SAYS ABOUT STARKVILLE

There are a lot of big games on our schedule, but I don't think there's any one game that is any bigger or more important to us than the Starkville game.

Mac Curlee

Tupelo Principal

Today, I think the Starkville-Tupelo rivalry is a friendly rivalry, unlike in the '80s when it was more hostile.

Danny Porter

Tupelo Athletic Director

There is no question about it. It's a huge game for us and the blood goes back a long way – long before I got here; but I feel it.

Eric Collins

Tupelo Head Football Coach

From Tupelo's perspective, it's a respectful rivalry. From Starkville's view, it's hostile.

James Sloan

Former Tupelo Head Football Coach

I have my sister's old "I Hate Starkville" t-shirt. A lot of people have "I Strongly Dislike Starkville" shirts.

Lindsay Purnell

Former Tupelo Cheerleader

When Starkville walked out on the field wearing their all-black uniforms, they were intimidating. They were always good, mean and very well coached. You knew it was a battle, no matter the sport, when you played Starkville.

Kirk Presley

Former Tupelo Football Player

Tupelo and Starkville are what I would consider the crown jewel cities in north Mississippi. Both have good schools, both have great athletes and great traditions, which is what makes this rivalry so good. There is a lot of respect on both sides.

David Garrett
Tupelo Booster Club President

Tupelo and Starkville have never liked each other. Growing up, you would walk around at high school football games and all you saw was, "I hate Starkville" t-shirts. It's pretty bad.

Chris Garrett
Tupelo Football Player

If you want to pinpoint one year where it all kind of happened, it was 1983. Willis Wright was the head coach at Starkville and Ricky Black was at Tupelo.

Bob Monroe
Former Tupelo Assistant Football Coach

They have great facilities, great hospitality and great spirit, just like it is here. That's why the rivalry is so good and positive, because there is so much respect between the two schools.

David Garrett
Tupelo Booster Club President

In the 22 years I've watched the rivalry, Starkville was more physical than Tupelo. They were always so talented athletically.

Will Kollmeyer
Former Tupelo TV Sportscaster

After we beat Starkville the first time, the school superintendent came down and shook my hand.

Eric Collins
Tupelo Head Football Coach

I remember the Starkville pep rally my first year as principal at Tupelo. There was a lot of energy in the gym. I remember seniors wore "I Hate Starkville" t-shirts and carried fly swatters.

Mac Curlee

Tupelo Principal

Now that I've been here four years, I understand it. Because of those epic battles that took place in the '90s, I know the Starkville game is special.

Eric Collins

Tupelo Head Football Coach

Starkville looked at us as the preppy, rich kids. I viewed them as a mean, dirty, "will hit you in the mouth and not think twice about it" team – just more of a blue collar "we're coming after you; you better get ready."

Kirk Presley

Former Tupelo Football Player

I'm sure Starkville thinks we're the rich people who are snobby and get everything we want, which is very untrue. Starkville always thought they were better than us in every sport – pretty cocky.

Chris Garrett

Tupelo Football Player

We don't have pep rallies for every game, but we always have a pep rally for the Starkville game because it's so big. We do skits and one of our guys dresses up like a Yellow Jacket. They attack him and he gets put in a garbage can.

Lindsay Purnell

Former Tupelo Cheerleader

Just knowing we are going to play Starkville gets everyone pumped up.

Chad Bumphis

Tupelo Football Player

When I was considering moving to Tupelo, my friend Willis Wright gave me some advice. He said, "Don't interview with the superintendent. Find out who the tailback is first."

Ricky Black

Former Tupelo Head Football Coach

There were some people who were convinced Coach Willis Wright was psychic.

Bob Monroe

Former Tupelo Assistant Football Coach

When Tupelo and Starkville play each other, all the records go out the window.

Samuel Bell, Jr.

Tupelo Fan

I think the Starkville-Tupelo rivalry is an excellent rivalry. I wish we had more of them.

Randy McCoy

Superintendent of Tupelo Schools

Some of Tupelo's rivalries have come and gone; Starkville hasn't.

Will Kollmeyer

Former Tupelo TV Sportscaster

What the Yellow Jackets Say About Tupelo

It's a good, healthy rivalry. It's good for us and it's good for Tupelo because we measure ourselves against them academically and athletically. From an administrative perspective, it's someone to measure yourself against and someone to strive to beat in a healthy sense of the word.

Kathi Wilson

Starkville Principal

We feel like Tupelo is a "preppy school." When their fans come here they say, "Oh, we're going to the ghetto." It's a put down.

Willie (Bill) Lee

Starkville Head Football Coach

They think they are better than we are.

Danny Carlisle

Starkville Assistant Football Coach

I get more fired up for the Tupelo game than I do for any other game.

Danny Ditta

Starkville Football Team Manager

Tupelo is one of the ones we've got to beat.

Carlton Fisher, Jr.

Former Starkville Student

I believe a lot of Starkville fans look at Tupelo as an elite program – a team they would like to emulate.

Don Foster

Sports Reporter

Starkville Daily News

We get the feeling they look down at us, and that fuels the rivalry even more.

Cleveland Hudson
Starkville Assistant Football Coach

Basically, Starkville is considered the blue collars and Tupelo the white collars.

Tee Milons
Former Starkville Player

We don't have any beef with them, but their fans hate us.

Ashley Allen
Former Starkville Cheerleader

The Tupelo fans are annoying. If they start winning, they start yelling and saying bad stuff, but we don't care.

Lake Jackson
Starkville Football Player

The crowd with Tupelo is very well mannered.

Kathi Wilson
Starkville Principal

I would rather go to Tupelo and beat them there.

Lake Jackson
Starkville Football Player

If Tupelo hates Starkville, that's fine with me.

Tee Milons
Former Starkville Football Player

TUPELO-STARKVILLE SERIES HISTORY

Year	Tupelo	Score	Starkville
1975	Dennis Waite	7-34	G.T. Thames
1976	Dennis Waite	17-19	G.T. Thames
1977	Dennis Waite	6-14	G.T. Thames
1978	Dennis Waite	0-34	Dog Owens
1979	G.T. Thames	*NA*	Dog Owens
1980	Ricky Black	27-6	Dog Owens
1981	Ricky Black	8-22	Willis Wright
1982	Ricky Black	7-14	Willis Wright
1983	Ricky Black	28-24	Willis Wright
1983*	Ricky Black	21-28	Willis Wright
1984	Ricky Black	14-29	Willis Wright
1984*	Ricky Black	34-14	Willis Wright
1985	Ricky Black	14-21	Willis Wright
1986	Ricky Black	24-36	Willis Wright
1987	Ricky Black	21-7	Tommy Lucas
1988	Ricky Black	13-6	Tommy Lucas
1989	Ricky Black	20-14	Tommy Lucas
1990	Ricky Black	16-19	Tommy Lucas
1991	James Sloan	20-23	Tommy Lucas
1992	James Sloan	31-24	Tommy Lucas
1993	James Sloan	23-19	Tommy Lucas
1994	James Sloan	7-55	Chuck Friend
1995	James Sloan	12-21	Chuck Friend
1995*	James Sloan	13-21	Chuck Friend
1996	Johnny Hill	21-35	Chuck Friend
1997	Johnny Hill	10-21	Chuck Friend
1998	Johnny Hill	14-21	Chuck Friend
1999	Johnny Hill	17-14	Chuck Friend
2000	Phil Ferguson	14-27	Chuck Friend
2001	Phil Ferguson	14-17	Bill Lee
2002	Phil Ferguson	10-35	Ronnie Cuevas
2003	Phil Ferguson	9-37	Ronnie Cuevas
2004	Eric Collins	21-20	Bill Lee
2005	Eric Collins	17-25	Bill Lee

Year	Tupelo	Score	Starkville
2006	Eric Collins	35-9	Bill Lee
2007	Eric Collins	38-35	Bill Lee

NA - Information Not Available

* Playoff Game

★★OFFICIAL GAME DAY PROGRAM $5.00★★

PASCAGOULA
VERSUS
MOSS POINT

PANTHERS

TIGERS

SINCE 1983

Utility Constructors, Inc.

JACKSON, MS

PROUD SPONSOR OF MISSISSIPPI HIGH SCHOOL FOOTBALL

FRIDAY, SEPTEMBER 12, 2008 ★ 7:00 PM KICKOFF

DANTZLER STADIUM ★ MOSS POINT, MISSISSIPPI

CHAPTER
11
CAT FIGHT ON THE COAST

Every time a Pascagoula football player leaves the locker room before practice or a game, he sees a sign by the door that reminds him of the immense responsibility that comes with his Panther uniform. The sign reads, "You are playing for all Panthers past and present. Represent them well."

For a present day player, there are certainly plenty of past Panthers to represent. The Pascagoula football program began back in 1919 under Coach Mack Morgan, and has established one of the finest high school football traditions in Mississippi in the 88 seasons since.

Pascagoula began its football life in the old Gulf Coast Conference before population growth allowed it to join the Big Eight Conference in 1946. During the 1930s, Pascagoula enjoyed its most successful decade, winning four Gulf Coast Conference championships in seven years and posting a .738 winning percentage under the combined head coaching efforts of C.C. "Hot" Moore, Tom Wells and V.C. Stripling. Pascagoula also proved to be a progressive football program during this period, as Coach Moore's 1934 team was one of the first in Mississippi to begin wearing numbers on their jerseys.

In 1944, Pascagoula landed future coaching legend Dobie Holden as its head coach. Holden was able to capture another Gulf Coast Conference crown in only his second season at the helm. In his third season, Holden's Panthers left the familiar confines of the Gulf Coast Conference and joined the ranks of the teams in the formidable Big Eight Conference. After two short seasons of play, the Panthers established themselves as a statewide football force as they posted a perfect 12-0 record and won the Big Eight. In fact, the 1947 team was so dominant that Coach Holden was presented the keys to a brand new 1948 Dodge Coupe at the end of the season. The next day, Coach Holden drove his new car to Pearl River Junior College where he accepted the head coaching position and ultimately secured his own coaching legacy.

During the greater part of the 1950s and 1960s, wins in the Pascagoula football program ebbed and flowed like the waters of the Gulf Coast as the Panthers rode a carousel of head coaches. Dutch Binion, Donald Gibson, Bruce Bradley, Ed Langford, Levaine Hollingshed and Aubrey Rozzell all tried their hand at guiding Panther teams, but none of them were able to establish any amount of sustained success or claim a championship. However, in 1974, a Pascagoula alum by the name of Johnny Woitt was able to bring some stability to the program.

After graduating from Pascagoula, Woitt went on to play college football at Mississippi State and then professionally with the San Francisco 49ers. When Woitt assumed the head coaching duties at Pascagoula, he was still one of, if not the, best athletes on the field, even though he inherited a rather talented bunch. The 1974 team included some of the best athletes ever to wear the Panther uniform. One player in particular stands out due to his abilities on the field and because of his colorful name – Ray Charles "Rooster" Jones.

Rooster was a dominant running back in his junior high days at Colmer and his reputation preceded him to Pascagoula High School. By the time the first game of the 1974 season rolled around, Rooster had already secured the starting running back position as a tenth grader. Over the next three seasons, Rooster added to his legacy and rewrote the Pascagoula record books. His football prowess ultimately landed him a scholarship to the University of Pittsburg, where he succeeded the legendary Tony Dorsett – but not before he helped Pascagoula produce one of its greatest seasons in 1976.

Walter Thornton, a 1977 graduate of Pascagoula High School, was an offensive and defensive lineman on the 1976 Panther team. Thornton relives his senior season:

> We had the best offensive line in the state and we had Rooster in the backfield. Our defense was supposed to be our weak link and we were not expected to do that much going into the season. Our first game we played a very talented South Natchez team in their stadium, which was called the "Snake Pit." They were ranked No. 4 in the state and they drove it down the field on us in their first possession. You could see that look in everyone's eyes like, "Oh, well, this is going to be one

of those games." However, Rooster scored on a sweep with about two minutes left in the game and our defense held on for a 14-8 win. We surprised ourselves. The next week we went back home and dismantled Laurel, who was always good. Week after week, we just kept taking teams out. North Natchez had James Berry and Hugh Green and we beat them in the regular season and then a second time in the playoffs. We played in the Big Eight championship game against Greenville and beat them 21-0 in the fog and cold. That was a very special season and the guys on the team remain close to this day. There isn't a single guy on that team I wouldn't help immediately if he gave me a call right now.

The 1976 team finished with a record of 12-0, equaling the record of the 1947 championship team. At the end of the season, Coach Woitt was given the keys to a 1977 Ford Grenada. Someone at the presentation immediately stood up and reminded Woitt of how Coach Dobie Holden left the Panthers at the altar 30 years prior when he was given a new car. Woitt responded by telling the concerned fan, "I promise you, I will still be here tomorrow."

Woitt did in fact stay another four seasons as head coach of the Panthers. By the time he left in 1980, his seven seasons at Pascagoula marked the longest coaching tenure in school history, and his 1976 championship team was the team by which all future Panther squads would be measured. However, in 1986, a relatively unknown coach from north Mississippi challenged Woitt's legacy.

A former football player at the University of Mississippi under Coach Johnny Vaught, Bill Matthews was the head coach at Cleveland High School in the middle of the Mississippi Delta when he received a call from a college friend. The friend informed him of a coaching vacancy over 300 miles away in Pascagoula. Matthews was not particularly interested in the job, since his son was in the junior high football program in Cleveland and his family had been there 11 years. However, Matthews' wife Peggy told him to go see what the position was all about, and to take a cooler so he could bring her back some fresh shrimp.

After his trip to the Coast, Matthews was still convinced the job at Pascagoula was not the right one for him. Nevertheless, Pascagoula was persistent, and Matthews was persuaded to make two subsequent trips down to the Coast. "Every time I went, I packed up that cooler and brought back more shrimp," said Matthews.

On his third trip, the Pascagoula brass took Matthews around to all the athletic facilities, including the football stadium. Recalls Matthews, "When they showed me the football stadium, I asked how they were able to coordinate scheduling with the junior college. At first, my question confused them. Then they said, 'No, Coach, this is our stadium. We don't share it with anyone.' It was at that point I really started paying attention. I don't think I was fully aware that Pascagoula was the largest school in the state at the time with around 2,500 students. I started to wonder if I could get out of my contract with Cleveland and how my son would feel about leaving all his friends."

It turned out that neither of Matthews' concerns were problems at all. Cleveland allowed him to break his contract to take advantage of the opportunity and his son immediately said, "Let's go." Matthews remembers having to temper his son's initial excitement. "I told him, 'Son, this is the largest school in the state and you're not automatically going to be the starting quarterback just because I'm the head coach. They play big-time football down on the Coast, and you're 5'8 and slow.' Then he told me, 'Don't worry, Dad, I'll be the starter.'"

Matthews and his family arrived in Pascagoula in April of 1986, just in time for spring training. During his first season as coach of the Panthers, Matthews' team posted a 3-7 record as the defenses on the Coast tore apart his ground-based veer attack. Says Matthews, "The linebackers down here were so big and fast that our offensive game plan just didn't have a chance. In the final game of the season, we lost to Moss Point 21-0. Afterwards, Coach Billy Wayne Miller came up to me said, 'Welcome to the Coast and big-time football.'" To add insult to injury, soon after the end of the season, the Pascagoula superintendent that hired Matthews informed him, "Head coaches down here last about three years, and superintendents last about two. You had better think about that, Coach."

Realizing that his approach needed an immediate emergency overhaul, Matthews went to work crafting a solution. "I knew we needed to get bigger and stronger, so I went to a strength and conditioning clinic and learned the system developed at the University of Nebraska by Boyd Eppley. At the time, the University of Georgia had a great defensive scheme, so our staff went there and brought that back. Finally, I knew we were going to have to throw the ball, so I called my friend

Archie Manning for advice. He put me in touch with a coach at Texas A&M who taught us a five-wide, single back attack. We ended up with a playbook that was about a foot thick," said Matthews.

In addition to revamping the offensive and defensive schemes, Matthews and his staff laid down the law to the players. Recalls Matthews,

> No one on the Coast was really throwing the ball, and certainly not to the extent we were about to. This complicated system was going to take total commitment by the players. We told them what we expected of them and that if they missed any practice or strength training workouts, they weren't playing. We just needed more discipline from top to bottom. Coming from the Delta, I wasn't used to all the earrings and long hair on the Coast. I told them if their hair was longer than mine, we were going to have a problem.

Many people in Pascagoula were not entirely convinced of Matthews' new approach. Matthews explains: "During the spring, people thought we had lost out minds. One of the assistant principals who was a friend of mine asked me, 'You have everyone split out. There is only one back in the backfield. Who is going to block?' I told him we were going to chunk it. If the defense made the wrong move, then we were going to pick it up and pick them apart."

When the 1987 season arrived, Coach Matthews' son, Shane, was comfortably situated in the starting quarterback position and thrilled to exchange his days as an option quarterback in the veer for the new high-flying attack. In the opening drive of the season, the new-look Panther offense zipped down the field and into the end zone. Said Matthews, "It was so easy it scared us. There were only a couple of thousand fans there to see it, since expectations were somewhat low after the previous season. Nevertheless, we put on a show. After that, word got out and we had 10,000 plus for every game for the rest of the season."

Pascagoula blistered their way to a perfect 14-0 championship season and a No. 14 ranking in the final *USA Today* national poll. The Panthers outscored their opponents 380-72 as the new offense worked to perfection. The following season, Pascagoula had what many considered an even stronger team, but they were upset in the playoffs on a late field goal by Gulfport in a driving rain. During this two-year period, the Panthers produced an amazing 20 Division I football players, including Terrell Buckley (Florida State), Shane Matthews (Florida), Keith Joseph (Mississippi State), Ricky Alexander (LSU), Frankie Godfrey (LSU) and Kez McCorvey (Florida State).

The 1987 Pascagoula team's 14-0 record stands as the greatest single-season mark produced by any team in school history. Coach Matthews' 11 seasons prowling the Panther sidelines remains the longest of any Pascagoula coach.

Says Walter Thornton, current assistant coach and member of the 1976 championship team,

> We preach history and tradition to the players at Pascagoula. We tell them they are playing for every guy before them that has coached or worn the Panther helmet since 1919 – everyone from Coach Mack Morgan to Coach Johnny Woitt, and from Rooster Jones to Terrell Buckley and Shane Matthews. When they walk onto the field, they have a responsibility to all the current and former players, but also to that guy who works down in the shipyard, or the guy in the McDonald's on Highway 90. They represent anyone who is a taxpayer in Pascagoula. What they do is important to so many people in this town; it always has been and it always will be.

****

"Who wants to play some football?"

"That's all it would take," recalls 1961 Moss Point High School graduate John Grafe. "You could walk out your front door and yell that, and in a matter of minutes you had enough kids around to play a football game; and you had more standing on the sidelines asking if they could play next. Moss Point was a great place to grow up as a kid. It was just a little industrial town where there were at least two kids in every house." Grafe continues, "We had a great school and we all loved sports. During the summer, we played football from dawn to dusk. Moss Point has always been a place where people are passionate about football from a very early age."

The little town of Moss Point is hidden in the southeast corner of Mississippi on a system of lakes just north of Pascagoula Bay. Mention Moss Point to football players, coaches and fans in Mississippi today, and they know exactly where it is and what it means in the world of high school football. For opposing teams, seeing the name "Moss Point" on your football schedule is the equivalent to taking out a big fat black magic marker and writing an "L" in your results column. If your team is unfortunate enough to be traveling to Moss Point, a loss may be the least of your worries; total annihilation is a distinct possibility – a gridiron death sentence, if you will. It's not just the players on the field. The whole town craves football year round. If the town had a choice between breathing clean oxygen or an aromatic mix of Friday night hotdogs, popcorn and cigars, well, that's not even a choice for people in Moss Point. The oxygen would simply have to go.

As dominant as the big blue Tigers of Moss Point have been over the past two decades, incredibly enough, there was a time when they found gridiron wins very hard to come by. The Tigers began playing football in 1925 under Coach A. Lumis Moore. During their first 46 campaigns, the Tigers suffered 30 losing seasons. Of the 16 non-losing seasons, only two of those teams produced win totals that were significantly greater than their losses: 1944 (8-2) and 1945 (10-0-1) under Coach Tom Swazey.

The exact reason, or reasons, for Moss Point's slow start have been unsuccessfully debated for decades. However, its citizens nearly unanimously agree upon the catalyst for Moss Point's rise to power. After spending one season as an assistant coach at Pascagoula under Aubrey Rozzell, the man who transformed Tiger football forever finally arrived on the Moss Point campus in 1971. The man was the one, the only, Billy Wayne Miller.

When Miller arrived in 1971, Moss Point High School was in the middle of a turbulent period of integration. The previous year, mandatory integration forced the combination of Moss Point and Magnolia High Schools. Like many places in Mississippi, the process was stressful for everyone involved, and not everything proceeded smoothly in the classroom or on the gridiron. In fact, many of the former Magnolia Monarchs felt they had been unfairly denied starting positions by the holdover coaching staff from Moss Point, and thus elected to leave the football team. To compound matters, Moss Point was losing football games at a rapid pace and finished the 1970 season a dismal 1-9.

Considering that black and white schools all over the state were combining their gridiron forces and producing more formidable teams, it was imperative that Moss Point quickly figure out how to overcome its internal rift if it were to have any chance at competing with the rest of the Big Eight Conference. Bringing his unique personality and style to the Tiger program, Coach Miller provided just what Moss Point needed at that point in time. Says 1976 Moss Point graduate, Dick Dickson, "Coach Miller came in and treated the black and white kids exactly the same – like s--t. He would scream and cuss at every one of us. We were all perfectly equal in his eyes."

Conventional or not, the coaching style of Billy Wayne Miller produced near immediate results for the Tigers on the field. Winning seasons were secured in his second and third campaigns, and in his fourth season in 1974, Coach Miller's Tigers blasted through their schedule a perfect 10-0, producing the first undefeated team in school history. The 1974 team was ultimately defeated in the Big Eight playoffs in the Shrimp Bowl by Laurel, a team Moss Point butchered 28-0 in the regular season. The loss denied Moss Point and Coach Miller their first state championship.

Miller continued to produce winners in the years that followed, but the year the Tigers finally reached the summit of Mississippi's high school football mountain was 1983. During this season, Moss Point opened with a pair of wins and then proceeded to drop three straight games to coastal foes Picayune, Biloxi and Gulfport. The team's reaction to the three defeats is a testament to the commitment of the coaching staff and the character of the players. The Tigers rebounded with three straight wins to pull their record to a respectable 5-3 before they hit the road for a showdown with No. 1 ranked Meridian in fabled Ray Stadium. When Coach Miller's boys were able to wrestle down a 14-7 win against the mighty Wildcats, the newspaper responded by labeling the victory a fluke. The Moss Point team answered by winning their remaining two regular season games and downing Meridian a second time in only a month, beating them 14-10 in the quarter-finals of the playoffs. The Tigers completed the dream season with a victory over Warren Central in the semifinals and a 6-0 victory over Starkville in the championship game. The victory earned the football-crazed town of Moss Point its first state title and marked the completion of the transformation of the program under Coach Miller.

Miller ultimately served as Moss Point's head coach for a school record 20 seasons, during which time the Tigers' losses outnumbered their wins only six times. Although Miller's mark on the Tiger program is evident in the record books, his less-quantifiable qualities make him a legend around the little Mississippi town.

One of Miller's greatest qualities was his ability to sell the Moss Point program. Moss Point 1990 graduate Lewis Sims recalls his first encounter with Miller:

> I had been in a private school in Waynesboro when my father's pig farming business went belly up. He told me the family would be moving to the Coast and asked me where I wanted to attend school. I had heard of Pascagoula and said that was my choice, but my father told me we were going to see Billy Wayne Miller instead. When I asked who that was, he said, "Only the best football coach in the state." When we got to the field house, we were taken back into Coach Miller's office, which was filled with cigar smoke. I had no idea what I had just stepped into, but within ten minutes of hearing Coach Miller talk about the Moss Point program, I was sold. He was so passionate and convincing that I didn't even have a chance. I never thought about Pascagoula again. From that point forward, I was going to wear the blue and white and be a Tiger.

Coach Luther Kuykendall, former Moss Point assistant coach, recalls Miller's unique personality, "Coach Miller was always the center of attention. That's the way he wanted it. When there was a group of people, everyone always wanted to listen to him, because he could tell a story in ways no one else could. He was a real personality and he used his personality to generate interest and attract attention to Moss Point football."

Anyone who ever spent time around Coach Miller seems to have a story about an unforgettable action or saying used by the Tiger coach. Lewis Sims recalls several of his favorite Billy Wayne Miller tales:

> I always remember Coach Miller with that cigar in his mouth. When he had his heart surgery, he switched to Levi Garrett chewing tobacco. He would have that wad of tobacco in his cheek just chewing and spitting away. He would get up in official's faces and his head would just be bobbing all around, stopping every now

and then to spit. Coach Miller was a stickler for certain things. I remember two things he always addressed were jocks and showers. We had one kid who had put his jock on over his underwear and his underwear was sticking out of the top of his pants at practice. Coach Miller went over to him with a pocketknife and cut off the waistband of the underwear and then ripped the kid's underwear off and threw them to the side. He said, "From now on you're going to remember to wear your jock and your jock only." He also told everyone, "Cleanliness is next to Godliness. When you leave this field house, you will be clean. It may be the only shower you have all day, but you will not leave this field house without a wet towel and a wet head. Your mamma sent you to me clean and I'm going to send you back the same way."

Amidst his antics and rough exterior, Coach Miller did have a very caring heart, especially when it came to matters of family and church. Recalls Dick Dickson, one of Miller's former players,

> You won't find anyone that played for him that didn't love him, as crazy as hell as he was. He did a lot for my family and me personally. My father died when I was 13. I had a single mom that was raising four kids ranging in age from 13 down to five. Coach Miller frequently stopped by our house to check on us and see if there was anything he could do to help. Even later when my younger brother was playing, he still came by and checked on things. This was a man who was much deeper than what people saw on the surface.

Raynard Robinson, 1980 Moss Point graduate, remembers one thing in particular that Coach Miller seemed to begrudgingly acknowledge being more important than football practice:

> On Wednesdays, I would have to leave practice a little early in order to make it to church. We would be in the middle of practicing hard and really getting after it. Coach Miller would be all riled up, and then I would go up and tell him that I had to leave so I could get to church on time. Now I was one of his starting linebackers, and I know he didn't like me missing that part of practice, but Coach Miller would look at me and

say, "Just go ahead on." I know he wanted me at practice, but he understood my priorities and he respected them.

Among the many influences Miller had on the Moss Point program was the improvement of the physical facilities. His contributions ranged from reconfiguring the football field so it correctly ran north to south, to helping push bond issues to upgrade and add school buildings. In fact, there were proposed bond issues that failed due to lack of support until Billy Wayne arrived. When the next bond issue came around, Miller offered his help if a small portion of the money would be set aside for athletics. When the superintendent agreed, Miller used his dynamic personality to get the athletic department and Touchdown Club on board, generating enough community support that the bond proposal passed. One of the results of the issue was the construction of the Moss Point field house.

When Coach Miller died on June 23, 1991, one might expect the Moss Point program to regress as a result of losing the most influential coach in school history. However, Moss Point football did not regress; it flourished. Credit for the future success of the program could also be laid at the feet of Coach Miller.

In 1975, Miller took note of a young coach at Gautier Middle School. The coach was originally from South Carolina and had recently played football and graduated from Delta State. After spending two years at Gautier, Coach Miller plucked the young coach out of the neighboring town and put him on the Moss Point High School football staff. Little did Miller know that when he hired Jerry Alexander, he had just ensured the future of Moss Point football for the next three and a half decades.

After serving as an assistant on the Tiger staff for 17 years under Miller, Jerry Alexander assumed the head coaching duties in 1991. In his first season as head coach, Alexander's team promptly went 12-2 and delivered the town of Moss Point its second-ever state championship. A few short years later, the Tigers played in back-to-back championship games in 1996 and 1997 against South Panola, defeating the powerful team from north Mississippi in both matches. In his first seven seasons at the helm, Alexander's teams won three 5A state championships and amassed a gaudy 82-13 record.

Coach Alex, as he is known to his players, may have come from the Billy Wayne Miller coaching tree, but he employs a far different approach with his team than did Miller. Using a more cerebral approach, Alexander is a constant teacher who emphasizes the total development of the player, not just the athlete. Says Alexander, "We emphasize to our players the six goals of character. The six goals are respect, responsibility, caring, citizenship, fairness and trustworthiness. When we have a couple of guys get into a little squabble with one another, I make each one of them teach the team about three of the six goals. The whole team then has to take a test. If the team doesn't score 100 percent, they have to re-teach the goals."

The character of the people of Moss Point was certainly put to the test in the 1990's when it began to lose some of the industry that employed a high percentage of its citizens. When International Paper and Rohm & Haas shut down their operations, the people of Moss Point could have cut and run, but instead they showed the same character preached by Coach Alexander and sunk their roots deeper. As the town battled economic challenges, it pulled closer together behind its football program and enjoyed the best decade of gridiron campaigns in the history of the school.

Says 1984 graduate Floyd Downs, "Losing some of the industry like International Paper really hurt Moss Point, but we can get through that. Now, if you took football away from Moss Point, the city would die. People here live for football."

****

If you want to know about the Pascagoula-Moss Point football rivalry, your best bet is to look for the warships. Since 1938, Northrop Grumman has built a wide variety of vessels utilized by the U.S. Navy. The $25 billion a year global defense enterprise is located in Pascagoula and employs over 10,000 people, making it the largest employer in the state of Mississippi. Because Moss Point is located a scant five miles from Pascagoula, a large percentage of the Northrop Grumman employees prowling the shipyard are either Pascagoula Panthers or Moss Point Tigers. Thus, the shipyard is a fertile environment for the exchange of information regarding both towns' favorite pastime – high school football.

Says Pascagoula alum Walter Thornton, "If you ever want to know what's going to happen in the Pascagoula-Moss Point game, go to the shipyard or to Chevron. There is always money exchanging hands over there on this game, and the line they keep is the most accurate one you can find. Vegas doesn't have anything on those guys."

The shipyard may be the best place to go for information on the annual gridiron collision between the Panthers and the Tigers, but the shipyard only arrived in 1938. This rivalry began all the way back in 1925. It was during that season that Pascagoula's D.M. Reagan took his Panthers to Moss Point for the first time and teed it up against Coach A. Lumis Moore's Tigers. The catfight on the Coast has been raging now for 83 years.

Pascagoula dominated the early part of the rivalry. During the first eight meetings, Pascagoula shut out Moss Point seven times. The best result achieved by the Tigers in that period was a scoreless tie in the third meeting in 1927. Finally, in 1933, Moss Point was able to get on the scoreboard in a 13-20 loss. However, more significant than Moss Point's offensive output was the brawl that took place. Although no one can recall why the fight began or who instigated it, its occurrence and ramifications are undeniable. After the 1933 contest, Moss Point and Pascagoula suspended their budding rivalry for 14 years.

During the suspension of the rivalry, Pascagoula won five Coastal Conference championships; and in 1944 and 1945, Moss Point lost a grand total of two games. Because both teams were excelling on the field, it was only natural that debates over which team was better would begin to fire up among the citizens. By 1946, the population of the two towns had grown, due in part to the addition of the shipyard (then named Ingalls), and school enrollments had swelled to the point that both Moss Point and Pascagoula joined the Big Eight Conference. Moss Point 1949 graduate, Francis Eugene "Dede" Dailey, Sr., remembers the conclusion of the 1947 season:

> Pascagoula had just gone 12-0 and won the Big Eight state championship, and Moss Point had just finished 3-8 that year. After that season, there was a big banquet held at the country club in Pascagoula and both teams were invited. It was a way of getting us all together and letting us get comfortable with one another and with the notion of the two schools playing each other again.

In 1948, the two schools renewed their rivalry in a game played in Pascagoula. Before the kickoff, there was a ceremony at midfield involving the bands and dignitaries from each school. Representatives of Moss Point and Pascagoula proceeded to dig a hole, insert an object in the hole and then cover it up. What was it that they placed in the hole? It was a hatchet, of course. They needed to bury it before football games could resume.

When play did resume after the burying of the hatchet, Moss Point notched its first win in the series by defeating the defending Big Eight champions by a score of 24-0. The Tigers followed up their inaugural win with a 21-0 shutout the following season before Pascagoula got back on track and proceeded to win 16 of the next 22 match ups. All of the games took place without any major incident, with the exception of the 1959 contest at Moss Point. Barry Bosarge, a player on that Moss Point team, recalls the game:

> There were some controversial calls in the 1959 game that really got the Moss Point fans riled up. They called a touchdown back late in the game that was crucial. Pascagoula ended up winning the game 7-6. When the game ended, I looked over my shoulder and saw fans coming over the fence. In particular, I noticed the mother and father of one of the kids on our team. Mr. Broome went out on the field, grabbed one of the referees, and took a swing at him. Mrs. Broome came running up behind with her high heel shoes in her hands and started hitting the ref with her heels. They finally had to get the refs off the field and put them in a car to get them out of there. When they did, some Moss Point students jumped on top of the car and caved the roof in.

The 1974 game at Moss Point saw first-year Pascagoula head coach Johnny Woitt unveil his hotshot sophomore running back, Ray Charles "Rooster" Jones, against the No. 1 ranked Tigers. During this game, the overmatched Panthers hung with Moss Point until late in the game, at which time Moss Point ran a tackle eligible play to ice the game 31-24. People in Pascagoula today are still adamant that the offensive formation was illegal and that two Moss Point players were in motion on the snap of the ball. In fact, you don't have to look far before a Panther loyalist offers to show you actual game footage to prove his contention. These same fans take obvious pleasure in pointing out what happened to Moss Point the following week. The Tigers agreed to play their first game of the Big Eight playoffs in Biloxi against Laurel in the Shrimp Bowl. After Moss Point had beaten Laurel 28-0 in the regular season, they were upset 10-7 and denied a state championship.

The mid to late 1970s was a volatile time for the rivalry, and many important figures were introduced to the cast of characters. Numerous accounts during this period have Moss Point students painting "MP" on all the stop signs in Pascagoula, as well as painting all of the Panther fire hydrants blue and white. Pascagoula students countered by using gasoline to burn a 40-yard-long "PHS" into Moss Point's football field. Moss Point responded by adding an "M" to the field graffiti and then allegedly delivering a beheaded rooster gift-wrapped in blue and white to the Pascagoula campus in honor of Ray Charles "Rooster" Jones. At one point or another, both schools ended up with commodes painted in respective school colors either chained to the front doors of the school or run up the flagpoles.

The stop signs, fire hydrants and schools were not the only targets; fans were targets as well. Many Pascagoula fans recall attending games at Moss Point and sitting in the visitor's stands that backed up to a wooded area. During the game, a hailstorm of eggs was occasionally launched skyward from the woods, raining down on the unsuspecting Panther faithful.

In 1975, Jerry Alexander was a first year assistant for Moss Point. Says Alexander, "Pascagoula had us down 28-0 at their place. It was late in the game and they faked a field goal to score another touchdown and go up 35-0. That was my first experience with this rivalry." Alexander's Tiger teams later punished Pascagoula for this early transgression.

Possibly no individual has been as involved, challenged and torn apart by the Moss Point-Pascagoula rivalry as coach Luther Kuykendall. Originally from Kosciusko, Kuykendall accepted a position as an assistant coach at Colmer Junior High, sight unseen, in 1971 after his graduation from Delta State. Kuykendall says,

> I had never been to the Coast and I didn't even know where Pascagoula was. When I was first asked if I would be interested in a job in Pascagoula, I said, "Sure. Where is Pascagoula?" When I finally got down here, I was just awestruck. The stadium, the weight room, everything was beautiful. My wife and I ended up buying a house four blocks from the Pascagoula stadium, where we have lived since 1974.

Kuykendall was moved from the junior high to the high school by Pascagoula's new head coach Johnny Woitt in 1974. Thus, his first experience with Pascagoula's rivalry with Moss Point was the 1974 game that Moss Point supposedly stole on the "illegal" play at the end of the game. Says Kuykendall,

> I had heard about the Pascagoula and Moss Point rivalry, but I didn't really know what to expect until 1974 when I first coached in it. A spot in the Big Eight playoffs was on the line and it was the biggest crowd I had ever seen. I saw people standing on buildings on the other side. They were lined up around the fence. Our entire coaching staff was brand new and we were really somewhat nervous when we came over. Moss Point is an intimidating place to play and we had heard all kinds of stories. One of our other assistants, Cooper Hogue, was considering bringing a pistol in his pocket in case we beat Moss Point and things got out of hand. Fortunately, we did talk him out of that.

In 1982, Pascagoula combined the positions of head football coach and athletic director and hired Kuykendall to the newly created post. Kuykendall immediately notched a 7-0 victory over archrival Moss Point, which was then led by the colorful Billy Wayne Miller. Recalls Kuykendall,

> I remember a game that we played at Pascagoula where the teams were evenly matched and the atmosphere was highly charged. During pre-game, Coach Miller walked out to the middle of the field and the Pascagoula fans started booing him. He stood there, raised his arm and shot their stands the bird. Everybody saw it, and he wanted them to see it. He knew he was going to get a rise out of it, and he did. It's like he was telling them, "When we're at Moss Point you do things our way, and when we're at Pascagoula, you will still do things our way. I'm in control." Who else would do that or get away with it other than Coach Miller?

During his years wearing the red and blue, Kuykendall became friends with a staple of the Pascagoula community, Neil Beckham. Beckham was a Pascagoula graduate who suffered from cerebral palsy and had a speech impediment. A diehard fan of Pascagoula football, Beckham handled all the Panther's video needs and traveled the state at his own expense. However, there was one particular skill of Beckham's that Kuykendall appreciated the most. Kuykendall elaborates:

> More so than anyone else I knew, Neil could get under Billy Wayne's skin. When we had to exchange game tape with Moss Point, I always sent Neil. Coach Miller would make Neil wait an hour before letting him into his office. When Neil finally got in there, he would tell Billy Wayne, "We're gonna whip y'all's ass this week." It was great, because Neil could get in Coach Miller's head and get him all worked up. Years later after Coach Miller died, Neil Beckham was one of the individuals that talked to the Moss Point superintendent about getting the Moss Point field house named after Coach Miller. That's the kind of love-hate relationship the two schools have between them.

Although Kuykendall found success against Moss Point in his first outing, his Panthers dropped the next three to the Tigers in tightly contested games. In 1985, Kuykendall was asked to resign after being at Pascagoula for 15 years. Some say his record against Moss Point cost him his job. Others cite a philosophical shift by the Pascagoula school district that led to a parting of the ways. Nonetheless, the move was important for two reasons. First, Kuykendall was a defensive genius, and it took Billy Wayne Miller at Moss Point about 30 seconds to make him a member of his own staff. Second, Kuykendall's dismissal did not sit well with many key supporters of the Pascagoula program, and many of them followed their old coach up Telephone Road and Main Street to fill key roles in the Moss Point program.

For Kuykendall, the move was a challenging one. He says,

> I had been at Pascagoula for a long time. When they asked me to leave, it broke my heart. I hated to leave, but I had to provide for my family. I had put in applications with Chevron and some of the other businesses on the Coast before Billy Wayne Miller offered me the defensive coordinator position at Moss Point. I had a daughter who was a 10th grader at Pascagoula and my son was in the 4th grade. I didn't want to uproot them from Pascagoula and go to Moss

Point, so I commuted each day.

In addition to the emotional challenge of switching to Moss Point, there was also a significant professional hurdle to overcome. Kuykendall was transitioning from a head coaching position at a 5A school to an assistant's position at a rival school under an unusually opinionated coach in Billy Wayne Miller. Regarding Miller, Kuykendall says, "Coach Miller was a strong-willed individual. For him to bring in the head coach from the rival school was a risky move. We definitely had our differences in coaching styles and we had our heated disputes about strategy, but he was interested in winning and so was I, and we always came out friends. He was a great, great friend and he was very good to me at a time my family and I needed it."

In his own unique way, Miller expressed his appreciation for Kuykendall after Moss Point's 21-0 victory over Pascagoula in 1986. At the end of the game, per Miller's instruction, the Moss Point cheerleaders displayed a large sign that simply read, "Kuykendall's Revenge."

Switching schools in 1986 and learning how to be an assistant under Coach Miller was certainly a tall order for Kuykendall, but both would pale in comparison to the challenge he faced in 1995. Remembers Kuykendall,

> In 1995, my son was a senior free safety at Pascagoula. We played them here at Moss Point and we had a really good team that should have won the state championship. The newspaper came out and took a picture of us together in the stadium – me in my Moss Point shirt and him in his Pascagoula uniform. My wife went to all of his games and supported him. I didn't get to see him play all year, except when we played them. Since he was playing defense and I was coaching our defense, I tried to watch every play I could when my guys were off the field. We won the game and I met my son on the field afterwards and gave him a big hug. That was a memorable moment for me. It was very emotional to have us split between the two schools.

In 1996, Moss Point entered the final game of the regular season against Pascagoula a perfect 9-0 and ranked No. 1 in the state and No. 14 nationally. The Tigers were also riding a five-year win streak against the rival Panthers. The week of the game, the *Mississippi Press* ran an article written by a Moss Point graduate. Moss Point's Jerry Alexander remembers the contents of the article:

> It said everything in it that a coach would never want to see in the paper, because it made great bulletin board material. It was extremely inflammatory and talked about how great Moss Point was and how Pascagoula had really taken a nosedive in recent years. It made analogies about how if both teams were showing up to a gunfight, Moss Point would bring a bazooka and Pascagoula would bring a water pistol.

The perfect upset scenario played out as if it were scripted, as Pascagoula dealt Moss Point its only loss of the season and stole the game 17-14 in two overtimes in Moss Point's stadium. The Tigers regrouped and ripped through the playoffs en route to the first of their back-to-back state championships.

Muskingum Barnes was a defensive tackle for the Tigers during the 1996 championship run. Says Barnes, "We were undefeated in 1996 and won the state championship, but we lost to Pascagoula in the last game of the regular season. I look at our championship ring and think, 14 and 1. Yeah, but Pascagoula beat us. I would rather have lost to Gulfport or somebody."

The 1995 and 1996 Moss Point teams are considered possibly the strongest in school history. They are often pitted against Bill Matthews' 1987 championship Pascagoula team in fictional games played out in barbershops in the area. The arguments typically center on the Moss Point defense's ability to stop the high-octane offensive attack engineered by Pascagoula's Shane Matthews. Muskingum Barnes offers his opinion on the fantasy match up:

> Everyone says Shane and those guys would have gone up and down the field on us; but we had possibly the best defensive line in the country that year, and I'm not sure Shane would have ever had time to get rid of the ball. Even if he did, I have to remind people that we had three Division I cornerbacks playing in our secondary. Personally, I don't think they would have stood a chance against our defense. But hey, I'm biased.

The 1996 upset victory over Moss Point would be the last Pascagoula would enjoy for a number of years. Part of their dry spell can be attributed to the quality of Jerry Alexander's Tiger teams during that time, and the fact that Pascagoula "kicked the hornet's nest," so to speak, in 1996. Another factor was that in 1997, Pascagoula High School lost over a third of its students when Gautier High School spun off. Pascagoula had grown so large that it was forced to have an "open" campus that allowed students to come and go as they pleased for lunch, since the cafeteria could not accommodate them all. After the split, Pascagoula remained a 5A school, but it lost enough students to instantly make Gautier a 4A school. It took the Panthers years to recover from this gash in the student population.

The past few years have brought some interesting changes to both the Moss Point and Pascagoula programs, and the general feeling is that the rivalry is entering a new phase of its history. After Katrina obliterated the Mississippi Gulf Coast, Pascagoula's coach, Dan Bland, decided to resign and move out of state. The head coaching vacancy was eventually filled by 1981 Pascagoula graduate, Scott Sisson. At Moss Point, the 2007 season marked the final year of the Jerry Alexander dynasty. The following season would be the first time in 37 years that someone other than Alexander or Miller would be running the Tiger program. Like Pascagoula, Moss Point also opted to fill their head coaching position with one of their own, 1990 graduate Lewis Sims.

Both Sisson and Sims are passionate about their alma maters and understand the importance of the rivalry. Sims still vividly recalls the day his father took him to visit Coach Billy Wayne Miller in a smoky field house office and how Miller instantly sold him on the tradition of the Tiger program. Similarly, Sisson recalls his father giving him money when he was in grade school so he could buy tickets to the Pascagoula-Moss Point game for the whole family that day at school before tickets sold out. Football tradition and pride runs deep in each family, and both men understand the responsibility they carry. They also understand each other particularly well. Sisson cut his teeth as a coach while an assistant at Moss Point under Alexander for a total of five seasons before taking the head job at East Central High School right up the road. When he left for East Central, Sisson took with him a young coach named Lewis Sims.

Says Moss Point's Lewis Sims,

There is tremendous pressure to succeed here at Moss Point. There are lean years everywhere, but they just refuse to accept them here. I tell people that I can get away a lot longer with being a bad athletic director than I can with being a bad football coach. The continuity of the coaching staff has brought Moss Point success over the years. We have so many guys come back here to coach as assistants and then, even when they get offers to go other places as a head, they choose to stay here because they have such a deep connection. Right now, there are six football coaches at the high school. Five of them are Moss Point natives with roots in the school. The two coaching staffs at Moss Point and Pascagoula right now know each other incredibly well. They all coached together for years at Moss Point. Everyone knows everyone else's tendencies. You aren't going to fool anyone. You just have to line it up and out execute the other team.

Unable to play football his junior and senior seasons at Pascagoula due to an injury, Sisson is now getting a chance to make his mark on this hotly contested rivalry as a head coach. "I remember going to Pascagoula games with my father as a young boy. Dad worked in the Ingalls shipyard and had great seats for the Pascagoula football games. He didn't go to Pascagoula High, but he was always an avid sports fan and loved having a team to follow. I know this job is one that he would have wanted me to take," says Sisson.

After assuming the head coaching duties for the Panthers in 2006, Sisson was able to stop Moss Point's three-game winning streak over his alma mater with a 20-10 victory over a very talented Tiger team. The victory over Moss Point came on Sisson's second try. Lewis Sims will take his first shot at Sisson's Panthers in 2008.

With the familiarity of the two coaching staffs, one might think that the Moss Point-Pascagoula rivalry will become a friendly rivalry. *Mississippi Press* sports editor, J.R. Wittner begs to differ. Says Wittner,

Some people say this is a friendly rivalry, but when they get on the field, I believe these people truly don't like each other for the full course of the game. It is a rivalry where the best way to settle the whole thing is to get out in a big open field, put a cage around them and let them go after it. There will always be the well-to-do handshakes after the game, but I think the coaches and players would just as soon go no holds barred for about 15 minutes and let the winner take all. When we did our photo shoot this year for the Coast's Most Wanted Players, we had kids from Ocean Springs, George County, Vancleave, Gautier, Moss Point and Pascagoula. All the kids were friendly to one another when we introduced them, but the kids from Moss Point and Pascagoula wouldn't even shake hands. They immediately started trash talking one another.

WHAT THE PANTHERS SAY ABOUT MOSS POINT

The Moss Point fans are incredible. They are probably the most loyal following of fans in the state. They don't ever give up on their team and they are always there to support them. There is no doubt that they love their Tigers.

Melinda Mitchell
Pascagoula Athletic Director

The cities of Pascagoula and Moss Point work very closely together in many political, social and economic arenas, but for that one Friday night in the fall, all bets are off.

Matthew Avara
Mayor of Pascagoula

I started playing Moss Point at an early age. They killed us in junior high; they really handed it to us. We came up short my first two years in high school, but that all made the win my senior year that much more enjoyable.

J.T. Tomes
Former Pascagoula Football Player

I don't think Moss Point fans are as bad as some people make them out to be. My family works at the shipyard. After this year's game, the Moss Point fans were telling them, "Y'all are the better team. Y'all earned it and proved it on the field." I know they love their team.

Eric Hollis
Pascagoula Football Player

The kids from Moss Point have gotten so arrogant recently. It's as if they know – no doubt in their minds – that they're gonna beat Pascagoula in whatever they do. They started taking us for granted. They don't feel that way after last year, though.

Jonathan DeFlanders
Pascagoula Football Player

The fact they dropped to 4A doesn't matter. Just because their student body dropped in size doesn't mean their football team is going to suffer. We know they are a powerhouse. We know they can take control of a game at any moment and blow you out. Them being 4A doesn't make us take them any less seriously.

Jonathan DeFlanders
Pascagoula Football Player

Pascagoula smells bad, but it's only because it's located so close to Moss Point.

Wayne Ferrell
Former Pascagoula Football Player

WHAT THE TIGERS SAY ABOUT PASCAGOULA

Oh, Lord, this has been a great rivalry. I would rather be on this end than the other. Early on, they had their day. There were a bunch of years they dominated, but lately, it's been really good for Moss Point.

Jerry Alexander
Former Moss Point Head Football Coach

Ocean Springs looks down on Gulfport; Gulfport looks down on Biloxi; Biloxi looks down on Pascagoula; and Pascagoula looks down on Moss Point. That's pretty much the pecking order on the Coast.

Lewis Sims
Moss Point Head Football Coach

The whole coaching staff at Pascagoula today may have graduated from Pascagoula, but they were all trained as coaches at Moss Point.

Vincent Norvell
Former Moss Point Football Player
and Current Assistant Football Coach

If you lost to Pascagoula, it was as if you just lost your life.

Floyd Downs
Former Moss Point Football Player

I have 40-year-old friends in Pascagoula that are still taking trash about games that were played 25 to 30 years ago.

Robert Henderson, Jr.
Former Moss Point Football Player

Moss Point and Pascagoula butt right up next to each other on Jefferson Street. We're right on top of each other. I can guarantee you they want to beat us as bad as we want to beat them.

Hugh Bodden
Former Moss Point Football Player

There are people at the shipyard who bet their whole paycheck on the Moss Point- Pascagoula game. To me, that's crazy. I would never let my financial wellbeing ride on the hormonal influxes of 16- and 17-year-old boys.

Lewis Sims
Moss Point Head Football Coach

I live in Gautier and I have to drive through Pascagoula to get to Moss Point. I hold my breath going through Pascagoula. I don't like it at all.

Robert Henderson, Jr.
Former Moss Point Football Player

PASCAGOULA-MOSS POINT
SERIES HISTORY

Year	Pascagoula	Score	Moss Point
1925	D.M. Reagan	42-0	Lumis Monroe
1926	J.O. Box	2-0	Lumis Monroe
1927	J.O. Box	0-0	Lumis Monroe
1928	J.O. Box	19-0	Lumis Monroe
1929	E.P. Sylvester	44-0	W.H. Cole
1930	Roy Biggers	53-0	Lamar Jones
1931	Roy Biggers	*Did Not Play*	Lamar Jones
1932	Roy Biggers	14-0	Lamar Jones
1933	C.C. Moore	20-13	Lamar Jones
1934	C.C. Moore	*Series Suspended*	Lamar Jones
1935	Tom Wells	*Series Suspended*	Eddie Khayat
1936	Tom Wells	*Series Suspended*	Eddie Khayat
1937	Tom Wells	*Series Suspended*	Eddie Khayat
1938	Tom Wells	*Series Suspended*	Eddie Khayat
1939	V.C. Stripling	*Series Suspended*	Eddie Khayat
1940	Tracy Walker	*Series Suspended*	Eddie Khayat
1941	Alton Woodward	*Series Suspended*	Eddie Khayat
1942	James Nesbit	*Series Suspended*	Eddie Khayat
1943	W.C. Hickman	*Series Suspended*	Tom Swayze
1944	Dobie Holden	*Series Suspended*	Tom Swayze
1945	Dobie Holden	*Series Suspended*	Tom Swayze
1946	Dobie Holden	*Series Suspended*	Tom Swayze
1947	Dobie Holden	*Series Suspended*	Dick Shields
1948	Felix Neal	0-24	Dick Shields
1949	Dutch Binion	0-21	Dick Shields
1950	Dutch Binion	19-19	Matt Floyd
1951	Dutch Binion	21-0	J.D. Stonestreet
1952	Dutch Binion	34-0	J.D. Stonestreet
1953	Dutch Binion	27-0	Earl Howell
1954	Donald Gibson	12-7	Earl Howell
1955	Donald Gibson	6-0	Red Davis
1956	Donald Gibson	18-0	Red Davis
1957	Donald Gibson	12-22	Red Davis
1958	Bernard Blackwell	0-20	Red Davis

Year	Pascagoula	Score	Moss Point
1959	Bruce Bradley	7-6	Red Davis
1960	Bruce Bradley	3-0	Red Davis
1961	Bruce Bradley	47-0	Bobby Holmes
1962	Ed Langford	14-13	Bobby Holmes
1963	Ed Langford	14-17	Bobby Holmes
1964	Ed Langford	20-6	Bobby Holmes
1965	Ed Langford	14-0	Bobby Holmes
1966	Ed Langford	7-7	Bobby Holmes
1967	Levaine Hollingshead	19-26	Bobby Holmes
1968	Levaine Hollingshead	27-0	Ray Freeman
1969	Aubrey Rozzell	42-8	Ray Freeman
1970	Aubrey Rozzell	30-15	Ray Freeman
1971	Aubrey Rozzell	6-0	Billy Miller
1972	Aubrey Rozzell	0-14	Billy Miller
1973	Aubrey Rozzell	13-35	Billy Miller
1974	Johnny Woitt	24-31	Billy Miller
1975	Johnny Woitt	35-0	Billy Miller
1976	Johnny Woitt	14-7	Billy Miller
1977	Johnny Woitt	21-14	Billy Miller
1978	Johnny Woitt	7-13	Billy Miller
1979	Johnny Woitt	6-26	Billy Miller
1980	Johnny Woitt	14-28	Billy Miller
1981	Mike Battles	20-17	Billy Miller
1982	Luther Kuykendall	7-0	Billy Miller
1983	Luther Kuykendall	8-14	Billy Miller
1984	Luther Kuykendall	10-19	Billy Miller
1985	Luther Kuykendall	7-14	Billy Miller
1986	Bill Matthews	0-21	Billy Miller
1987	Bill Matthews	14-0	Billy Miller
1988	Bill Matthews	31-6	Billy Miller
1989	Bill Matthews	0-26	Billy Miller
1990	Bill Matthews	10-8	Billy Miller
1991	Bill Matthews	6-14	Jerry Alexander
1992	Bill Matthews	7-25	Jerry Alexander
1993	Bill Matthews	18-20	Jerry Alexander
1994	Bill Matthews	14-30	Jerry Alexander
1995	Bill Matthews	0-25	Jerry Alexander
1996	Bill Matthews	17-14	Jerry Alexander

Year	Pascagoula	Score	Moss Point
1997	Jamie Kelly	31-53	Jerry Alexander
1998	Jamie Kelly	0-30	Jerry Alexander
1999	Joe Gaddis	6-24	Jerry Alexander
2000	Joe Gaddis	7-43	Jerry Alexander
2001	Dan Bland	0-33	Jerry Alexander
2002	Dan Bland	12-35	Jerry Alexander
2003	Dan Bland	37-14	Jerry Alexander
2004	Dan Bland	0-34	Jerry Alexander
2005	Dan Bland	13-27	Jerry Alexander
2006	Scott Sisson	14-28	Jerry Alexander
2007	Scott Sisson	20-10	Jerry Alexander

★★ OFFICIAL GAME DAY PROGRAM $5.00 ★★

ACKERMAN
VERSUS
EUPORA

Trustmark
Banking and Financial Solutions

PROUD SPONSOR OF MISSISSIPPI HIGH SCHOOL FOOTBALL

FRIDAY, OCTOBER 17, 2008 ★ 7:00 PM KICKOFF
WOFFORD FIELD ★ EUPORA, MISSISSIPPI

CHAPTER

12

CRADLE OF COACHES

William Foots Ford died February 14, 2008 – on Valentine's Day. Considered by many Eagle supporters to be Eupora's number one fan, Mr. Ford had cheered for the school's athletic teams for over 50 years. The elderly black gentleman in his early eighties with a raspy voice and hands that had become withered due to diabetes still possessed a spirit just as vibrant as the teenagers he encouraged. He was the kind of man people rallied around – a man who truly cared for young people – a man who made a difference in his community.

Junior Graham recalls Mr. Ford's warning on the first day of his job as Eupora's head football coach: "Now, Coach, we've got to beat Ackerman." While every game was big for Mr. Ford, the Ackerman game was especially important. To make sure Coach Graham and his staff heeded his warning, Mr. Ford attended practice every day and wouldn't hesitate to add his commentary regarding the progress of the team. Mr. Ford had a special interest in two of the players on the 2007 team – both senior starters and both his grandsons. Coach Graham didn't disappoint Mr. Ford. The Eagles posted their first undefeated regular season with a perfect 10-0 record.

Unfortunately, there was a time during the season when Mr. Ford was unable to attend the daily practices and weekly games. Because of his deteriorating health, he was confined to the hospital and wasn't able to keep an eye on the coach. Fortunately, Coach Graham provided Mr. Ford with video tapes of the games while he was "out of action." Graham recalls the week after the Eagles posted their 10-0 season. Mr. Ford, who had just been released from the hospital, came to visit him. Coach Graham says, "He was so excited and thrilled with the perfect season. You would have thought we had just won the Super Bowl."

Coach Graham also remembers a situation when one of his players failed to show up for class: "I contacted Mr. Ford immediately and told him the situation. He said in that raspy voice, 'I'll find him.' Before the school day was over, Mr. Ford had rounded up the kid and had him seated in his desk at school." Coach Graham continues:

> Mr. Ford wouldn't let you get sorry. It's easy to blow off things and get your priorities out of order. Football was really big to him and he was gonna make sure if there was any way he could help, he would. Mr. Ford knew every kid in the community, especially the black kids, because he knew their parents and grandparents. He did not hesitate to talk to them straight out. When he got through talking to a kid or their parents, they understood the message. You need people like that in the community who maybe aren't politically correct – just correct.

As Mr. Ford's health declined, it became more difficult for him to move around in the bleachers. Consequently, he became comfortable sitting in a metal folding chair in the west end of Eagle Stadium on the lower terrace.

Sadly, Mr. Ford is gone. While his presence will certainly be missed, Eagle fans attending future Eupora football games will have a visual reminder of the elderly black gentleman with the raspy voice who cared so dearly for his Eupora Eagles – an empty metal folding chair in the corner of the end zone.

Prior to the start of the 2008 season, Eupora High School will retire No. 1 from its football roster. The school will encase a jersey bearing No. 1 in a glass box in the Eagles' field house in honor of Eupora's number one fan – William Foots Ford.

****

While formal records are not available to verify the date Eupora High School began playing football, there is evidence to establish a football team at the school in 1933. It is probable that Eupora fielded a team prior to this date – maybe as early as 1910.

One interesting bit of trivia that can be confirmed surrounds the mascot, or mascots, associated with Eupora's athletic teams. From 1933 – and probably earlier – until 1946, Eupora's mascot was the Yahoo. Former Eupora football player Pete Fortner, Jr., who played in the late

'40s, says, "I looked it up in the dictionary. A yahoo is a person who doesn't conform to anything – almost like an outlaw." In 1947, Coach Mike Mahalic changed the mascot to the Black Bears. He also changed the school's colors to black and white. After only one year, Coach Grady McCool followed Coach Mahalic. He immediately changed the mascot to the Eagles and the school colors back to the original maroon and white. Since 1948, the Eupora mascot has remained the Eagles and the colors have remained maroon and white, leaving behind the Yahoos and the Black Bears.

Coach McCool also made another appearance in Eupora's school history in connection with the old gymnasium on the campus. Pete Fortner explains:

> The gymnasium was originally at Camp McCain over in Grenada. It was built in the late '30s and used during World War II. After the war ended and all the buildings at the camp were auctioned off, the gymnasium was torn down and brought over here where it was reassembled in the late '40s. When Coach McCool first came here and changed the mascot to Eagles, he worked from a ladder to paint the Eagle on the wall of the gym. It's still there today.

Over the years, Eupora has been blessed with an unusually large number of legendary coaches. The consistent production of big time coaches from this town is staggering when you consider its population (2265, according to 2000 U.S. Census) and the fact that its high school plays in the second smallest size classification in Mississippi (2A).

Starting in the late '40s, Grady McCool literally left his mark on the Eupora football program when he painted that Eagle on the gymnasium wall. Next came Hollis Rutter, considered by many football fans to be one of the greatest coaches to ever come out of Mississippi. Rutter led Jackson's Provine Rams to their glory days in the '60s, in addition to having successful stints at Morton, Greenwood, Pillow Academy and Brookhaven Academy.

In the '60s and early '70s, Eupora had a succession of big time coaches, beginning with Doug Sullivan and, later, Reuban Walker. Both of these men were successful in keeping the Eagles' football program soaring. During the late '70s and until 1988, Eupora football was under the direction of Coach Jerry Brantley. Phillip Smith, a former player for Coach Brantley for three seasons (1977-1979), comments about his former coach: "He was hardnosed. He believed in running it down the other team's throat. Coach Brantley was a community leader." Then in 1990, a young coach over at Ethel who had played his high school ball at Ackerman, of all places, took over the Eupora program. The arrival of Ricky Woods put Eupora on the fast track to gridiron success. Eventually, Coach Woods left Eupora to return to his hometown to become the head coach of the Ackerman Indians, Eupora's hated rival. After a highly successful run at Ackerman, Coach Woods took over the program at perennial 5A powerhouse, South Panola. Woods' Tiger teams not only won four consecutive state championships; they also set a national record for successive wins.

After Coach Woods' departure to Ackerman, Eupora was reclassified up to 3A and had to compete with larger schools, most of which had already been playing at the higher level. At the end of Eupora's first season at the 3A level, the team was able to post an impressive 10-1 record under the leadership of Coach Jimmy Pittman.

Following Coach Pittman as leader of the Eagles was hometown boy Lance Pogue. A 1987 graduate of Eupora High School, Pogue played offensive and defensive tackle for Coach Reuban Walker. Coach Walker recalls, "Lance was energized at all times. He gave you 110 percent." Under Coach Pogue, the program moved to yet a higher level. During the Pogue years, the games with archrival Ackerman, coached by former Eupora coach Ricky Woods, took on all the characteristics of a world war. Some of the classic games in the series between these two schools occurred while Pogue was at the helm of the Eupora Eagles. Ironically, when Pogue left Eupora in 2007, it was to succeed Coach Woods at South Panola. His first year there he extended the Tigers' 60-game winning streak started by Woods to an amazing 75 consecutive wins in route to leading South Panola to an unprecedented fifth straight 5A state championship.

When Coach Pogue left for South Panola, Eagle fans were concerned about his replacement. The prevailing question throughout the Eupora community was how many times could they catch lightning in a bottle and again snare another big time coach. However, in Eupora lightning can strike again – and again – and again. This time, lightning appeared in the form of a 5'6", 150-pound soft-spoken guy from just over the county line in Weir with a "good ole boy" name of "Junior."

From the moment Junior Graham arrived on the Eupora campus, everyone knew why Weir football was the most successful 1A program in the state. While soft-spoken and low key, Coach Graham exudes a confidence that is contagious. Once again, the community of Eupora caught lightning in a bottle. Under Graham in 2007, Eupora posted its first undefeated regular season. The Eagles finished the season 10-1, having lost in the playoffs.

Jimmy Pittman, the superintendent of Eupora schools and the person primarily responsible for hiring Coach Graham, says, "You just can't get any better than Junior Graham. He's the real deal."

Former Eupora head football coach Reuban Walker sizes up Junior Graham:

> He is a unique individual. Junior takes the kids to heart and they really respect him. He is a perfect fit for this community. This past season he took a group of players who, at the beginning of the year, I thought would be lucky to win five games, and he molded them into a pretty good football team. They went undefeated. No way should that team have won all those games, but they did. Junior could coach the rest of his life in Eupora if he wanted to. The people in this little ole town just love him.

Beginning in 1948 with Coach Grady McCool, followed by Rutter, Sullivan, Walker, Brantley, Woods, Pogue and Junior, 60 years later, Eupora can be legitimately labeled as "The Cradle of Coaches in Mississippi" – that is, half of the cradle. The other half of the cradle is located just 17 miles down Highway 9 on the reservation of the Ackerman Indians.

****

The folks in Ackerman may have the highest "FIQ" of anybody in Mississippi. Every one of the 1700 people in the community seem to have a natural ability to grasp the concepts, language and mathematical probabilities associated with the complex science measured by FIQ testing. Regardless of gender, age, race, religious affiliation or economic status, everyone appears to be gifted. Year after year, the FIQ test scores coming out of Ackerman are in the upper percentile. When it comes to FIQ, Football Intelligence Quotient, the folks in Ackerman know their stuff, particularly everything about the Ackerman Indians.

Many football aficionados (i.e., know-it-alls) regularly theorize about the cause of this high concentration of football intelligence in such a small town. After much debate, it seems to boil down to five things. First, the majority of men in the community played high school football for the Indians. Second, the Ackerman teams have historically been well coached; consequently, the people recognize good coaching and quickly eliminate poor coaches. Third, many in the community have family members who have coached or are coaching somewhere, thus creating a football-savvy town. Fourth, the football history of Ackerman is steeped in tradition and brings a wellspring of pride to the community. Last, the Eupora Eagles, the rival up the road, keep the residents of Ackerman in constant pursuit of football excellence, or just call it "bragging rights."

Current Ackerman head football coach, Adam Dillinger, recalls the first weeks in town after he was hired:

> For about five days we spent every afternoon going around town to the businesses, just meeting the people in town. We met everybody who was interested in Ackerman football. We went out to talk to everybody because of all the interest in football here. It was almost as if they needed to approve whoever the new person was. So it was like I had the job, but I had to sell myself to the community.

Of course the scene described by Coach Dillinger doesn't seem too abnormal, given the importance placed on hiring a new head coach to take custody of the town's prized possession – its football team. However, Coach Dillinger was describing the routine when he was hired as an *assistant* football coach. Coach Dillinger continues, "They really understand the dynamics that it's not one coach that does everything – it's an entire staff. They want to know who the O-line coach is and who will be coaching DBs – all of the coaches. This community has a high football IQ. Football is so important to them."

When it comes to great coaches, Ackerman and Eupora have a parallel history. Dating back to 1947 under Coach Dale Davidson, Ackerman fielded its first undefeated team. At the end of the 1947 regular season, four teams in the state remained undefeated – Picayune, Meridian, Amory and Ackerman. During the first weekend in December of '47, Ackerman and Amory collided in the Magnolia Bowl in Meridian. That same weekend, Picayune and Meridian put their undefeated records on the line. When the dust settled from these two head-on collisions, Ackerman and Picayune remained standing. Unfortunately, the Mississippi High School Activities Association did not want to extend the season and refused to allow the two super teams to play for a mythical state championship. Ten players from Ackerman's 1947 team signed football scholarships with colleges. One of the players on the Ackerman team, Bo Reid, was a High School All-American and later received similar honors as a player at Mississippi State University. Reid's teammate, Felt Montgomery, played at Ole Miss and was the Most Outstanding Defensive Player in the 1951 Sugar Bowl.

Exactly ten years after the '47 team ran the table to its 13-0 record, another future legendary coach was graduating from Ackerman High School. Mancel Fulce was to spend the next 30 years as a head football coach at Sturgis High School, Holmes Junior College and then back at his alma mater, Ackerman. Not once in his career did Coach Fulce serve as an assistant coach. The first year of the new state championship format, Coach Fulce led the Sturgis Lions to the 1981 Mississippi 1A championship. Coach Fulce says, "I started off as the head man and I ended up that way. I never was an assistant coach. I just did what I thought was right."

While at Ackerman, Coach Fulce had a young assistant coach who left his hometown Indians to lead the Eagle football team up the road in Eupora. However, Ricky Woods would eventually return to Ackerman to coach the Indians to some of the most impressive achievements in the school's football history.

A 1978 graduate of Ackerman High School, Ricky Woods returned to coach at his alma mater in 1995, staying seven seasons and departing in 2002 for South Panola. During those seven seasons, Ackerman beat Eupora five times and lost only twice to the Eagles. Coach Woods took the Indians on a wild state championship ride that few Ackerman fans will ever forget.

Michael Montgomery, a former Ackerman player during Coach Woods' first three season, recalls, "My sophomore year in 1995 we went 10 and 3. My junior year we went 14 and 1 and lost to Bruce in the state championship game. My senior year, 1997, we went 15-0 and won the state."

The 1997 Ackerman team became the first team in Mississippi history to go through the entire playoffs without giving up a single point. The 1997 team was so dominant that the only close game they had all year was a regular season match against Choctaw Central. Trailing 22-8 at halftime, Coach Woods was able to engineer a thrilling 28-25 come-from-behind victory.

Over the remainder of his career at Ackerman, Coach Woods won all of the Indians' regular season games except for one – a loss in 2001. However, that same year, Ackerman won its second state championship.

Many people include Ricky Joe Black, a 1967 graduate of Ackerman High School, in a very select group of coaches in Mississippi – the few coaches people refer to as "the best." After playing for three successive coaches while attending Ackerman High, Black and his teammates found success his senior year, going undefeated in the regular season. The only blemish on the Indians' record was a loss to Starkville High School in a postseason bowl game in Columbus.

After graduating from Ackerman High School in 1967, Black played two years at Holmes Junior College and then completed his education at Mississippi State University. He served as an assistant coach for three years at Kosciusko before becoming their head coach at age 25. During Black's five-year head coaching career at Kosciusko, his teams recorded 49 wins and only 6 losses. In 1980, Black moved to Tupelo to lead the Golden Wave football program for the next 11 seasons. By 1983, the Tupelo program had risen to prominence, as the Golden Wave recorded a perfect 10-0 season record. From the mid-'80s on, Tupelo was a contender every year for the north 5A championship. Black left Tupelo for college ball, accepting a position on the staff at Mississippi State. Following six years of big time SEC football, he decided it was time to do something else. As a favor to two old friends, Walter Shelton and Louis Grubbs, Black interviewed at Jackson Preparatory School.

Today, Ricky Black is still the head football coach at Jackson Prep where, in his 11-year tenure, he has led the Patriots to ten MPSA state championship games, winning five.

The Indians' current head football coach, Adam Dillinger, found his way to Ackerman by way of Jill McClure and Ricky Woods while attending Mississippi State University. Dillinger had the good fortune of doing his student teaching at Ackerman in 1997 under the supervision of Coach Woods. After Dillinger did a short stint at Coffeeville High School, he received an offer from his mentor, Coach Woods, to return to Ackerman. Dillinger accepted the offer for two good reasons. First, Ackerman and Coach Woods were riding the wave of success in Mississippi football at the time. Second, the new Mrs. Adam Dillinger, formerly Jill McClure, was a diehard Indian fan since birth and had family firmly rooted in Ackerman. Jill's dad, Jimmy McClure, an Ackerman graduate and former Ackerman mayor, sums up the attitude of his hometown regarding its football program: "Ackerman is a football town. If you don't win, you don't stay long. You can get by with a lot of things, but you can't get by with being a losing coach." Those are very comforting words for his son-in-law, Coach Dillinger. However, Coach Dillinger and his wife, Jill, fully understand the importance of the football program to this community. Dillinger comments:

> Football is a good metaphor for many people here. This is an area of the state where you have to work hard. There are not a lot of different industries in the area, so people have to work blue-collar jobs. They farm, log and work in the coal mine. We have a lot of rough jobs that our people grew up with. Football, more than any other sport, gets people ready for that type of work. Football is more physically demanding than other sports and attracts a kid that's tougher and has some aggression. That's the way it has been here. I think our kids are just tougher and have more of a natural work ethic than other places in the state. Our kids don't have an easier option. If they don't play football, they are going to be working.

It's not surprising that young coach Adam Dillinger is at Ackerman, given his pedigree and the folks at Ackerman's ability to recognize great coaches. Adams' dad, Jimmy Dillinger, is the legendary head football coach at Baldwyn. Adam's older brother, Ricky, is the new head football coach at Wheeler, and his younger brother, Patrick, is an assistant football coach at Ethel. The Dillingers are a football family for real. Adam fully understands the mindset of the Ackerman community because he shares the same values. "Football is so engrained in everybody's life. That is why we take so much pride in it. This is what we love," states Dillinger.

The key phrase spoken by Coach Dillinger – "This is what we

love" – is the reason the folks of Ackerman selected him as the head football coach of their Indians. With their high FIQ, they recognize that football is what Coach Dillinger loves.

****

There is an old tattered football in the trophy case at Eupora High School bearing the date "1953." What appears at first glance to be a non-descript piece of leather is probably the most prized artifact in the town of Eupora. Embedded among dozens of glittering brass trophies and plaques commemorating athletic accomplishments of past Eagle teams, the old football represents the ultimate prize. Any tour of the Eupora athletic facilities inevitably starts, or ends, in front of the trophy case protecting this priceless Eupora football relic. There, under the glass for the Eagle faithful to see, is evidence of the greatest football victory ever achieved by a Eupora team. The old ball bearing the year "1953" also has a score painted on it – "Eupora 26 Ackerman 20." The ball represents the Eagles' first victory over the Indians since 1935, thereby breaking Ackerman's 18-year death grip on Eupora.

While the records memorializing the early years of the football programs of both teams are sparse, the old football represents a tangible starting point for the Eupora-Ackerman rivalry. Prior to 1953, the Indians dominated the series. However, that 26-20 Eupora victory under head coach Hollis Rutter jumpstarted one of the most intense football series in Mississippi. Located only 17 miles apart, many of the people in both communities work and attend church together. Since most of the residents of these two communities have lived there all their lives, the men have all played in this rivalry and passed on the hatred to their sons. As Coach Ricky Woods explains, "You teach them at a young age – you've got to beat Eupora."

Although the rivalry is more of a friendly one today, during the early years it was quite hostile. Back in the '40s and '50s, it was common for fights to break out at the games. During that same period there were also considerably more pranks pulled on the two campuses. During the Eupora-Ackerman game week, scarecrows dressed like Indians were hung from the Ackerman goal posts. In retaliation, dead buzzards could be found hanging on the school buildings at Eupora. Even though Eupora's mascot is the Eagle, Ackerman fans derisively refer to them as "buzzards" or "chickens." Still today, both teams take turns posting signs for each other along Highway 9. Visiting teams are greeted by the signs designed to depress their spirits and rattle their cage.

Of course, each team today implements countermeasures to the other's psych-out techniques. For example, when Coach Ricky Woods traveled to Eupora, he had the Ackerman police cars escorting the team buses turn on their sirens when they arrived at the Eupora city limits. "It sort of made them mad in Eupora when we did that. I also told my team to snap their chin straps, put their mouth pieces in and get ready," recalls Woods.

Each school over the years has played shenanigans on the other, regardless of all their denials. However, oftentimes the scandalous acts perpetrated on one side have been orchestrated by a coach or fan to pump up their own team while accusing the other side of the misdeed. In fact, such an incident did take place during Coach Woods' third year at Eupora. A Eupora fan, who to this day wishes to remain anonymous, wanted to make sure the Eagle team was "fired up and really mad" for the upcoming Ackerman game. According to the anonymous source, he waited until about 2:00 on the Friday morning before the game. He then went to the market, purchased a few dead chickens and hung them from the goal posts to get the Eupora players' attention. To add insult to injury, this rabid Eagle fan bought several pillows and scattered the white feathers all over the field and around the field house. The next morning, Coach Woods discovered the mess and made his players clean up to the feathers supposedly left by the Ackerman invaders. The ploy worked. The Eupora players were fighting mad and they whipped Ackerman that night.

Throughout the Eupora-Ackerman series there have been those special games that are still talked about years, and in some instances, decades later. One such game occurred in 1997 when the Eagles came to Ackerman for the annual slugfest. You have to go back two years to appreciate fully the 1997 game.

In 1995, Ricky Woods left Eupora to return to his alma mater in Ackerman. In the first meeting between Coach Woods' Ackerman team and his former team at Eupora, the Eagles won decisively – 28-0. It was to be the worst defeat of a Woods-coached team during his career.

Michael Montgomery, a player on the 1995 team, recalls Woods' first game as the Indians' coach his sophomore year:

Our team that year was mostly underclassmen, and Eupora was loaded with juniors and seniors. On one play, Eupora sacked our quarterback close to our sideline. I was standing beside Coach Woods when it happened. After the play, a Eupora player pointed at Coach Woods and said, "We're gonna make you regret that you ever left Eupora." After the game, all of the sophomores on the team went to Coach Woods and told him, "Never again will you lose to Eupora as long as we are on this team."

The next year, Ackerman beat Eupora at Eupora in a 14-13 nail biter. Michael Montgomery recalls the turning point in that big game his junior year:

Winning 13-7, the Eupora quarterback dropped back to pass and one of our defensive ends, Conner Stevens, came off the corner and hit the guy so hard it knocked his helmet and the bandana he was wearing under his helmet ten yards down the field. One of our other defensive players picked up the bandana and put it under his jersey. After we won the game, the teammate who retrieved the bandana gave it to Conner Stevens as a trophy. The whole team went to the middle of the field and danced around the bandana, celebrating like Indians around a freshly taken scalp.

In 1997 it happened – the two teams collided again at Ackerman to settle the score. Each team had a victory in the two previous years. The 1997 game would be the tiebreaker. As the pre-game activities began, everything proceeded in routine fashion, except for one thing – there was no Ackerman team. Just prior to the playing of the "National Anthem," the Eupora team blasted through its crash sheet and took its position on the visitor's sideline. However, still no Ackerman team. After the Ackerman band played the "National Anthem" and just minutes until kickoff – no Indians. People were everywhere. The stands were packed to capacity and the end zones were stacked three deep. At that point, a hush fell over the crowd, an almost immediate recognition that something was wrong. Where was the Ackerman team? Maybe, as odd as it might seem, there would be no game that night. Then, unceremoniously, a bus pulled up over by the home ticket booth and the door opened. Beginning with Ackerman's quarterback, one by one the Ackerman team walked single file into the stadium. According to eyewitness Ronda Huffman, "You could have heard a pin drop in that stadium. It was total silence. They marched one by one all the way up that sideline and went out and lined up for the kickoff. They beat the stew out of Eupora."

According to many Eupora fans, the Eagles were beat before they ever got on the field. Ackerman's entrance into the stadium was a total psych out. They just swaggered onto the field for the kickoff. To this day, the Ackerman fans still refer to the 1997 Eupora game as "The Death March." Ackerman beat Eupora 56-3 that night, fulfilling the promise made by Michael Montgomery and his sophomore teammates to Coach Woods two years earlier.

In every great rivalry, the pendulum swings back and forth between victory and defeat. As fate would have it, the 2001 regular season Eupora-Ackerman game proved to be special for Eupora fans. Having lost to Ackerman for five consecutive years leading up to the 2001 game, Eupora was itching to spoil Ackerman's 62-game winning streak. However, the prognosticators considered Ackerman the overwhelming favorite and didn't give the Eagles much of a chance of winning. As expected, late in the game Ackerman was ahead 21-18 with Eupora in possession of the ball at midfield. On its final drive of the game, Eupora's quarterback launched a Hail Mary to his deep receiver who was covered up by defensive backs. The quarterback had thrown the pass high, requiring the receiver and all three defenders to leap for the ball. The rest of the play turned into a nightmare for the Indians. The Eagle receiver out-jumped the defensive backs and snared the ball. As he landed on the turf, he spun off the would-be tacklers and raced into the end zone. Final score: Eupora 25, Ackerman 21.

Tommy Gladney, a Eupora fan, was sitting on the cemetery terrace of the end zone with some of the old timers. He recalls, "It was like he ran the ball right into our laps. I was shouting; then I was crying. I called my wife and said, 'You want to know the score?' She said, 'Yeah. How bad did we get beat?' I said, 'Eupora won the ballgame 25-21.' I ran out on the field; I was still crying."

It was a great day in Eupora's football history, but a dark, dark day for the Indians. To make matters even worse for Ackerman fans, the win in 2001 rejuvenated Eupora, who proceeded to beat Ackerman six times in the next eight years. However, despite Ackerman's heartbreaking loss to Eupora in the fourth game of the regular season, the Indians regrouped and went on to post a 14-1 record and win another state championship in 2001. Recalls Woods, "We were proud of that state championship, but that was a heartbreaking loss. I wish somebody else other than Eupora would have been the one to beat us."

When the senior football players at Ackerman got together after winning the state championship in 2001 to decide on the design of the team's championship ring, they faced a dilemma. Should the ring have the team's impressive 14-1 record etched into it, or simply the words "State Champions" without the record? Unanimously, the seniors decided on foregoing the record and engraving the ring with "State Champions." The reason? They could not bear to be reminded of the loss to Eupora, regardless of winning the state championship.

WHAT THE INDIANS SAY ABOUT EUPORA

Back in the '70s and '80s, it could have gotten out of hand quickly. That's when you had your pulpwood boys coming to town on Friday nights. They didn't mind getting crossed up with somebody if they had a different opinion.

Frank Black
Former Ackerman Football Player

Used to, you didn't go up there a lot. If you did, you wouldn't go by yourself; you would go in a group. Today, most people in Ackerman and Eupora are friends.

Jimmy McClure
Former Ackerman Football Player

We have Mourn for Eupora Day – Mourn the Eagles, which is like the death of the Eagles. Everybody wears black. Last year we actually had a funeral where we had an Eagle in a casket.

Jennifer Cooper
Ackerman Cheerleader

I think there are many similarities between the towns, the schools and the people. It's a lot of people that are alike.

Jill Dillinger
Former Ackerman Student
and Wife of Head Football Coach

The Eupora-Ackerman game is a huge deal. It's the Saturday morning talk at the coffee shop and they talk it year round – it's not just during football season.

Ronda Huffman
Ackerman Principal

I think this rivalry is steeped in football pride.

Adam Dillinger
Ackerman Head Football Coach

If you want to know the truth, I really got my start at Eupora.

Ricky Woods
Former Ackerman Football Player
and Head Football Coach

One time back in the '50s, Eupora beat Ackerman something like 60-12. Twenty years later, the folks in Ackerman were still paying them back for that game.

Ricky Black
Former Ackerman Football Player

I played sports in the seventh grade through my senior year. I played two years at Delta State University. I was only involved in one on-the-field fight. That was in the Ackerman-Eupora game my junior year.

Dale Reid
Former Ackerman Football Player
and Public Address Announcer

You don't lose the Eupora game. There are no excuses.

Ricky Woods
Former Ackerman Football Player
and Head Football Coach

The Eupora-Ackerman game completely defines the meaning of "rivalry."

Jennifer Cooper
Ackerman Cheerleader

WHAT THE EAGLES SAY ABOUT ACKERMAN

If you don't win down there, then you go to the house real quick.

Reuban Walker
Former Eupora Head Football Coach

Because of the football rivalry, we don't socialize with Ackerman people.

Blakelee Parsons
Former Eupora Student Body President

There's not much in Ackerman. Well, there is a girl in Ackerman that does good hair.

Molly Pittman
Eupora Cheerleader

A lot of rivalries seem to hit a lull and fizzle out, but this one has not. Our kids still make a big deal out of it. Everything about the rivalry with Ackerman is special.

Jimmy Pittman
Former Eupora Head Football Coach
and Superintendent of Webster County School District

I've eaten at Pap's fish house once and it wasn't that good.

Kody Knight
Eupora Football Player

There is always going to be something special about the Eupora-Ackerman game, no matter what happens the rest of the season. When it's over, everybody starts thinking about the game next year.

James Mason
Former Eupora Student and
Eupora Principal

Ackerman is the toughest opponent Eupora has had down through the years.

Tommy Lott
Former Eupora Student and Mayor of Eupora

The Eupora-Ackerman game is the biggest event in Webster County.

James Mason
Former Eupora Student
and Eupora Principal

Every time I have traveled to Ackerman to play, there have been signs all along Highway 9 saying they are going to beat us.

Jonathan Holmes
Eupora Public Address and Radio Announcer

It has been a huge rivalry all of my life. You have to beat Ackerman. It doesn't matter about any other game.

Suzanne Graham
Former Eupora Student and
Wife of Head Football Coach

When we play Ackerman, I tell our kids, "You're going to get their 'A' game. Kids in Choctaw County know how to play in big games; so get ready."

Junior Graham
Eupora Head Football Coach

There is nothing in Ackerman unless you want to get a Philly from Bumpers. That's about it.

Blakelee Parsons
Former Eupora Student Body President

It's a friendly rivalry, but each side likes to rub it in when they win. It's like the Ole Miss-State thing.

Phillip Smith
Former Eupora Football Player
and Sheriff of Webster County

I've heard they have Eupora Skank Day the week of the game. They probably dress like they normally come to school.

Blakelee Parsons
Former Eupora Student Body President

I think the kids live the rivalry all year, but the adults on both sides who are such enemies on that one Friday night are friends again the following Monday – for the most part.

Jimmy Pittman
Former Eupora Head Football Coach
and Superintendent of Webster County School District

I don't know how it got started – probably by the cheerleaders – but every year since I've been affiliated with the school, one day during the week of the game is Ackerman Hick Day. Our students wear straw hats. Some girls wear pigtails and freckles.

James Mason
Former Eupora Student
and Eupora Principal

The Ackerman game is always more intense than any other game we play. You want to win that game like the state championship.

Kody Knight
Eupora Football Player

ACKERMAN-EUPORA
SERIES HISTORY

Year	Ackerman	Score	Eupora
1934	Coach Sanders	12-0	Coach Rowe
1935	Coach Sanders	0-18	Coach Hine
1936	Coach Sanders		*No team*
1937	Coach Sanders		*No team*
1938	Coach Sanders	13-6	Coach Phillips
1939	Coach Sanders	33-6	Coach Phillips
1940	Frank Branch	19-7	Coach Phillips
1941	Frank Branch	13-6	Coach Phillips
1942	Frank Branch	*Did Not Play*	Coach Hunter
1943	Frank Branch	14-0	Coach Wilson
1944	Frank Branch	26-6	Coach Crawford
1945	Frank Branch	34-0	Coach Wright
1946	Dale Davidson	39-0	Coach Wright
1947	Dale Davidson	*Did Not Play*	Mike Mahalic
1948	Dale Davidson	40-0	Grady McCool
1949	Dale Davidson	28-6	Grady McCool
1950	Dale Davidson	34-7	Grady McCool
1951	Dale Davidson	13-13	Coach Gunn
1952	Dale Davidson	47-6	Hollis Rutter
1953	Dale Davidson	20-26	Hollis Rutter
1954	Dale Davidson	19-19	Hollis Rutter
1955	Prentiss Irvin	13-39	Hollis Rutter
1956	Prentiss Irvin	19-61	Hollis Rutter
1957	Prentiss Irvin	12-59	Coach Garner
1958	Prentiss Irvin	0-40	Coach Garner
1959	Jeff Gardner	7-27	Coach Nichols
1960	Jeff Gardner	0-28	Coach Nichols
1961	Sam Kendricks	6-33	Coach Nichols
1962	Sam Kendricks	20-7	Coach Nichols
1963	Sam Kendricks	12-14	Doug Sullivan
1964	Sam Kendricks	0-0	Doug Sullivan
1965	Billy Newman	28-12	Doug Sullivan
1966	Jim Brown	50-27	Doug Sullivan
1967	Parker Dykes	0-32	Doug Sullivan

Year	Ackerman	Score	Eupora
1968	Parker Dykes	7-13	Doug Sullivan
1969	Parker Dykes	6-20	Doug Sullivan
1970	Art Nester	0-21	Reuban Walker
1971	Art Nester	35-12	Reuban Walker
1972	Ronnie Ware	6-7	Reuban Walker
1973	Ronnie Ware	0-0	Reuban Walker
1974	Ronnie Ware	29-0	Coach Hamby
1975	Ronnie Ware	42-3	Coach Hamby
1976	Ronnie Ware	40-0	Coach Hamby
1977	Ronnie Ware	28-22	Coach Brantley
1978	Ronnie Ware	8-41	Jerry Brantley
1979	Larry Harms	7-35	Jerry Brantley
1980	Larry Harms	7-14	Jerry Brantley
1981	Larry Harms	7-20	Jerry Brantley
1982	Randy Martin	0-55	Jerry Brantley
1983	Randy Martin	7-0	Jerry Brantley
1984	Randy Martin	7-13	Jerry Brantley
1985	Randy Martin	13-0	Jerry Brantley
1986	Johnny Fulce	6-34	Jerry Brantley
1987	Johnny Fulce	0-23	Jerry Brantley
1988	Johnny Fulce	7-13	Jerry Brantley
1989	Johnny Fulce	14-14	Jerry Brantley
1990	Johnny Fulce	14-6	Ricky Woods
1991	Johnny Fulce	50-25	Ricky Woods
1992	Bill Scott	13-25	Ricky Woods
1993	Bill Scott	0-35	Ricky Woods
1994	Bill Scott	14-28	Ricky Woods
1995	Ricky Woods	0-28	Jimmy Pittman
1996	Ricky Woods	14-13	Jimmy Pittman
1997	Ricky Woods	56-3	Jimmy Pittman
1998	Ricky Woods	54-0	Lance Pogue
1999	Ricky Woods	14-7	Lance Pogue
2000	Ricky Woods	33-6	Lance Pogue
2001	Ricky Woods	21-25	Lance Pogue
2002	Steve Denson	28-19	Lance Pogue
2002	Steve Denson	34-35	Lance Pogue
2003	Steve Denson	15-18	Lance Pogue
2004	Steve Denson	8-7	Lance Pogue

Year	Ackerman	Score	Eupora
2004	Steve Denson	9-15	Lance Pogue
2005	Steve Denson	12-21	Lance Pogue
2006	Adam Dillinger	27-54	Lance Pogue
2007	Adam Dillinger	6-23	Harold "Junior" Graham

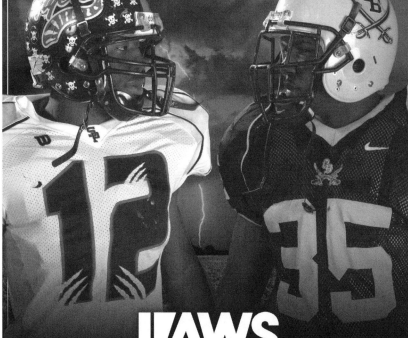

★★ OFFICIAL GAME DAY PROGRAM $5.00 ★★

SOUTH PANOLA
VERSUS
OLIVE BRANCH

L/AWS
CONSTRUCTION

PROUD SPONSOR OF MISSISSIPPI HIGH SCHOOL FOOTBALL

FRIDAY, OCTOBER 3, 2008 ★ 7:00 PM KICKOFF
POOL FIELD ★ OLIVE BRANCH, MISSISSIPPI

CHAPTER
13

THE KING AND THE CONTENDER

Hanging on the walls in the corridor leading into the Olive Branch football complex are photographs of previous Conquistador teams. What is remarkable about this collection of team photos is the number – 82 in all – dating back to the first Olive Branch football team of 1926. To fully appreciate the deep sense of pride this town in north central Mississippi has for its football program, one has to carefully study the 1930 team photo. There, second from the left on the back row is Jack Bell, grandfather of Olive Branch's current head football coach, Scott Samsel. Pictured in the 1928 team photograph is Frank Brigance, the great uncle of Kyle Brigance, the current principal of Olive Branch High School.

The Brigance family helped settle the Olive Branch area in the 1800s. According to Kyle Brigance, there were four Brigance brothers who came over from France on a ship that landed in North Carolina. When they arrived in the United States, one brother stayed in North Carolina, one brother migrated to Oklahoma, another brother went to Florida and the fourth Brigance brother settled in the Olive Branch area. During the Civil War, the Brigance household served as a hospital. Still located on the homestead today is the family cemetery. Brigance roots run very, very deep in Olive Branch. They are extremely proud of their community.

Kyle attended school at Olive Branch and, while in high school, played quarterback for the legendary Coach Leslie Pool. After graduation from college, Kyle returned to Olive Branch and started his coaching career. Kyle's dad, Lemoyne Brigance, was the principal at the elementary school, and his mom taught at the intermediate school in Olive Branch. His coaching career eventually brought Kyle back in contact with his former coach, Leslie Pool. When Coach Pool retired from coaching in 1998, Kyle moved into school administration. Today,

Kyle Brigance is the principal of Olive Branch High School – a dream fulfilled and another proud Blue and Gold legacy. To boot, Kyle's wife, Allyson, is a teacher at the Olive Branch middle school.

Another disciple of the legendary Coach Pool is one of his former players, Scott Samsel, now the Olive Branch head football coach. Scott played for the Conquistadors under Coach Pool from 1976 to 1978 and then served as an assistant to Pool from 1985 to 1989. After Coach Pool's retirement in 1998, two coaches, Mike Moore and Jamie Mitchell, followed before Coach Samsel returned. Both Coach Moore and Coach Mitchell helped maintain the Olive Branch football legacy between 1999 and 2005. Coach Pool tells the story of how he tried to recruit Samsel to follow him upon his retirement:

> Scott and I were good friends. We hunted together when he played for me and later when he was one of my assistant coaches. I had a great deal of faith that Scott would maintain the program in the way the community had grown to respect and expect. Scott and I drove around town for several hours, talking about the opportunity for him to become my successor. Eventually, we ended up at Scott's grandmother's house and talked some more. In the end, Scott turned down the job. However, two coaches and several years later, he is finally home.

That's one more Samsel added to the photo wall showcasing the storied Conquistador legacy.

The legacy chain of the Olive Branch football program remains stronger than ever. Currently coaching the 7th-grade team, Rob Pool, son of Coach Leslie Pool, directs the development of future Conquistadors. According to Rob, "We actually run the same offense my dad ran years ago. It's just from a spread formation. The same reads I made when I played high school football, I am teaching to the kids I now coach. The more things change, the more they stay the same." Add another link in the Olive Branch football legacy.

The Conquistador football legacy is fueled by a storied past and the dreams of gridiron glory in the minds of youngsters all over Olive Branch. One such youngster back in the early 1970s was Sammy Jones. Sammy was a running back for the Conquistadors between 1976 and 1979, setting a single-game rushing record (298 yards) that still stands today. Jones describes his thoughts about playing for Olive Branch when he was eight years old:

> The football field was close to my house, so I could hear the public address announcer on Friday nights in the fall. I sat on the front porch with my mama and listened to the game. Everyone in our house was at the game except for me and Mama. I told myself, "One of these days they are going to be announcing my name on that loud speaker." I knew then – when I was eight – that I was going to play football for the Conquistadors. When it came my time, I was determined to be on that field wearing the blue and gold. I just loved sitting on the porch with Mama listening to that announcer and dreaming about what it would be like to hear, "Touchdown by Sammy Jones" and the roar of the crowd.

The single-game rushing record set by Sammy Jones in 1978 becomes even more important in Olive Branch football history, considering it was in the Conquistador's first victory over . . . South Panola.

Forty years after Sammy Jones sat on his front porch with his mama listening to the public address announcer and dreaming of his football heroics, another Olive Branch youngster is living out his dream playing for the Conquistadors. Clint Wilson, Olive Branch's current quarterback, has wanted to quarterback the Blue and Gold since he was a kid growing up in Olive Branch. Clint's dad, Andy, says, "That's been my son's goal ever since he was a child. Clint was born in Olive Branch and we have been going to Conquistador games together his entire life." He's yet another Olive Branch youngster chasing the dream and wanting to be a part of the legacy – another photograph on the wall.

The entire Olive Branch community is committed to supporting the Conquistador football program and helping its young men chase their dreams. As Olive Branch Mayor Sam Rikard points out, "The football program is a point of community pride. It is the billboard of our community." To fully appreciate the support the team gets, one must visit the Olive Branch weight room. Upon entering the new facility for the first time, any visitor unaware of where he was would assume he was standing in a state-of-the-art weight room at a major university. However, what makes this facility so special is that it was designed and built by two former Conquistador players. Willie Anderson and Dustin Bobbitt worked together to make every piece of equipment in the training facility except the bars and plates - everything hand-built and custom made for the Conquistadors. The Olive Branch weight room is tangible evidence of the commitment by the community, its former players and the booster club to the youngsters wearing the Blue and Gold, and to future Conquistadors dreaming about hearing their names called out over the public address system on those special Friday nights in the fall at Leslie Pool Field.

The community's commitment to the Olive Branch football program has paid dividends. The Conquistadors have advanced to the north Mississippi championship game twice as many times as all the other schools in DeSoto County combined.

****

Approximately 60 miles southwest of Olive Branch is Batesville, a small Mississippi town with a population of 8,000. Located in Batesville is one of the premier high school football programs in America – the South Panola Tigers, or as they have become known, the "University" of South Panola. Currently, the Tigers are riding an incredible 75-game winning streak that leads the nation. From 2003 to 2007, South Panola has won an unprecedented five straight Mississippi 5A championships. In addition to their amazing state championship run, the Tigers captured additional titles in 1993 and 1998. Every year, the South Panola football program produces double-digit numbers of players heavily recruited by colleges and universities across the country. As a testament to the intense loyalty Tiger fans and players have for South Panola, former Tiger great Deshea Townsend announced the "University" of South Panola as his college alma mater during pre-game introductions of the Pittsburgh Steelers' defensive unit prior to Super Bowl XL.

Unfortunately, along with the success of South Panola's football program have come the critics. Regardless of the target of their criticism, high school athletics in general, or South Panola football specifically, the critics are quick to condemn all athletic accomplishments. The foundation for arguments against successful high school athletic programs rests on the presumption that a school can not achieve consistent success and stay within the rules. Thus, critics arrive at the conclusion that the successful teams must be cheating, either in the form of improper recruiting, playing ineligible players or paying off referees, along with a myriad of other accusations. In other words, success seems to bring with it an automatic presumption of guilt!

A close examination of the South Panola football program reveals that these typical criticisms don't apply to the Tigers. Instead, one finds that the reason for the unusual success of the Tiger program is based on an unusual work ethic – a work ethic rarely found in college football programs, let alone high school programs.

Obviously, the extended success of South Panola football has been greatly aided by a roster of highly talented and dedicated coaches. As far back as 1968, Coach Runt McMinn was building the foundation for South Panola's winning teams of today. Continuing into the modern era of Mississippi high school football (i.e., the advent of the state championship playoff system in 1981), outstanding coaches such as Willis Wright, Ed Stanley, Ricky Woods and current head coach Lance Pogue have all won one or more state championships. In addition to outstanding coaches, Panola County has provided the Tigers with an unlimited stock of highly-talented athletes. However, the best-kept secret surrounding the success of South Panola's football program is the Tiger's junior high coaching staff. Meet Coaches Robert Lightsey and Will Roberson, both of whom have coached South Panola's junior high teams for the past 27 years. That's right. The same coaches have been in the same junior high positions for their entire careers. Coaches Lightsey and Roberson coach the 7th, 8th and 9th-grade teams, which involve over 225 players, along with 6th-grade P.E. classes.

According to Coach Lightsey, "Around Christmas, we select the top 50 athletes in the 6th grade and send them to the weight room. After we max them out to determine their strength levels, we put them in groups and start them on a six-week training cycle." Lightsey and Roberson don't have to beg the kids to lift weights because every boy at South Panola dreams of playing for the Tigers. The kids are already motivated. So to earn your Tiger stripes, it is understood that working out in the weight room is essential.

Coach Lightsey describes the drill: "We place them in groups of three and everyone in the group is responsible for each other. The kids monitor each other. We find out real quick who the leaders are. We don't put up with any messing around. The kids discover if a player doesn't make his grades he will not play. They wake up to that concept real quick." Coach Lightsey continues, "Another aspect of the work ethic is discipline. If a teacher has any problems with one of our players, that player gets three licks with the board and then I ask him what happened." Coaches Lightsey and Roberson run a no-nonsense classroom and weight room program. The players either accept their policy or they don't become Tiger football players. Lightsey says, "It's all about discipline. We're tougher on players now more so than we used to be. Kids today can be hardheaded. They have so many distractions – cell phones, computers, television and X Boxes. But it always gets back to discipline."

Coach Lightsey's no-nonsense approach is quite evident in the weight room. Once he and Coach Roberson get the three-man groups organized, the lifting techniques taught and each player on a training routine, the players are on their own. If a player does not meet his lifting goal at the end of a six-week cycle, then out comes the board. Every player in the three-man group gets punished, even though the other players may have reached their respective goals. Explains Coach Lightsey: "We do this to teach them team concepts. Being on a team is about helping your teammates. It is extremely important that our kids understand their responsibility to each other. We constantly stress that the team is more important than the individual." Of course every player has the option of leaving the program if he chooses. However, most of Coach Lightsey's players comply with the classroom and weightlifting demands and eagerly set out to earn their Tiger jerseys. "The kids in our program are not about to turn in that jersey. We stay on them every day about working hard, keeping their grades up and their responsibility to the team and the community. Everyone understands what we are trying to accomplish. It's all about molding them into good, responsible citizens," states Lightsey. Coaches Lightsey and Roberson receive the full support of their players' parents, mainly because the parents are byproducts of the same system. Most of the players' parents were coached by Lightsey and Roberson. "Many of our kids come from disadvantaged backgrounds; however, our football program gives them certain advantages, like pride. That is what motivates them in the classroom. They learn lessons in the weight room and on the football field that cannot be learned in the classroom. For our kids, the classroom, weight room and football field work together to build their self-esteem," says Coach Lightsey.

Upon his arrival at South Panola, first-year head coach Lance Pogue immediately noticed the difference in the work ethic. Pogue says,

"The biggest thing I found is these kids have unique work habits. They are physically tough. It's unbelievable. They work so hard physically that they distance themselves from the competition. We have some talent, but the work ethic is the big difference – strictly blue collar and proud of it."

Long-time Tiger public address and radio announcer, George Carlson, describes a typical day in the South Panola weight room: "There are no coaches present. The older players are in control. Everybody is working hard. Nobody slacks off. They work hard at working hard. Their mentality is to do what it takes."

Dixie Pogue, Coach Pogue's wife, teaches P.E. classes at Pope Elementary School, one of the feeder schools to South Panola. Dixie describes her young students as "competitive – so competitive. They want to be the fastest and strongest – just so competitive. Most all of my students have dads, uncles, brothers and cousins who have played for the Tigers. They want to out-do them."

Because so many former Tiger players have made a name for themselves at the collegiate and professional levels, the pride associated with playing for the Tigers is infectious throughout every level of the South Panola football program. Take for example what a high school player must do to earn his name on the back of his game jersey. Each player must attend a predetermined number of off-season workouts to get his name on the coveted Tiger jersey. According to Dixie Pogue, "Most of the workouts are at 7:00 a.m. The majority of our kids don't have cars, but they will find a way to get to those workouts at 7:00 a.m. They want their names on that jersey. It's all about pride, and the kids are willing to work hard to earn that respect."

Many critics of successful high school football programs often argue against their educational value. Those accusations include winning at all costs, elevating football over all other athletic and academic programs, lower graduation rates for athletes and the pampering of football players. School administrators everywhere have heard these common complaints. As South Panola's football program has achieved more and more success, especially at the national level, its school administrators have heard all these criticisms. However, a close examination of the Tiger football program reveals the contrary.

Consider several noteworthy facts. In 2007, first-year head coach Lance Pogue benched his Parade All-American running back prior to the most important game of the regular season against South

Panola's biggest rival. After following Coach Ricky Woods' four consecutive state championships and a 60-game winning streak, Coach Pogue inherited a monster. The pressure to maintain the Tiger program at its championship level was a challenge of the highest order. At stake were his coaching reputation and the confidence of his players. Coach Pogue set aside all the pressure on him and focused on the greater good of the team and the player who was benched. He sent a message about priorities. Coach Pogue's action was a tangible demonstration that he did not buy into the "win at all costs" philosophy.

Frequently, the allegations of improper recruiting and playing ineligible players are made against successful football programs. However, anyone who is remotely familiar with South Panola is aware of the bloodlines – the Sanfords, Barksdales, Townsends, Conners and Burdettes, just to name a few – all homegrown. The South Panola bloodlines span over 40 years. The short answer to this criticism is that South Panola doesn't need to recruit. Its Tigers are all homegrown with numerous Tiger cubs in the weight room getting ready for their chance to compete on the gridiron.

The current principal at South Panola, Gearl Loden, provides some interesting facts about the Tiger athletic programs. According to Principal Loden, "We try to balance all our athletic programs to make sure we offer a lot of opportunities for our kids." In addition to the standard sports (i.e., football, basketball, baseball, soccer and track), South Panola has added archery, bowling and girls' golf and cross country. Both boys' and girls' powerlifting are also offered. The South Panola varsity cheerleading squad is currently ranked sixth nationally. Interestingly, South Panola conducts only one pep rally a season, and that is during its annual homecoming festivities.

Principal Loden describes the academic support system at South Panola for all of its students: "We try to match our kids with good mentors so you have an adult other than a parent reinforcing the values of being on time, making good grades and being responsible. We have tutorial sessions three days a week and run buses for those kids who need transportation. There are a number of our teachers who give extra time, even on weekends, to help students. We have a good school."

As far as graduation rates are concerned, South Panola ranks 21st out of 151 school districts in Mississippi. "If someone is about to drop out, we get that student in our GED program and do our best to encourage them to stick it out. Most of the time, we are successful. If a student drops out, we are all failures," states Loden. "The stark reality is that due to the success of our football program, everything we do at South Panola is put under a microscope. Everyone watches us. If we make a mistake, the whole world sees it and points at us," explains Loden.

Finally, for all those critics claiming that high school football players are pampered and coddled, those misguided folks need to report to the South Panola weight room at 7:00 a.m. and ask for Coach Robert Lightsey or Coach Will Roberson. Enjoy your pampering!

****

The Olive Branch-South Panola rivalry began in 1972. South Panola High School came into existence in 1963 with the consolidation of area schools brought about by integration. At the time South Panola High School began, it became a member of the Delta Valley Conference and did not compete against Olive Branch. However, in the early '70s, South Panola joined the Chickasaw Conference and met Olive Branch for the first time on the gridiron in 1972, defeating the Conquistadors 29-0. For the following five seasons, the Tigers won the annual game against Olive Branch. However, in 1978, Olive Branch defeated South Panola 42-16 for the first time behind the record-setting performance of junior fullback Sammy Jones. After defeating the Tigers again in 1979, the Conquistadors lost the next five games to South Panola in close, hard-fought contests. Then to reverse the trend, Olive Branch High School won the next five games against South Panola from 1984 to 1989. The two schools traded victories in 1989 and 1990. Between 1991 and 1998, the Tigers and Conquistadors did not play each other due to Olive Branch being reclassified as a 4A school, while South Panola remained in the 5A classification. The series resumed in 1999 with South Panola defeating Olive Branch 35-7. The Conquistadors returned the favor in 2000 with a thrilling 17-16 win over the Tigers. Since the victory in 2000, Olive Branch has not defeated South Panola, although they have met in 10 games (7 regular season and 3 playoff games). The 2007 season marked the third in a row that the Conquistadors made it to the 5A north Mississippi championship game to face South Panola. All of the recent games between the Tigers and the Conquistadors have been classics. South Panola and Olive Branch represent big-time high school football at its finest. At the conclusion of the 2007 playoffs, these two powerhouse teams had played 32 times in the rivalry dating back to 1972. South Panola leads the series with 23 wins to Olive Branch's 9.

According to Olive Branch Mayor Sam Rikard, "It gets down to this; you can't find a better football game than Olive Branch playing South Panola. I believe the rivalry has grown to where it is today because of the quality of both football programs. The rivalry between the two schools is intense, but respectful, because of the level of excellence of both programs."

Batesville Mayor Jerry Autrey comments:

> I've probably seen every Olive Branch-South Panola game played. Olive Branch is a progressive town with a big population. They've got the students and the players. South Panola is going to have to beat them every year, probably twice, to advance to the state championship. The two communities have a good relationship. All of us know we are going to see a great football game. It's great for the teams and for the state to have a rivalry like South Panola and Olive Branch.

Myra Bean, sports reporter for *The Panolian*, comments, "The rivalry has been amazing. It's so intense. In many ways, South Panola has pushed all the other teams in the district to become better."

When South Panola and Olive Branch take the field against each other, the crowds swell to ten, eleven and twelve thousand spectators. According to Mayor Rikard:

> The whole football program is a point of community pride. The South Panola game is where you are able to put your best against their best. We have been able to play our best football against one of the best football programs in the nation. Both teams play as hard a football as you'd ever want to see; but when it's over, you know the team that scored the most points won. They shake hands and walk off respecting each other.

The sentiment flowing from both the South Panola and Olive Branch supporters is that a Tiger and Conquistador football game is at a higher level than a typical high school game. As Mayor Rikard states, "It's big league football. All these other games are warm-ups for the

South Panola game. South Panola is usually ranked No. 1 in the state and Olive Branch, No. 2. South Panola is consistently ranked in the top ten teams nationally. To me, that means Olive Branch is up there among the elite high school football teams in America."

Mayor Autrey comments about the Olive Branch rivalry: "Both programs can compete with the big dogs. It's not a hate rivalry; it's one of respect, because each team is capable of beating the other on any given night. Everyone knows both teams are talented and well prepared. We have respect for each other."

Interestingly, Olive Branch and South Panola are the other's biggest fan as long as they are not playing each other. The South Panola folks want Olive Branch to stay strong and keep winning so the classic games with South Panola will continue. At Olive Branch, they want to be the team that ends the South Panola winning streak and dethrones the Tigers of the 5A state championship.

Coach Samsel's wife, Kellie, described the reaction of their nine-year-old son, Jack, when it was announced during an Olive Branch game that Columbus was beating South Panola during the 2007 regular reason. "He got real upset and said, 'I don't want Columbus to beat them. I want to be the one to beat them.' At age 9 he knows it's a special game."

Olive Branch principal, Kyle Brigance, speaks highly of the South Panola school administrators: "They have always been very hospitable to us. It's just a wonderful atmosphere in which to play football. They have a huge set of stands and we pack our side. Tickets for the game are sold in advance. It's just an electric atmosphere. The anticipation for the South Panola game is unbearable." Former Olive Branch player, Sammy Jones, described his experience playing at South Panola. "They were well-mannered. The fans treated you real nice. There was no rowdy behavior like throwing stuff at you or getting cussed out from the stands."

Jamie Mercer, *DeSoto County Tribune* reporter, says, "I have never seen any kind of rivalry that has sustained its intensity as long as South Panola and Olive Branch. This rivalry doesn't seem to be dwindling at all. If anything, it is getting more intense. There is so much intensity and respect when South Panola and Olive Branch get together. I think that bleeds over to the fans. After the game, the players from both teams are shaking hands and talking. The coaches are all out on the field talking. The parents and fans on both sides are all on the field shaking hands and talking. You can hardly tell who is for whom."

Jamie continues, "I've talked to some other coaches in the area whose teams play South Panola. Often, they have the attitude that the Tigers are unbeatable and they wish there was some way to get them off the schedule. It's not that way at Olive Branch. Our mindset is: here's the date, circle it in red and get ready. The attitude at other schools is, 'If we beat South Panola;' but here at Olive Branch, we talk about 'When we beat the Tigers.' Around Olive Branch, the South Panola game is bigger than the Super Bowl."

Former legendary Olive Branch head football coach Leslie Pool describes the big game:

> I think everyone can actually feel the excitement when you come into the stadium. The players have more bounce in their step and are just more pumped up. As the game begins, you see a very aggressive style of play. For people who love football, watching Olive Branch and South Panola play is a totally positive experience. The fans get into it, the cheerleaders are into it and so is the band. It's the total package for anybody who loves high school football.

Coach Pool's experiences as a spectator of the game after his retirement bear out the description that the Olive Branch and South Panola game is all about respect and good sportsmanship. "I don't think I can recall any game getting out of hand. The reason is because both schools have quality coaching staffs that demand sportsmanship and citizenship. It's a mutual respect, not only from the coaching staffs, but also from the players," says Pool.

Olive Branch and Batesville represent small town Mississippi at its best when it comes to high school football. Despite the typical economic, social and religious divides that can exist in communities anywhere, the success of the Conquistador and Tiger football programs has created a sense of pride in both towns. According to Mayor Autrey, South Panola football has had positive effects on the Batesville community in many ways. Two examples touch on race relations and work ethic. "We have a good black-white relationship in Batesville. When the kids are young they all play together for a common goal – victory for South Panola. I think that attitude – everyone pulling together for a common goal – carries over as they get older, graduate and stay in Batesville," states Mayor Autrey. As to the work ethic taught by the rigors of the Tiger football program, the mayor says, "The young kids see how hard the players work, not just during the season, but all year. It spills over into their work ethic and study habits." This attitude is echoed by junior Tiger David Conner. "Everybody in our school and town is so encouraging. That's why we go out and play hard. We want to keep the streak going for them. Our fans inspire us to keep playing harder and harder. Playing for South Panola is just a dream come true for me. I want to live here all my life. I love everybody."

The bond to Olive Branch is just as strong for Conquistador Carlos Wilson as it is for David Conner to Batesville. When asked if he could reverse the 2007 playoff game loss to the Tigers, would he then exchange the win for a make-believe payment of $10,000, his response was an emphatic, "Burn the money." When the ante was upped to $100,000, Carlos responded again, "Burn it." When the jackpot was increased to $1,000,000, his response was, "I want the win. Burn the money." Carlos went on to say, "This is the place I want to be. Olive Branch is a great place to live, work and play football."

Olive Branch and Batesville – two communities; the Conquistadors and Tigers – two teams; Carlos Wilson and David Conner – two high school football players. They all demonstrate the intense loyalty and pride engendered by their football programs. The Olive Branch and South Panola rivalry is based on respect for the excellence of the other and pride in one's community.

WHAT THE TIGERS SAY ABOUT OLIVE BRANCH

All that pointing at opposing players and trash talking like "I'm gonna get you" isn't real smart, because God doesn't like ugly.

David Conner
South Panola FootballPlayer

Olive Branch is the school most determined to beat us.

Jamie Battle
South Panola Cheerleader

Olive Branch is capable of beating us every year, because they have the numbers and the quality of players.

Jerry Autrey
Mayor of Batesville

I admire Olive Branch. If I couldn't go to school at South Panola, I would want to go to Olive Branch. I want them to win all their other games like they have been doing; because the more they win it inspires me.

David Conner
South Panola Football Player

Olive Branch has always had a proud football tradition. It goes all the way back to Coach Leslie Pool.

George Carlson
South Panola Radio Announcer

Our weight room may not be better than their weight room, but as long as we work hard, we don't need all that fancy stuff.

David Conner
South Panola Football Player

I think there is no question that Olive Branch is the second best 5A team in Mississippi – not just the past year, but over the last several years. South Panola has just been fortunate to be a little bit better.

Lance Pogue
South Panola Head Football Coach

After the playoff game this past year, the Olive Branch players wished us "Good luck. Hope you win it all." They showed good sportsmanship. It really meant a lot coming from our biggest rival.

Marvin Burdett
South Panola Football Player

The two schools respect each other. It is a very intense rivalry and a lot of fun. You won't find nicer people than the folks in Olive Branch.

George Carlson
South Panola Radio Announcer

The Olive Branch fans probably think we are really cocky because we are undefeated and have the long winning streak. We really don't think like that at all. We just like to win. Batesville is just a town that loves its football. It's not just the school. It's the whole town.

Jamie Battle
South Panola Cheerleader

The fans at Olive Branch think South Panola has won so often that we don't care very much anymore. They are wrong!

Myra Bean
Sports Reporter for The Panolian

WHAT THE CONQUISTADORS SAY ABOUT SOUTH PANOLA

South Panola has an unusually large number of quality players. I think they have gained the confidence needed to win close games. The opponent comes in thinking maybe they can't win. In close games, South Panola's players seem to have the backbone and character to reach back and go to another level to get that win.

Coach Leslie Pool
Former Olive Branch Head Football Coach

I think their kids work hard in the weight room. Their kids expect to win. From the time they are in the 7th grade, they know there is something special about them because they wear that "SP".

Coach Rob Pool
Olive Branch Assistant Football Coach

Coach Willis Wright is a winner.

Kellie Samsel
Wife of Olive Branch Head Football Coach

I think their sense of community is still intact. There is a lot of family history and family tradition in South Panola football. Their young men feel a lot of pressure from relatives and the community because it is so tight knit. They feel pressure from the community to not just play football, but to excel in playing football. I believe that is the motivating factor in the weight room. It's a big deal to the community.

Coach Scott Samsel
Olive Branch Head Football Coach

South Panola's big criticism of Olive Branch is that we play so many teams out of Tennessee. However, we have a difficult time scheduling games every year.

Andy Wilson
Olive Branch Booster Club President

When South Panola scores a touchdown, it's almost like, "Okay, wow, another touchdown." They aren't as excited as we are when Olive Branch scores.

Carley Wilson
Olive Branch Cheerleader

I think South Panola is getting complacent. All good things come to an end, and especially if you are cocky.

Carlos Wilson
Olive Branch Football Player

South Panola's secret to success is hard work and determination. Winning has become contagious. I think people are intimidated by them.

Clint Wilson
Olive Branch Football Player

South Panola has always had that mystique and tradition that means so much to their community.

Jimmy Woods
Olive Branch Play-by-Play Announcer

South Panola has discipline, focus and commitment to their football program.

Sam Rikard
Mayor of Olive Branch

SOUTH PANOLA-OLIVE BRANCH
SERIES HISTORY

Year	South Panola	Score	Olive Branch
1972	Darrel Arnold	29-0	Jesse Weeks
1973	Darrel Arnold	31-0	Jesse Weeks
1974	Darrel Arnold	32-6	Jesse Weeks
1975	Darrel Arnold	21-0	Jesse Weeks
1976	Darrel Arnold	18-15	Leslie Pool
1977	Darrel Arnold	14-0	Leslie Pool
1978	Darrel Arnold	16-42	Leslie Pool
1979	Darrel Arnold	22-45	Leslie Pool
1980	"Runt" McMinn	12-7	Leslie Pool
1981	"Runt" McMinn	13-9	Leslie Pool
1981^	"Runt" McMinn	23-6	Leslie Pool
1982	"Runt" McMinn	14-6	Leslie Pool
1983	"Runt" McMinn	12-2	Leslie Pool
1984	"Runt" McMinn	6-24	Leslie Pool
1985	"Runt" McMinn	0-21	Leslie Pool
1986	"Runt" McMinn	0-20	Leslie Pool
1987	"Runt" McMinn	10-37	Leslie Pool
1988	"Runt" McMinn	0-21	Leslie Pool
1989	"Runt" McMinn	14-10	Leslie Pool
1990	"Runt" McMinn	22-44	Leslie Pool
1991	Willis Wright	*Did Not Play*	Leslie Pool
1992	Willis Wright	*Did Not Play*	Leslie Pool
1993	Willis Wright	*Did Not Play*	Leslie Pool
1994	Willis Wright	*Did Not Play*	Leslie Pool
1995	Ed Stanley	*Did Not Play*	Leslie Pool
1996	Ed Stanley	*Did Not Play*	Leslie Pool
1997	Ed Stanley	*Did Not Play*	Leslie Pool
1998	Ed Stanley	*Did Not Play*	Leslie Pool
1999	Ed Stanley	35-7	Mike Moore
2000	Ed Stanley	16-17	Mike Moore
2001	Ricky Woods	28-6	Mike Moore
2002	Ricky Woods	27-13	Jamie Mitchell
2003	Ricky Woods	38-10	Jamie Mitchell
2004	Ricky Woods	28-10	Jamie Mitchell

Year	South Panola	Score	Olive Branch
2005	Ricky Woods	27-3	Jamie Mitchell
2005*	Ricky Woods	26-0	Jamie Mitchell
2006	Ricky Woods	12-7	Scott Samsel
2006*	Ricky Woods	35-13	Scott Samsel
2007	Lance Pogue	17-3	Scott Samsel
2007*	Lance Pogue	43-28	Scott Samsel

^ *Chickasaw Conference Championship Play-off Game*

* *North Mississippi Class 5A Championship Game*

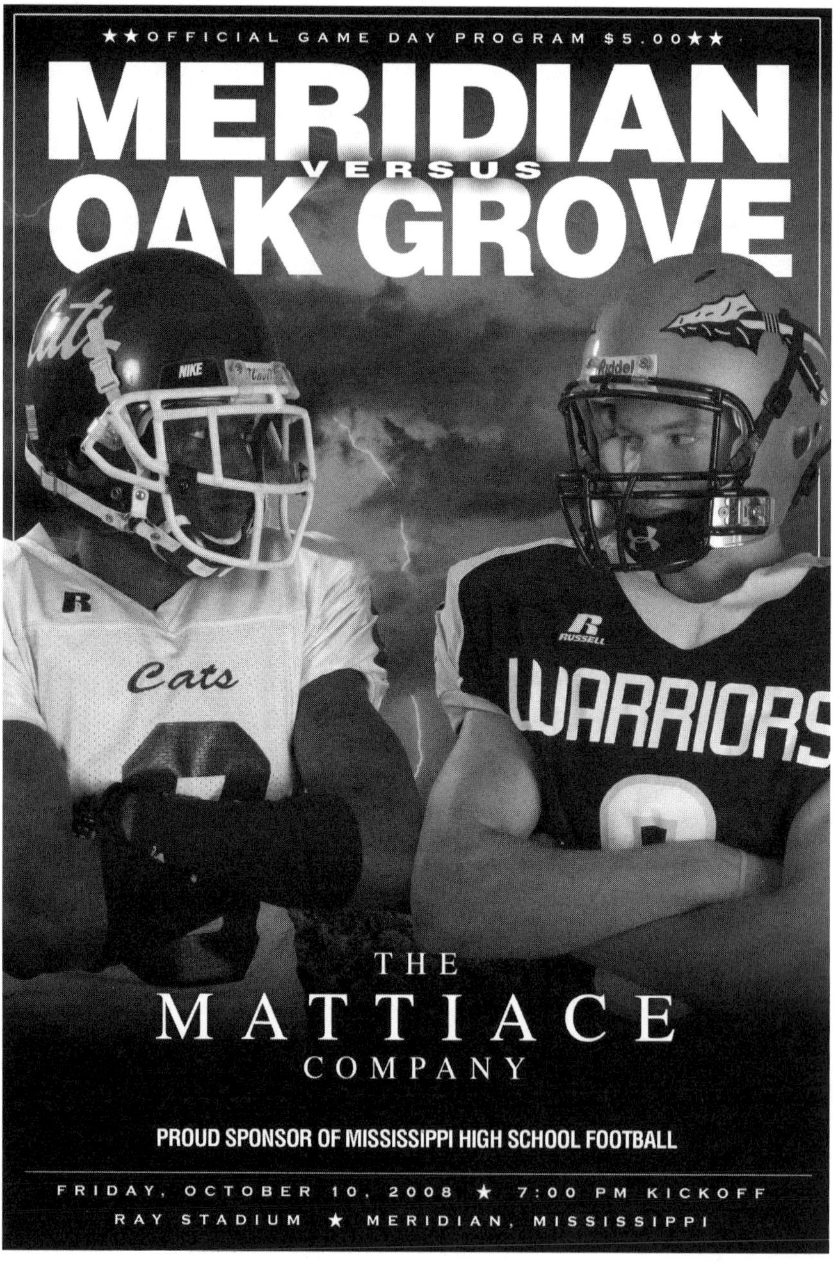
★★OFFICIAL GAME DAY PROGRAM $5.00★★
MERIDIAN
VERSUS
OAK GROVE
Cats
NIKE
Cats
WARRIORS
RUSSELL
THE
MATTIACE
COMPANY
PROUD SPONSOR OF MISSISSIPPI HIGH SCHOOL FOOTBALL
FRIDAY, OCTOBER 10, 2008 ★ 7:00 PM KICKOFF
RAY STADIUM ★ MERIDIAN, MISSISSIPPI

14

AN ARMY OF GHOSTS & THE IMPOSSIBLE TEAM

When you play against the Meridian Wildcats, you also play against their history. An endless army of ghosts follows Meridian teams onto the field for every football contest – ghosts of the 1927 championship team, ghosts of the 1931 championship team. The school from the Queen City has amassed an amazing 21 state football titles, and the ghosts from each of those historic teams follow today's Meridian Wildcats to the gridiron on Friday nights. No other Mississippi high school boasts as rich a history or legacy of football excellence as Meridian; and when the Wildcats play football, they play inspired by the champions that came before them. Today's Wildcats feel the presence of former Meridian players who have long since stepped into the record books. Their opponents feel the presence as well. The feeling is unavoidable. The tradition is too strong.

Meridian High School was originally formed in the late 1880s, but did not start playing football until 1914 under Coach Ben Cameron. However, it did not take long for football to become an important component of the school's identity. By 1927, Meridian had established itself as a force within the Big Eight Conference and took home the conference crown that year under the guidance of Coach N.C. Young. The following season, Jim Baxter replaced Young as head coach of the Wildcats. Baxter led the team for 14 seasons and captured five Big Eight titles. In his final four seasons from 1937-1940, Baxter's teams amassed an impressive 38-3-2 record.

Undoubtedly, one of the most emphatic gestures that could possibly be made to indicate Meridian's commitment to high school football came in 1936. That was the year the school built Ray Stadium, a colossal structure with concrete stands that seats approximately 15,000 people. No high school stadium in Mississippi during the 1930s came close to matching the size of Ray Stadium. More impressive is the fact that no high school stadium built in the next 80-plus years in Mississippi would equal the size of the "Ray." Any school willing to invest the money to build such a monument to its gridiron team is unquestionably committed to long-term, sustained football excellence, and the school would have it.

Over the next 35 years, the Wildcats piled up more victories and conference championships in their new stadium under coaches like Doby Bartling, Obie Brown, and Claude Jennings. After a couple of break-even type seasons, the now spoiled Wildcat faithful grew impatient with Jim Tait, their coach of only two years, and went searching for a replacement. The replacement came from Senatobia, Mississippi, and he was surprised that the Wildcats called his number.

Coach Bob Tyler had hopped around north Mississippi as a head coach at Water Valley, Okolona, Corinth and Senatobia. Like most young coaches who were climbing the professional ladder, he was always looking to move up a rung when the opportunity presented itself. Tyler applied for the Meridian job when it opened up, but didn't expect he would get a call. Tyler says, "There were certain jobs that were considered the plums, and Meridian was at the top of the list. I knew I would love to coach there, but I felt as if they could choose from a long list of candidates and would probably find one they liked more than me." However, Tyler had a secret weapon that even he didn't know he possessed. He says, "I was always a fan of Johnny Vaught at Ole Miss, even though I never played for him. No matter where I was coaching, I always tried to steer my guys to Ole Miss to play for Coach Vaught. I went to Ole Miss games and Coach Vaught tripped over me on his way to the field, because I was always underfoot."

When Tyler received the job as Meridian's head football coach and athletic director, he was able to look through the files detailing the search for the new coach. In his own files, he found comments about recommendations made in his favor by Coach Vaught. Remembers Tyler, "At the time, I had no idea that Coach Vaught would do something like that for me. Later, I realized why. Meridian had more talent than any other school in the state. Who better for Coach Vaught to have as the head coach at that particular school than an enthusiastic young coach who wants all his players to go to Ole Miss?"

Coming from Senatobia, Coach Tyler was used to managing teams with less than 30 players. He could never have dreamed of what he would find at Meridian. Tyler recalls,

> I got to football practice and there were athletes
> everywhere – good athletes. That first spring we had
> around 150 kids out for football. The following spring
> we had over 200. When we practiced, we literally took
> up every field on Meridian's campus - the football
> field, band field, baseball field, everything. The interest
> in football and the number of talented athletes was
> staggering.

One of the unique challenges Tyler found at Meridian was managing the numbers on the huge squad. Comments Tyler, "How do you figure out who your best 11 are out of 200? I had never been forced to think and coach like that."

Whatever Tyler's methods were, they worked. His first season he found plenty of fast athletes that could catch the ball and at least one athlete that could throw it. Says Tyler, "Our whole offense was basically built around throwing the bomb, not short crossing routes like are used today, not intermediate passes, but the bomb." Tyler's first team in 1966 went a perfect 10-0 and destroyed Provine 34-0 in the championship game. His starting quarterback, Bob White, earned a scholarship to Ole Miss (the same year as Archie Manning), and his two starting receivers, Grady Coleman and George Ranager, received scholarships to Delta State and Alabama, respectively.

After his first season, Tyler thought he had surely lucked up and caught one of those special classes laden with ability that make coaches look good. However, this was Meridian, a place where talent just keeps showing up in waves. Tyler's second season, his team went 9-0-1, tying only Billy Brewer's team at Columbus Lee and defeating Murrah 37-7 for the championship. That season, Tyler's starting wide receivers, Ted Gullette and David Bailey, earned scholarships to Delta State and Alabama, and his quarterback, Wally Hudnall, was given a football scholarship to play at Tennessee. Amazingly, it was almost an exact repeat of the 1966 season, except that this year Tyler's starting tight end, Smylie Gebhart, was also awarded a scholarship to Georgia Tech.

As great as the talent at Meridian was, there were also so many other pieces in place that made success possible for Tyler. Meridian's principal, Charlie Armstrong, was committed to football excellence and helped Tyler and the program in any way he could. Says Tyler, "When you have 200 guys out for football, making sure you have enough equipment and uniforms is no small task. We had to have at least two buses for our travel team alone. Mr. Armstrong always made sure we were taken care of."

In addition to the school administration, the Wildcat program also had the support of the community. Shorty McWilliams, former All-American at Mississippi State University and a 1940s graduate of Meridian High School, owned and operated Meridian's famous Weidman's restaurant and was a major contributor to the football program. Tyler says,

> If we needed something and the school couldn't provide it, Shorty and several other key boosters made sure we got it. Comparatively speaking, I had access to more extras at Meridian than I did at any other program during my career. One of our football banquets even featured Paul Hornung as the guest speaker. We ate our pre-game meals at Weidman's, where they had an incredible bourbon pie that our players really liked. When the school said the guys couldn't eat something called bourbon pie, Shorty changed the name to Wildcat Pie, but I'm pretty sure it still had bourbon in it.

After two short, wonderful years, Tyler's mentor, Johnny Vaught, asked him to join the Ole Miss staff as the wide receivers coach. Even though he was in love with the Meridian program, Tyler could not turn down the opportunity. The choice proved a good career move, as Tyler coached with Vaught at Ole Miss, then took an assistant's job at Alabama where he coached with the Bear, and finally ended up at Mississippi State as the head coach of the Bulldogs from 1973-1978.

So dominant were Tyler's two Meridian teams, that schools in the powerful Big Eight Conference began shying away from playing the Wildcats even after Tyler left. By 1969, Meridian couldn't even schedule enough games within the Big Eight to be eligible for the conference crown. The Wildcats were soon forced out of the Big Eight central division and into the coastal division. The move made no sense geographically, and could almost certainly be blamed on the Jackson schools who wanted no part of the Wildcats.

During Tyler's final season, a young sophomore quarterback

named Mac Barnes paid close attention to the way the Wildcat program was being run. The son of two Meridian High graduates, Barnes completed a stellar career under Coach Charlie Garrett and then returned nine short years later to assume the post as Meridian's twentieth head coach. Barnes is widely credited by Meridian faithful as the architect of Meridian's modern day success. During his tenure, the Wildcats won Big Eight championships in 1978 and 1979, and then captured state championships under the new playoff system in 1985 and 1990. Barnes' teams produced dozens of NFL and college players, as well as the incomparable National Player of the Year, Demetrius Hill.

Says Barnes,

> I was fortunate to be coached and mentored by some of the best people to ever come through Meridian High School. When I think back on individuals who left a lasting impression on this program, I think of Principal Charlie Armstrong and Coach Earl Morgan. Those men set such high expectations for everyone who came through Meridian. They expected excellence in everything, not just sports. It is that mentality and approach that I felt the responsibility to uphold when it was my turn to lead the program. You want kids to strive for excellence, not only because it helps perpetuate the tradition of this school, but also because it will guide them and help them to succeed in everything they do for the rest of their lives.

Jermaine Brown took over as Meridian's athletic director in 2005. A graduate of Hattiesburg High School, he appreciates and understands Meridian's tradition. Brown says,

> People in Meridian are very connected to the school and especially to the sports programs. At one time there was a big movement to pass a bond issue to build a new high school in a new location. The question kept coming up, "What are we going to do with Ray Stadium?" No acceptable answer was ever offered, and the new school has not been built. That stadium is truly sacred around here. There are some schools like Oak Grove that haven't played in Ray Stadium for very long, and they don't necessarily know the history. That's why we are making an effort to commemorate and display

in the stadium all of the championships that have been won around here starting back in 1927. It also helps to educate our own kids, but I want our opponents to realize this is what we have done since the 1920s. How dare you think you are going to come in here and beat us?

Possibly no one is better qualified to comment on what the high school means to the city of Meridian than its mayor, John Robert Smith. A 1967 graduate of Meridian, Smith did not play football, but was an avid supporter of the team. Says Smith,

> Back in those days, the high school was your identity. "Who are you? I am Meridian High School." Even today, Meridian is known around the country for many things: Jimmy Rogers, the father of country music; Peavey Electronics and the Naval Air Base. People nationally and internationally know those things about Meridian, but in Meridian, the high school and its sports teams still rank right there at the top. Meridian football games are important to everyone in Meridian. The town rehashes Friday night's game at least through Wednesday. By Wednesday night church, we kind of let it go. It's like an exorcism on Wednesday night so you can be ready for the next holy experience on Friday.

Mayor Smith's two grandchildren have graduated from Meridian, so he no longer has a family connection. However, according to Smith, "I still go to the football games, because it's Meridian High School. You may leave it, but it never leaves you."

****

Numerous baseball state championships, an all-superior band, a championship drama department, one of only 15 schools in the nation to be awarded three National Blue Ribbon Awards by the United States Department of Education – these are only a few of the mile-long list of accomplishments that can be claimed by Oak Grove High School. It is an amazingly decorated school from top to bottom, and the excellence of its faculty and students manifests itself in virtually every activity in which the school chooses to participate. However, it wasn't always that way with football.

Originally a small community just outside of Hattiesburg, Oak Grove established its high school over 100 years ago in 1898. The school began competing in football in the early '60s, but found little success as its team lived squarely in the middle of the territory ruled by the Hattiesburg Tigers. As Hattiesburg's population began to grow towards the southwest, Oak Grove grew as well. While the additional population helped fuel further success for Oak Grove in almost every school activity, it did not result in a transformation of the football program. In fact, by the 1990s, Oak Grove football was making a name for itself due to its futility.

Sandie Brock had the dubious honor of presiding over the booster club during the late 1990s. Brock, who had a son on the football team, describes the state of affairs:

> We were playing teams and just getting our brains beat out. There was very little to get excited about and the best we could hope for was that we might score a touchdown and not get shutout. We were getting beat so badly that no one wanted to come to the games. There may have been 300-400 people at the games, but most of those left after the band played at halftime. It got to the point where the good players we did have were moving out of the district so they could play for Hattiesburg or Petal. It was awful.

Over the years, steady population growth had pushed Oak Grove from the smallest classification steadily up the ladder until they reached 4A, the next to largest size class for high school sports in Mississippi. As the turn of the century approached, Oak Grove's student enrollment continued to swell due to its geographic location and proximity to Forrest General Hospital, Wesley Hospital, Camp Shelby, the University of Southern Mississippi, Pearl River Community College, Jones County Junior College and William Carey College. By the time the Mississippi High School Activities Association (MHSAA) began preparing to update its size rankings for member schools in 2001, it was obvious to everyone that Oak Grove would be moving up once again and would soon be classified as a 5A school.

Playing 5A football would mean regularly taking on powerhouse teams such as Wayne County, Hattiesburg, Meridian and Brandon.

People in the Oak Grove community wondered how they were supposed to compete with such 5A goliaths when they had only managed to win a handful of games at the 4A level over the past decade. Newspaper articles reported that such a transition was at best impossible and, at worst, dangerous for the kids at Oak Grove. In addition, the Oak Grove football facilities were nowhere near the quality of those at other 5A schools. Some members of the Oak Grove administration discussed the possibility of abandoning football altogether in the face of such a hopeless situation.

Oak Grove principal, Mrs. Carolyn Adams, decided to go against popular opinion and opted to draw a line in the sand when it came to Oak Grove football. Mrs. Adams decided that a school as excellent as Oak Grove should not settle for mediocrity in any activity in which it chose to participate, and she charged a select group of people with the task of overhauling the program. Says Sandie Brock, a member of the football task force, "Mrs. Adams took a lot of heat and criticism for her decision. It was a risky position to take, but she is the one who decided to make football at Oak Grove a priority."

It didn't take long before the search committee began to zero in on the man they believed could solve their problem – the man they believed could do what many said was impossible.

Coach Nevil Barr is originally from Purvis, Mississippi, and had made a name for himself over the past decade as the head coach at Petal High School, a 4A team that had dominated Oak Grove for the past half century. After several backroom meetings with the Oak Grove search committee, Barr decided he liked what he was hearing and called his good friend Tim Heldt, who was the head coach at Lumberton High School at the time. Like Barr, Heldt was also a graduate of Purvis High School and had coached with Barr at both Sumrall and Petal. Heldt remembers the call from Barr:

> The phone rang and Nevil told me he was thinking about taking a new job. He said the school was also looking for an athletic director and that he didn't want anything to do with that. He asked if I would serve as an assistant on his football staff and also take the AD's position. I said, "Okay, where is it you want to go?" When he told me the place was Oak Grove, I paused for a second and asked, "What? Why would we want to go there?"

Jeff Waits was a 1980 graduate of Oak Grove High School and was an assistant coach on the Warrior football staff before Barr arrived. In an interview with Barr that would essentially decide whether Waits would be asked to continue coaching at his alma mater, Waits turned the table on Barr. Waits says, "I love Oak Grove and I want what's best for it. I was really confused about why Nevil would want to come here. During our meeting I asked him point blank, 'You have a talented group of ninth graders coming up at Petal and the future there looks bright. We're struggling and we don't have good facilities. Why do you want to come here?'" Jeff Waits made the cut and remained on staff at Oak Grove.

According to Barr, a number of positive factors led him to Oak Grove. "I really liked and trusted the people who were in charge at Oak Grove, and they were in the process of upgrading their facilities. I just felt as if there was positive momentum under the surface and that we could get this thing turned around. I thought it might take a while, but I thought we could get it done. It was a wonderful opportunity and challenge," says Barr.

Bob Byrd was a graduate of Petal High School and an assistant coach under Barr. Even though he was coaching at his alma mater, and Petal was moving up to 5A with Oak Grove in 2001, Byrd elected to accept Barr's offer to go with him to Oak Grove. Byrd comments on the decision:

> I felt like we had done all we could do at Petal and I really felt like Oak Grove was serious about getting in the football business. There was no doubt that Petal was better prepared for the jump to 5A football than Oak Grove was. I remember looking at the schedule and all the teams we were going to have to play and thinking to myself, My God, we are going to have to play Meridian. Can you imagine us playing Meridian?

Jesse Lang was another coach from the previous Oak Grove staff that Barr elected to keep on board. Remembers Lang,

> We had some outstanding athletes playing baseball at Oak Grove, but they didn't play football because they didn't want to jeopardize their chance to play baseball. Football was always a secondary sport

here. We had great kids playing football, but they just didn't have any speed. We were running the Wing T and a bunch of misdirection because we felt as if it gave our kids the best chance to succeed. However, when one of our kids broke the line of scrimmage, the defensive players got up off the ground and caught them from behind.

Interestingly, Barr and his staff had also been running the Wing T at Petal for a number of years, so the offensive philosophy of the new staff and the experience of the players seemed to be a perfect fit. However, the coaches saw things differently. Says Coach Byrd, "The Wing T requires toughness and discipline that takes a number of years to develop. We didn't think that was the right fit for Oak Grove. This was a baseball school and we knew there were kids here that had great hand-eye coordination. Athletes with those type characteristics don't dictate that you run the Wing T."

Similar to the previous coaching staff, Barr agreed that Oak Grove did not have the type athletes needed to line up and run straight at the likes of Hattiesburg and Meridian, and that they would need to do something a little different. Recognition of this need led Barr and his staff to Middle Tennessee State where they met with Larry Fedora to learn the spread offense. Regarding the new offense, Barr comments, "We came in and put in the spread, which was a 180-degree shift for both the coaches and the kids. We never get in the huddle and we never get under center. If it's fourth and goal, we're in the shotgun. It's a wide-open offense. It's like basketball on grass."

The spread offense was a better fit for the athletic skills of the Oak Grove kids, but, more importantly, it was a tremendous selling point for Barr and his staff. Says Bob Byrd, "The spread is much more fun to practice than a traditional offense is. It's different going out to practice the spread every day where you are throwing the ball all over the place, as opposed to lining up against one another to just pound, pound, pound."

The implementation of the spread offense, coupled with Barr's approach to leadership, immediately caused an explosion of the Oak Grove team to an 80-man roster. For the first time in school history, the football program enjoyed the benefits of being in a high population growth area, as well as the services of some of its most talented athletes who had before dedicated their services exclusively to the baseball diamond. Barr made training speed and quickness, rather than strength and bulk, a priority for his team. He also encouraged athletes to play multiple sports in order to maximize their overall athleticism. Both techniques served to increase participation and generate athletes perfectly suited to run the new offensive attack.

Barr's coaching philosophy and approach with players are equally as important as his ability in the Xs and Os department. He makes the Golden Rule the foundation of his entire program, and he makes it his mission to make every player feel as if he is important and has a hand in the success of the team. Says Barr,

> Morale is a huge part of football. I always consider that my number one job. The way I treat the least talented guy on the team dictates the morale for our entire team. If we have a guy who's not a very good player, but he is out there busting his butt everyday and I don't treat him the same as the guy everyone in the country is looking at, the kids see it and it affects their morale.

Mitchell Williams, sports director of WDAM, has four sons who have played, or will play, football at Oak Grove under Barr. Says Williams,

> Coach Barr has won everywhere he has been, and it's not necessarily because he has better athletes than everyone else. He is a hands-on guy who believes in having a great staff around him. His players love him and would fight for him. Coach Barr is this tall statesman who walks around and shakes people's hands in a genuine way. He's great at convincing guys that are in the band playing the tuba that they should come out and play football. He made my oldest son believe he could do things that even I, as his father, couldn't convince him of.

In an effort to protect the fragile football egos of his Oak Grove players, Barr made another against-the-grain decision prior to his first season with the Warriors. Says Sandie Brock,

> Coach decided that we wouldn't play in any

spring or pre-season jamborees. Many supporters
questioned his decision, but Coach Barr told them,
"There is no reason to put our kids in the spotlight of
a jamboree before they are ready. They don't need to
suffer more losses. Instead, we will focus on installing
our new system and will scrimmage against ourselves.
In time, we will show up and play."

By the time the 2001 season arrived, the entire Oak Grove
community was on the edge of their seats waiting to see what type
product Barr and his crack group of assistants would put on the field.
Would they be demolished by their 5A opponents? Would this whole
adventure ultimately be a failed experiment that would lead Oak Grove
to discontinue football? Or, would the spread offense work? Could
skilled baseball players become great football players?

Going into the tenth week of the season, the Warriors were an
unimpressive 4-5. However, two of their losses were narrow defeats at
the hands of No. 1 ranked Brandon and perennial power Wayne County.
In addition, Barr's Warriors had dismantled historical nemesis Petal by
a score of 28-0. With two games remaining, Oak Grove was amazingly
in a position to capture the fourth and final playoff spot in their region,
a feat the Warriors had not accomplished at any point in school history.
However, they would need to win both games, and the next game was
against the Meridian Wildcats.

Says Coach Tim Heldt,

When we came to Oak Grove, we knew we would
have to play Meridian. We were always conscious of the
fact that Meridian was on our schedule and the gravity
of what that meant, but the true reality of it didn't set
in until we got to the game. They came out on the field
and were twice as big as we were. All of our coaches
just looked at one another during pre-game. You could
see that we were all thinking the same thing: Can you
believe we are about to play Meridian High School?

****

As fans began to gather at the Oak Grove stadium, the anticipation
and excitement grew with each passing moment. For the first time in as
long as anyone present could remember, Oak Grove was about to play

a football game that mattered. A win tonight would bring them to an even 5-5 for the season and would give the Warriors an opportunity to secure the school's first-ever playoff berth the following week in the season finale. The football team had played beyond expectations all year, and the fans dared to dream of the implications of a win. Had their new coaching staff really been able to accomplish the impossible and turn horrid Oak Grove into a 5A playoff-caliber football team in less than a year? Was it possible that the outstanding baseball players traditionally produced by the school really could transfer their talents to the gridiron? Might Oak Grove eventually escape from the shadow of neighboring Hattiesburg High School? It all seemed strangely plausible in the moments leading up to kickoff on that fall evening.

Then, the Meridian cheerleaders arrived at the game . . . in a limousine. It was a simple act that said a mouthful. Meridian had been the gold standard for high school football in Mississippi for nearly an entire century. They owned more football state championships by far than any other team in the state. They boasted a football stadium that was the largest of any high school stadium in the state and, in fact, bigger than many colleges. This football match-up was beyond the "haves and the have-nots", it was the "have-everythings and the have-nothings." Simply by the arrival of Meridian's cheerleaders, the Oak Grove fans were quickly reminded of the chasm that separated their two schools. For goodness sakes, even their cheerleaders have a limousine, thought the Oak Grove fans. What did the Oak Grove fans have to welcome the visitors from Meridian? They had a football facility that was sub-par compared to the 4A schools the Warriors had been playing against before moving up to 5A. The stadium was so dated and small that Oak Grove's own assistant coach, Bob Byrd, nicknamed it "the dungeon."

According to Byrd, "When teams arrived at our place, you could see it in their eyes. They were thinking, Is this the right place? Is this where we are supposed to play? It really screws with the mind of the other team when they go from thinking about the game to wondering, Good Lord. Do they have toilets or porta potties? The place really was pretty rough."

As the Meridian team was left to wonder about the condition of their locker room facilities, Oak Grove's coaching staff focused their team on weathering the initial shock of being on the field with the Wildcats. Coach Barr knew that if his guys could take Meridian's opening body shots, they would quickly gain confidence in their ability to stay on the field and eventually win the game. The approach worked, and as the final seconds ticked off the scoreboard in "the dungeon," Oak Grove had notched the most important win in the history of its football program. Final score: Oak Grove 27, Meridian 13.

Coach Byrd remembers his thoughts as he stood on the field after the game, "Everyone on the field felt a weird combination of excitement and stunned disbelief at what had just happened. I thought to myself, We just beat Meridian. I can't believe this. We just beat Meridian." Coach Barr reflects on the significance of the win over Meridian:

> The Meridian team was composed of a bunch of hard-nosed kids that could just jam the ball down your throat. We had tremendous respect for their program and we made a big deal to our kids about beating them. We told our team, "You just beat the school considered by most to be the greatest all-time football program in the state of Mississippi." The confidence they gained from that game was phenomenal. The following week, we had to beat Hancock by eight points to guarantee we would make the fourth and final spot in the playoffs. Our kids met the challenge and beat them by 28 points.

The following season marked the first time Oak Grove would travel to Meridian and play in famed Ray Stadium. With Oak Grove's coaching staff being new to 5A football, this would be the first time for most of them to coach in Ray Stadium as well. The 2002 season also marked the first for Meridian's new head coach, Ed Stanley. One of the more accomplished coaches in the state and the architect of much of South Panola's early success, Stanley was more than capable of guiding the storied Wildcat program.

Similar to the 2001 match-up, the key for Oak Grove was to get past the bigness and history of Meridian's stadium and to weather the initial storm. Trailing 13-7 at halftime, the Warriors began to show signs of a championship team in that they found ways to win that weren't necessarily part of their original game plan. Although it was their high-octane offense that was receiving all the attention, their defense produced a pair of long touchdowns in the second half to down the Wildcats 34-27. The upstart Warriors were now the proud owners of an unlikely two-game winning streak over the vaunted Meridian program. In addition, the 2002 season ended with Oak Grove playing for the south state championship against Wayne County – an amazing accomplishment considering where the Warrior program had been just a short 24 months prior.

By 2003, the Meridian program was now squarely under the control of Ed Stanley, and the Wildcats were beginning to find that dominating groove to which they had grown so accustomed over the years. In the eighth game of the season, Meridian once again traveled to Oak Grove to take on the Warriors. However, unlike the first meeting two years earlier, this time the Warriors were undefeated. On the second play from scrimmage, Meridian gashed the Warrior defense with an 81-yard touchdown run. The Wildcats controlled the game all night until the Warrior defense was able to make a critical stop late in the game that put the offense in excellent field position. Oak Grove was able to capitalize on the field position and punched the ball across the goal line to take their first lead of the game 28-21 with precious little time remaining. The strong Meridian offense immediately went to work and pushed the ball down the field to Oak Grove's 2-yard line. Depending on whom you ask, the game then ended on a controversial play where either Meridian's young quarterback made a mental error and spiked the ball on fourth down, or the referees lost track of downs and robbed Meridian of a final shot at the end zone. In either instance, Oak Grove escaped with yet another victory over Meridian.

Fortunately for the Wildcats, they only had to stew over the loss to Oak Grove for about a month before they got a shot at revenge. With both teams hitting on all cylinders, they met in the second round of the playoffs in Meridian at Ray Stadium. Unfortunately for Meridian, the Oak Grove offense had fully matured into a well-oiled, quick-strike weapon of mass destruction, and halftime saw the Warriors with a commanding 24-0 lead. Although Meridian put up a couple of second-half scores, they never really threatened to take control of the game. Oak Grove claimed another victory by the score of 31-16. This marked the first time in the young rivalry where one of the teams dominated the other, and the fact that it happened in the playoffs made it much more difficult for Meridian to swallow, as tempers flared during post-game handshakes. Says Stan Caldwell of the *Hattiesburg American*, "That was the first time Meridian lost to Oak Grove in a situation like that, and I don't think they were quite ready for it. Losing in the playoffs is different from losing in the regular season. There is finality to it." Oak Grove used the victory to catapult itself through the playoffs and into its first ever championship game against South Panola and a 14-1 season.

Still feeling the sting of the playoff loss from the year before, Meridian met Oak Grove in the eighth game of the season in 2004 and made quick work of the Warriors. Meridian used their powerful running attack to pound the Warrior defense unmercifully in traditional Meridian style and claim a long-overdue victory over Oak Grove in the process. That year's Wildcat team was sending talented athletes to the field in droves, and many people were already chattering about their chances of making it to the championship game and being the team to knock off the defending champs, the Tigers from South Panola.

Oak Grove dropped a few games during the 2004 season, but was able to secure a spot in the playoffs and claw its way into a third-round game against Meridian. In customary fashion, Meridian jumped out to a quick 14-0 lead and set the table for the predicted blowout. However, Oak Grove hung around and used an interception return for a touchdown to put the score at 21-19 in the third quarter. With six minutes to go in the game, both teams began a scoring frenzy, each putting up two touchdowns and bringing the point total to 35-33. With less than a minute to play and the ball on their 27-yard line, the gritty Warrior offense then began its assault on a skilled Meridian defense. After a few quick completions, Oak Grove's Taylor Lovitt nailed a 27-yard field goal to take the lead, end the scoring, secure the victory and send Oak Grove to its third straight south state championship game. Meridian's match-up with South Panola never happened, and the sting of losing to Oak Grove reached a new high.

By 2005, the match-up between Oak Grove and Meridian had turned into a full-blown, red-hot rivalry as each school continued to field exceptional teams and each game seemed to have serious playoff implications. Even the student bodies began taking the games very personally, and, as with any rivalry, creativity began to show. Meridian students produced "Oak Grove Sucks" t-shirts and Oak Grove students welcomed the Wildcats to Warrior stadium in 2005 by "blacking out" the entire stadium. Says former Oak Grove football player, Travis Payton, "My junior year, our students got everyone to wear black to the game. People were dressed in black from head to toe. They even dressed their babies in all black. Many of our students painted their faces black, too, so they were completely covered. It looked so good from the field. It was an awesome atmosphere – definitely intimidating." There was also a large sign in the stadium greeting the Wildcats that read, "Go back to Meridian. You're wasting your time." Proud of their now 5-1 record against the Wildcats, Oak Grove students and fans had long since moved past the inferiority complex generated by the discrepancy in football tradition between the two schools. While many Warrior fans acknowledged Meridian's incredible tradition, they now seemed to believe that Oak Grove was immune to it.

After losing to the Warriors in the 2005 regular season match-up, Meridian powered through the rest of its schedule to force a rematch in the south state championship game. Meridian's athletic director, Jemaine Brown, recalls the big game:

> Oak Grove was undefeated when we played them for south state, but we knew we had an outstanding team as well and we really needed this win to get ourselves back on track. Everyone at Meridian put so much energy into preparation for that game. There was certainly a feeling of, We have to get this thing done right now. No more excuses. We have had enough of losing to Oak Grove.

The game didn't disappoint and produced the typical point explosion that had become the standard in this series. Many fans on both sides of the rivalry remember this game as the best played between the two teams to date. As the Wildcats and Warriors traded scoring blows the entire game, it was ultimately the bruising running of Meridian's All-American running back, Cordera Eason, and an uncharacteristic six turnovers by the Warriors that proved decisive. Remarkably, even with Eason's running and the multiple turnovers, Oak Grove had a chance to win the game on the last play when a Kirk Lance pass sailed just beyond the outstretched hands of Torris Magee in the end zone. Final score: Meridian 46, Oak Grove 40.

It was as if the Meridian tradition and all the ghosts from the previous championship teams finally showed up for a game against Oak Grove. The Meridian win sent the Warriors home and propelled the Wildcats to the championship game for an uncountable number of times in school history. Says Jermaine Brown,

> The 2005 victory was one of the best I have ever been a part of anywhere. The attitude of our team and fans on the field after the game was like, We finally did it.

You could tell everyone was physically and emotionally spent. It took everything we had, and it showed the next week against South Panola in the championship game. It's just really difficult for a team to get that high two weeks in a row.

Voice of the Wildcats, Ray Matheny, remembers the excitement of the south state championship game, "It was a truly remarkable performance by both teams. I remember going home after the game and writing a post on a message board that I frequent. It was such a stunning game, all I could think to write was 'I just saw the best high school game I have ever seen.'"

If the Meridian tradition made a cameo appearance in the 2005 south state championship game, it made a full fledged return in 2006 when Larry Weems replaced Ed Stanley as the head coach of the Wildcats. Having spent nearly 20 years as an assistant coach at Meridian, Weems returned to lead the Wildcats after serving as the head coach of the Pearl Pirates for the past six seasons. Weems immediately hired North Panola's head coach, Demetrius Hill, to serve as an assistant on his staff. Hill was a favorite son of the Meridian faithful as he led the team to a state championship in 1985 and captured the honor of First Team All-American Player of the Year. Weems stocked his staff with former Meridian players who fully understood and appreciated the school's unique tradition. The staff promptly began teaching the intricacies and responsibility of the Meridian tradition to the players.

Equally as important as the coaching staffs' deep roots in the Wildcat program was Weems attitude towards offensive football. Weems says,

When I was at Pearl, I knew that I would not have an overpowering amount of athletic talent to work with. My background is as a defensive coordinator, so I asked myself, What type offense is it that has given you the most problems over the years? I knew the answer was any offense that stretched the field both horizontally and vertically, so that's what I decided to do at Pearl. By the time I came back to Meridian, I was comfortable with the scheme and we installed it here too. Coach Stanley had a big ole line and a couple of monster running backs that he could run over teams with, but we went in the exact opposite direction. Now we come out in a no-huddle shotgun and spread the ball all over the field. It's a difficult scheme for people to stop in a game because they can't replicate it in practice to get their defense ready. They may know the plays and the formations, and they may be able to get their scout teams to line up correctly, but unless your team runs the same type attack every day, it's impossible to create a scout team that can execute like we do on Friday night.

When Demetrius Hill returned to Meridian, he was surprised at what he found:

When I got here, I was prepared to get everyone ready for the big rivalry game against Laurel, but the players told me the team they really wanted to beat was Oak Grove. I kept asking guys, "Who is Oak Grove?" When we went down to their place that season, their students met our bus and started shaking it. They were all wearing t-shirts that said "Meridian – overrated." I realized that this new kid on the block was trying to start something. They actually beat us that game, but I knew we also had a number of key players who missed the game, and that we would probably catch them again in the playoffs. In fact, we did get them in the south state championship game at our place for the second year in a row. Our attitude was "Okay, you want a rivalry. Fine. You started this, now we're going to finish it." We beat them 27-20 and went on to play for another state championship.

Prior to the 2005 meeting in the south state championship game, the principals of both schools organized a meeting between some of their students. The games between the schools were becoming so heated that they felt there needed to be somewhat of a get-to-know-you session. The get together took place at a neutral location in Laurel, and both schools sent a busload of students in to have breakfast and talk about the rivalry. Says Jermaine Brown, "The schools are located almost 100 miles apart, so it's not like the students interact with one another on a regular basis. All many of them know about one another is what they see the couple times a year we play football."

In 2007, Weems' Wildcats took another one from Oak Grove in a 36-35 shootout. Says Meridian's Ray Matheny, "This game used to be about a clash of styles. Now, with Coach Weems, both teams are running the same offenses and it has produced even more exciting match-ups. They are both so familiar with what the other is going to do, it's all about execution now."

Coach Demetrius Hill's initial confusion towards the rivalry with Oak Grove is understandable. Over the years, Meridian has been rivals with many schools, such as Laurel and Hattiesburg. Starkville, Moss Point and Biloxi have also challenged Meridian at times. During the 1960s, a game against any team from Jackson was considered a must-win game for the Wildcats. Meridian has been playing football at a very high level for nearly a century, but no school has demonstrated the staying power necessary to merit a long-term rivalry. In essence, Meridian's attitude towards Oak Grove can be compared to Western European countries' attitude towards American history: 1776? Oh, that's cute, America. Have you ever heard of ancient Rome or 1066 and William the Conqueror?

Although the rivalry between the two schools may not have proven that it can stand the test of time, there is no doubt that it has been one of the most important match-ups in the state over the past seven years. Either Oak Grove or Meridian has played in the south state championship game in each of the past six years, and they have played in a combined three state championship games during that same period. With the continuing growth of Oak Grove and the presence of Larry Weems at Meridian, it is likely the rivalry will continue for the near future.

Says Oak Grove's Mitchell Williams, "I don't know what the future holds, but I do know about the past. They have an unbelievable football history, and we don't – yet. To go back only seven years and think about where our program was, it's amazing that I can sit here and talk about Oak Grove having a rivalry with anyone, let alone Meridian."

WHAT THE WILDCATS SAY ABOUT OAK GROVE

Oak Grove may not be able to beat you based on pure athleticism, but their coaching staff does an amazing job of preparing those kids and putting them in a position to be successful. The results speak for themselves.

Jermaine Brown
Meridian Athletic Director

Their stadium is very nice, and it's set up so you feel like they are looking down on you. It's a pretty intimidating place to play.

Olivia Chisolm
Meridian Cheerleader

Oak Grove has that wide-open offensive attack. You can never relax against them.

Ray Matheny
Voice of the Wildcats

So many of the games against Oak Grove are high-scoring contests decided by razor-thin margins. They are wonderful games for the fans.

John Robert Smith
Mayor of Meridian

Oak Grove people are pretty cocky, but, then again, so are we.

Olivia Chisolm
Meridian Cheerleader

Oak Grove has a great new stadium, especially their home stands. I love when our team plays in their stadium.

Demetrius Hill
Meridian Assistant Football Coach

To think that Oak Grove ever considered dropping football is incredible. You can talk yourself into some dumb things sometimes. They were obviously selling themselves short, because that's a darn good program.

Larry Weems
Meridian Head Football Coach

You would think our defense would be prepared for their offense since they see us run the same type plays everyday at practice, but Oak Grove always finds a way to put in a new wrinkle that makes their offense very hard to stop. They have some very smart coaches.

Tyler Russell
Meridian Football Player

Fans from both schools travel strong. If the home crowd doesn't come to the game ready, they will get out-yelled by the visitor's stands.

Ray Matheny
Voice of the Wildcats

Meridian has been playing football for almost 100 years and established a name that others want to say they have beaten. We get everyone's best shot every week, and our kids have to fight their rear ends off every game. We don't get an off week.

Larry Weems
Meridian Head Football Coach

WHAT THE WARRIORS SAY ABOUT MERIDIAN

Meridian and Oak Grove started out as opposites. We were the finesse team and they were smash mouth and physical.

Nevil Barr

Oak Grove Head Football Coach

Meridian is huge and they have talent galore. When we get together and play, you are going to get your money's worth.

Bob Byrd

Oak Grove Assistant Football Coach

My freshman year we were marching off the field and the Meridian fans were booing us and throwing stuff on the field.

Katie Folkes

Oak Grove Band Member

Football at Meridian is all about power running. They always have some big boys in the backfield.

Travis Payton

Former Oak Grove Football Player

The first time we played Meridian our kids had big eyes. I had never coached against them and I had big eyes. We knew all about their tradition and long history of success.

Jeff Waits

Oak Grove Assistant Football Coach

They're big and strong and they have numbers. The only way to beat them is to outwork them and take their spirit away. Otherwise, they will pound you.

Mitchell Williams

Sports Director, WDAM

My ideal scenario is to beat Meridian in the south state championship game in the final seconds. I don't want to beat them bad, just by a point at the very end. That way it will hurt worse.

Bob Byrd
Oak Grove Assistant Football Coach

You just want to beat Meridian in everything. It bothers me when we lose to them. We got beat by them in softball yesterday and it bothers me.

Katie Folkes
Oak Grove Band Member

People at Meridian probably think every student at Oak Grove drives a Lexus.

Stan Caldwell
Hattiesburg American

I'm going to say this as nicely as I can. They are not very gracious winners.

Bob Byrd
Oak Grove Assistant Football Coach

We don't have to do much to get our guys focused for the Meridian game. They already know it's going to be a four-quarter battle. They know they are in for a war.

Nevil Barr
Oak Grove Head Football Coach

Ray Stadium is one of those great old rustic stadiums in the state. When we go to Meridian, even as a broadcaster, I'm pumped.

Kelly Sanner
Oak Grove Radio Play-By-Play Announcer

There is non-stop head butting between these two teams. They both have great athletes and want to be the best in the district.

Sam Thomas
Former Oak Grove Football Player

Meridian has a great team, but Oak Grove is better. Meridian is definitely overrated.

Currie Fletcher
Oak Grove Cheerleader

Oak Grove has always had a lot of interest in beating Hattiesburg because they are right next door; but the measuring stick of whether or not you're going to the playoffs is Meridian.

Mitchell Williams
Sports Director, WDAM

If you can't get excited about an Oak Grove-Meridian game, then you just don't like high school football.

Stan Caldwell
Hattiesburg American

MERIDIAN - OAK GROVE
SERIES HISTORY

Year	Meridian	Score	Oak Grove
2001	Bill Sartin	13-27	Nevil Barr
2002	Ed Stanley	27-34	Nevil Barr
2003	Ed Stanley	21-28	Nevil Barr
2003*	Ed Stanley	16-31	Nevil Barr
2004	Ed Stanley	35-21	Nevil Barr
2004*	Ed Stanley	35-36	Nevil Barr
2005	Ed Stanley	30-41	Nevil Barr
2005*	Ed Stanley	46-40	Nevil Barr
2006	Larry Weems	7-27	Nevil Barr
2006*	Larry Weems	27-20	Nevil Barr
2007	Larry Weems	36-35	Nevil Barr

Playoff Game

★★ OFFICIAL GAME DAY PROGRAM $5.00 ★★

CLINTON
VERSUS
MADISON CENTRAL

Madison
the city

FamilyCircle
BEST TOWN
FOR FAMILIES

PROUD SPONSOR OF MISSISSIPPI HIGH SCHOOL FOOTBALL

FRIDAY, SEPTEMBER 26, 2008 ★ 7:00 PM KICKOFF

JAGUAR FIELD ★ MADISON, MISSISSIPPI

CHAPTER

15

TOP THAT

The man was a jinx. He had to be fired; and he was fired, just hours before the 2006 Clinton-Madison Central game.

The strange chain of events leading up to the termination of the employment of the man responsible for so much grief at both Clinton and Madison Central began seven years earlier. In 1999, J. Reeves was the principal at Madison Central High School. During his three-year tenure as principal at Madison Central, the Jaguars lost to archrival Clinton every year in football. In 2003, immediately following his position as principal at Madison Central, Reeves became the principal at Clinton. Over the first five years of his tenure as principal at Clinton, the Arrows lost four football games to the Jaguars. Was all of this mere coincidence or was there something more sinister at work? Dr. Tommye Henderson, Superintendent of Clinton Schools, was concerned about this phenomenon. She was very troubled about the incidence of success of the team opposite Reeves in the Clinton-Madison Central football series. Dr. Henderson, who is an avid Arrow fan, was compelled to protect the interests of her students, and beating Madison Central in football was of vital interest to her students. She had to do something, so she conducted an investigation of Reeves' past employment and a statistical analysis of the won-loss ratios of the teams opposite Reeves. Her findings were alarming. Based on her research, she formulated a theory, which became widely known throughout the greater Clinton area as the "Reeves Jinx Theory." Today, many social scientists and experts in paranormal activities refer to the "Reeves Jinx Theory" as simply "RJT." Consequently, Dr. Henderson moved quickly and aggressively to eradicate any impediment posed by the RJT in the upcoming game against Madison Central in 2006. She simply could not allow the Jaguars to have any unfair advantage, albeit unknown to Madison Central that such advantage existed.

Dr. Henderson attended the pep rally in the Clinton High School gym the morning before the game that night. At the beginning of the pep rally, Dr. Henderson informed the students jammed into the gym that she had an important announcement to make. Little did J. Reeves know that his life was about to change forever. Dr. Henderson explained the results of her investigation and the dark background of Principal Reeves involving the Clinton-Madison Central rivalry. She revealed to the students at the pep rally the coincidental – or maybe not so coincidental – nature of the affiliation of the losing team to Reeves. She reduced all of her investigation and research to the "Reeves Jinx Theory" or "RJT." In short, Reeves was a jinx and he had to be fired. Mustering all of her courage, Dr. Henderson struck the first blow to eradicate the evil forces at play when she announced, "Mr. Reeves, you're fired!" The assembly of students reacted with utter delight and joy that someone had finally stepped up to combat the dark forces that had plagued the Arrow team over the past five years. Immediately following the announcement, former principal J. Reeves was escorted from the school grounds under heavy security – banished, so to speak – to a place where, hopefully, he could do no more harm to the Arrows.

The Arrows proceeded confidently into the game with Madison Central that evening, knowing Dr. Henderson had removed the jinx. However, as the Jaguars maintained a lead late in the fourth quarter, Clinton fans started to feel twinges of guilt that maybe they had falsely blamed Reeves for the prior losses based on the "Reeves Jinx Theory."

Then it happened. With Madison Central in possession of the ball and the lead, the Jags fumbled. As the ball squirted out of the hands of the Madison Central ball carrier, the events that followed started moving in slow motion. An Arrow player scooped up the loose football and raced down the field into the end zone to score the winning touchdown as time on the scoreboard evaporated. Such was the dramatic swing of events.

Just moments before the fluke Jaguar fumble, Clinton fans were second-guessing the Reeves Jinx Theory. Then, in a span of less than ten seconds, they had tangible proof of the validity of RJT – a victory over Madison Central. The events of the day were hard evidence that the forces of evil in the underworld of high school football were using J. Reeves as a medium – a conduit – to direct the outcome of this special game every year. However, due to the diligence and courage of Dr. Henderson, the grip of the evil forces on J. Reeves had been broken – at least for now.

On the Monday following the big victory over the Jaguars, Dr. Henderson rehired J. Reeves as Principal of Clinton High School. Unfortunately, the Reeves story has a sad ending. The next year – 2007 – Dr. Henderson, for whatever reason – perhaps a lapse in judgment, forgetfulness, or maybe just pure sympathy – failed to terminate Reeves before the Madison Central game. The result was disastrous. The Arrows suffered their first loss on their new football field at the hands of Madison Central by a heartbreaking one-point margin.

The conspiracy theorists in the Clinton community are now totally convinced Reeves, Henderson and possibly other unknown persons, are involved in a grand plot to defeat the Arrows.

While the conspiracy theorists are certainly in the minority, the majority of Clinton fans, along with the scientific community, believe the Reeves Jinx Theory has been completely validated. In order to control the supernatural forces at play, the link between these evil forces and J. Reeves must be cut every year on the day of the game for Clinton to have a fair chance of beating Madison Central. A fringe group of Clinton fans wants to retire Reeves, or better yet, transfer him to Madison Central.

****

The Clinton Arrows have played on four home fields during their storied history. In the early days, the Arrows shared Robinson Field with Mississippi College when that facility was located where the Baptist Healthplex is presently situated on the Clinton Parkway.

Ironically, the opening of the new Arrow Stadium in 2007 came exactly 50 years to the date (1957) of the completion of the Arrows' first stadium of their own, S.R. Crane Field. The stadium was located adjacent to then Clinton High School on Fairmont Street.

In 1963, Clinton High School was relocated to Lakeview Drive. Seven years later, a new stadium was built. On September 25, 1970, the Arrows played their first game at the new Roy Burkett Field. The popular Burkett, who retired following the 1971 season, had been the Arrows' head coach since 1956. At the time of his retirement, he had won more games than any coach in Arrow football history. During the time the Arrows played their 211 home games at Roy Burkett Field, they won 144 games with a 67 percent winning percentage.

James "Booty" Sloan followed the legendary Burkett and built the Arrow program into a dynasty in the Little Dixie Conference. Clinton won, or shared, North Division Championships in 1971, 1972, 1973, 1974, 1975, 1976, 1977 and 1980. Four times – in 1972, 1975, 1977 and 1980 – the Arrows were crowned Overall Little Dixie Champions. Coach Sloan's 1977 Arrows finished 11-0, posting the only perfect season in Arrow football history.

Under Coach Jerry Lyons, Sloan's successor, the 1980 Arrows finished 9-1 and were voted the No. 1 team in the state by the final United Press International Coach's Poll. After the Arrows' short stint under Jerry Mahon in 1983 and 1984, Booty Sloan returned to Clinton in 1985. Sloan's 1987 Arrow team finished 11-2 and was ranked No. 2 in the state by the Associated Press final poll. Sloan resigned following the 1990 season with a 73 percent winning percentage, which remains the best in Arrow football history.

David Bradberry became Clinton's fifteenth head coach in 1991 and led the Arrows to the playoffs nine times over the next 11 seasons. The Arrows reached their highest level ever in 2000 with a 14-1 record and a No. 23 ranking in the *USA Today* Prep Poll. Bradberry led the Arrows to their only North 5A Championship and an appearance in the 5A State Championship finals in 2000. Coach Bradberry retired in 2002 with a stellar 86-48 record and a 65 percent winning percentage.

In April 2002, Pete Hurt became Clinton's sixteenth head coach. His 2002 Arrows won the Region 2 5A Championship. In 2004, Hurt led the Arrows to the 5A North Championship game and a No. 10 ranking in the Associated Press Final Poll.

Scott Brown, the Arrow's current head coach, became Clinton's seventeenth head coach in April 2005. In 2007, Brown led the Arrows to a 9-4 record, advancing to the second round of the playoffs. Today, Brown's Arrows occupy the new Arrow Stadium, which many high school football fans consider the best facility in the state.

Over the long history of Clinton High School football, many rivalries have evolved and then dissolved. During the time the Arrows were in the Little Dixie Conference, the games with Brandon and Magee became crucial to winning the conference championship. For a time in the '70s, the Clinton and Jackson St. Joseph game developed into a hot rivalry. However, looking back at the Arrows' football history, there are three particular rivalries that stick out. In the '50s and '60s, the annual game with Forest Hill was a classic. Fans still tell stories to this day about the hostility between Clinton and the Rebels. Beginning in 1965, the Arrows developed a heated rivalry with Warren Central, particularly during the years legendary coaches Lum Wright and James Sloan were leading the Vikings and Arrows, respectively. A number of the Clinton and Warren Central games during this era were classics. Today, the two teams still play, but the Madison Central and Clinton game has upstaged the old rivalry with Warren Central. Beginning in 1993 and continuing through today, the Clinton and Madison Central rivalry is the hottest game every year for both schools. According to Clinton Mayor Rosemary Aultman, "Yes, Madison Central now is by far the biggest rival and creates the largest crowd both here and there."

Clinton High School is located in Clinton in Hinds County, Mississippi. The Clinton Separate School District was formed in 1970, and the community has always stayed focused on its school system. Mayor Aultman says, "Actually, our community grew during the '70s around the school system; so the community has stayed very dedicated to it. All the way through, there is a strong focus in our community on quality schools. That builds a real cohesiveness and support system with parents and booster club members that have formed the bedrock of the Clinton community."

Former Clinton head football coach, David Bradberry, comments, "I came to Clinton in 1991 as athletic director and assistant football coach. Clinton was a great draw at the time. It was one of the best school districts in the state. Coach Sloan had put together an athletic department that was a total package."

Mayor Aultman comments further about the importance of Clinton High School to the entire community:

> The high school is the focal point in our community. Although students are developing all through the system, the high school is where they really have an opportunity to exhibit their skills, whether it's in athletics, academics or any type of extracurricular activity. That is the focal point of the community. Clinton High School is really the beacon in this town. I love it when I go to a ballgame on Friday night and there are people there who have attended games for 35 years. Their children were seniors in high school when I first started going to ballgames. They are 80-something years old now, but they are still there and they have a

real loyalty and dedication to it. That is typical here. Then you have young couples at the football games that don't have any children yet. It's a real rallying point and selling point for the community. We sell it every time we have new people come into town. They built the school in the middle of a field. There were no houses anywhere near the site. Today, there are houses everywhere with more neighborhoods under construction. People want to be close to the high school.

Clinton High School has produced its share of great coaches over the years in Roy Burkett, Jerry Lyons, James Sloan, David Bradberry, Pete Hurt and now Scott Brown. Along with outstanding coaches have come a host of big time Arrow players, such as Kyle Morris, Clarence McDougal, Coco Hodge, Donte Walker, Andrew Shapley and Dominick Douglas, just to name a few. The Clinton High School Arrows are a proud football program based on deep tradition embedded in a community clearly focused on the overall excellence of its schools.

****

The architect of the Madison Central High School football program built it from the ground up. Beginning in 1993, Madison Central came into existence through the consolidation of Madison-Ridgeland High School and Flora High School. Overnight, the two smaller schools morphed into a large 4A school with more growth expected. In a very short period, Madison Central grew into a giant 5A school, becoming the largest high school in Mississippi. The architect of the Jaguar football program pushed for rapid completion of his project, which included a new super-sized football stadium, a modern field house and the creation of a new cross-county rivalry to stimulate fan support. The architect wanted it all and wanted it fast. The blueprint for gridiron success designed by the architect worked. Only six years after his plan had been implemented, the Jaguars achieved their ultimate objective – a 15 and 0 perfect record and Madison Central's first 5A state championship. However, to appreciate fully the design of the Jaguar football program, its rapid implementation and the resulting success, one must first learn something about the talented architect of this project – Mike Justice.

Born and raised in the little community of Beans Ferry in Itawamba County, Mississippi, Mike Justice attended Fulton High

School. While at Fulton, he played fullback and linebacker for the legendary coach Ben Jones. Justice's dad, who was a pulpwood hauler, and Coach Jones both taught from the same "book of life." The message was the same, even though it was delivered in different ways. He learned common sense and no-nonsense principles to guide a young man through life, such as be on time, work hard, don't expect anything without working for it, finish what you start and respect all men.

After high school, Justice attended Itawamba Junior College where he played football and baseball. While Justice was at Itawamba, his high school coach, Ben Jones, became the head football coach. Jones recruited Justice to hang around after his playing eligibility had expired to help him with scouting reports and other assistant coach duties. It was then and there Justice realized, This is what I do best – coaching.

Following his college graduation, Justice immediately embarked on his coaching career, accepting his first assignment as an assistant coach at Caledonia High School. One year later, at the age of 25, Mike Justice was the head football coach at the little school in Lowndes County. Justice next took over the program at Calhoun City High School and led them to the state championship game in 1983. From there, Justice went to Louisville, where he led the Wildcats to back-to-back state championships in 1985 and 1986. In 1993, Justice began the process of building the new Madison Central High School football program from scratch. Six years later in 1999, the Jaguars captured the 5A state championship and ended the year ranked No. 12 nationally.

Every program Mike Justice touched, with the exception of Madison Central where there was no program, was in a state of disarray when he arrived. According to Justice, "I like doormat programs because they will let you do what you want to. I have spent my career going to places where they needed a coach. I am a hardcore philosophy person. I do it a certain way – my way."

The Justice way is based on the principles taught him by his dad and his coach when he was a young man. However, no words better sum up the Justice philosophy than his famous quote repeated time and time again: "No work, no win."

Many words have been used to describe Coach Mike Justice. Depending on whom you ask for a description of him as a coach, you will get different answers. Critics of Justice might describe him as boisterous, brash, arrogant or cocky. The more middle-of-the-road comments might include intense, self-confident and direct. However, the people closest to Coach Justice consistently refer to him as colorful, one-of-a-kind, funny, dedicated to his players and one hell of a football coach.

Edith Mitchell, the current principal at Madison Central High School, comments about her experience in dealing with Coach Justice while she was a counselor at Madison Central. She says, "Coach Justice was very confident in his football teams. He believed they could win and instilled that attitude in his players. There is something many people may not know about Coach Justice. During my early years at Madison Central, I was a counselor. He was in the counselors' offices at least once a day, checking on his players. He wanted to know about their grades. He always knew where his kids were academically. Coach Justice wanted his boys to do well academically. He always tried to find out where they were before they slipped too far. That is a part of his personality not too many people know about."

Principal Mitchell continues, "Coach Justice started this program. He built it from the ground up. We would not have an athletic program of this caliber without his vision. He initially took a lot of flak for our stadium, because it was not the typical high school stadium; but he had a vision and he built toward that vision."

To be a great architect, one must have vision, and that is why Mike Justice's fingerprints are, and forever will be, all over the football program at Madison Central High School.

When Coach Justice departed Madison Central in 2003, he left the football program in the capable hands of his trusted assistant coach, Ted Taylor. Under Coach Taylor, the Jaguar program continued the success established by Justice in the early years. Remarkably, when Ridgeland High School was created in 2002, which resulted in a significant reduction in the student population at Madison Central, Taylor was able to maintain the Jaguar program at its highly competitive level.

The official motto of Madison Central High School is "A tradition of excellence." However, Principal Mitchell says, "The real motto that we operate by is, 'If you are keeping score, we are playing to win.' What that means is that we want to win at everything we do – athletics, academics and the arts. We instill that level of expectation and that desire to excel in all our students. That even carries over to the community. Mike Justice gave us that quote, because that's what he lives by."

In 2006, Bobby Hall became head coach at Madison Central. While the coaching styles of Justice and Hall are distinctly different, there are some remarkable similarities between the two men.

Coach Hall also hails from a small town in Northeast Mississippi – Guntown – just 13 miles north of Tupelo on Highway 45. Like Justice, Hall attended a relatively small high school – Baldwyn – and played for a big time coach by the name of Hubert Tucker. Both Hall and Justice attended Itawamba Junior College. Following college, Hall, like Justice, went directly into coaching. In 1978, he took his first job at Fulton High School, Justice's alma mater. After two years as an assistant coach, Hall became the head football coach at Raleigh High School at age 25. After three years at Raleigh, Hall coached at Amory from 1984 to 1989. During that time, his teams played for, but did not win, the state championship in 1987 and 1988. After Amory, Hall succeeded Justice at Louisville. In 1991, Louisville defeated Stone County to win the state championship. In 1993, Hall returned to Amory and led the Panthers to an incredible 86-8 record over a seven-year stretch. During this remarkable run, Hall's Amory teams captured three state championships, with each team posting a 15-0 record. Immediately following his tenure at Amory, Hall jumpstarted a struggling Wayne County program before trading in high school coaching for college coaching. After a stint at Northeast Mississippi Community College and Murray State University (Kentucky), Hall accepted the offer to become the head football coach at Madison Central in 2006.

Mike Kent, Superintendent of Madison County Schools, comments regarding Coach Hall: "Coach Hall is really, really good. I have been in this business a long time, and Coach Hall is the complete package. He is a great football coach and a great athletic director. He is the best I've ever worked with."

According to Mark Carlson, Madison Central Booster Club President, "Bobby is almost a preacher at heart. He loves talking to groups and he is very much about the kids."

Superintendent Kent comments, "Coach Hall wants his teams to perform well. He wants his kids to represent the school and community well. Many coaches are not concerned with all of the minutia. They just want to win the ballgame. He wants to win and look good in the process."

One of the highest compliments paid to Coach Hall and the Jaguar athletic programs comes from Mark Carlson, Madison Central

Booster Club President. Carlson says, "People think of Madison Central as a small college. I attribute that to Bobby Hall's vision. We really have almost become like a small college in our athletic programs."

When Coach Mike Justice and Coach Bobby Hall arrived at Madison Central, they both had experience, confidence and a fistful of championships to their credit. More importantly, they both had vision. While Mike Justice is considered the undisputed architect of the Jaguar football program, Bobby Hall is now the engineer who is renovating and expanding the Madison Central athletic programs. Together, these two visionary coaches can claim co-ownership of one of the elite high school athletic programs in America. From its very beginning in 1993 until today, everything that is representative of Jaguar athletics is colored orange and blue and covered with the fingerprints of Mike Justice and Bobby Hall.

****

The two coaches stood at midfield as the rain came down in sheets – both men faced each other, dripping wet, cold and shivering, with each wearing a short-sleeved shirt and no jacket.

Debbie Turman, an Arrow fan, remembers the first meeting of Madison Central and Clinton at the old Madison-Ridgeland field on Highway 51 in Madison in 1994. She recalls, "It was early in the season and it was our first time to play them in Madison. Their visitor's stands were very small. I remember that it was one of those days where you knew it was going to rain at any time. Right before the game started, it began to rain. Then it came in sheets. Everybody got drenched."

J. Reeves also remembers that Friday night in Madison back in 1994 and the weather conditions at the time of kick off: "It started raining so hard you couldn't see the other sideline; then the rain turned cold, making playing conditions miserable."

In the midst of the bone-chilling, drenching rain, the opposing coaches, Mike Justice of Madison Central and David Bradberry of Clinton, stalked their respective sidelines, glaring and yelling across the field at each other. While the players covered up in rain gear and the fans wrapped themselves in ponchos and raincoats, the two coaches directed the gridiron warfare, each wearing a short-sleeved shirt. At the end of the game when Justice and Bradberry met at midfield, Coach Justice asked Coach Bradberry, "Why didn't you put on a rain coat?" Bradberry responded, "I wasn't putting on a coat until you put one on."

That one scene at midfield in Madison in 1994, with the two opposing coaches for Madison Central and Clinton facing each other as the downpour continued, reflects the Jaguar-Arrow rivalry better than words can. Starting with the two head football coaches, Justice and Bradberry, and permeating down through the players, cheerleaders, bands, students, fans, administrators, mayors and communities, when Madison Central and Clinton compete in anything, it's on.

The rivalry started in 1993 with the new upstart school in Madison defeating tradition-rich Clinton High School 14-7. The next year, the first game between the schools played on Jaguar turf, Clinton unloaded on Madison Central, defeating the Jaguars 27-7 in a cold downpour that persisted from the beginning to the end of the game. Throughout the game, Madison Central's coach, Mike Justice, yelled across the field to his counterpart, David Bradberry, admonishing him for running up the score. In 1995, Justice and the Jaguars got revenge by shutting out Clinton 35-0. The 1995 game is the only shutout in the 15-year history of the series. The schools swapped wins from 1996 through 1998, establishing a characteristic of the Arrow-Jaguar series with consistently close margins of victory.

In 1999, one of the most thrilling games in the series history was played at Roy Burkett Field in Clinton. With both Clinton and Madison Central ranked, the last game of the regular season drew a crowd in excess of 10,000 people. Coach Scott Brown, now Clinton's head football coach, was an assistant on David Bradberry's staff the night of the monumental game. He recalls, "When we came out of the dressing room an hour before game time, both sides were full. Everyone was cheering and it felt like a college atmosphere. There was so much community hoopla about the game." The Arrows engineered a commanding 31-8 lead with 9 minutes to go in the fourth quarter, only to lose the game 37-31 to the Jaguars. Madison Central went on to win its first 5A state championship, riding the momentum created by the sensational come-from-behind win over Clinton.

Coach Brown painfully recalls the 1999 game against the Jaguars: "The 1999 game was the worst loss I've ever been a part of because we just collapsed." However, in the 2000 game played at Madison Central, a record-breaking crowd in excess of 12,000 people witnessed a thrilling win by Clinton over Madison Central. As the clock was running down, Madison Central's quarterback was blindsided and fumbled when an Arrow defender scooped the ball off the turf and ran it in for a touchdown. Clinton won 31-24. Just like the year before, the momentum of beating Madison Central propelled Clinton into and through the playoffs, taking the Arrows to the championship game against Moss Point.

Longtime Clinton P.A. announcer, Danny Davis, says, "I think the two biggest games in the Clinton-Madison Central series were the games in 1999 and 2000. Both games featured big time players, big time crowds and lots of excitement."

The games played from 2001 through the most recent game in 2007 have all been decided by a touchdown or less, except in 2005 when the final score was Madison Central 17, Clinton 7. The rivalry has always been competitive. The 2007 game was played in Clinton's new Arrow Stadium against an 0-4 Madison Central team. Clinton was the heavy favorite due to Madison Central's dismal record; however, Arrow coach Scott Brown warned his team all week to beware. Clinton assistant coach Danny Davis recalls the warnings of Coach Brown: "All week, Coach told the players, 'Look who Madison Central lost to in those first four games – all very good teams.' We ended up losing 18 to 17." The loss hurt the Clinton faithful, because it was the first loss ever in the new stadium after winning three games in a row in there. To lose was bad enough, but to lose to Madison Central was a blow. For Madison Central, the win over Clinton was the catalyst to turn their season around. Madison Central Coach, Bobby Hall, says, "We just went over there and played well and won a very, very close game. There was a huge crowd. It was their first loss in their new stadium, which is the nicest high school stadium I've ever coached in. We went on and won six of our last eight games."

Clinton Mayor, Rosemary Aultman, expresses her thoughts regarding the 2007 Clinton and Madison Central game: "I was sick we gave the game away. We should have won it. It turned Madison Central's whole season around when they beat us that night."

The Clinton-Madison Central rivalry is only 15 years old, but it has created a competitive environment between the two communities in everything, each trying to top the other. David Bradberry, former Clinton head football coach, tells the story about Mike Justice calling him one day and asking if he could come tour his field house. Coach Justice admired Clinton's facility, and since Madison Central was in the process of planning the construction of a new field house, he wanted to take a closer look at the Arrows' field house. Coach Bradberry graciously invited his colleague over for a visit. After touring the Clinton field house, Justice informed Bradberry that he was so impressed with the facility that he was going to recommend that Madison Central duplicate it with one exception. Bradberry, of course, asked Justice what aspect of his field house would he not duplicate. Justice said, "The size. I'm going to make ours five feet longer and wider so that our field house is bigger than yours." That's exactly what Coach Justice did. Coach Bradberry states, "That's the way the school districts look at each other. I think it is a healthy rivalry. It doesn't matter if it's football or checkers, Madison Central versus Clinton has always been a knockdown, drag out for bragging rights in the community."

Mayor Aultman comments on the rivalry:

> When we were working on the bond issue here for our athletic complex, it was very important to the people in this community that we have a complex that we felt was the best in the state. You can translate that into "better than Madison Central" if you want to. We wanted to make sure it was something that represented our community and that it was something in which the students felt they had ownership. When we proposed the bond issue for not only the school, but the stadium as well, both issues passed – one by 89 percent and one by 88 percent. The community understands the value of the school and its athletic programs.

Coach Bradberry echoes Mayor Aultman's sentiments regarding the community rivalry. He says, "Whether we put it on paper or whether Madison puts it on paper, the measuring stick was the other group. Whatever they did, we were thinking, How are we going to beat Madison? I know they were the same way – What do we need to do to get ahead of them? That's the way it went with everything."

Mark Carlson, Madison Central's Booster Club President, says, "Clinton and Madison are affluent areas. Because of that, the facilities at both schools are tremendous. There is a lot of parental involvement and excitement at both schools. When you have parents involved – parents that care about their kids and spend time with their kids – that creates a fan base with a lot of excitement and a lot of interest."

Madison Central head football coach Bobby Hall weighs in on

the competitiveness of the two communities:

> As the head coach, if you told me I could only win one game, Clinton is the one I would want to win. I think it goes much deeper than football. We are arguably two of the best school districts in the entire state. We both try to do things first class. Our academics are the best. Besides the athletic competition, we compete academically as well. It gets down to the fact that we both have great school districts.

When Clinton opened its new stadium in 2007, the Arrows were proud to unveil an all-weather turf field. Once Coach Hall at Madison Central became aware of the state-of-the-art enhancement at Clinton, he immediately started a campaign to upgrade the field at Jaguar Stadium. Due to the support of the Jaguar Booster Club and the Mayor of Madison, Mary Hawkins-Butler, an avid Jaguar supporter, Coach Hall fully expects to have Madison Central's new all-weather playing surface installed and ready for the upcoming Clinton game in 2008. However, neither one of these schools is prone to accept the status quo. Once a balance of power is achieved, it would not be surprising if campaigns were begun at either school to increase its seating in order to claim the "biggest stadium" prize. Anything goes when Clinton and Madison compete. Perhaps Coach Hall reveals some of his strategic thoughts when he says, "I really think the Madison community would consider additional enhancements to our facilities." Madison Mayor, Mary Hawkins-Butler, comments, "I support Coach Hall's efforts to elevate our football program to the same status as our city (a top ten city in America) – with a national ranking." As Coach Hall quipped, "No high school in Mississippi has built a domed football stadium yet!"
Where will it end?

WHAT THE ARROWS SAY ABOUT MADISON CENTRAL

If either school knew how similar they were to the other, they would be disgusted with themselves.

J. Reeves
Clinton Principal

The 1999 loss to Madison Central was the worst loss I've ever been a part of. We just collapsed.

Scott Brown
Clinton Head Football Coach

Clinton High School football is a big deal in Clinton. The community is involved with every game, but when it comes to Madison Central, they turn it up a notch.

C.J. DeLoach
Former Clinton Cheerleader

I was stopped in the hall at school one day by an administrator who commented, "You are wearing an orange shirt." I immediately responded, "No, it's not – this is salmon. I do not own anything orange."

Debbie Turman
Clinton Booster Club Treasurer

They say it's not as big a deal to them as it is to us. I will go to my grave saying they want that game just as much as we do for the rivalry aspect.

Brett Robinson
Clinton Assistant Football Coach

Overall, we don't like Madison.

Amber Smith
Former Clinton Cheerleader
and Student Body President

I would say Clinton people think the people from Madison believe they are a little better than we are.

Danny Davis
Clinton P.A. Announcer

It was an intentional thing last year (2007) when the Madison Central players and fans came onto our field to celebrate and would not leave. It was as if they were thinking, Let's go stomp all over that big arrow! It infuriated all of us.

Debbie Turman
Clinton Booster Club Treasurer

My guy friends who know girls from Madison Central say they are preppy or they think highly of themselves.

Anna Kate Jackson
Clinton Cheerleader

The rivalry got started when Coach Justice and Coach Bradberry were going after it.

Brett Robinson
Clinton Assistant Football Coach

The people in Madison probably think Clinton is riding its tradition and isn't as good as it used to be in the old days.

Danny Davis
Clinton P.A. Announcer

Personally, I try not to like them.

Amber Smith
Former Clinton Cheerleader
and Student Body President

WHAT THE JAGUARS SAY ABOUT CLINTON

Before this school was built, Clinton was the trophy school in Mississippi. We think we are the trophy school now. I'm sure they will argue that point, but we think Madison Central has replaced them. This rivalry goes much deeper than football. It's about everything. It's about our communities, our schools, our academics and our athletics – the whole pie. Football is just a piece of it.

Bobby Hall
Madison Central Head Football Coach

We consider Clinton a historical rival. Clinton gauges their year on whether they beat us.

Mark Carlson
Madison Central Booster Club President

Clinton and Madison Central's visions are the same. We both want to turn out National Merit Finalists, and we want to do well at everything we do. It's obvious that they take a lot of pride in their school. The same thing is true over here.

Mike Kent
Superintendent of Madison County Schools

They look at it like, "Those guys at Madison Central have everything." There is a jealousy factor. It's kind of funny because they are the ones that just got the beautiful new stadium with turf.

Steve Metz
Madison Central Assistant Football Coach

We worry about Clinton one week out of 52; they worry about us 54 out of 52.

Tim Shramek
Madison Central Assistant Football Coach

It's a very goodhearted rivalry, but there is a rivalry there.

Mark Carlson
Madison Central Booster Club President

There is a lot of mutual respect between the two schools.

Bobby Hall
Madison Central Head Football Coach

Our school is an infant compared to Clinton in terms of tradition.

Tim Shramek
Madison Central Assistant Football Coach

I always tell the people in Clinton, "Rivalry? We don't care about y'all. We don't even have a pep rally before we play y'all!" Boy, they get mad. I'm just egging them on because it does matter here; but it kills them when I say, "You're just another game!"

Tim Shramek
Madison Central Assistant Football Coach

Sometimes we refer to them as the Clinton "Errors."

Mark Carlson
Madison Central Booster Club President

Everywhere J. Reeves has been they have lost.

Steve Metz
Madison Central Assistant Football Coach

They have more of a generational legacy in Clinton, and they probably regard us to some extent as an upstart.

Mark Carlson
Madison Central Booster Club President

CLINTON-MADISON CENTRAL
SERIES HISTORY

Year	Clinton	Score	Madison Central
1993	David Bradberry	7-14	Mike Justice
1994	David Bradberry	27-7	Mike Justice
1995	David Bradberry	0-35	Mike Justice
1996	David Bradberry	9-21	Mike Justice
1997	David Bradberry	18-14	Mike Justice
1998	David Bradberry	23-25	Mike Justice
1999	David Bradberry	31-37	Mike Justice
2000	David Bradberry	31-24	Mike Justice
2001	David Bradberry	16-14	Mike Justice
2002	Pete Hurt	19-16	Ted Taylor
2003	Pete Hurt	18-21	Ted Taylor
2004	Pete Hurt	10-13	Ted Taylor
2005	Scott Brown	7-17	Ted Taylor
2006	Scott Brown	21-14	Bobby Hall
2007	Scott Brown	17-18	Bobby Hall

★★OFFICIAL GAME DAY PROGRAM $5.00★★

BILOXI
VERSUS
GULFPORT

BILOXI

TFIC
INFRASTRUCTURE CONSTRUCTION

PROUD SPONSOR OF MISSISSIPPI HIGH SCHOOL FOOTBALL

FRIDAY, NOVEMBER 7, 2008 ★ 7:00 PM KICKOFF

MILNER STADIUM ★ GULFPORT, MISSISSIPPI

CHAPTER
16

AS OLD AS THE SEA

There is a glow that rises above the trees across the bayou. It is distinctly different and foreign to the rest of the landscape, and it is what many people fix their stares upon on warm, humid fall nights in the city of Biloxi. To the many citizens that toil in the demanding seafood industry, the glow signals the end of another backbreaking week of work on the Gulf Coast. It means that it is time for the fathers who work around the clock on shrimp boats to finally get a dry change of clothes, and for the mothers who pick shrimp in one of the many factories during the day to come home to their families. The city of Biloxi may have its economy firmly anchored in the waters of the Gulf Coast, but its heart is drawn to that glow above the trees.

Henry "Spud" Wieniewitz remembers looking at the glow when he was a kid growing up in Biloxi, Mississippi: "We were a fishing family and we lived in a housing project on the bay. There was a white housing project and a black project that were separated by a bayou. To the south you could see that bright light and you could hear the crowds of people beneath it. Then, the announcement, 'Good evening, football fans' would echo through the neighborhood."

The glow above the trees was generated by the lights of Biloxi's Yankie Stadium. One of the most beautiful football stadiums in the state, the concrete stands surrounding the gridiron could accommodate over 8,000 enthusiastic fans. This was the location of the famous post-season Shrimp Bowl and, more importantly, the home of the Biloxi Indians football team.

During the time Wieniewitz stared at the glow as a kid, the Indians were being led by Coach John Williams. During his tenure as head coach at Biloxi from 1964-1971, Williams commanded one of the most imposing football forces in the state of Mississippi. Clad in their red and white uniforms, the Indians took the field at Yankie Stadium in droves. Line after line of Biloxi players would form on the field for pre-game warm-ups until half of the turf was covered in Indians standing shoulder to shoulder. Mammoth squads boasting an astonishing 150 players or more were the rule, not the exception, under Williams. In fact, Williams remembers one game against Picayune where his team jumped out to a 50-0 halftime lead. During the intermission, he sent 35 of his players to the stands and had a fresh 35 take their uniforms and dress out for the second half. Williams says,

> We didn't always have enough uniforms to dress everyone out at the same time. When we traveled, we had to take four buses to accommodate our entire team. Football was a big, big deal on the Coast during that time, and we were particularly strong. There was one season when we were forced to play six of our eleven games against out-of-state opponents, because no one else would play us.

Originally from Port Gibson and a graduate of Mississippi College, Williams was coaching at Magee when the Biloxi superintendent called him out of the blue. The superintendent told Williams that Biloxi had an opening for a head football coach and athletic director, and that he was going to suggest Williams to the school board as the man they should hire. When Williams revealed that he had never been to the Coast before, the superintendent quickly persuaded him to come down and take a visit. Remembers Williams, "They gave me a tour of the campus and everything was so impressive. Then they took me to Yankie Stadium. It was like nothing I had ever seen. It was better than the stadium I played in at Mississippi College. After I saw Yankie Stadium, I knew I was in hog heaven and I couldn't accept the job fast enough."

One of the great traditions at Yankie Stadium was the collection of photographs that it housed. Every kid from Biloxi who went on to play college football was immortalized with a framed photograph hanging in the inner hallways of the stadium. The tradition was kept current through the mid-1960s until John Williams began producing college players at such a rapid pace that the stadium couldn't keep up. Said Williams, "At one point we had 17 kids that were playing in the SEC alone. Either it got too expensive or too difficult to keep pace, but they stopped adding the photos." John Tapper, 1968 Biloxi graduate, recalls the photo gallery, "It was something that motivated you as a kid to perform to the best of your ability. Next to the photos, there was a sign that read 'Who's next?' I was fortunate enough to go on and play football at Southern Mississippi, so I got my photo added to the wall. I was actually the last one added before they stopped the tradition."

Yankie Stadium continued to serve as home to the Indians through the turn of the century before it was retired for a newer, more modern facility. In 2003, Biloxi built a brand new school on a new campus. The school was funded primarily with money generated by the eight casinos in the city. With the new school came a state of the art on-campus stadium. The new stadium featured an all-weather track, synthetic turf, spacious home and visitor stands and a giant press box. It quickly became regarded as the best facility in the state, and Yankie Stadium was forgotten, for a moment.

In August 2005, Hurricane Katrina obliterated the Mississippi Gulf Coast. Tens of thousands of people were displaced or saw their homes destroyed. Immediately after the storm, organizations such as FEMA, the Salvation Army, Red Cross and the National Guard began moving in people and supplies. The proud confines of Yankie Stadium answered the call and served as a massive staging area for many of these groups and the services that provided immediate assistance to the community.

Biloxi principal Pamela Manners describes the weeks following Katrina:

> All the school facilities were crucial in the recovery effort. Yankie Stadium was overrun with relief personnel and we turned the new campus into a working hospital and shelter. We literally had families that were living in the new football stadium and in the gym. We opened the drama department to find clothes for people, and we used clean rags and duct tape from the janitor's closet to diaper babies. The whole experience was surreal. One of the advisory groups from Florida sent to help us recover said that the single most important thing we could do was to reopen the school. If the school was open, the kids could go on with their normal day, almost as if nothing happened. This allowed the parents time to work out issues with the insurance companies. We worked extremely hard to make that happen.

Once the school reopened and the children were back in class, the next step taken by the school may not have been so clear to the advisory group from Florida, but it was crystal clear to the school administration - restore the glow above the trees.

Just as the glow generated by Yankie Stadium in years past had symbolized the end of the workweek, recreation and community pride, the glow from the new stadium did the same, albeit at a far more crucial time in the city's history. As soon as the new lights were fired up for the first time after the storm, the people of Biloxi responded the same way they always had – they showed up to see the Indians play. The glow of the lights comforted the people of Biloxi and assured them that life would return to normal, and that, maybe, it wasn't so far from normal after all.

Pamela Manners recalls the first football game after Katrina:

> Once we got everything cleaned up and sanitized, one of the first things we did was have a football game. I don't even remember who we played; I just know it was packed and it was a great distraction and treat for everyone. People were socializing and going to the concession stand. It was almost like a throwback to the '40s and '50s before all the big, modern entertainment developed. It was a wonderful healing event for the people in Biloxi, and it was the first fun thing many of them had done in weeks. It wasn't as if you could go home and watch TV.

****

Gulfport High School is preparing to celebrate its 100th year of high school football in 2008. During its storied history, countless individuals have contributed to the success of the Commodore/Admiral program, but there is one name that has been so instrumental in the development of the program over the course of so many years that he stands alone as the most important figure in Gulfport history. That individual is Mr. Gulfport himself, Coach Lindy Callahan.

As synonymous a figure as Callahan is with Gulfport, he is, surprisingly, not originally from Gulfport. Callahan grew up in Meridian and played football for the Wildcats in famed Ray Stadium before taking his talents to Ole Miss, where he played and studied under Johnny Vaught. After playing a little bit of semi-pro baseball, Callahan was offered a job at Gulfport by Roland Dale, whom Callahan knew from Ole Miss and who was the current head football coach at Gulfport. After two seasons, Dale left, and at the young age of 26, Callahan was promoted to head coach and athletic director in 1955.

Callahan ultimately served as the head coach of the Commodores for 11 seasons. During this period, the Commodores competed in the powerful Big Eight Conference, which Callahan's alma mater, Meridian, regularly dominated. By his ninth season, Callahan had built the Gulfport program into a bona fide power, and the Commodores captured their first Big Eight championship in 1963. In addition to building a dominant 35-game winning streak, Callahan's boys followed the 1963 season with an encore performance in 1964 and won a second conference championship, firmly establishing the Gulf Coast as the current stronghold of high school football in Mississippi.

Just as Callahan seemed to be hitting his stride as a football coach, the Gulfport school district made a surprising and far-reaching decision. Forced integration was just around the corner, and those in charge of the Gulfport school system knew it would create a unique problem. Gulfport High School was already operating at near maximum capacity, and the addition of students from 33rd Avenue High School would push existing facilities beyond capabilities. Rather than operate one giant school, administrators decided it would be better to divide their forces and operate two smaller schools. Thus, in 1966 a large number of the students from Gulfport High School were sent to the newly formed Gulfport East High School.

As part of the restructuring process, the Gulfport High football staff was equally divided between the two schools. Coach Callahan, possibly the only man capable of doing the job, was placed in the position of athletic director over all three Gulfport schools: Gulfport, Gulfport East and 33rd Avenue.

In 1969, 33rd Avenue was closed and the bulk of its students were sent to Gulfport High. A testament to Callahan's administrative ability, in its first year fielding a fully integrated team, Gulfport High won its third ever Big Eight championship in 1970 and then added a fourth in 1972. Further, Callahan was able to bring order and keep the peace in a potentially chaotic situation where former teammates at Gulfport were now competing against one another with some of them now attending Gulfport East.

Continuing to serve as athletic director, Callahan also presided over Gulfport athletics when school administrators decided to reverse their earlier decision and bring the city's two schools back together in 1977. Individuals who were once hurt when they were told they could no longer wear the blue and white of the Gulfport Commodores, were now hurt a second time when they were forced to give up their newly formed pride in the orange and white of the Gulfport East Vikings. Callahan was instrumental in bringing both sides back together and reuniting the Gulfport family under the blue and orange of what became the Admiral athletic program.

Callahan's guidance during the reuniting of the two schools provided a stability and comfort that may have been impossible to find anywhere else. Just like the season that immediately followed integration, the first united Gulfport team in 1977 went on to win the Big Eight championship. Head football coaches may have changed over the years, but the athletic director remained consistent, and so did the results.

During this time, Callahan sought to build excellence at every level of the program, not just on the gridiron. One of his unique and memorable techniques was how he handled players who just couldn't seem to stay on the path of the righteous. If a player continuously broke team rules or generally failed to live up to Callahan's high expectations, the player would be given a special card to put in his wallet. The front of the card read: "Because of your lack of self discipline, poor attitude and not fulfilling your commitment to the Admiral athletic program, this is your... ." When you flipped the card over, the other side read "LAST CHANCE!" The card served as a constant reminder to the athlete that he had come to the end of the line and any further transgressions would result in his dismissal. The card also served as proof to potentially angry parents that their son had been given fair warning and opportunity to conform to the standards set by Callahan himself.

Of the 100 years of Gulfport football, Lindy Callahan has been directly involved in 55 of them. Not only has Callahan logged a staggering number of years in the Gulfport program, but he has also been around for the most important events in the program's history. Regarding his long association with Gulfport High School, Coach Callahan says, "Life has been good. The journey has been great. I worked 12-hour days Monday through Sunday, but it was always a pleasure to go to work. The association with the players, the community, the school staff and the administrators I was under – it has all been a great experience. My years at Gulfport have all been so wonderful and I cherish them very much."

****

Biloxi High School first formed a football team in 1907. However, due to the lack of high school football teams on the Coast, they were unable to find an opponent until November of the following year. Finally, on Thanksgiving Day of 1908, Biloxi's football team, led by Coach Cleveland Huggins, took the field for the first time. The game was played at 3:00 in the afternoon against a group of boys from neighboring Gulfport High School. Thus began the longest running high school football rivalry in the state of Mississippi.

Newspaper accounts of the game estimate that attendance at this historic event was approximately 250 people. Cost of admission was 25 cents for what the paper dubbed "the only special event on Thanksgiving day with the exception of church services."

Gulfport won the opening coin toss and opted to kick the ball to Biloxi. Spectator accounts indicate the Biloxi players were a bit larger and better conditioned than the players from Gulfport were. Despite this supposed advantage, it was Gulfport's left halfback, Joe Milner, who notched the first score of the game and the series. Milner's touchdown made the score 5-0 and his extra point stretched the Gulfport lead to 6-0. Biloxi's fullback, Ashby Long, was able to put the ball across the goal line shortly thereafter, accounting for the first score in Biloxi history and knotting the score at 6-6 at halftime.

The superior conditioning of the Biloxi team showed in the second half as the Gulfport players were gasping for air and stretching on the ground at every opportunity. Students began yelling cheers at one another across the field and the rest of the crowd joined in. Biloxi ultimately added three more touchdowns and closed out the game with a 24-6 victory.

A newspaper article the following day expressed surprise at how much interest and enthusiasm was generated by a football game played by the Biloxi High School team. With football being relatively new to the Coast, and observers still trying to decide how to feel about the sport, the author of the newspaper article expressed the following opinion: "Football is a game which arouses an entirely different spirit than that manifested in baseball. While baseball is the national game, football is essentially a college game and it arouses college spirit and community pride as nothing else will."

To arouse the spirit even more, less than 24 hours after the first meeting between Biloxi and Gulfport, controversy was introduced to the rivalry. The Gulfport superintendent made a statement that the group of individuals who played the previous day against the Biloxi High team was not the "official" team from Gulfport High School. Because the parents of the players had not signed the required consent forms, the team was not technically authorized to represent Gulfport High School, and therefore a rematch should be scheduled. A newspaper article, which was clearly written by a Biloxi supporter, showed no interest in the superintendent's claim and responded to the statement by saying, "The team that came here yesterday was regarded as the team of Gulfport High School and will continue to be so regarded."

A second game was quickly scheduled nonetheless, and was played in Gulfport. The second game took place on Saturday, December 12, and this time resulted in a Gulfport victory. While accounts of the first game reported the Biloxi players to be "a bit heftier" than Gulfport's, accounts of the second game describe Gulfport's players to be "much heavier" than the Biloxi players, a rather suspicious observation since the two games took place a mere 16 days apart.

With the infant series already locked at one game apiece, the two communities apparently could not wait until the following season to play a tiebreaker. A third contest was immediately scheduled between the purple and white of Biloxi and the blue and gold of Gulfport. Controversy and disagreement began before the opening kickoff as the referee failed to show, and then Biloxi arrived with only ten players and tried to dress out a non-student to fill the eleventh slot. After an hour of waiting and debate, fans began asking for their money back. Finally, a compromise was made between the coaches and the game was played, but it was agreed that it would not count as an official high school game. Shortly after the game began, Biloxi took exception to a call that went against their team and a debate ensued between the referee and the coaches. Soon fans joined in the debate and it didn't take long before the frustrated referee decided to end the game and award a victory by way of forfeit to Gulfport.

In addition to describing the game as a "fiasco" and insinuating that Gulfport displayed poor sportsmanship by accepting a victory due to forfeit, the byline of the following day's newspaper article read,

"Game is Forfeited by Referee to Gulfport – Football Game Turned into Gabfest, Very Unsatisfactory Outcome to Saturday's Inter-Scholastic Event."

Although documentation cannot be found to definitively prove it to be fact, it is widely believed that Biloxi and Gulfport continued their football contests with each other the following year in 1909. Scores to the series resurface in 1920 and show that the teams were in fact still playing one another twice a year through 1924. The rivalry remained balanced for the next 30 years, as each team experienced short streaks of success before the other went on their own run and rebalanced the series totals. It is interesting to point out that in the 23 meetings from 1921-1940, there were an incredible 22 shutouts. Gulfport shut out Biloxi five games straight on two different occasions, while Biloxi shut out Gulfport in seven straight meetings. During Biloxi's run of shutout victories, the Indians experienced possibly their greatest period of football success as they also captured four straight Big Eight Conference championships from 1927-1930.

Located only 13 miles apart on Highway 90, Gulfport and Biloxi were certainly destined to become rivals. When the schools first played football in 1908, Gulfport had approximately 1,000 residents, while Biloxi had just over 5,000. In the 100 years since, the populations of the two cities have ballooned to 71,000 and 50,500 respectively, and are now the second and third largest cities in Mississippi. Located on the water, the economies of both communities are anchored in marine-based activities, such as traffic from their ports and the seafood industry.

Geographic proximity and other similarities help fuel the rivalry between the two cities, but so do their differences. Residents of the Coast have always regarded Gulfport as a white-collar city, while Biloxi and its seafood industry place it in the blue-collar category. Historically, Gulfport was the place to go for the yacht club and downtown shopping, while Biloxi was the hot spot at night for juke joints, strip clubs and illegal gaming. The people of Gulfport have traditionally been a bit more homogenous and tilt towards the Protestant faith. Biloxi's residents are often more diverse and are more strongly influenced by early French settlement, tourism and the Catholic religion. Says 1994 Gulfport graduate Brad Palazzo, "My father-in-law is from Biloxi and he sounds like he is from Louisiana. People from Biloxi sound completely different from people in Gulfport, and we're only separated by a few miles."

Keith Williams, a 1982 Gulfport graduate, remembers his high school days: "The Robert E. Lee and the Fiesta were two Biloxi nightclubs where Gulfport people sometimes went. When preppy Gulfport guys showed up at those places, it was pretty obvious they were on foreign turf. There were plenty of altercations that took place."

Even current Biloxi mayor and 1958 Biloxi graduate, A.J. Holloway, recalls his early adventures into Gulfport: "Gulfport had drive-ins on the beach and the yacht club where we liked to go on the weekends. The yacht club hosted dances that involved a lot of the high schools kids from Biloxi and Gulfport. The dances usually ended up in a fight."

The football contest between Biloxi and Gulfport turned out to be the ultimate conduit in which to funnel the communities' competitive spirit towards each other. During the week of the game, the city of Gulfport would conduct a giant parade through downtown. Because the game was traditionally played on Thanksgiving, the parade took place the day before on Wednesday. Remembers 1942 Gulfport graduate, Frank Bertucci:

> The parade started at Gulfport High, which is now the courthouse, and went all through town. The cheerleaders got on top of the roof of Jones Brothers Drug Store and did their cheers. There were no other real activities, so everyone in Gulfport was in the streets for this event. People walked behind the parade and followed it though town. There were even a couple of theaters the parade would march through. It was a big deal. Whatever else you had planned for Thanksgiving Day, the football game was a priority part of it.

Business throughout town showed their support for their team by decorating their storefronts in the appropriate colors. The week of the game also produced a widespread display of "GGG" and "BBB" signs, buttons and stickers throughout the communities. These cryptic little abbreviations are clear indicators of an individual's allegiance to Biloxi or Gulfport. Stop to purchase a cup of coffee in Gulfport during the week of the Biloxi game and the cashier may have a BBB sticker on her lapel. What is her sticker saying to you? "Beat Biloxi Bad." The roadside sign of a restaurant in Biloxi may drop the posting of the blue plate special and replace it with GGG. What's more important than food that particular week? "Get Gulfport Good."

The exact origination of the monikers is unknown, and supporters of both schools adamantly claim to have invented theirs first. What is undisputed is the frequency with which the letters are used as windshield decorations, t-shirt designs, vandalism graffiti and countless other displays meant to better define the boundary lines of the rivalry.

By 1956, the series score totaled a near perfectly balanced mark of 19-21-4. The rivalry was approaching the half-century mark and was deeply entrenched as one of the most important annual events for each city. Says Gulfport's Lindy Callahan, "I can't think of a single event that was more important during the year than our annual football game with Biloxi."

The maturity of the rivalry meant that men who once played for Biloxi and Gulfport in the early part of the century were now sitting in the stands cheering on their sons and grandsons against the neighboring school. This dynamic produced as much or more intensity in the stands as on the field of play. By the time of the 1956 contest, this intensity was quickly building towards a tipping point that soon led to a series of events that left a permanent mark on the rivalry equivalent to a giant impact crater on the surface of the moon.

During the 1956 game, Biloxi's A.J. Holloway posted an early score to grab a 6-0 lead for the Indians. Holloway describes his memory of the ensuing kickoff:

> I ran down the field and was in on the tackle of Gulfport's return man. When I was getting up, someone shoved me from behind. As I was turning around to see who it was, the ref grabbed both of us and threw us both out of the game. I didn't do anything. A Gulfport player just shoved me and I got thrown out of the game. At least that's what I remember, and I'm sticking to my story.

Gulfport ultimately came back to win the game 7-6 on a last-minute cutback sweep that Chuck Morris took 81 yards for a touchdown. Forced to play the remainder of the game without their star running back due to a controversial call, Biloxi fans left the stadium with a bitter taste in their mouths. The bitterness festered for the next 12 months and then turned downright rancid by the time the teams met again.

The 1957 game was played in Gulfport in its customary afternoon slot on Thanksgiving Day. Tom Freeman was a junior player on Gulfport's team for the contest and remembers the events that transpired:

> The game was incredibly rough and we took an early 10-0 lead. At halftime, players were complaining to Coach Callahan that Biloxi players were hitting them in the piles and taking some dirty shots at them. Coach Callahan told us, "We're not going to retaliate. We're going to play good football." Biloxi had a real fine team and they ended up taking the lead 19-10 in the second half. Late in the fourth quarter, they had control of the game and were running out the clock. Our middle guard, Doug Medley, jumped off sides and knocked their center into their quarterback. There was a little tussle between the players and the referees got everything worked out, but you could feel the tension in the air all around you. The stadium was a powder keg. At that point, they probably should have called the game and sent everyone to the locker rooms, but they insisted that we run one more play to properly run out the clock. That's when the fight happened. It may have started with the players, but the fans quickly got involved and emptied out of the stands. There was no fence around the field, so you could step right out of the stands and be on the sidelines. The stands just spilled onto the field. There was not that much security present for a football game back in those days, so the whole incident got ugly fast. It was really pretty scary.

After being "unfairly" ejected from the game the previous year, Biloxi's A.J. Holloway led the comeback victory over Gulfport as he accounted for all three of the Indians' touchdowns. Holloway went on to earn a football scholarship to Ole Miss and later became Biloxi's mayor. Interestingly, it is widely rumored through both communities, though unconfirmed, that A.J. Holloway is the individual that threw the first punch that started the epic brawl.

Some people refer to the events at the 1957 game as a fight between players; others describe it as nothing less than a war between the two towns. Regardless of the description, the event resulted in the suspension of football games between the schools for a full decade. The suspension of the biggest annual event in either town began in 1958 and lasted until 1968. Towards the end of the suspension, in 1966, Gulfport

High School split itself into Gulfport and Gulfport East. During the next two seasons, neither of the schools in Gulfport was allowed to play Biloxi in football. Recalls 1968 Biloxi graduate John Tapper, "During the years we didn't play, there was some really bad tension. It was as if both teams blamed the other for starting the melee. We played them in basketball and, since we knew we weren't going to play in football, it made the basketball games even more intense and physical."

The suspension of the rivalry was made more difficult by the fact that both Gulfport and Biloxi were members of the Big Eight Conference. Since the schools were not allowed to play, and because both were fielding highly competitive teams during the years of the suspension, deciding the prestigious Big Eight championship became an awkward matter. Biloxi claimed the crown in 1962 and Gulfport snared back-to-back titles in 1963 and 1964. Without a mechanism for settling the matter on the gridiron, debate over who had the better team intensified.

By the late 1960s, the two schools began talks of resuming their football rivalry. Gulfport's coach during the infamous 1957 game, Lindy Callahan, was now the athletic director over the Gulfport schools and his work spearheaded the renewal of the rivalry on the western front. The business director for the Biloxi schools helped mend feelings from the east. This individual was none other than A.J. Holloway.

The rivalry finally resumed in 1968 at Biloxi's Yankie Stadium. Because Gulfport had begun to play Gulfport East in the final game of the season, the 1968 game with Biloxi was played as the fifth game of the year rather than on Thanksgiving Day, as it had been in the past. Gulfport East coach Jerry Gundlach remembers attending the game and the unusual way in which it started, "They actually had the teams shake hands before the game. They got this out of the way first, just in case they had to rush the teams off the field quickly after the game was over. There was at least some lingering concern over how everyone was going to handle the whole event."

Buddy Palazzo was a senior quarterback for Gulfport during the game in 1968. Says Palazzo,

> It was still a rivalry, even though we had not played each other for ten years. There was so much built up anticipation from all the fans. There were over 10,000 people packed into that stadium and it felt like a

college atmosphere. The one thing I vividly remember about the game is that it was one of the cleanest games I have ever played in. Everyone felt like they had to be on their best behavior or we may never get to play each other again.

The 1968 game ended in a 26-14 Biloxi victory that helped catapult the Indians to their sixth overall Big Eight championship.

Another possible reason for the renewal of the rivalry was the fact that integration was looming on the horizon. Knowing that unique challenges would certainly confront their schools during this period, both schools probably felt they needed to heal old wounds before new challenges could be met. The very next year, in 1969, 33rd Avenue High School in Gulfport was closed and its students were sent to either Gulfport or Gulfport East. However, Nichols High School, the counterpart black school in Biloxi, did not close until after the 1971 school year. Therefore, for a couple of years, Gulfport enjoyed somewhat of a personnel advantage over their rivals in Biloxi, who had yet to unite their black and white football forces. Gulfport had fallen just behind in the overall series with Biloxi, but used the period following integration to immediately grab four straight victories and reclaim the series lead. Says 33rd Avenue graduate and former Gulfport athletic director, Prince Jones, "The talent level between Gulfport and Biloxi was not even close after integration. They simply couldn't match the raw skill we were putting on the field during that period of time." The Gulfport teams were so talented that they won Big Eight championships in 1970 and 1972.

The rivalry took another important turn in 1977 for a multitude of reasons. First, 1977 marked the first year that Gulfport and Gulfport East merged back into one school, thus bringing Gulfport truly back to full strength. Second, Gulfport achieved immediate success in 1977 by winning its fifth overall Big Eight championship. However, the most important occurrence of 1977 took place when Gulfport's head coach, J.E. Loiacano, hired a former Gulfport player as his offensive line coach.

Ronnie Cuevas was a 1972 graduate of Gulfport High School who had a distinguished football career at Mississippi State, where he made a name for himself as the smallest offensive lineman in the SEC. More importantly, Cuevas loved Gulfport football and had a special passion for beating Biloxi. During his senior season in 1971, Cuevas's Commodore team was a disappointing 0-4 going into their annual grudge match with Biloxi, who was 4-0 and ranked No. 1 in the state. Excited by and focused on the game with Biloxi, Cuevas attempted to take a test at school the day of the game. In every blank on the test, Cuevas repeatedly wrote the only answer that seemed appropriate to him on that particular day: "Beat Biloxi."

That night, Gulfport upset Biloxi 16-6. Scoring less than perfect on his test, Cuevas was allowed to retake the exam once he had cleared his head of pigskin residue and replaced it with contents that were more academic. Even when there wasn't an officially scheduled game against Biloxi, Cuevas still craved competition with the rival town. Says Cuevas, "I couldn't get enough of the rivalry. We would go down to where the old President Casino used to be and there was some beautiful Bermuda grass. We would meet a bunch of the guys from Biloxi and we would play tackle football there every weekend. Football and fistfights – that's what it was every weekend."

Cuevas exhibited the same intensity and desire once he became a coach, and his attitude left its mark on the longstanding rivalry. After serving as a Gulfport assistant under J.E. Loiacano and Tom Freeman, Cuevas took over the head coaching duties in 1990. During the 27 years Cuevas spent coaching at Gulfport, the historically balanced series record spiked sharply in favor of the Admirals as Gulfport won 23 and lost only four to Biloxi. Unlike the approach of some coaches, Cuevas made it known to his players that playing Biloxi was not just like any other game, and that beating the Indians was a priority. On the day of games against Biloxi, Cuevas had the school use the Biloxi fight song in lieu of the traditional bell to signify the time to change classes.

It is appropriate that the first year Cuevas took over the head coaching duties, Gulfport and Biloxi were forced to play each another twice in the same season and in back-to-back games at the end of the season, no less. Fielding a team of only 35 players for the 1990 season, Cuevas struggled to find qualified personnel at each position, especially at kicker. During a particularly frustrating special teams practice in the middle of two-a-days, the Gulfport kickers couldn't hit the broad side of a barn. That's when Cuevas snapped. He turned to his manager, Chad Edwards, and barked, "Chad, go see the doctor at 1:00 for a physical and have your butt back out here ready to kick this afternoon."

A regular on the Admiral's soccer team, Edwards passed his

physical and then passed Cuevas's test to become the starting place kicker. However, Edwards did retain his job as the head manager for the team. Said Edwards, "I practiced special teams with everyone at the beginning of practice and then took care of my duties as manager the rest of the practice."

Cuevas was committed to his Wing T offense, and it was extremely rare that he sent his field goal unit onto the field unless it was absolutely necessary. In fact, by the time Gulfport met up with Biloxi in the final game of the season, Edwards had attempted only one kick, albeit a blast that defeated Meridian 3-0.

The 1990 season also marked the beginning of the "Best of the '90s Trophy," conceived by Gulfport's Lindy Callahan as a mechanism to help generate new interest in the rivalry. Late in the fourth quarter, Biloxi held a 20-18 lead and prepared to punt the ball from mid-field to pin Gulfport deep in their own territory. Because Gulfport had no timeouts remaining, execution of the punt was to be the final move before checkmate was achieved. Knowing the outcome of the game was all but finalized, Coach Callahan began making his way towards the Biloxi sideline with the newly minted game trophy. The Biloxi punter then unexpectedly dropped the ball and touched his knee down at mid-field, giving Gulfport surprising field position and a shot to win the game. Gulfport quickly hit a couple of passes and worked the ball to the Biloxi 25-yard line with 6 seconds left on the clock. Cuevas elected to send in his field goal unit led by manager-turned-kicker Chad Edwards.

Gulfport's sophomore holder Joel Smith recalls the field goal attempt, "I was just the holder for the kick and I was nervous. When I put my hand down and looked back at Chad to make sure he was ready, he just kind of stared blankly at me. I thought, If he's not ready now, he never will be; so I told the center to snap it. Chad nailed it, and the rest is history." Says Edwards, "That was a great moment for the team and for me personally. I also played baseball, and I think I was hit by more pitches in games against Biloxi that season than the rest of my career combined. Maybe it was just coincidence."

In a twist of fate, Gulfport had to play Biloxi again the very next week in the first round of the playoffs. Leading late in the game once again, Biloxi shot themselves in the foot and Gulfport stole another come-from-behind victory, winning 16-12. Cuevas immediately stopped using the Biloxi fight song during class changes in favor of the radio replay of Edwards' kick. By the time Cuevas left Gulfport as a head coach, he had beaten Biloxi 12 of 14 times and, in his last attempt, dealt the Indians a 56-0 defeat, which stands as the most lopsided victory for either team in the history of the rivalry.

Undoubtedly pleased to see Cuevas leave Gulfport, it took Biloxi a couple more years and one very special player before they found themselves back on the winning end of a game against the Admirals. In 2005, it was the running ability of Biloxi's Damion Fletcher that helped the Indians break a tough seven-year losing streak to Gulfport. Fletcher gashed the Admiral defense for 267 yards and led Biloxi to a 35-12 victory. The uniqueness of Fletcher was truly unveiled the following season when, as a freshman running back for the University of Southern Mississippi, he enjoyed the second most prolific season rushing total in school history and hit the Maxwell Award "watch list," all before his sophomore season in 2007.

Many individuals have made their mark on this longstanding rivalry between the two coastal schools, and undoubtedly, many more will follow. As the schools currently undergo periods of change and rebirth, the rivalry appears to be in good hands. In his first year as head coach of Biloxi in 2007, Steve Jones and his Indians beat Gulfport 48-44 in the highest-scoring game in series history and the one that also marks the greatest number of points ever scored by a Biloxi team against Gulfport. Interestingly, Jones's passion for the rivalry was taught to him by a Gulfport man. Says Jones,

> My father was a coach at Gulfport during the 1960s. He always told me, "Know who your rival is and make sure you beat them the majority of the time." Dad was well aware of the importance of this rivalry and he passed it on to me. Even though I went to school in Starkville, I have always felt a deep connection to the Biloxi-Gulfport game. It is the best rivalry in the state of Mississippi and I want to keep the tradition going.

WHAT THE INDIANS SAY ABOUT GULFPORT

Football gets talked about all year round in Biloxi, but you don't talk about Moss Point, and you don't talk about Pascagoula. You don't talk about anybody except that Biloxi-Gulfport game.

John Tapper
Former Biloxi Football Player

My grandmother doesn't know anything about Biloxi football, but she knows when we are going to play Gulfport.

Tyler Hailey
Biloxi Football Player

I think Gulfport is bitter because our school district gets so much money from the casinos and they don't.

Tiffany Langlinais
Biloxi Student Body President

If my truck ran out of gas in Gulfport, I would push it back to Biloxi before I'd buy gas there.

Don Powers
Biloxi Booster Club President and
Former Biloxi Football Player

We'll go over and do a little cheer on the Gulfport side and their cheerleaders will do the same for us. We are actually pretty civil to each other – surprisingly.

Dori Waltz
Biloxi Cheerleader

They look like us and they act like us, but there is just something about them. You just hate people from Gulfport.

Tyler Hailey
Biloxi Football Player

The Biloxi-Gulfport game is intense. The fans are at each other's throats, the players are at each other's throats and the coaches are at each other's throats. It's the biggest game of the year on the Coast, if not in the whole state.

Camal Petro

Biloxi Student

I always try to shake opponents' hands after the game, but it's hard for me to shake hands with a Gulfport player. I don't think I could ever really be friends with a Gulfport player.

Sean Murphy

Biloxi Football Player

From kindergarten all the way through high school, everybody really wants to beat Gulfport. It's like the number one thing a Biloxi student has to do.

Tiffany Langlinais

Biloxi Student Body President

Debuys Road divides Gulfport and Biloxi. We didn't go over there and they didn't come over here. You didn't get caught in either town at night; they would give you something you couldn't wash off.

John Tapper

Former Biloxi Football Player

WHAT THE ADMIRALS SAY ABOUT BILOXI

I have friends in Gulfport that won't shop at Edgewater Mall because it is in Biloxi. They say they want to leave their tax money in Gulfport.

Jimmy Tucker

Former Gulfport Football Coach

When I was a football player at Gulfport, there was no way you could get away with dating a Biloxi cheerleader. It was absolutely inconceivable. By the time my son played in the mid-1990s, things had changed. Heck, he didn't just date one; he married one.

Buddy Palazzo

Former Gulfport Football Player

Biloxi's new stadium is pretty good, but no matter what they build, it will never be better than Milner Stadium.

Bryant Lavender

Gulfport Football Player

I played on a youth baseball team with some guys from Biloxi. They always kind of separated themselves from the rest of us and we wondered why. Then I got to high school and realized that Biloxi-Gulfport is probably the biggest rivalry in the state.

Andrew Rose

Gulfport Football Player

The rivalry is still intense today. If players today see a guy in the mall with a Biloxi hat on, they will look over there and try to figure out who it is; but those players from 40 years ago probably would have run over there and cold-cocked the guy in the back of the head.

Chad Edwards

Former Gulfport Football Player

When we played Biloxi, we knew we were going to win. When things got tough, they folded and we didn't. We were just tougher than they were.

Sid Wilkinson

Former Gulfport Football Coach

It must be hard for those Biloxi players to pull off those big white shrimping boots so they can put on their cleats.

Joel Smith

Gulfport Booster Club President

and Former Gulfport Football Player

We had a highway patrolman come talk to our student body about drinking and driving. He talked about how the Coast was his home and how he was concerned for everyone's safety. Then he mentioned that he was from Biloxi and everyone started booing him.

Michael Lindsay

Gulfport Principal and

Former Gulfport Football Coach

When you cross Debuys Road into Biloxi, you have to set your watch back a couple of hours.

Buddy Palazzo

Former Gulfport Football Player

When we play Biloxi, the crowds are bigger, the band is louder, the cheerleaders are sharper and the football team is quicker. It brings out the best in every component of the school. It's good old-fashioned family fun, with a little bit of aggression served on the side.

Glen East

Superintendent of Gulfport School District

and Former Gulfport Student

BILOXI VS. GULFPORT
SERIES HISTORY

Year	Biloxi	Score	Gulfport
1908	Cleveland Huggins	24-6	Carl Gates
1908	Cleveland Huggins	*NA*	Carl Gates
1908	Cleveland Huggins	*NA*	Carl Gates
1909	*NA*	*NA*	Carl Gates
1910	*NA*	*NA*	Coach Newton
1911	*NA*	*NA*	C. A. Galloway
1912	*NA*	*NA*	*NA*
1913	*NA*	*NA*	Coach Hudson
1914	*NA*	*NA*	Carl Gates
1915	*NA*	*NA*	*NA*
1916	*NA*	*NA*	*NA*
1917	*NA*	*NA*	*NA*
1918	*NA*	*NA*	*NA*
1919	*NA*	*NA*	*NA*
1920	*NA*	0-0	Roy Bridges
1920	*NA*	6-14	Roy Bridges
1921	*NA*	7-18	Roy Bridges
1921	*NA*	0-0	Roy Bridges
1922	*NA*	39-0	V.P. Ferguson
1922	*NA*	38-0	V.P. Ferguson
1923	*NA*	0-32	V.P. Ferguson
1923	*NA*	0-9	V.P. Ferguson
1924	*NA*	0-19	Coach Wilson
1924	*NA*	0-6	Coach Wilson
1925	*NA*	0-6	Coach Wilson
1926	*NA*	7-6	Robert Laird
1927	*NA*	6-0	Robert Laird
1928	*NA*	6-0	Robert Laird
1929	*NA*	0-0	Robert Laird
1930	*NA*	13-0	Robert Laird
1931	Coach Hair	19-0	Robert Laird
1932	*NA*	19-0	Bryan Smith
1933	*NA*	7-0	Bryan Smith
1934	*NA*	0-7	Bryan Smith

Year	Biloxi	Score	Gulfport
1935	*NA*	0-20	Bryan Smith
1936	*NA*	0-7	Bryan Smith
1937	*NA*	0-28	Nick Duncan
1938	*NA*	0-0	Nick Duncan
1939	*NA*	7-0	Nick Duncan
1940	*NA*	12-0	Nick Duncan
1941	*NA*	6-20	Nick Duncan
1942	*NA*	26-0	James Landrum
1943	*NA*	7-0	James Landrum
1944	G. Dace Davis	0-24	James Landrum
1945	*NA*	6-8	James Landrum
1946	*NA*	13-0	James Landrum
1947	*NA*	6-0	James Landrum
1948	*NA*	13-14	James Landrum
1949	*NA*	13-26	James Landrum
1950	*NA*	20-27	Buddy Watkins
1951	*NA*	19-7	Buddy Watkins
1952	*NA*	20-6	Buddy Watkins
1953	*NA*	0-19	Roland Dale
1954	*NA*	6-20	Roland Dale
1955	*NA*	14-7	Lindy Callahan
1956	*NA*	6-7	Lindy Callahan
1957	*NA*	19-10	Lindy Callahan
1958	*NA*	*Series Suspended*	Lindy Callahan
1959	*NA*	*Series Suspended*	Lindy Callahan
1960	*NA*	*Series Suspended*	Lindy Callahan
1961	*NA*	*Series Suspended*	Lindy Callahan
1962	*NA*	*Series Suspended*	Lindy Callahan
1963	Willie D. Wiles	*Series Suspended*	Lindy Callahan
1964	John Williams	*Series Suspended*	Lindy Callahan
1965	John Williams	*Series Suspended*	Lindy Callahan
1966	John Williams	*Series Suspended*	Charles Elzy
1967	John Williams	*Series Suspended*	Charles Elzy
1968	John Williams	26-14	Charles Elzy
1969	John Williams	20-8	Charles Elzy
1970	John Williams	7-19	Leon Regal
1971	John Williams	6-16	Leon Regal
1972	Joe Sabbatini	19-34	Leon Regal

Year	Biloxi	Score	Gulfport
1973	Joe Sabbatini	10-20	Leon Regal
1974	Joe Sabbatini	14-7	Leon Regal
1975	Joe Sabbatini	16-10	Paul Pounds
1976	Joe Sabbatini	14-8	Paul Pounds
1977	Joe Sabbatini	7-17	J.E. Loiacano
1978	Joe Sabbatini	21-7	Tom Freeman
1979	Joe Sabbatini	6-7	Tom Freeman
1980	Joe Sabbatini	24-21	Tom Freeman
1981	Joe Sabbatini	0-9	Tom Freeman
1982	Joe Sabbatini	7-17	Tom Freeman
1983	Lum Wright, Jr.	16-13	Tom Freeman
1984	Lum Wright, Jr.	13-7	Tom Freeman
1985	Lum Wright, Jr.	6-20	Tom Freeman
1986	Lum Wright, Jr.	14-21·	Tom Freeman
1987	Larry Weems	20-21	Tom Freeman
1988	Larry Weems	17-26	Tom Freeman
1989	Larry Weems	18-19	Tom Freeman
1990	Danny Cowart	20-21	Ronnie Cuevas
1990*	Danny Cowart	12-16	Ronnie Cuevas
1991	Danny Cowart	7-31	Ronnie Cuevas
1992	John Williams	0-20	Ronnie Cuevas
1993	John Williams	14-13	Ronnie Cuevas
1994	John Williams	16-20	Ronnie Cuevas
1995	John Williams	7-20	Ronnie Cuevas
1996	John Williams	10-35	Ronnie Cuevas
1997	John Williams	31-24	Ronnie Cuevas
1998	Mike Battles	6-49	Ronnie Cuevas
1999	Mike Battles	14-32	Ronnie Cuevas
2000	Mike Battles	21-39	Ronnie Cuevas
2001	Mike Battles	7-24	Ronnie Cuevas
2002	David Russell	0-56	Joey D'Angelo
2003	David Russell	24-28	Joey D'Angelo
2004	David Russell	6-32	Joey D'Angelo
2005	David Russell	35-12	Joey D'Angelo
2006	David Russell	22-27	Marcus Wood
2007	Steve Jones	48-44	Marcus Wood

NA - Information Not Available

* Playoff Game

★★ OFFICIAL GAME DAY PROGRAM $5.00 ★★

Y'ALL vs US

Trustmark
Banking and Financial Solutions

17

NOT JUST ANOTHER GAME

An authentic rivalry game is not just another game; quite the contrary, it is a special game – very special. Some coaches and school administrators try to downplay a rivalry, or better still, attempt to ignore it; however, the stark reality is, they cannot. It's like trying to make believe the 600-pound gorilla in the room really isn't there. The problem, however, is when King Kong decides to play, you best be ready to entertain him. If every game on a schedule is equally important, then there is no rivalry. That's too bad, because the players, students and fans are missing one of the true pleasures of high school football. In many ways, a true rivalry is like a rare treasure that should be guarded and protected. Not every school has an authentic rivalry to circle on its calendar every year – a game that, from the final whistle this year to kickoff next year, is on everyone's mind. These special games have the potential to create lasting memories in the lives of the young people who are playing for, and supporting, their team. Rivalry games energize the spirit of the community. These are the games the little grade school kids hanging on the fence fantasize about playing in someday. Rivalry games stir up memories 10, 20 and even 40 year later in those who played in them. Yes, rivalry games are special and should be savored, enjoyed to the fullest and treasured. To do otherwise is to deny players, fans and the entire community the sheer delight of a gift not everyone receives.

Two veteran school administrators share their perspectives regarding the importance of rivalry games. Mac Curlee, Principal of Tupelo High School, says, "You look to see when the rivalry game is going to be played each year, and it becomes a red letter date on the calendar. Those games are able to etch out a little special place in your mind that you take with you for a lifetime."

Buddy Bailey, Principal of Brandon High School, says, "I think in any great rivalry it becomes a representation of the two communities. The communities fully support and believe in their kids, and the kids represent what the community stands for. I believe that is the theme of every great rivalry. The game becomes an anchor that reminds people of the spirit of the community and of the relationship of the community to their children."

Malcolm White, a 1970 graduate of Booneville High School and a former Blue Devil football player under the legendary Jim Drewry, offers a poignant description of his experience when Booneville defeated the Baldwyn Bearcats his junior year in 1968. His remarks are noteworthy, considering that White is now in his mid-50s, a highly successful businessman, currently serves as Executive Director of the Mississippi Arts Commission and is the founder of the St. Paddy's Day Parade in Jackson, the largest social gathering in Mississippi each year outside of a football game. White says, "I moved to Booneville in the summer of 1965. From the moment I arrived, it was clear that Baldwyn was the enemy. I learned to hate them early, even though I didn't know anyone from Baldwyn – that was irrelevant."

White started participating in sports immediately after his family moved to Booneville when he was in the eighth grade. He learned quickly that football was the game in which he had a chance to excel, and he took advantage of his ability. White had the opportunity to play a lot as a sophomore, and started at fullback and defensive end his junior and senior years. He was also the place kicker, wearing No. 3 in honor of Jan Stenerud, the kicker for the Kansas City Chiefs, Green Bay Packers and Minnesota Vikings. White recalls the game against Baldwyn his junior year:

> We always played our best against the Bearcats, and every game was a close one. Neither team ever handily beat the other. I remember beating them my junior year and going back to the field later that night. I stayed there in the stadium throughout much of the night, reliving the game. It was so incredibly special to beat Baldwyn. It was a big deal. The rivalry was so intense that it permeated all of the social orders. There were often fights at the games—on the field and off – and anywhere else you could find to fight them. It's really funny now. You grow up and think how crazy all that was, but it was so important to you at the time. The

night I went back to the field after beating Baldwyn, I knew even then, that moment was special. Sitting on the field in the darkness to relive the sounds and the smells, even at that early age, I was able to understand I didn't want the night to end. I just wanted to stay in that moment as long as I could, because I knew how special it was. I knew memories were made of unique feelings like that. Here I am – all these years later – I can still remember the dew had already set and what it felt like to be out there. It was just remarkable – and it still is.

Being able to participate in a big rivalry game has provided unlimited fond memories for countless numbers of players, students and fans, while stirring the dreams of young people as they wait for their turn to take part in the tradition. Rivalries give communities something to get involved in and look forward to. Rivalries evoke emotion and passion in people and make life fun and entertaining. For instance, there is an elderly lady who grew up in Baldwyn, married a Baldwyn guy, had children and raised them in Baldwyn. Of course, this lady, her husband, her children and now her grandchildren are all Bearcats. Over the years, she developed a true love for Baldwyn, its school and particularly Bearcat football. The annual Booneville-Baldwyn game is still special for her. Beating the Blue Devils makes her year, while losing to them is just "the pits." Either way, she is passionate and enjoys the rivalry to this day at age 88. However, the rivalry has dealt this elderly Bearcat grandmother a strange twist of fate. Sadly, she has developed early stages of Alzheimer's and now lives in a nursing home in, of all places, Booneville. Her family dares not tell her she's in Booneville for fear of upsetting her. As a family member says, "Our grandmother knows she's in a nursing home, but she doesn't know she's in Booneville; so we just don't tell her where she is. It's best that way."

Football in the Magnolia State is all about traditions, and the rivalry games every year are a special part of the richness of Mississippi's football culture. Randy McCoy, Superintendent of Tupelo Public School District, says,

Our history and our traditions are what inspire us. While looking to the future is exciting, we still have to make sure our kids understand the past. A community's traditions demonstrate the excellence we aspire to. The only way we can influence the future is by what we do right now. For example, to win next year's big rival game, we have to work hard today, next week, next month. The effort has to be given today – now. We tell the stories about the past to connect to the future – to make the present more important – because that's really all we have to work with – today.

In every football game you have an adversary. Quite often one adversary becomes more than an opposing team on Friday night. That team becomes a passion – or an intense rival. *Y'all vs. Us* is the story of fifteen of the most intense rivalries that exist in Mississippi and the impact those rivalries have had on individuals and their communities.

Last year the Mississippi High School Activities Association worked with the authors Mike Frascogna and his two sons – Mike III and Marty – to produce Gridiron Gold, the story of Mississippi's legendary high school football coaches. That book was a huge success, but those coaches made us aware that football is about more than the coach. Repeatedly these gridiron leaders talked about rivalries, and they talked about the importance of communities to building a successful football program. They said communities and their football are inseparable, and both impact the other.

With Gridiron Gold I expressed concern that we would omit deserving coaches. Each day I remember coaches who should have been included in that book. With this book I again had that same apprehension as we listed the many football rivalries in the state. The list was long and included such rivalries as Greenville vs. Greenwood, Hattiesburg vs. Laurel, and Magee vs. Mendenhall that are not included in the book. However, the authors couldn't address a hundred rivalries. They had to narrow the list to fifteen so that they could adequately tell the story of each, and that narrowing of the list was a difficult job. I apologize that we had to omit some of the deserving matchups. My reaction is that this subject of Mississippi football rivalries requires more than one book; we need several books to analyze this topic completely.

I am so proud of all of the football programs in our state. I know that football builds good citizens for the future of our state. As Knute Rockne said, "Four years of football are calculated to breed in the average man more ingredients of success in life than almost any academic course he takes." However, this book clearly demonstrates that this "game" we call high school football also builds communities and community spirit.

We have seen another benefit of football as a great bonder and healer. Football helped us as a state to cope with integration, 9/11, and the aftermath of Hurricane Katrina. These intense rivalries also brought out the best of our coaches' skills as they worked to develop character, dedication, and loyalty in their players.

I thank our schools and their community members for their willingness to share their feelings and their remembrances of their competitions. I thank our authors for their hard work on this book. They have once again captured the determination and the passion of our Mississippi people through the stories of these thirty rivals. This book will be one that is read years from now because of its historical value, and we at the Mississippi High School Activities Association are proud to be a part of continuing to honor our Mississippi communities, their passion through their rivalries, and their strength of character.

Ennis H. Proctor, Executive Director
Mississippi High School Activities Association